India and the Cold War

THE NEW COLD WAR HISTORY

Odd Arne Westad, editor

This series focuses on new interpretations of the Cold War era made possible by the opening of Soviet, East European, Chinese, and other archives. Books in the series based on multilingual and multiarchival research incorporate interdisciplinary insights and new conceptual frameworks that place historical scholarship in a broad, international context.

A complete list of books published in The New Cold War History is available at www.uncpress.org.

INDIA

and the Cold War

EDITED BY

Manu Bhagavan

THE UNIVERSITY OF NORTH CAROLINA PRESS

Chapel Hill

© 2019 The University of North Carolina Press

Designed by Jamison Cockerham
Set in Arno, Scala Sans, Chippett, and Neue Kabel
by Tseng Information Systems, Inc.

Manufactured in the United States of America

The University of North Carolina Press has been a member
of the Green Press Initiative since 2003.

Jacket photographs: John F. Kennedy, Library of Congress Prints and
Photographs Division; Nikita Khrushchev, photo by Herman Hiller,
New York World-Telegram and the Sun Newspaper Photograph Collection,
Library of Congress; Jawaharlal Nehru, 1947, Royroydeb/Wikimedia
Commons; atomic bombing of Nagasaki, 9 August 1945, photo by
Charles Levy, Wikimedia Commons.

LIBRARY OF CONGRESS CATALOGING-IN-PUBLICATION DATA
Names: Bhagavan, Manu Belur, 1970– editor.
Title: India and the Cold War / edited by Manu Bhagavan.
Other titles: New Cold War history.
Description: Chapel Hill : University of North Carolina Press, [2019] | Series:
    The new Cold War history | Includes bibliographical references and index.
Identifiers: LCCN 2018058261 | ISBN 9781469651163 (cloth : alk. paper) |
    ISBN 9781469651170 (ebook)
Subjects: LCSH: India—Foreign relations—20th century. | India—Politics and
    government—1947– | Cold War.
Classification: LCC DS448 .I523 2019 | DDC 327.54009/045—dc23
    LC record available at https://lccn.loc.gov/2018058261

FOR THE DREAMS OF MY FATHER

Contents

Acknowledgments   *xi*

Introduction   *1*
Manu Bhagavan

PART I   THE HOME AND THE WORLD, CIRCA 1947–1956

1   Journeys of Discovery: The State Visits of Jawaharlal
     Nehru and Liaquat Ali Khan to the United States   *19*
     Pallavi Raghavan

2   The Soviet Peace Offensive and Nehru's India,
     1953–1956   *36*
     Swapna Kona Nayudu

3   Faiz, Love, and the Fellowship of the Oppressed   *57*
     Syed Akbar Hyder

PART II   DOVES OF PEACE, DOGS OF WAR, CIRCA 1950–1969

4   The Accidental Global Peacekeeper   *79*
     Waheguru Pal Singh Sidhu

5   A Missed Opportunity? The Nehru–Zhou Enlai
     Summit of 1960   *100*
     Srinath Raghavan

6   Nuclear Ambiguity and International Status:
India in the Eighteen-Nation Committee
on Disarmament, 1962–1969   *126*
Rohan Mukherjee

PART III   THE DEVELOPMENT OF IMAGINATION,
CIRCA 1950–1980

7   Promoting Development without Struggle:
Sino-Indian Relations in the 1950s   *153*
Anton Harder

8   Indira Gandhi, the "Long 1970s," and the Cold War   *178*
Priya Chacko

PART IV   EPILOGUE

9   Bertrand Russell in Bollyworld: Film,
the Cold War, and a Postmortem on Peace   *199*
Raminder Kaur

10   Hindu Nationalists and the Cold War   *229*
Rahul Sagar

Contributors   *255*

Index   *259*

Figures

Jawaharlal Nehru visits with two diplomats
during his visit to Washington, D.C.   24

Pakistani prime minister Ali Khan speaking with
U.S. secretary of state Dean Acheson   27

Bertrand Russell meets Gautam Das   200

A medical graduate, Gautam Das (played by
Rajendra Kumar), venerates a photograph of
Bertrand Russell   202

Gautam and Meloda (played by Saira Banu) in
the Hiroshima Memorial Museum   212

Clocks at the Hiroshima Memorial
Museum stopped at 8:16 A.M.   213

Meloda lays a wreath while a dove looks on   214

Meloda recalls the day of the atomic attack against
its reproduction from a Japanese film   214

Gautam's body on the way to the funeral
pyre in the center of New Delhi   219

Jawaharlal Nehru's funeral procession through
the capital city of New Delhi   220

Gautam's funeral procession through the
capital city of New Delhi   220

Acknowledgments

This book has grown out of many conversations large and small that I have had with friends, colleagues, and students over the past several years. I have learned so much first and foremost from the contributors to this book and feel privileged to have collaborated on this project together. For their insights and encouragement, and thoughtful criticisms, I am grateful to: Karna Basu, Kanchan Chandra, Ellen Chesler, Ramachandra Guha, Donna Haverty-Stacke, Sunil Khilnani, David Lelyveld, David Ludden, David Malone, Pratap Bhanu Mehta, Uday Mehta, Shivshankar Menon, Raja Mohan, Nirupama Rao, Sanjay Ruperelia, Samir Saran, Shyam Saran, Mrinalini Sinha, Rupal Oza, Yasmin Saikia, John Torpey, and Barbara Welter. My colleagues Benjamin Hett, Elidor Mëhilli, and Jonathan Rosenberg improved my understanding of the Cold War with their expertise and sharpened the prose with their careful editing. Thanks also to Mary Roldán for her consistent support both as chair of my department and as my friend, and to everyone at Hunter College who help to make it a fine academic home, including Associate Provost Christa Acampora, Provost Lon Kaufman, Dean Andy Polsky, and President Jennifer Raab. An award from the college's Shuster Fund facilitated production.

Everyone at the University of North Carolina Press has worked tirelessly to make this book better. There is no finer team than: Dino Battista, Anna Faison, Chuck Grench, Cate Hodorowicz, Jay Mazzocchi, and Dylan White. A special thanks to Odd Arne Westad for his guidance. My agent, Matthew Carnicelli, makes it all happen.

I am lucky to have an amazing, funny, and brilliant extended family, who help in every way imaginable: S. Mitra Kalita, Vikas Bajaj, Arun Venugopal,

Meera Nair, Nitin Mukul, Sumathi Reddy, Dev Benegal, Kiran Desai, Tim Reedy, Aseem Chhabra, Molly Jo Felde, Paola Guevara, Sandeep Junnarkar, Shobana Ram, Ash Rao, Jonathan Rockoff, Sucheta Sachdev, and Hari Sreenivasan. A special shout-out of love to Belur Bhagavan, Minni Gopal, and Sharad Ramadas, and the larger clan. Sree and Priyanka are my everything.

India and the Cold War

Introduction

MANU BHAGAVAN

I

Writing just over ten years ago, Odd Arne Westad changed the way we think about the Cold War. While the conflict was certainly about the struggle between the two superpowers, he observed that it was truly global in scope. To actually understand the clash, we had to go beyond narrow understandings of the bilateral relationship and stop limiting our focus to sites of conventional warfare. By looking at Soviet and American interventionism in the Third World, as well as the reactions that such interventions generated, Westad established that the Cold War was a grand phenomenon with multiple actors shaping and reshaping international politics based on various domestic agendas and foreign policies. Asia, Africa, and Latin America were not peripheral to the main show but were each a key stage on which the drama unfolded.[1]

India's role in the Cold War has classically been defined as having been rather minimal, circumscribed by a policy of non-alignment and a basic insistence that Third World interests lay outside the two rival power blocs. No major battles were fought on the subcontinent, so the region was seen as marginal to the superpower standoff. To make matters worse, the moral high ground India claimed proved shaky. Its colorful denunciations of power politics took on the hue of posturing when its outlook soon came to be seen as having a pro-Soviet tilt. Such hypocrisy undermined India's credibility in myriad ways, such that the country, despite its massive size, population, and strategic location, has remained little more than a footnote in Cold War history.

Over the past decade, synchronous with Westad's breakthrough insights, this view has begun to change. Independent India, it turns out, was actually quite influential in the first two decades of its existence, which coincided with the emergent development of U.S.-Soviet bipolar hostilities. The chapters in this book take advantage of newly accessible archival material and the latest research to offer a richer and more nuanced narrative of India's role in the Cold War, with a special focus on this early period.

II

India's significance stemmed in measure from its legendary founding figure, Mahatma Gandhi, who was assassinated in 1948. Gandhi was widely heralded as larger than life with a kind of saintly legitimacy, and the afterglow of his halo continued to shine on his country after his death.[2]

Additionally, India's great stature in this early period was due to its dashing, debonair, and dazzling first prime minister, Jawaharlal Nehru. Nehru wore the mantle of Gandhi's hand-picked successor with ease, shaping and recasting his mentor's vision of nonviolent politics for international appeal and global impact.

From the earliest days of the Cold War, Nehru saw the collision of superpowers as an existential threat to all life, the ultimate culmination, in his view, of a teleology produced by nationalism that led to violence, to war, and finally to total destruction. A certain kind of nationalism for Nehru was fundamental and necessary in the historically specific context of imperialism, whereby European states vied with one another for spheres of influence, economic and military control, and supremacy. Anticolonial nationalism demanded liberty and the right to self-determination for colonized people. But for Nehru and many of his brethren, the nation-state was not the end game.[3]

From the end of World War I, Nehru had been trying to reconcile his Fabian socialist outlook with an emergent subcontinental critique of nationalism, eventually settling on a protean understanding of internationalism as the best, and indeed only, way forward. In conversation, and sometimes in argument, with fellow Indian political intellectuals, especially Gandhi, Nehru's internationalism evolved from a broad cosmopolitanism, in which the best ideas of each people simply would be celebrated, to an embrace of world federation and, by the late forties, specifically federal world government. What exactly such a federated government would look like was intentionally left vague, as Nehru believed that the details would have to evolve from everyone invested. Generally, though, he hoped for some kind of ex-

Manu Bhagavan

ecutive, legislative, and judicial structure that would sit atop national states, unifying them all.[4]

Global union did not preempt or undermine the need for political responsiveness to local needs. Rather it sought to streamline the demands of individuals, groups, and nations with universal principles of human dignity. This goal found a means of expression in the emergent discourse of *human rights*, which Nehru saw as a way to bind states and peoples to a code of proper action. India played a pivotal leadership role in developing a consensus around these new norms, and in crafting the instruments through which they would be popularized and made legal.[5]

Human rights were premised on the idea that state sovereignty was not absolute, and that the international community could intervene in the domestic affairs of states if they did not live up to their obligations to their people, as their authority was fundamental and beyond that of any one state. Of course, this did not mean that such rights were above controversy. Indeed, as the effort to codify human rights gained momentum in 1947 through the official sanction of the new United Nations, fissures between the "East" and the "West" soon became readily apparent. A major fault line emerged over what precisely constituted "human rights." Western powers pushed for political and civil liberties while those from the "non-West" favored economic, social, and cultural rights. If the committee chaired by former U.S. first lady Eleanor Roosevelt started its work with much fanfare and hope, it quickly devolved into acrimony and contentious debate, lines generally drawn along those of the Cold War blocs. It was in this committee, and under such conditions, that India found its footing.[6]

The decolonizing country's U.N. representatives were highly trained, the elite products of the upper echelons of the British Indian system. They were initially led by Nehru's sister, Madam Vijaya Lakshmi Pandit, who had achieved celebrity status a few years earlier through a series of high-profile and high-stakes showdowns. She had debated and defeated Winston Churchill's parliamentary secretary Robert Boothby on a popular American radio program; she had led a counterdelegation representing colonized societies and colored peoples to the San Francisco U.N. Conference in 1945, winning a moral victory; and in her biggest achievement, she had gone head-to-head with Jan Smuts in the U.N. General Assembly over South African law and won the first "Asian victory" of the modern era with a supermajority vote in favor of her position. Brilliant, charming, sophisticated, sharp-tongued, and not incidentally quite beautiful, Madam Pandit brought high-wattage star power to Indian diplomacy and was the country's best-known face aside from Nehru himself. In a telling move following Madam Pandit's break-through role as inaugural head of the U.N. delegation, her brother appointed her the country's first ambassador to the Soviet Union, and then, a year later in 1949, as the first woman ambassador to the United States. Although she was heralded in both places, her appointment was particularly well received in the United States.[7]

India saw it as its mission to play global peacemaker, not only to pre-vent total annihilation under a mushroom cloud, but also to serve a larger human ideal. In the human rights committee, India eventually argued that there were two kinds of rights — negative, those political and civil rights re-quiring no action by the state other than a guarantee of protection, and posi-tive, those economic, social, and cultural rights requiring some state action to engineer. Each had a different genealogy. Nor did these two types of rights mirror a permanent division of east and west or north and south, as Eleanor Roosevelt herself had defensively pointed out. Two of FDR's Four Freedoms were from want and fear, and much of the New Deal was premised on gov-ernment intervention. So rather than a clash of antithetical ideas, India saw negative and positive rights as distinct forms of heritage, different sets of ideas that reflected the pluralism at the heart of the human condition. Any human rights framework had to respect and accommodate these different systems without trying to erase either one, for that was the only way to vali-date the principle of diversity and to create lasting harmony.

So it was India that led the effort to break into two the legally binding covenant that followed the 1948 Universal Declaration of Human Rights, creating separate but mutually reinforcing documents. The success of India's initial efforts to walk the Cold War tightrope, and to balance the views of both sides, is reflected in the fact that, even as tense human rights negotia-tions were ongoing, Madam Pandit, who had recently returned to her pre-vious position as head of India's U.N. team, was nominated and elected to the presidency of the U.N. General Assembly in 1953, with the unanimous support of the United States, the Soviet Union, and the Commonwealth.[8]

The election capped a milestone year that reinforced India's emergent position as a trusted superpower go-between. The Cold War's first major hot conflict had been raging since 1950 on the Korean peninsula. From the start, India had counseled restraint and warned of the dire consequences of escalation, while also arguing that efforts to isolate and blame China for aggression would ultimately prove counterproductive. With what historian Vineet Thakur describes as an entrepreneurial spirit spearheaded by savvy diplomats B. N. Rau and V. K. Krishna Menon, India persevered, shuttling back and forth between the warring sides and their allies, eventually negotiating an acceptable settlement crafted in the armistice that went into effect in mid-1953.[9]

Some of India's momentum that year was generated by the death of Joseph Stalin, whom Nehru had always distrusted, even as he pursued engagement guided by the belief that a caged bear was always the most dangerous. Nikita Khrushchev's assumption of power afforded new possibilities and channels of communication, and a burst of sunshine amid otherwise gloomy forecasts. Nehru really believed that a turning point had been reached, or at least was near, not just in terms of bilateral relations, but in broader Cold War terms as well.

Nowhere was this general optimism more apparent than in the simultaneously dramatic efforts to solve the primary challenge that India continued to face at home and abroad: the fraught relations with its neighbor Pakistan produced by the partition of the subcontinent, especially over the unresolved status of the contested territory of Kashmir. A flurry of activity occurred between India and the United States following a complex but related debate in the United Nations over the question of self-determination. The Human Rights Committee had agreed, following its decision to create twin covenants on political and civil liberties and on economic, social, and cultural rights, to make the right to self-determination the first right listed in both documents. There had been widespread agreement among Global South delegates that the concept was thought of in relation to empire, inasmuch as freedom from imperial control was seen as a necessary precondition for any kind of human rights to be effectual. But *how* the public will necessary for self-determination was to be judged remained unclear. Although India initially agreed that plebiscites were the only real mechanism available, it later went along with a push from the United States to allow elections to count as well. Nehru was adamant about keeping India in line with international norms. This change allowed him to approach the Kashmir matter from a different angle, and so, in consultation with U.S. Secretary of State John Foster Dulles and members of his own team, and crucially with Pakistani support, he pursued a final settlement with Pakistan and Kashmir. This essentially would have solidified the status quo, allowing Pakistan to incorporate the portion of the state under its control, and India to do the same, with elections used as a means to legitimize the process. But Cold War exigencies simply proved too great: the United States and Pakistan concluded an accord by the end of that year, throwing power relations in the subcontinent into imbalance and torpedoing the deal.[10]

India for its part opted to stay the course, convinced that nuclear holo-caust was the only alternative to its serving as an active, impartial advocate of global peace. It had good reason for thinking this. Robert Oppenheimer, a renowned theoretical physicist who played a leading role in the develop-ment of atomic weapons as part of the U.S. Manhattan Project, had secretly contacted both Madam Pandit and her brother, warning of even more ter-rible weapons then in development. Oppenheimer beseeched Nehru to save the world, arguing that only he possessed the stature and goodwill neces-sary to fend off catastrophe.[11] While working on the Korean armistice and attempting to resolve its neighborhood problems, India helped establish a disarmament subcommittee through the U.N. General Assembly, expanded its contribution to worldwide peacekeeping forces, and began a serious push to eliminate the nuclear threat.[12]

At the same time, however, India was investing in expanding its scien-tific prowess and in furthering its own power needs. The physicist Homi Bha-bha helped the country make its own great strides in nuclear science from his perch as founding director of the Tata Institute of Fundamental Research. Some of this work opened India to charges of two-facedness, as it seemed to hold everyone to a different standard while pursuing its own self-interest, including, ultimately a nuclear weapon.[13]

The 1950s proved challenging in other ways. While there were no doubt diplomats and politicians in both the United States and the Soviet Union who genuinely believed that India was an honest broker and were grateful to have an open channel to the opposing camp, others were more hard-nosed. They saw both India and Nehru as naive, pompous, and overbearing. From this perspective, India was seen as a potential but prickly strategic asset, a geographically important, large state that was too reluctant to pick a side. In 1950, for instance, the United States offered India a permanent seat on the U.N. Security Council, in place of newly communist China. Nehru im-mediately rejected this offer for fear of alienating his large northern neigh-bor, undermining the United Nations itself, and contributing to greater ani-mosity in the world. In 1955, the Soviet Union and the United States each broached the subject again, but Nehru remained firm that he would do noth-ing that threatened the fragile stability and viability of the United Nations as an institution. Reordering the Security Council, he believed, would require a review of the U.N. Charter, a dangerous proposition given that so many were chomping at the bit to make changes. From their perspective, each super-power remained keen on wooing India to its side, or at least to leverage the policy of non-alignment to its advantage.[14]

Significantly, 1955 was also the year of the Bandung Conference in Indonesia, in which the Non-Aligned Movement was born. This was a moment of Third World solidarity, a chance for the peoples of the colonized world to come together and assert themselves. The West felt left out of the conference and the Americans were particularly skeptical and concerned about the event. Not surprisingly, the Soviets gave a full-throated endorsement, roaring in support of the anticolonial claims of the attendees.[15]

Khrushchev's mid-decade outreach to India just months after Bandung, and his warm embrace of Nehru, might thus be read either way, or as a bit of both: a relieved acknowledgment of India's larger role in keeping the Cold War in check, and/or a careful management of a desired asset. Both countries traded state visits, with Nehru given a spectacular reception in Moscow. This was in keeping with the way he fared wherever he went, a rock star before the age of rock. But in this case, it was clear that the Soviets were pulling out all the stops. For his part, Nehru was trying to further his post-Stalin efforts to build a more open and trustworthy relationship with the Soviets. And so India, too, received Khrushchev rapturously, though privately Nehru confided that he was upset by counterproductive anti-Western tirades.[16]

Things came to a head the following year with the twin crises of Suez and Hungary. Through the early part of 1956, President Dwight Eisenhower maintained a high personal regard for Nehru, as someone who could be believed, who (almost) stood above politics. So when Israel, Great Britain, and their allies attacked Egypt over Gamal Abdel Nasser's decision to nationalize the Suez, the American president reached out directly to the Indian prime minister, indicating that his help was required to solve the crisis peacefully. But at the same moment, the Soviets invaded Hungary, and fate twisted in the winds of the Cold War. India's ambassador to Hungary had fallen sick, and Nehru thus was unable to independently verify any news about what was happening there. His plodding response came across as purposeful flat-footedness when contrasted with his much nimbler pushback against the Suez Crisis, and the double-quick time it took Krishna Menon to make a fiery speech in the United Nations denouncing the West while defending Soviet action as a domestic matter. Indian officials warned Nehru immediately of the way things appeared. Nehru himself proceeded to equate the two events, but the damage had been done. For those who never could believe India's rhetoric, who saw it as a thin veil for much more mundane posturing and plotting, and for those who saw Nehru as a holier-than-thou preacher, this moment was a welcome humbling.[17]

Perhaps no one was watching with keener interest than China. Nehru had gone out of his way to defend the Asian giant, unfailingly calling the India-China bond unbreakable. Two years before, the countries had signed the Panchsheel (Five Principles) Agreement, signaling mutual respect for each other's sovereignty and territory, though for Nehru this was in the context of larger internationalist strategic objectives. But China had its doubts about Nehru personally, and about India's position more broadly, seeing its southern neighbor as a potential threat, a reality that India never grasped. Moreover, China actually contested portions of the border, through the fifties constructing infrastructure in the Aksai Chin region and claiming the territory as its own in maps that India discovered shortly after the Suez Crisis and failed Hungarian Revolution. Nehru was convinced that this was all a misunderstanding and referred the matter to the United Nations, expecting neutral arbitration to clarify right and wrong. But the Dalai Lama's daring 1959 escape to India humiliated China and made the United Nations' pro-India findings irrelevant.[18]

Over the coming months and years, things deteriorated still further. Krishna Menon, up for reelection to parliament, was challenged by a beloved Gandhian. Nehru defended his friend but, in the process of shoring up his bombastic defense minister, was seduced into a military confrontation with the Portuguese, despite the prime minister's repeated assurances that there was no alternative to nonviolence there. When India reclaimed Goa through this maneuver, Menon chortled about his prowess and turned his rhetorical cannon toward China, his words echoing through its local media and further incensing its leadership. Despite other serious diplomatic efforts to cool tensions, China finally invaded India in 1962, slicing through its defenses like butter, with Delhi apparently ripe for the taking. Then suddenly, and inexplicably, the Chinese withdrew, their primary objective achieved, the abject embarrassment of Nehru and the discrediting of India on the world stage.[19]

India then suffered two body blows, the first when Nehru, now a mere shadow of his former self, died in 1964. The country lost its greatest beacon of idealism and moral clarity. Two years later, Homi Bhabha died in a plane crash, just months after he had proclaimed that India could build nuclear weapons if it wanted to and if it became necessary.[20]

Indira Gandhi assumed power that same year, determined to live up to her father's name while not making the same mistakes. India, she concluded, must never be seen as weak again. As a first step, she helped usher in the Green Revolution to make India self-sufficient in food production.[21]

But the real test of her resolve came in 1971 when fissures between East and West Pakistan finally fractured the country into warring halves. Mrs.

Gandhi's role in rallying the international community to her side, in sheltering Bengali refugees, in liberating East Pakistan, and in the creation of an independent Bangladesh has become legend in the region. But the historian Gary Bass has revealed just how much Cold War dynamics drove the entire affair. Dhaka-based American official Archer Blood famously sent a telegram to President Richard Nixon and Secretary of State Henry Kissinger warning that Pakistani military action in the region was veering into a genocide, but the American leadership was simply too invested in its Pakistani counterpart to abandon or condemn the regime, a commitment made all the more stark by the Nixon administration's visceral dislike of the Indian prime minister.[22]

Indira Gandhi used this to her advantage as she scored a decisive victory against her country's long-standing regional nemesis. She emerged stronger than ever, and now with an actual tilt toward the Soviet Union, rationalized by the American betrayal. But internal controversies and personal shortcomings soon led Mrs. Gandhi to declare an emergency and suspend democracy. She called this off in 1977, but the country was now so mired in domestic squabbles that it began to focus most of its energies inward.

India would still make noise on the international stage, but it was no longer effective at advancing an agenda. Short-sighted and sanctimonious, the country lost any sense of strategic purpose and remained marginal for the remainder of the Cold War.[23]

But the gradual collapse of the Soviet Union, and its economy, over the 1980s, and the emergence of the United States as a more dominant, unilateral power, changed the equation in New Delhi. Policies of economic liberalization begun in the eighties dramatically expanded in 1991, setting the country on an altogether new course, the effects of which continue to be seen today.[24] As a potential new Cold War emerges, a confident, muscular India, now the world's seventh largest economy, but on track to become the second, looks to play a major role, even as it confronts the legacy of Nehru and bitterly argues over its own commitment to pluralism and democracy.

III

The chapters in this book engage with and expand on various aspects of this historical account. Collectively, their central intervention is to invert how we see the Cold War. Rather than looking at the Third World solely through the eyes of the superpowers, on the receiving end of political machinations, this book asks that we see the Cold War from the perspective of the so-called developing world. India was an actor in its own right. How did the newly independent country craft its foreign policy in such a hostile climate? What did India want out of the United States and the U.S.S.R.? How did it interpret American and Soviet designs? How did the Cold War shape India's hopes for a rising Asia and for decolonization more broadly? Did India's claims to act as a peacemaker have substance? And how did other countries, like China and Pakistan, in turn see India?

To answer these questions, the essays draw on a wide array of new material, from fresh archival sources to literature and film. Authors then meld different approaches, from diplomatic history to development studies, to present a holistic analysis of India's approach to the Cold War, to explain the choices it made, and to frame decisions by its policy makers.

The chapters are grouped into several thematic sections and arranged in loosely chronological, overlapping fashion. Traditional Cold War narratives unfold along timelines set by various American and Soviet foreign policy decisions, in a fairly logical sequence of action and reaction. Looking from India's perspective, however, we see not only new dimensions in the story but multiple stories happening at once, altering our sense of where, when, and how the Cold War begins and ends. Indian foreign and domestic policy in this context was broadly concerned with great power politics, peacemaking, and economic development, and the book is laid out to reflect this.

Part I focuses on the interplay of a bifurcated subcontinent with the polarized superpowers. Pallavi Raghavan begins by comparing and contrasting the visits of the subcontinental heads of state to the United States soon after independence. Within months of each other over 1949–50, Nehru and his Pakistani counterpart, Liaquat Ali Khan, journeyed to Washington to make the case for their respective agendas. Raghavan explores the motivations behind the visits, along with their reception and impact, to argue that clear-cut distinctions between both countries' aims based on ideology or outlook is impossible. Complex undercurrents also informed each decision.

Swapna Kona Nayudu then looks deeper into the way the Indo-Soviet relationship evolved a few years later, following Stalin's demise. She demonstrates that Soviet premier Georgy Malenkov was keen on communist-capitalist coexistence, in synch with India's broad vision for the world. At the same time, the Soviets saw support for decolonization as a means to draw newly forming nation-states into their sphere of influence.

Through an examination of the life and writings of Faiz Ahmed Faiz, one of the subcontinent's most cherished poets, and Nehru's favorite, Syed Akbar Hyder concludes this section by traversing cultural terrain that overlay political boundaries, crossing the lines separating Pakistan from India, the Soviets from other countries. Faiz rejected negating oppositions, and through his writings, which stemmed from the Islamic mysticism he embraced, he helped inform a nascent type of world citizenship.

Part II highlights the spaces in which India's airy idealism hit the pavement of realpolitik. Waheguru Pal Singh Sidhu writes about India's peacekeeping efforts in light of its broader peacemaking goals. The Korean War, the U.N. Emergency Force, and the Congo all became important sites for Indian interventions, as well as opportunities for the country to shape international rules. Significantly, this fit in not only with Nehru's high-minded hopes but also with India's immediate strategic needs.

Srinath Raghavan's chapter flows from Sidhu's, taking a deep dive into Indian efforts in 1960 to stave off a conflict with China over the decade-long border dispute. Nehru and Zhou Enlai held a summit in April that year. China offered compromises in that meeting, but Nehru walked away, leading some analysts to remark on Nehru's hypocrisy. This chapter explains the hard realism that guided Nehru's judgment in this case and concedes the notion that unjust compromise would only embolden an aggressor further. Raghavan in the process reminds us of how impenetrable the fog of war can be and of the dangers of oversimplified analysis.

Rohan Mukherjee focuses attention on India's nuclear policy and the country's participation in the larger disarmament debates of the 1960s. Many have seen a disjuncture between these two, India all too willing to talk a good game while ruthlessly pursuing its own interests at home. Mukherjee dismisses such allegations, proposing instead that India accrued status benefits from its nuclear ambiguity. It used this to further with sincerity its disarmament aims. Yet India's rejection of the Nuclear Non-Proliferation Treaty (NPT) in the late 1960s seemed to provide its critics clear proof that the country had always been after a nuclear weapon. To the contrary, Mukherjee ties India's rebuff of the NPT to the country's long-standing rejection of imperial Great Power politics, to ensure that its voice would not be locked out of a future select club that would dictate and determine the future of all others.

Part III looks at the ways in which domestic economic and political developments were deeply intertwined with external relations, ideologies, and interventionism during the Cold War. Anton Harder dissects India's attitudes toward the superpowers, in conversation with Pallavi Raghavan, Swapna Nayudu, and others, to underscore India's commitment to its ideals. The country was working to establish a "third way" in its internal development as a means to actually build the bridge to all countries it saw as its primary diplomatic purpose and tactical foreign policy objective. China played an important role in India's imagination (as the chapter illustrates), but despite Nehru's genuine efforts at outreach and reconciliation, the Chinese, led by Mao Zedong, gradually came to see India as a threat more existential than physical. For the way India chose to structure its economy—capitalism tempered by progressive socialism—undermined the necessity of violent revolution for social development. For Mao this was inconceivable. It was India's development model, Harder claims, that poisoned the country's relations with its northern neighbor and that played a consequential role in the Sino-Soviet split and, thus, the larger Cold War.

Priya Chacko examines some of these same issues while carrying us into the era of Indira Gandhi. She argues that consensus on India's economic policy ended by the late 1960s, resulting in a period of crisis and reform as part of the "long 1970s," when utopias around the world collapsed. International pressures affected domestic Indian development policy and contributed to the form of state capitalism that emerged, with consequences extending down to the present.

The final part serves as something of an epilogue. The Hindi film *Aman* (Peace, 1967), Raminder Kaur proclaims, is an elegy to the Nehruvian era. Inflected by the appearance of British philosopher Bertrand Russell, the film follows a tragic hero on a doomed quest to rid the world of nuclear weapons. Kaur sees the funeral for the hero at the end of *Aman* as a cultural coming-to-terms with the death of India's great leader. The dark storm clouds of the Cold War always threatened to rain down nuclear missiles on a helpless humanity. What would follow the loss of the only one who saw this clearly?

In the last chapter, Rahul Sagar offers a counterhistory that traces the foreign policy vision of the Hindu right in India. Throughout the Cold War, these religious nationalists stood outside the main power structures in India, gradually moving from marginalized figures to main Opposition, and subsequently becoming the dominant political force in the country. According to Sagar, this very evolution helped structure sympathetic intellectuals' ideas on India and the world, ones that confronted Nehruvian policies, co-opting them in places and rejecting them in others, and that have since given some shape to an alternate paradigm for India to follow. But opposition gave Hindu nationalists' international outlook a coherency that masked significant internal inconsistencies. Now that they stand at the precipice of full power, unshorn of domestic coalition partners, Sagar asserts that a day of reckoning is coming.

Taken together, then, these chapters reveal an India that was proactive in the early Cold War. The new country tried to develop foreign relations that would help in its internal development while also mitigating conflict and reducing tensions overall in the world. Popular artists reached across boundaries, helping to forge a loose cultural consensus around certain ideals.

The superpowers drove the conflict, but individual states interacted with the Americans and the Soviets, and with each other, with their own interests and ideologies in mind. The United States and the U.S.S.R. were each also wary of the other, and so their relations with large and (potentially) powerful countries like India were often bipolar: they were warm and friendly at opportunities for alliance and dominance but were chilly and paranoid about suspected enemy influence and partnership. India, for its part, remained undeterred and carried on with its policy of determined independence, seeking out agreement wherever possible but refusing to approach any problem with some predetermined result in mind, confident that honesty and transparency were humanity's only hope in such a destructive atmosphere of mistrust.

India's achievements overall were significant, yet its misfires were notable as well. Nehru emerges from all of this a wise, tall statesman, though not an infallible person. He led his country with hope in a time of great fear, seeking to balance virtuous purpose with the grim realities of power politics. Surprised, ultimately, by China's response to this worldview, India pulled back from its commitment to international cooperation, settling for the world as it was rather than as it hoped it to be. Since then, it has adopted more classical defenses even as it has ceded much of the authority it once wielded.

More recently, India has begun to rise once again on the world stage, reconsidering what role it wants to play and what values, if any, it stands for. This book, therefore, comes at a timely moment. Helping to understand India's role during the Cold War—the stature it held, the goodwill it generated, the animosities it contained, and the new frictions it caused—will, it is hoped, shed light on matters of peace, security, prosperity, and a future that all people must share.

NOTES

1. Odd Arne Westad, *The Global Cold War: Third World Interventions and the Making of Our Times* (Cambridge: Cambridge University Press, 2005).

2. Cf. David Hardiman, *Gandhi in His Time and Ours* (New York: Columbia University Press, 2003); and Claude Markovits, *The Un-Gandhian Gandhi: The Life and Afterlife of the Mahatma* (London: Anthem Press, 2003).

3. Manu Bhagavan, *India and the Quest for One World: The Peacemakers* (Basingstoke, UK: Palgrave Macmillan, 2013).

4. Ibid. See also Manu Bhagavan, "Towards a Strategic Vacuum," *Outlook* (New Delhi), 21 August 2017; and Bhagavan, "Reflections on Indian Internationalism and a Postnational Global Order: A Response to Partha Chatterjee," *Comparative Studies of South Asia, Africa, and the Middle East* 37, no. 2 (August 2017): 220–25.

5. Bhagavan, *India and the Quest for One World*, 65–74, 105–13.

6. See ibid.

7. Ibid., 14–65, 113–16.

8. Ibid., 105–16.

9. Vineet Thakur, "India's Diplomatic Entrepreneurism: Revisiting India's Role in the Korea Crisis, 1950–52," *China Report* 49, no. 3 (2013): 273–98; David Malone, *Does the Elephant Dance? Contemporary Indian Foreign Policy* (New Delhi: Oxford University Press, 2011), 252; Stanley Kochanek, "India's Changing Role in the United Nations," *Pacific Affairs* 53, no. 1 (1980): 48–68; cf. Rudra Chaudhuri, *Forged in Crisis: India and the United States since 1947* (New York: Oxford University Press, 2014), 49–77.

10. Manu Bhagavan, "Indian Internationalism and the Implementation of Self-Determination: Kamaladevi Chattopadhyay and the United Nations Human Rights Commission," in *A Passionate Life: Writings by and on Kamaladevi Chattopadhyay*, ed. Vinay Lal and Ellen DuBois (Delhi: Zubaan, 2017), 424–44.

11. Nayantara Sahgal, *Jawaharlal Nehru: Civilizing a Savage World* (Delhi: Penguin, 2011), 40–42.

12. Priya Chacko, *Indian Foreign Policy: The Politics of Postcolonial Identity from 1947 to 2004* (New York: Routledge, 2012), 42; Vijay Prashad, *The Darker Nations: A People's History of the Third World* (New York: New Press, 2007), 42; Kochanek, "India's Changing Role," 50.

13. George Perkovich, *India's Nuclear Bomb: The Impact on Global Proliferation* (Berkeley: University of California Press, 1999), 16–22; M. V. Ramana, *The Power of Promise: Examining Nuclear Energy in India* (Delhi: Penguin Viking, 2012), chap. 1.

14. Anton Harder, "Not at the Cost of China: India and the United Nations Security Council Seat, 1950," Cold War International History Project Working Paper no. 76 (11 March 2015); Manu Bhagavan, "India and the United Nations, or Things Fall Apart," in *The Oxford Handbook of Indian Foreign Policy*, ed. David Malone, C. Raja Mohan, and Srinath Raghavan (Oxford: Oxford University Press, 2015), 602.

15. See Seng Tan and Amitav Acharya, eds., *Bandung Revisited: The Legacy of the 1955 Asian-African Conference for International Order* (Singapore: National University of Singapore Press, 2008); Prashad, *Darker Nations*, 31–50; Westad, *Global Cold War*, 97–109; Odd Arne Westad, *The Cold War: A World History* (New York: Basic Books, 2017), 432–34.

16. Bhagavan, *India and the Quest for One World*, 116–21.

17. Ibid., 121–24.

18. Westad, *Cold War*, 430–32; Bhagavan, *India and the Quest for One World*, 121, 128.

19. Ramachandra Guha, *India after Gandhi* (New York: Ecco, 2007), 331–33; Bhagavan, *India and the Quest for One World*, 128, and n. 3; cf. Paul McGarr, *The Cold War in South Asia: Britain, the United States and the Indian Subcontinent, 1945–1965* (Cambridge: Cambridge University Press, 2013), 119–82; Andrew Kennedy, *The International Ambitions of Mao and Nehru* (Cambridge: Cambridge University Press, 2012), 217–37.

20. Conspiracy theories have since abounded that he was assassinated. Deathbed allegations made by a former operative of the CIA that the agency was involved, and that the action was taken to ensure that the subcontinent did not pass the atomic

developmental threshold, have added further grist to the rumor mill. See Gregory Douglas, *Conversations with the Crow* (self-pub., Basilisk Press, 2013). This book continues to generate sensational media reports. See, e.g., Srinivas Laxmani, "Operative Spoke of CIA Hand in 1966 Crash: Report," *Times of India*, 30 July 2017.

21. Cf. John Perkins, *Geopolitics and the Green Revolution: Wheat, Genes, and the Cold War* (New York: Oxford University Press, 1997), 183, 186; Vandana Shiva, *The Violence of the Green Revolution* (Lexington: University Press of Kentucky, 2016).

22. Gary Bass, *The Blood Telegram: Nixon, Kissinger, and a Forgotten Genocide* (New York: Vintage Books, 2014); cf. Srinath Raghavan, *1971: A Global History of the Creation of Bangladesh* (Cambridge, Mass.: Harvard University Press, 2013).

23. Bhagavan, "India and the United Nations," 604–7.

24. Akash Kapur, "India's Path Was Paved by Soviet Fall," *New York Times*, 19 November 2009; cf. Vinay Sitapati, *Half-Lion: How P. V. Narasimha Rao Transformed India* (Delhi: Penguin Viking, 2016), 107–39.

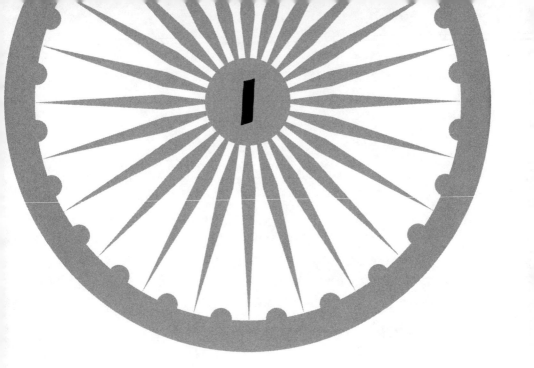

The Home and the World,
circa 1947–1956

Chapter   *One*

Journeys of Discovery

The State Visits of Jawaharlal Nehru and
Liaquat Ali Khan to the United States

PALLAVI RAGHAVAN

The process of decolonization across large parts of Asia and Africa in the 1950s and 1960s set up an important series of conversations about the extent to which colonial networks of influence over trade, military alliances, and international politics could continue to be used. For India and Pakistan, in the years that immediately followed the transfer of power, their relations with the United States were based on strategies that had been honed and developed by the government of India under the British. In this chapter, I present aspects of India's and Pakistan's early dealings with the United States explicitly in terms of a continuation of the geopolitical legacy of colonialism. Rather than viewing these interactions solely in terms of the dispute between India and Pakistan, we must also locate their foreign policy in other considerations that were more entrenched over a longer period of time that preceded the transfer of power.

What is also remarkable is the extent to which both India and Pakistan, despite frequently adopting postures that were critical of colonialism and the subjugation of South Asia under the British, nonetheless went about actively tapping into and embracing strategies that perpetuated preexisting colonial ideas about the best ways of leveraging their position. The dynamics of the Cold War—the rivalry between the United States and the Soviet Union—shaped the foreign policy interactions of India and Pakistan from the earliest years of their existence. Indeed, in Asia, the Cold War represented as much of an opportunity as a challenge. Policy makers in South Asia used the dynamic of the Cold War to further leverage their positions to one, the other, or both superpowers, to extract the maximum benefits for their countries, in maneuvers that were quite unrelated to their own ideological commitments toward communism or capitalism. In fact, the Non-Aligned Movement—wherein nations adopted a calculated equivalence toward both superpowers, and to which both India and Pakistan subscribed—was also built precisely on these considerations. Contrary to the perception that the Cold War entered into the foreign policy calculations of India and Pakistan only after 1954—the year that Pakistan entered into a mutual defense treaty with the United States—considerations about how best to tempt the United States to take a more active presence in India, as well as Pakistan, were actively part of the calculations of both countries almost from the moment of their creation.

It is also striking how strongly the early contacts that India and Pakistan set up with the United States were based on similar objectives. Both countries were tempted into their positions in the Cold War by a combination of similar ingredients: colonial precedent, a hunger for funding and developmental infrastructure, and a precarious question of how to justify this in the eyes of critical domestic audiences. Indeed, a detailed examination of the matrix within which India and Pakistan carried out their early foreign policies reveals that many of the patterns of interactions among India, Pakistan, and the United States had been set well before the transfer of power.

These trends were also manifested in the initial visits of Nehru and Liaquat Ali Khan to the United States as prime ministers of India and Pakistan. Both prime ministers had elected—and the timing of their decisions was more then merely coincidental—to visit the United States less than seven months apart, one in October 1949 and the other in May 1950. Both leaders, in more or less straightforward terms, asked for greater aid from the United States and painted stark pictures of how disadvantageous it would be if the Soviet sphere of influence were to extend into South Asia. Both also touted their geographical position as an asset of strategic value to the United States. The valuation that the United States made of this geographical positioning, moreover, hinged on assumptions that borrowed heavily from the assessments made by the British over the nineteenth and twentieth centuries. Rather than attempting to dispel these ideas, both Nehru and Liaquat Ali Khan closely built on them, in order to secure greater assistance from the United States. The developments around Nehru's and Liaquat Ali Khan's visits to the United States therefore presents a more unsettled picture than a straightforward polar opposition between the ideological orientations of the leadership of India and Pakistan with regard to foreign policy.

President Harry Truman's State Department, during the early 1950s, deliberated on how to bring within the U.S. ambit countries that had thus far been under British or French rule.[1] For several years after colonial transfers of power, what State Department officials mostly preferred to do was to take directions from European colonial nations in determining what U.S. responses to situations in Asia, the Middle East, and Africa ought to be. The concern was that, with the departure of the West, newly decolonized states would be ripe breeding grounds for the growth of communism. Increasingly, it became imperative for the State Department to examine ways in which this could be avoided. Indeed, it was evident that U.S. policies toward South Asia in the 1950s were marked by continuity rather than change. Chester Bowles, a famously ardent advocate of closer ties between the United States and India, as well as the American ambassador to India from 1951 to 1953, characterized the nature of U.S. concerns in South Asia thus: "In effect, we have taken over the traditional foreign policy which the British had maintained since the war of the Spanish succession."[2]

A memo for Henry Byroade, the assistant secretary of state for Near Eastern, South Asian, and African affairs, explored how the United States could thread together the disparate interests of the South Asia region: "Or, to put it another way, to keep the support and friendship of rising nationalism in the NEA [Near East–Asia] area without undermining legitimate local positions of our two strongest allies in NATO, the UK and France."[3] Furthermore, this note pointed out: "The decline and weakness of the UK and of France in various sections of NE Asia have left a growing vacuum which should, from a U.S. point of view, be filled, as far as possible, by elements friendly rather than hostile to the free world."[4]

That economics would be a critical plank by which these concerns could be met was also widely evident by the 1940s. The first U.S. ambassador to India, Henry F. Grady, argued in a speech in 1952 that "if our foreign policy is such as to ensure the development of stability and peace in the world, it naturally affects business favorably. . . . Because this is true, it is most important that business make its own contribution towards making a foreign policy that will give it security and conditions favorable to its progress."[5] Chester Bowles for his part forged an influential argument about the long-term wisdom of greater economic collaboration between India and the United States.

While motivating Congress to approve aid for India, he pointed out: "Today Indo-China is on fire and we are spending some $500 million annually. . . . If India was in an equally desperate situation, a panicky Congress could undoubtedly spend even greater amounts of money to save the situation there. However, by that time not only does the cost multiply many times over, but the chances of success are greatly diminished."[6] A stable and relatively prosperous India was in the U.S. interest, and sending financial aid to secure this purpose now would be cheaper in the long term.

Many of Nehru's senior officials at the Ministry of External Affairs were products of the Indian Civil Service—their experience, as well as professional connections were deeply embedded within the worldview of the colonial state. These officials also worked hard to achieve a more secure footing for India in the Americans' considerations. Following a meeting with Indian finance minister C. D. Deshmukh, "a conservative, thoughtful individual," Chester Bowles pressed the State Department to expedite food and developmental loans to India. Deshmukh, indeed, had had decades of experience in the Civil Service and, in 1943, had been appointed governor of the Reserve Bank. For its part, by the early 1950s the State Department did make efforts toward securing larger loans for the Indian government. Deshmukh told Bowles in 1952 that it would be impossible for India to carry out its minimum economic plans without substantial U.S. aid.[7] In fact, for all of India's insistence on non-alignment, Nehru and his officials had gone out of their way unofficially to assure U.S. representatives that, in the event of a world conflict, India would stand with the United States.[8]

Non-alignment undoubtedly held considerable sway in India: it was seen as a useful bargaining chip through which, it was hoped, the superpowers could be induced to compete in providing South Asia with more resources and developmental aid in an attempt to reduce the influence of the other. At the Asian Relations Conference held at the Indian Council for World Affairs in March 1947, for instance, Nehru had signaled his intentions to conduct an independent foreign policy without brooking any colonial interference from the British after their date of departure. This, along with a pronounced socialist slant within some sections of the Congress's top leadership, gave Nehru enough room to craft a political persona that was studiously aloof from the language of brinksmanship being adopted in other theaters of the Cold War. Yet, given such positions, what is also striking is how much Nehru's government adopted stances that contradicted these principles. Nehru himself, as well as senior officials in his foreign ministry, such as Girija Shankar Bajpai, eagerly exploited existing connections with the United Kingdom with the aim of using its proximity to the United States for their benefit.

By many accounts, Nehru's visit to the United States in the winter of 1949 was successful. Among other things, Nehru used the occasion to renew India's request for a million tons of wheat from the United States. Accompanying Nehru were Foreign Secretary Bajpai, M. O. Mathai, Indira Gandhi, and Minister of Finance Deshmukh. He was also followed by a retinue of journalists — K. Rama Rau from the *Hindustan Times* and D. R. Mankekar from the *Times of India*. In his joint address before the House of Representatives, Nehru, while pointing out that his government had just passed major land reform legislation to improve India's agricultural economy, was blunt in his request for developmental aid and financial assistance: "Though our economic potential is great, its conversion into finished wealth will need much technical and mechanical aid." Moreover, he argued, such cooperation would be of immense value, not just for India but also for the United States, owing to India's pivotal position in Asia: "Whichever region you take [while talking about Asia's geography], India inevitably comes into the picture. . . . It has a great deal to do with the Middle Eastern World, with the Chinese World, and with South East Asia."[9]

During a meeting with Dean Acheson, Nehru expressed his intention to try to reduce the price of wheat in India by 10 percent. Legislation would accordingly need to be passed in the United States to permit sales of government wheat at lowered prices. Truman was happy enough to acquiesce to this request. At a meeting at the White House with Nehru and Bajpai, Truman pointed out that the percentage of the U.S. population dependent on agriculture for their livelihood had in fact halved and that, moreover, the United States now produced more than double of what the purchasing power of the rest of the world could procure.[10] Truman himself campaigned energetically to push through legislation that would enable India to procure wheat from the United States at reduced rates, arguing that "we must counter the false promises of communist imperialism with constructive action for human betterment." Securing this legislation, moreover, was the only way to keep India stable and democratic, an objective that would always be in the U.S. interest.[11]

A State Department cable on the eve of Nehru's visit noted that commercial exchange with India had strong potential. "Government leaders, particularly the Prime Minister have become acutely aware of the need for foreign investment, but, due to political reasons to defer to the popular attitude and

Jawaharlal Nehru (*right*) visits with two diplomats during his visit to
Washington, D.C. (Copyright unknown, courtesy of Harry S. Truman Library)

have accordingly not taken a firm stand in welcoming an inflow of capital."[12]
Nonetheless, this was not an insurmountable hurdle. "Responsible members
of the cabinet have assured our High Commissioner that the government is
prepared to enter into individual agreements with United States investors
which would guarantee practically all of the safeguards which we hoped to
obtain by a general treaty."[13] Furthermore, the United States assisted India in
acquiring hefty loans from the International Bank: during Nehru's visit, the
bank approved $34 million in grants for railway maintenance and $10 million
for the purchase of agricultural technology.

At the same time, however, Truman was warned that the United States
could not meet all of India's demands for military aid.[14] "We should, how-

Pallavi Raghavan

ever, tell Nehru that we may not be able in the near future to make available to India any large quantity of military equipment. . . . It results from our heavy commitments to other parts of the world."[15] This memo argued that American efforts in the region to provide military, technical, or infrastructural assistance should be strengthened. At the same time, it was crucial to reassure the Indians that the United States would always be available to help India should the situation arise. "Should extraneous developments place serious and unexpected strains on the Indian economy, this government would stand ready to consult with the government of India with respect to cooperative measures which might be taken to solve these extraordinary problems."[16] Yet this appraisal was also, to some extent, based on assumptions that were rooted in the colonial period. Investments for defense in the region, the thinking went, were useful to the extent that they protected the outer flanks of the subcontinent—along its northeastern and northwestern borders, where Soviet threats against the United States were at their most pressing. Within India, the calculation was, other types of investment would go further.

The central plinth in Harry Truman's policies toward South Asia was the Point Four Program, and his administration went to substantial trouble to get it passed in 1948. Writing in his memoirs years later, Truman described the program: "Point Four was conceived as a worldwide, continuing program of helping underdeveloped nations to help themselves through the sharing of technical information already tested and proved in the United States."[17] Its logic was superficially simple: if developing countries were offered aid and technological assistance, then the chances of their becoming breeding grounds for communism were lessened. The legislation, which Truman sponsored in 1948, enabled the United States to offer economic and technical aid to developing countries and received bipartisan support. By 1952, Point Four was extended to India.

Extending the program to cover the subcontinent had the same basic logic: an extension of the U.S. economic footprint to create closer and more interdependent relations based on the dollar economy. The agreement called for an "interchange of technical knowledge and skills in related activities designed to contribute to the balanced and integrated development of the economic resources and productive capacities in India."[18] In February 1951, World Bank chairman Eugene Black famously called Tennessee Valley Authority director David Lilienthal about exploring how the Indus water basin could be developed collaboratively under the bank's auspices. In fact, a particularly successful example of the logical extension of aid-giving programs to developing countries crystallized a full decade later with the signing of the Indus Waters Treaty. For Chester Bowles, Point Four's most significant political message was about keeping India "democratic and free." Indeed, exchange programs between India and the United States were rich during this period, including a proliferation of information about U.S. cultural centers and the transmission of radio programs sponsored by the U.S. government. For his part, Bowles also recorded his anxiety about the prospect of the spread of communism through student-led mobilizations that, he said, were spreading across the country, leaving its inhabitants "directionless and dazed."[19]

Expanding Point Four was not the only piece of business between India and the United States during Nehru's visit. In 1951, Truman announced to Congress that he seek the passage of a bill to send enable emergency aid to India. Chester Bowles congratulated Truman on the bill's passage, noting that it would be an effective strategy in the fight against communism. He argued further that the only way to cement the U.S.-India relationship was to enter into plans modeled along the lines of the Marshall Plan: "The Indian Government quite often fails to do what we would like, but there is no question of its devotion to democracy, nor is there any question as to what side it will fall on once it has built a solid economic foundation and developed the full confidence and support of its people."[20] India, then, was to be cultivated by the United States, based on an assessment that it was a valuable potential ally in the struggle to limit the influence of communism in Asia.

At the same time, the United States had not forgotten about India's western neighbor. Different methods were used to shape alliances with Pakistan, but appraisals of the nation's use to the United States were made along identical lines and borrowed liberally from practices put in place by the British.

Liaquat Ali Khan made a vigorous appeal for the potential in Pakistan's economy in almost every speech he made in the United States: "Its economy is sound, its successive budgets have been balanced, and it has a favorable trade balance with the dollar area. It is fast educating itself, sending its men and women abroad for training and utilizing the help of technical experts from abroad."[21] Pakistan, moreover, was also a beneficiary of the Point Four Program, and under its terms, the country was entitled to developmental aid in "agriculture, geological surveys, transportation, light industries, etc."[22] After the agreement was signed, Liaquat Ali Khan was lavish in his praise: "For we believe that this would be the most courageous, the wisest and the most far reaching method by which your country can assure the world of its goodwill and international outlook."[23]

Prime Minister Ali Khan (*second from right*) speaking with Secretary of State Dean Acheson. (U.S. Department of State, courtesy of Harry S. Truman Library)

Yet, on the eve of Liaquat Ali Khan's visit to the United States, U.S. officials warned the State Department that Pakistan had had established trading and diplomatic missions with many nations in Eastern Europe, including Hungary and Poland—something the United States had repeatedly warned its international allies against doing. A case could be made, therefore, for limiting U.S. interactions with Pakistan. But that case was severely outweighed by larger strategic considerations. "Located on the East and West of the subcontinent of South Asia, [Pakistan] occupies two flanks of one of the largest non-communist areas of Asia and controls one of the routes from Sinkiang, and one of the major routes from Tibet. Eastern Pakistan, lying relatively near to Communist China, has importance in relation to possible Communist expansionist tendencies. Western Pakistan has inherited the primary responsibilities of the defense of the North Western Frontier Province."[24] All in all, then, it made no sense to cut off trade contacts with Pakistan.

Liaquat Ali Khan had been accompanied by his wife, Rana Liaquat Ali Khan, M. A. H. Ispahani, Pakistan's ambassador to the United States, and

M. Ikramullah, his foreign secretary. During his visit, Liaquat, like Nehru, made a speech to Congress and visited the joint chiefs of staff at the Pentagon. His trip extended over three weeks, and he visited business leaders, journalists, traders, military personnel, and students in Washington, Boston, and Chicago and across California. His speeches about the role that the United States could play in Pakistan were straightforward:

> To the western world we look for two things, that it will maintain
> world peace and that it will help the underdeveloped countries by
> throwing open to them the fullest advantages of its experience, its
> technical knowledge and technical skill. Indeed, the two aims are
> the same. For it is difficult to see how peace can be maintained when
> there is such glaring economic disequilibrium in the world. And it
> is difficult to see how this disequilibrium can be removed in time
> to save the world from the catastrophe of the war, unless the more
> advanced countries in the world take an elevated and enlightened
> view of their moral responsibility.[25]

Not only was Pakistan situated along an important border of the Middle East, he argued, but its eastern flank overlapped with Burma and Southeast Asia. Both regions needed a stabilizing influence to counter the threat of communism, and Pakistan could help to establish this. In fact, he pointed out, unsubtly, "Pakistan's military manpower would enable it to make a significant contribution to the Middle East's capacity to resist Soviet aggression."[26] This potential opening for a strategic partnership with the United States was certainly felt in Pakistan in the years that followed the transfer of power. Hussain Haqqani charts out how Pakistan's relations with the United States were from the beginning an energetic campaign about its utility in the region against the spread of Soviet influence.

Successive governments of Pakistan insistently reminded the United States of its usefulness in the region, including, for instance, the uninterrupted use of an air force base in Badaber, from which Soviet activities could be monitored. During his three-week tour of the United States, moreover, Liaquat Ali Khan repeatedly touted "the fighting qualities of [Pakistan's] anti-communist Muslim warriors." He added that Pakistan's western territory, bordering Iran and Afghanistan, could be an important location for "communications to and from the old bearing areas of the Middle East."[27] In many ways, Khan's assessment matched Henry Grady's: "The broad objectives of the British and ourselves are identical in that we want to protect ourselves and the world against the ruthless expansionist policy of the Soviets.

. . . The securing of agreement on the all-important problem of the Middle East is one of pressing amount."[28]

The historian Anita Inder Singh shows that the aftermath of decolonization in Asia concentrated the efforts of the British and their American allies in retaining a strategic influence in the defense of the subcontinent against a potential Soviet threat. She argues that the British effectively had a tactical retreat in mind: they planned to continue their influence over subcontinental strategic affairs in effect if not in name. It was these traditions of strategic thought that the United States as well as Pakistan consistently tapped into during the Cold War decades. Similarly, Narendra Singh Sarila, an aide-de-camp to Lord Louis Mountbatten, wrote years later that the transfer of power negotiations were aimed at ensuring that western Pakistan would remain a British defensive asset. During the deliberations over the interim government, for example, Field Marshal Bernard L. Montgomery, chief of the Imperial General Staff, described the possibilities offered by the creation of Pakistan: "From the broad aspect of Commonwealth strategy it would be a tremendous asset if Pakistan, particularly the northwest, remained within the Commonwealth. The bases, airfields, and ports in northwest India would be invaluable to Commonwealth defense."[29]

Especially influential in early U.S. machinations in South Asia was Olaf Caroe, governor of the North Western Frontier Provinces until 1946 and foreign secretary to the government of India from 1939 to 1946. Caroe later became a key adviser to the State Department on its policies on South Asia and was close to Assistant Secretary of State Henry Byroade.[30] Indeed, several commentators laid the responsibility for the Baghdad Pact squarely at the door of a monograph written by Caroe and published in 1951, titled *The Wells of Power*—a reference to the oil fields in the Middle East and the struggle over their control. Caroe had correctly assumed that the big international struggles in the coming decades would be based on the search for oil, and that the pursuit of these interests would entail a continuation of older trends in geopolitical thinking. From the middle of the nineteenth century, he pointed out, "the external policy of the British government in India was directed mainly at the stabilization of the Middle Eastern frontiers, and to safeguarding the continued existence of Persia and Afghanistan, against the forces of Russian expansionism."[31]

These arguments were repeatedly made in the 1950s. At a regional conference of American consular personnel in South Asia in 1951, a variety of ways to harness South Asia's international relevance were discussed. Echoing almost exactly the strategic wisdom of developments half a century later,

Captain E. Millner, U.S. commander of Middle East Forces, declared: "Although Afghanistan is in a weak position militarily, it occupies a position of strategic importance; in the event of war, it would be to our advantage to have Afghanistan determined to resist Soviet invasion."[32] Furthermore, Millner pointed out, also in line with Caroe's argument, "The most effective military defense of South Asia would require strong flanks. Turkey, Iran and Pakistan are of primary importance in the West, and Indo-China in the East."[33] He concluded, "However far this region appears to be from the front line today, in this generation (if the Soviets can effect it), and certainly in the next, South Asia will play a major role in our destiny."[34]

The concept of a ringed system of defense around the edges of the subcontinent—which created so-called frontier territories along both the east and the west that were considered to be removed from mainland systems of administration—had been a key factor in the making of South Asia's historical foreign policy. In the nineteenth century, for instance, the ringed system of defense had been designed to contain the spread of hostile influence from tsarist Russia into the subcontinent. By the time of the first military pact between the United States and Middle Eastern countries in 1954, the idea to use the terrain of what constituted West Pakistan as a defensive frontier against the spread of Russian influence was at least a century old. In the current period, Caroe pointed out that Pakistan was also well situated for the struggle over the security of the "wells of power." During World War II the country had served as a source of manpower and training for the British army, as well as a base for securing Iran and Iraq, and this had only emphasized its potential to combat the spread of the Soviet influence. All things considered, Caroe wrote, "Pakistan had inherited much of undivided India's responsibility in guarding its interests in the Indian subcontinent, the Persian and Arabian gulf, as well as the Middle East." In short, Caroe firmly believed that Pakistan could become an integral part of the United States' strategies in South Asia.

The U.S. government, in short, believed that tapping into British traditions of strategic thinking was essential in building a strong presence in the Middle East. One option was for a Middle East Command to be established along the lines of the North Atlantic Treaty Organization, which could protect Anglo-American interests for oil and a strategic presence. At a meeting of British and American representatives at the White House in January 1952, Winston Churchill pointed out that the pursuit of Western interests in Asia would have to be recalibrated, seeing that "this position has been deeply altered by the disappearance of the Indian Army as a British military instrument as a result of Indian independence."[35] British operations in the Middle East region, Churchill continued, including in Egypt and Iran, had thus far relied extensively on the organizational capacities of the Indian army. For the Middle East Command to remain in operation and have an active presence in the region, it would have to work more closely with Turkey, Britain, France, and the United States. In 1952—within a year of dialogues initiated following Liaquat Ali Khan's visit to the United States—Pakistan had entered into an alliance with the United States and Iraq, Afghanistan, and Turkey that was designed specifically to prevent Soviet influence from spreading beyond the Middle East.

Given such detailed strategies about Pakistan's key role in the defense of the free world, what was also apparent was the staunch opposition within critical sections of opinion within Pakistan about the proposed treaty. This opposition, moreover, hinged on arguments over how much assistance was needed to acquire Pakistan's loyalty. Many argued that the resources offered so far, particularly for developmental aid, were insufficient. These concerns were relentlessly hammered home to U.S. officials visiting Pakistan in the early 1950s. George McGhee, the assistant secretary of state for Near Eastern, South Asian, and African affairs, and an important point person in Truman's and Eisenhower's State Department with regard to relations with South Asia, repeatedly encountered these arguments during a visit to Karachi in 1951. In preparation for the formalization of the Middle Eastern Defense Organization—a precursor of the Central Treaty Organization—McGhee had visited Karachi after a monthlong tour of Saudi Arabia, Turkey, and Iraq. McGhee met with the editor of the *Dawn* newspaper, Altaf Hussain, who was scornful of the slowness of progress in the U.S. efforts in the cultivation of its relations with Pakistan, and its attempts at enfolding Pakistan into a multilateral defense-treaty system with the United States. Hussain, in remarks that—intentionally, perhaps—sent chills down the spine of many State Department officials, airily remarked at a dinner party that the onslaught of communism in South Asia was merely a matter of years, a decade at most. Certainly, American attempts at combating it were feeble at best.[36] The telegram from the U.S. embassy—which described and analyzed this conversation in full—conceded that there seemed to be some truth to Hussain's hidden suggestion: "The long delay in Congressional approval for Point IV; the small sums of money mentioned; and the continual emphasis on what the nations of Asia must do apparently dissipate what little hopes may be left."[37] On the basis of conversations with influential sections of opinion in South Asia, McGhee concluded that the United States should increase its technical, financial, and military involvement in Pakistan.

But any agreement between Pakistan and the United States to prevent the presumed Soviet onslaught would be less than effective, it was argued, unless it also took into account the threat from India. Domestic opposition to the defense treaty in Pakistan was substantial. What, the *Dawn* asked, was the point of an arms treaty unless it contained specific wording on the pledge of support in the eventuality of a war with India? The governor general, moreover, summoned the U.S. ambassador to complain that the treaty's vagueness undermined his authority. Critics, including the influential political thinker Hans Morgenthau, also pointed out that the treaty would be useless in safeguarding the ultimate interests of the United States in the subcontinent: although it might help in a regional war between India, Pakistan, and Afghanistan, it would be of little use if India were indeed to fall under communism.[38]

Notwithstanding these arguments, however, the idea of a system of mutual defense was explored repeatedly by the United States, Pakistan, Afghanistan, Iraq, Iran, and Turkey from the early 1950s. By mid-decade, moreover, Pakistan was formally a member of two pacts for mutual defense in South Asia. Signed in Baghdad and Manilla, each provided for defensive assistance from the United States in the event of hostilities from the Soviet Bloc. Called the Central Treaty Organization (CENTO) and Southeast Asia Treaty Organization (SEATO) Pacts, they enabled Pakistan to participate in the defense of Middle Eastern and Southeast Asian nations against outside threats.

In India, the signing of the Baghdad Pact in 1955 was seen as further proof of Pakistan's determination to ally itself with the United States in a bid to gain more power in the subcontinent, even as India remained neutral to Cold War rivalries. An article in the Indian newspaper *Anandabazaar Patrika* speculated that the misguided choices being made on India's foreign policy and the "foolhardiness of the policy of non-alignment" could lead to India being surrounded by hostile forces.[39] An adherence to non-alignment, the writer warned, would simply lead the United States to cultivate anticommunist alliances with other countries, leaving India out in the cold. At the Bandung Conference of nonaligned nations in 1955, Nehru gave full rein to his displeasure, declaring: "Indeed, it is an intolerable thought to me that the great countries of Asia and Africa should come out of bondage themselves or humiliate themselves in this way."[40] The narrative for a differentiated approach to foreign policy by India and Pakistan was more or less set by then.

Yet, evaluating the impact of the inheritances of colonialism in shaping the foreign policies of India and Pakistan raises other questions. After the transfer of power, neither the Indian nor the Pakistani government was particularly averse to maintaining linkages with colonial networks — including, for example, the Commonwealth — as well as preexisting patterns of strategic thinking in furthering their international pursuits. But policies of continuing imperial traditions of geopolitics in India and Pakistan can also be read in a different way: what characterized their international positioning in the years that followed the partition, was as much an attempt to consolidate and build on inheritances that were deeply entrenched, as it was an embarking on a set of decisions specifically and exclusively geared toward perpetuating their hostility with one another.

The circumstances surrounding the early years of the U.S. relationship with India and Pakistan are important to analyze how the rhetoric about transnational alliances for protection against threats from cross-border movements came into place. But what they also reveal is that, for India and Pakistan, ideology itself was of not an insurmountable obstacle in the shaping of their relationships with the superpowers. This ought to further problematize characterizations about how international alliances protect rights to freedom or individual liberties, since, frequently, these are also shaped by patterns of continuity in strategic thought that well precede the particular moment in which the alliance is formally forged. In the evaluation of many commentators who observed India's and Pakistan's dealings with the world, it usually was held that Pakistan was opportunistic and militaristic, while India was nonaligned and aloof. This article has tried to explore the complexity of the manifold considerations that shaped both India's and Pakistan's foreign policy during the Cold War, and shown that, in some respects at least, the nature of motivations governing their choices were remarkably similar.

NOTES

1. The history of the relationship between India and the United States has been the subject of excellent scholarly analysis in recent years. See, e.g., Rudra Chaudhuri, *Forged in Crisis: India and the United States since 1947* (London: Hurst, 2014); Paul McGarr, *The Cold War in South Asia: Britain, the United States and the Indian Subcontinent* (Cambridge: Cambridge University Press, 2013); Nicholas Cullanther, *The Hungry World: America's Cold War Battle against Poverty in Asia* (Cambridge, Mass.: Harvard University Press, 2010); Manu Bhagavan, *The Peacemakers: India and the Quest for One World* (New Delhi: HarperCollins, 2012); and R. J. McMahon, *The Cold War and the Peripheries: The United States, India, and Pakistan* (New York: Columbia University Press, 1996). See also Denis

Kux, *Disenchanted Allies: The United States and Pakistan, 1947–2000* (Baltimore: Johns Hopkins University Press, 2001).

2. Chester Bowles to Raymond Allen, 15 July 1952, Chester Bowles' Correspondence, Psychological Strategy Board Files, 1951–1953 Harry S. Truman Archives (hereafter HSTA).

3. Regional Planning Adviser, Bureau of Near Eastern, South Asian, and African Affairs (Hoskins) to Assistant Secretary of State for Near Eastern, South Asian, and African Affairs (Byroade), memorandum, Washington, D.C., 7 April 1952, Official File 426, Harry S. Truman Papers (Truman Papers), HSTA.

4. Ibid.

5. Summary of Remarks from the speech of Henry Grady at the University of California, Berkeley, April 1952, box 1, Henry F. Grady Papers, HSTA.

6. Bowles to Averill Harriman, September 1952, Official File 426, Truman Papers, HSTA.

7. Ibid.

8. See, e.g., McGarr, *Cold War in South Asia*, chap. 1.

9. Background Memoranda on Visit to the United States of Jawaharlal Nehru, October 1949, box 158, Foreign Affairs File, 1949–1953, President's Secretary's Files, HSTA.

10. Ibid.

11. Truman, Address to U.S. Congress, February 1952, Truman Papers, HSTA.

12. Background Memoranda on Visit to the United States of Jawaharlal Nehru, October 1949.

13. Ibid.

14. Ibid.

15. Ibid.

16. Ibid.

17. Raymond H. Geselbracht, ed., *Foreign Aid and the Legacy of Harry S. Truman* (Kirksville, MO: Truman State University Press, 2015), 206.

18. "Point IV General Agreement for the Technical Cooperation between India and the United States of America, Signed December 1950," in *Select Document on India's Foreign Policy and Relations*, ed. A. Appadorai, vol. 2 (New Delhi: Oxford University Press, 1985), 73.

19. Bowles to Truman, 20 September 1952, Official File 426, "Aid to India," Truman Papers, HSTA.

20. Ibid.

21. Background Memoranda of Visit to the United States of Liaquat Ali Khan, May 1950, Pt. VII, "United States-Pakistan Relations," box 141, Foreign Affairs File, 1949–1953, President's Secretary's Files, HSTA.

22. Ibid.

23. "Town Hall Speech, 8 May 1950," in Liaquat Ali Khan, *Pakistan: The Heart of Asia* (Cambridge, Mass.: Harvard University Press, 1950), 31.

24. Background Memoranda of Visit to the United States of Liaquat Ali Khan, May 1950.

25. Speech to the Chicago Council on Foreign Relations, "Pakistani Policy: Domestic and Foreign," in Khan, *Pakistan*, 48.

26. Cited in Hussain Haqqani, *Magnificent Delusions: Pakistan, the United States, and an Epic History of Misunderstanding* (Cambridge, Mass.: Harvard University Press, 2014), 48–50.

27. Ibid., 49.

28. Henry F. Grady and John T. McNay, *The Memoirs of Ambassador Henry F. Grady* (Columbia: University of Missouri Press, 2009), 117–36.

29. Narendra Singh Sarila, *The Shadow of the Great Game: The Untold Story of India's Partition* (New Delhi: HarperCollins, 2005).

30. See, e.g., Peter J. Brobst, *The Future of the Great Game: Sir Olaf Caroe, India's Independence, and the Defense of Asia* (Akron, Ohio: University of Akron Press, 2005).

31. Olaf Caroe, *The Soviet Empire: The Turks of Central Asia and Stalinism* (New York: St. Martin's Press, 1953).

32. South Asia Regional Conference of United States Diplomatic and Consular Officers, Ceylon, March 1951, box 2, George McGhee Papers, HSTA.

33. Ibid.

34. Ibid.

35. *Foreign Relations of the United States, 1952–1954*, vol. 6, pt. 1, *Western Europe and Canada*, ed. David M. Baehler et al. (Washington, D.C.: U.S. Government Printing Office, 1986), Document 340.

36. South Asia Regional Conference of United States Diplomatic and Consular Officers, Ceylon, March 1951.

37. Ibid.

38. Haqqani, *Magnificent Delusions*, 49.

39. South Asia Regional Conference of United States Diplomatic and Consular Officers, Ceylon, March 1951.

40. Amitav Acharya, *Whose Ideas Matter? Agency and Power in Asian Regionalism* (Ithaca, N.Y.: Cornell University Press, 2009), 58.

Chapter Two

The Soviet Peace Offensive and Nehru's India, 1953–1956

SWAPNA KONA NAYUDU

Now we say loudly: Indo-Soviet friendship
zindabad; world peace zindabad.[1]

INTRODUCTION

This chapter explores intellectual changes in the Indo-Soviet relationship between 1953 and 1956. This is an account of the view from New Delhi, the central argument being that this period should be studied as one of intense politicization of relations. On both sides, there were various strands of thought and action that constituted this transformative period.[2] A flurry of diplomatic activity took place back and forth from Moscow during these years. Jawaharlal Nehru attempted to reciprocate the thaw with the goal of expanding India's relations with the Soviet Union from purely bilateral to multilateral interactions and, indeed, institutionalizing Indo-Soviet relations by pushing forth his advocacy of the United Nations as being as accessible and amenable to the Soviet Union as much as it was to other powers.

The history of Indo-Soviet relations is often written as a narrative of the crises faced by the Soviet Union during the Cold War and India's responses to those crises. This narrative usually begins with a history of the Hungarian Revolution of 1956. As a result, the period from India's independence in 1947 to 1956 receives little critical attention. Rather than taking that approach, this chapter treats that period as foundational to Indo-Soviet relations, focusing on the four years between Joseph Stalin's death in 1953 and the end of the Hungarian Revolution in 1956. The end of the Stalin era precipitated a moment of intense internal upheaval in the Soviet Union, so there are many moments to choose from. This chapter limits itself to events with consequences for India, and therefore for the Indo-Soviet relationship, starting with a discussion of the peace offensive. The processes of de-Stalinization culminated quite quickly in the internationalization of Soviet foreign policy for the first time extending well outside the socialist bloc, with particular emphasis on peaceful coexistence with the United States.[3] This new approach was also extended to the countries of the Third World, led by Moscow's strong and unambiguous overtures toward India.[4] The "internationalization of foreign policy" is in itself a strange concept, pointing to the particularity of Soviet politics in this period, and makes for an interesting leitmotif of the thaw, discussed in detail here. Aid and trade formed a large part of this growing relationship, but the focus here is limited to the ideological negotiation that constituted the bedrock of other avenues of collaboration.

The year 1954 saw the first major event that the Soviet Union attended post-Stalin — the Geneva Conference of April–July 1954 — where India had a significant presence and played a major role.[5] All major players left the conference somewhat dissatisfied with its outcomes. The fallout of the Geneva Conference set the tone for the rest of that year, and indeed for world politics until the simultaneous crises in the Suez and in Hungary in 1956.[6] In 1955, the leaders of India and the Soviet Union had taken extended tours in each other's countries. Both occasions together formed a great spectacle, one that caused a great deal of alarm in the First World and led to some frankly hysterical appraisals of India's supposed seduction by the Reds.[7] It cannot be denied, however, that the Soviet star was on the ascendant in India until the Hungarian Revolution had the dramatic effect of throwing a spanner in the works. The aftermath represents a moment of quiet assessment that followed the diplomatic crescendo reached by the mutual visits of 1955. The chapter ends by pulling together these various oscillations.

As archival material becomes increasingly available, it is clearer than ever before that both parties to this partnership recalibrated their approach to world politics to accommodate each other — their foreign policies in general were affected to some degree by their conduct toward the other state. This mutual influence has not been studied as extensively as it should be. The United States, for instance, regarded this growing partnership with great trepidation as the opening of a new Cold War front in South Asia, and formed its policies accordingly. Naturally, the relationship between India and the Soviet Union affected and grew not only out of their policies toward each other but through the policies of other states toward both of them.

While it is true of all foreign policies per se that they do not exist in a vacuum of bilateral relations, the beginnings of a substantial Indo-Soviet relationship have not received much attention. The period from 1953 to 1956 was one of great excitement, certainly, but also one of constant appraisal of a strange and new friendship. This chapter engages with some of the more exacting details of that time.

NEHRU, KHRUSHCHEV, AND THE THAW

A cult of personality was not only fundamental to the politics of the Soviet Union but also rather significant in postindependence India. On the Russian side, Joseph Stalin, Georgy Malenkov, and Nikita Khrushchev struggled internally for leadership of the Soviet Union and externally for the international socialist movement. On the Indian side, there was Jawaharlal Nehru, and Nehruvian non-alignment carried forward by a small network of diplomats, including Subimal Dutt and K. P. S. Menon. At the United Nations, New Delhi and Moscow's positions on various issues were put forward by Krishna Menon from India and for a short while after the thaw had begun, by Andrey Vyshinsky from the Soviet Union. Much of the narrative of this four-year period has been reconstructed through examining a series of correspondence between these people. These have been made available by the opening of the archives in two phases in Moscow and through an ongoing process of declassification in New Delhi.[8] Nehru had had a long-standing interest in foreign policy going back well before 1947, which manifested itself institutionally when he kept for himself the portfolio of foreign affairs and immediately pushed forth the idea of Indian non-alignment. This policy was framed in opposition to an ideological organization of the world system of states but designed with the two Cold War superpowers particularly in mind.[9] Even so, in the early years India cultivated relations with both the United States and the Soviet Union.[10] Initially without much positive consequence, relations with both great nations began to improve due to India's mediation in the post–Korean War negotiations, particularly with respect to the divisive question of the settlement of the prisoners of war.[11] India had a significant impact on the eventual signing of the armistice agreement between parties to the conflict at Panmunjom, a contribution acknowledged by the Soviets.[12]

India's mediation between both superpowers and overtures toward the Soviet Union had in fact started much earlier, in the summer of 1950. This period between 1950 and 1953 marks the beginning of the painfully slow thaw in relations between the two countries, eventually accelerated in 1953.[13]

Swapna Kona Nayudu

Nehru had attempted without much success to open channels of communication with the Kremlin, symbolically by sending his own sister, Vijaya Lakshmi Pandit, as his first envoy to Moscow and substantially by opening talks on trade and industry.[14] Although Madame Pandit made little headway and was not received by Stalin during her tenure, Indo-Soviet ties did begin to open up especially in the context of the Moscow Economic Conference organized in April 1952, to which India sent one of the largest delegations present, comparable to those from France, Great Britain, and China,[15] with some estimates putting the number of Indians in attendance at twenty-eight.[16] The Soviet Union reciprocated soon after by sending a delegation to Bombay to the International Industrial Exhibition held in May 1952.[17] Meanwhile, Sarvepalli Radhakrishnan, an eminent philosopher, had replaced Madame Pandit as India's ambassador to the Soviet Union. Stalin received him twice — in January 1950 and again in April 1952.[18] At the first meeting, Stalin asked repeatedly and in some detail about India's relations with the Commonwealth, worrying that there might be a tendency to be overly dependent on the United Kingdom, but Radhakrishnan reassured Stalin that India would soon be a republic.[19] At the second meeting, Radhakrishnan thanked Stalin for the Soviet Union's aid to India in form of the wheat made available in a time of acute crisis. Stalin replied that India "could count on [their] help" and that the Soviets had "been educated in the equal treatment of Asian people."[20]

The difference in the issues discussed at the two meetings itself points to the development of an already somewhat more nuanced understanding of India by the Soviets. Radhakrishnan's stint coincided with the peak of the Korean War — these meetings, especially in the context of Stalin's reluctance to receive other diplomats, signaled that Stalinist Russia was warming up to the idea of nonaligned India, a prospect the Soviet Union fully explored only in the years after the death of Stalin.[21] While Stalin was still alive, K. P. S. Menon, previously India's first foreign secretary, replaced Radhakrishnan as India's ambassador in Moscow. Stalin met him on 18 February 1953, almost as soon as Menon had arrived in Moscow and less than a month before Stalin passed away.[22] Menon continued with the tone and temper set by his predecessor and proved to be a rather enthusiastic votary of improved relations between the two countries. In his reports back to New Delhi, he compared Stalin to Voltaire, although conceding that the former was rather "bucolic" (Voltaire certainly was not) and best described as a "mixture of a peasant and a wild cat."[23]

The following month, Stalin fell into a coma and died soon after, leading to a dramatic leadership crisis in the Soviet Union that was followed closely from New Delhi, although usually with less than a clear understanding of what exactly was unfolding due to the Iron Curtain. Against this backdrop, Malenkov announced on the ides of March 1953 what came to be known as the "Peace Offensive."[24] As the duumvirate between Malenkov and Khrushchev began to take shape, New Delhi was occupied with the negotiation talks over Korea at the United Nations, where Krishna Menon had begun to work in consultation with Vijaya Lakshmi Pandit, then the elected president of the General Assembly, and Andrey Vyshinsky, permanent representative from the Soviet Union to the United Nations. Vyshinsky was previously Russia's foreign minister, a diplomat with a keen sense of the new direction of Russia's foreign policy. This triangulation of Krishna Menon (long suspected by the West of being a communist), Madame Pandit (India's first ambassador to the Soviet Union), and Vyshinsky lent a distinct positive note to the negotiations for the Soviets, who saw India less and less as a liability, evidenced by their influence on the Chinese to cooperate with India and use Nehru's good offices to negotiate a settlement with the West.[25] Nehru was jubilant, but cautious, and saw India's role as the triumph of its non-aligned politics, remarking soon after, "The turn that international events have taken has brought India into the picture and cast a heavy responsibility upon her. The independent policy that we have pursued and our constant attempts to remain friendly with all countries have borne fruit. The Great Powers look upon us with respect and realize that what we say will be listened to by many."[26]

When Stalin was alive, Nehru had appealed to him to end the war and had received a response, leading to speculation in the Western press that Nehru was suited for the task of global mediator.[27] It had been hard enough to break through to Stalin, and with him gone and the new Soviet leadership in place, India became increasingly confident in its new role in world politics, particularly based on its bettering relationship with the Soviet Union. The United States and Europe were quite critical of this choice and made it quite clear that they thought it unwise for a newly independent India to befriend "a temporary state."[28] The Indian diplomatic establishment was concerned with this question, too, albeit in slightly differing terms, wondering in 1954 whether "from the point of view of internal security, it [was] safe to have too friendly relations with a Communist State, of which their ultimate objective is world revolution."[29] Interestingly, the conclusion of this assessment from K. P. S. Menon was that "world revolution [was] receding as a practicable goal, even from the minds of ardent communists."[30] Menon also emphasized to New Delhi that the Russians felt that their assistance to India through aid and trade would "fetch dividends not only in Rupees and Roubles, but in India's goodwill, which is worth much to them, especially at a time when the U.S.A. is picking off one weak or compliant Asian State after another and hitching it to its wagon."[31] India thus had an assessment not only of the Cold War as it played out in the West but also of its imminent arrival in South Asia. The Indian establishment was also aware of the Soviet Union's "muscling in on Santa Claus" in an effort to eliminate American influence from the sub-continent.[32] By the end of 1954, the Soviet Union had invited Nehru to make a state visit.

The year 1954 was, indeed, the most efficacious for Indo-Soviet relations. Beginning in May, the Soviet Union began to mention India first in its greetings at the Kremlin to all noncommunist countries. On all three big issues of global concern — the Korean War, the Indochina War, and the issue of arms control — Moscow backed Indian participation.[33] Having tested its first thermonuclear device in 1953, the Soviet Union had finally corrected its nuclear asymmetry with the United States but was stronger on the conventional side. This led it to become more and more involved in the disarmament initiatives undertaken at the United Nations, of which India was a staunch advocate. At the Geneva Conference, the Soviet Union asked for active Indian participation on the supervisory bodies formed to manage the aftermath of both conflicts.[34] On the International Control Commission, formed to deal with French withdrawal from Vietnam, Molotov pushed for Indian chairmanship on 15 June 1954. Not only did the Soviet Union encourage and insist on Indian participation, but Moscow did this in the face of staunch Western opposition, based mostly on U.S. objections to Indian's nonaligned position. This had the inadvertent consequence of effectively pushing India toward the Soviet Union, seeing in it a potential equal partner. Nehru had already harbored doubts about the Anglo-American attitude toward India, which were not assuaged in the least by successful U.S. efforts at lobbying to keep India out of the peace conference on Korea. Nehru was flabbergasted by this attitude, remarking to Vijaya Lakshmi Pandit, "People in England and America are very courteous to us and friendly but in the final analysis they treat India as a country to be humored but not as an equal. Indeed, the United States hardly treats any other country as an equal."[35] This was not an exaggerated estimation, evidence by the U.S. response to the first Asian African Conference held in April 1955.

Nehru attended the Bandung Conference of Asian and African Cooperation and played a significant part in the drafting of the Bandung Declaration, which emphasized peaceful coexistence, keeping out of the two camps, and the social and economic progress of the newly decolonized countries. The Russians saw Bandung as a positive step, away from the Western bloc.[36] Editorials in *Pravda* during the conference said, "The peoples of Asia and Africa are on the eve of an important political event," and one in *Izvestia* summing up the conference said, "Bandoong was a sign of our age."[37] *Pravda* summed up the Soviet official response, which was, "The people of the Soviet Union have complete understanding for the struggle of the Asian and African countries against all forms of colonial rule, for political and economic interdependence."[38] Nehru then traveled to Moscow in June 1955 and was impressed by the "intense urge for peace" he witnessed.[39] On this visit, Nehru and Khrushchev discussed a host of issues that had hindered India-Russia relations, including the place of Indian communists and Soviet support on the problems of Goa and Kashmir.[40] The favorable view of Bandung taken by the Soviets continued, with Moscow issuing statements saying, "You are following your own road."[41] K. P. S. Menon sent one more of his detailed reports back to New Delhi making the following striking points: Russian leader Nikolai Bulganin had broken tradition and traveled in an open car with Nehru, showing that Nehru's visit had brought the Soviet leaders closer to their own people; all speeches made on the visit were extremely solemn, which meant that they were serious statements of policy, recognizing Nehru's role as a "harbinger of peace"; and, most of all, the Soviet government, which had previously viewed the world only in terms of black and white, had now been shown that "grey, too, has a virtue of its own."[42]

Later that year, Bulganin and Khrushchev traveled through South Asia, spending a significant amount of time in India.[43] Nehru thought their trip to India was a "historic event . . . because of its political aspect and the possible consequences" that would follow from it.[44] Khrushchev liked Nehru's anticolonialism and socialist disposition and expressed Soviet support for economic and military cooperation with the Third World in general and India in particular.[45] In public speeches, the Soviet leaders even called India "an ally."[46] Nehru's high regard for President Eisenhower led him to distance India from this language of alliances, emphasizing that Indo-Soviet cooperation was not directed against any other country.[47] It is interesting to note that the growing relationship was cast in contradictory terms in Moscow and in Delhi.[48] While Nehru attempted to hold on to the gains India had made in Indo-U.S. relations, Khrushchev justified these moves to the Communist Party of the Soviet Union (CPSU) as a strategic balancing of U.S. interest in the Third World and sought to remind his audience of the Leninist prediction that the East would emerge as a "new, powerful factor in international relations."[49] Menon was of the opinion that the visit of the Soviet leaders to India had shown the Indian people that the Soviets were "not the ogres the Western governments had painted them to be" and that the meeting between all the leaders could only be described as *drushba velikih narodov*, or a meeting between great peoples.[50] Certainly, the mutual visits energized the relationship beyond compare and spurred on more collaboration—in the month of September 1955 alone, these included: visits from an oil delegation, a delegation headed by the minister of natural resources, a steel mission, a delegation of scientists headed by Homi Bhabha, an Air India delegation concluding an agreement with Aeroflot, a delegation of Indian educationists in company with representatives from UNESCO, a group of statisticians, a textile trade union delegation, a Kisan Sabha delegation, a traveling handicrafts exhibition, and a visiting football team.[51]

The frenzy continued, and on the eve of 1956, the Indian establishment seemed to believe that in the event of an emergency, "the Russians would give us anything."[52] Then came Khrushchev's CPSU speech of February 1956, in which he referred to further democratization in the Soviet Union's relations with its satellite states and to the new doctrine of "peaceful co-existence."[53] Nehru was careful to distinguish the Soviet concept from the Indian Panchsheel (Five Principles), which he saw as more positively constituted. Yet the speech seems to have had some effect on him: he thought that "even the communist version of socialism and the way to achieve it, which have been rigid dogmas, are in process of undergoing some change."[54] In particular, Poland and Hungary were showing reformist tendencies in the wake of democratized narratives emerging from the Soviet Union.[55] On 25 October 1956, Nehru made his first public statement regarding the uprisings in Poland and Hungary, which he called a "nationalist upsurge" and "a feeling that they themselves are going to fashion their policies and not necessarily others." He did not want to "interfere in any way even by expressing an opinion on the internal affairs of these countries."[56] Yet the situation in Hungary was getting out of hand, and as Soviet troops and tanks began to arrive, by 28 October, international condemnation and pressure was reported from the meeting of the U.N. Security Council. The council voted on a resolution put forward by the United States, which went against the Soviets by 9 to 1, with Yugoslavia abstaining on the grounds of noninterference in Hungarian affairs but opposition to the use of force. Nehru refused to align himself with this U.S. initiative and remained silent on the matter, instead focusing his condemnation on the Suez Crisis, which had broken out simultaneously.[57] Concerns were being expressed on what looked like his partisan approach to these situations of international crises playing out in parallel.[58] The Americans, certain that Nehru was in the wrong and in time would come to that realization, began to discuss Nehru's imminent pro-West sentiment that "we would want to nurture and promote," while finding him a "face-saving device."[59]

The main events of the Hungarian Revolution lasted for a little more than two weeks, ending by November. This coincided with the exact duration of the Suez Crisis, and India's response to that situation took precedence over the uprising in Hungary, which to Nehru seemed opaque and, in any case, to be resolving itself.[60] India didn't have a full ambassador in Budapest at the time of the events,[61] but M. M. Rahman, the chargé d'affaires, continued to send detailed reports, which reached New Delhi belatedly.[62] In the absence of full information, Nehru delayed taking a stand condemnatory of Soviet action.[63] The Indian government was clearly "firm in its belief that when the Soviets announced withdrawal of their troops, they in fact intended to withdraw completely."[64] In fact, Nehru seemed completely taken aback by this return to Stalinist policies that went against the grain of what the new Soviet line seemed to be, especially as Soviet actions in Hungary ran contradictory to the Soviet denunciation of the crisis in Egypt.[65] The Indian policy on this issue was to stress the futility of condemnation and the complicated nature of the situation, although Nehru did refer to the situation as a "civil conflict."[66] On the contrary, as Hungary and the Soviet Union began to hold talks on Hungary's withdrawal from the Warsaw Pact, the Americans hailed these developments as the "dawn of a new day" in Eastern Europe.[67]

Thus, it was much to the consternation of the West[68] and disappointment of his own diplomatic corps[69] that Nehru had yet to condemn Soviet suppression of the Hungarian uprising, although he did ask K. P. S. Menon to convey to the Soviet leadership that their actions were unacceptable. As events spiraled, Nehru, now increasingly outraged, appealed to Moscow to say that Soviet suppression had to stop, "not only because they appear to be [in] violation of Panchsheel which so many countries have loudly proclaimed but also because they have [an] adverse effect on [the] Egyptian situation."[70] Nehru's instructions to Arthur Lall, India's permanent representative and ambassador at the United Nations, were to support the right of Hungarian people "to decide for themselves without external intervention or pressure" but, in the absence of "full facts," to avoid condemnation of the Soviet Union.[71] When the U.N. General Assembly met on 4 November for an emergency session, the house passed a U.S.-sponsored resolution condemning the use of Soviet military forces in Hungary and requesting the

Swapna Kona Nayudu

secretary-general to investigate and observe the military situation through his representatives.[72] India abstained, much to the shock of Western countries, in particular the Canadians, who failed to see why India would take such a strong view against the actions in Egypt but not in Hungary.[73]

Subimal Dutt, who was then the foreign secretary, writes in his account of events that although the instructions had been sent to Arthur Lall, he had not yet received them when voting on the resolution began, and he considered it best to abstain, given the resolution's heavy condemnation of the Soviets.[74] Nehru explained this vote to G. L. Mehta, the Indian ambassador in the United States, saying, "It seemed to us unwise to interfere when a settlement like Poland appeared likely."[75] However, Nehru's support was essential in bringing the situation in Hungary to a peaceful resolution, since "no one else could speak for the whole of Asia"[76] and because the Hungarians were themselves "asking India to intervene and our Prime Minister to come out and bring peace."[77] The Americans considered enlisting Nehru's support in the problem of Hungary but thought that Nehru was either supportive of the Soviets or did not yet have a fully considered policy on the matter.[78] This changed somewhat when, in a speech at the UNESCO General Conference held on 5 November, Nehru took the opportunity to speak out against the situations in Egypt and Hungary but also made a pointed criticism directed at the Soviet Union by referring to countries that subscribed to the Panchsheel, saying, "Those five principles are also mere words without meaning to some countries who claim the right of deciding problems by superior might."[79] Once Nehru made this statement, the Americans, particularly Eisenhower, began to court his support.[80]

However, a renewed correspondence from Bulganin and Nehru at this juncture convinced Nehru to some extent of the Soviet line, and he began to refer to the situation in Hungary as a "civil conflict" with "mutual killings."[81] The Americans were convinced that Nehru had been brainwashed by the Soviets, especially when Nehru referred to the situation in Hungary as being "obscure."[82] Eisenhower was convinced that "Nehru seemed to be falling for the Moscow line — buying their entire bill of goods."[83] After what was being referred to as Nehru's "Bulganization," the West dove into a state of panic. This crisis of confidence was complicated by India's voting on the three resolutions of 8 and 9 November at the U.N. General Assembly.[84] India voted against the first resolution sponsored by Italy, Ireland, Pakistan, Peru, and Cuba, which came to be known as the Five Power Resolution, because it called for elections to be held in Hungary under U.N. auspices.[85] On a second resolution sponsored by the United States condemning Soviet actions in Hungary, India abstained.[86] India voted in support of a third resolution sponsored by Austria, calling for increased aid to Hungary.[87]

The West was shocked that India had been the only noncommunist country to abstain in the vote on the U.S.-sponsored resolution. However, it was clear why India had voted against U.N.-supervised elections in Hungary: this was different from a "fact-finding team," which Nehru opposed on the grounds that if today they were allowed in Hungary, tomorrow they would want to go into Kashmir.[88] Indeed, Nehru considered this proposal "not only unconstitutional but dangerous precedent for other countries," but sought to explain that the procedure of voting meant that even though India criticized Soviet actions, it had had to vote on the operative part of the resolution, which concerned itself foremost with U.N.-supervised elections.[89] Nevertheless, there was widespread criticism of the Indian vote in many countries, and not least in India.[90] Finally, on 16 November, Nehru made a speech in the Lok Sabha on the situation in Hungary, declaring, "There was no immediate aggression in Hungary in the sense of something militarily happening as there was in the case of Egypt. It was really a continuing intervention of Soviet armies in Hungary based on the Warsaw Pact. The fact is that as subsequent events have shown, the Soviet armies were there against the wishes of the Hungarian people."[91] This and events following in the next few days marked the beginning of the "de-Bulganization" of Nehru.[92]

Between 1954 and 1956, Nehru had begun to rely on General Tito of Yugoslavia considerably in gaining an understanding of Europe from a European and of the Soviet Union from one of the socialist bloc.[93] The Soviets, too, cultivated Tito as a bridge to the rest of the socialist bloc but also to the newly opened up Third World, the vast uncommitted political space with memberships in the United Nations. But by 1956, relations between Yugoslavia and the Soviet Union became more strained. Imre Nagy, the Hungarian leader in exile, had been seeking asylum in the Yugoslav embassy, and Tito had made a public speech criticizing the first Soviet intervention (of October) but declaring the inevitability of the second one (of November). Nehru disagreed with Tito's assessment, saying that "the first one is a catastrophe; the second one is an evil,"[94] and so relied less and less on his consul in the days to come.[95] Nehru and Krishna Menon agreed that India would maintain its position of noninterference in Hungarian internal matters and that it was "for the people of Hungary to decide what government they should have."[96] Sensing a loss of Indian support, the Soviets sent the ambassador in Delhi to call on Nehru to remind him of Soviet support on the question of Kashmir at the United Nations, in a form of "gentle blackmail."[97] Yet Indian efforts at diplomatic solutions continued; Nehru wrote to Menon, saying, "If war comes, it will come in spite of us."[98]

Tito having turned against the Soviets,[99] and with Rahman's incessant reports detailing the injustices imposed on the Hungarian population,[100] Nehru began to advise restraint all around, saying, "We should try to avoid giving needless offence or aggravating a situation that is bad enough."[101] In the next phase of diplomatic activity at the United Nations, two resolutions were passed on 4 and 12 December 1956. The first resolution demanded the withdrawal of Soviet troops from Hungary; the second declared that the presence of Soviet troops was violating the political independence of Hungary. Nehru and Krishna Menon widely debated India's position on the resolutions in the United Nations that were demanding the withdrawal of Soviet troops from Hungary.[102] Eventually, when India abstained on both resolutions, Menon explained it in the General Assembly on 10 December, saying that India's "objection was to the use of Soviet forces in the Hungarian internal affairs" and that what had "happened in Hungary was a national uprising."[103] Menon was of the opinion that even though India was abstaining on the resolutions, "this is an occasion when, independent of the resolution, we should express ourselves fully and critically about the Soviet Union."[104] Nehru agreed with Menon, saying that although the justification provided by the Soviets could be seen from their point of view, it was "certainly contrary to Panchsheel."[105]

CONCLUSION

A few months after the events of the Hungarian Revolution had taken place, Nehru wrote to K. P. S. Menon, saying that "a succession of foolish actions" by the Soviet Union had disrupted "the idea of real peace in our generation."[106] These and numerous other assessments put forth by Nehru in his many writings emphasized continuously how it was important to cultivate good relations with the Soviet Union, as it was India's policy to do so with all nations, but also quite significantly that it was important to take the initiative in organizing these relations because they would lead to a further opening up of the Soviet Union itself. Whether Western commentators and policy makers at the time considered non-alignment immoral or ineffective, they paid less and less attention to the sort of foreign policy approaches that nonaligned India attempted during the Cold War. After the death of Nehru, and India's defeat at the hands of the Chinese in a border war, the nonaligned approach became riled with controversy and disorientation, leading to fewer studies of what it constituted. Thus, most exhaustive accounts of India's Cold War politics belong to the era in which that politics was played out and are mostly from that time. They also tend to focus, particularly in the case of Indo-Soviet relations, on building a narrative of the bilateral relationship through the lens of studying India's international relations and solely for that purpose.[107] Although these were useful at the time, the subsequent opening of the Indian archives helps us newly contest the concept of the Cold War as a whole, not only where it is concerned with a discussion of India's national interests.[108] These new challenges will position themselves within international relations literature, and can do well to take advantage of the historical turn under way in the field. Previous studies in this vein have had a rather Eurocentric approach and consider the Cold War a Western phenomenon, fought in a closed theater, with some concessions being made to accommodate perspectives from Red China.[109]

The Indian account of the Cold War in South Asia and more broadly globally has much to contribute by way of offering a fresh archival perspective but also by bringing new theoretical lenses to the study of the Cold War. Even where Indian archives are opening up and being used to write new histories, they are often underused in their theoretical potential. For instance, in lamenting Soviet actions in Hungary, Nehru remarked in two separate sets of correspondence, "It will be very difficult for the Soviet Government to outlive this black mark."[110] Previous interpretations have suggested that Nehru was claiming that India's relations with the Soviet Union had suffered and that he was proved wrong because in the future, New Delhi's relations with Moscow only grew more robust.[111] In fact, a broader reading of Nehru's letter suggests otherwise—that, in fact, he was disappointed that the Soviet Union had breached any chances of peaceful settlements *with the West*. Certainly, Nehru was concerned with India's relations with the Soviet Union, but he took in the case of this relationship the same bird's-eye view that he adopted elsewhere. Asian and African nations were rapidly decolonizing but were emerging into a Cold War context. Nehru constantly laid stress in his writings on the need to diffuse that larger climate of war. This led him to regard not only communism but also any other political approach with some degree of suspicion. In his political thought, these states had all willingly participated in either colonial or Cold War enterprises or, indeed, in both. Thus, there was no question that India would naturally collaborate with either bloc but would follow a course that suited the country. That was, in fact, the essence of non-alignment—an accent on holding political concepts up to scrutiny, irrespective of their ideological or geographical origin. Thus, the emergent archive can only be read to full use if the political thought and debates prevalent in the Indian establishment at the time are understood more deeply.

This is clearly evident in India's approach to de-Stalinized Soviet foreign policy. It is clear from the discussion above that the Indian diplomatic establishment headed by Nehru sought to delink Soviet communism from Soviet foreign policy—some like K. P. S. Menon thought it was possible, while others like Subimal Dutt thought it needed much more doing. For the most part, there was a systematic probing of master narratives and a radical attempt at saying that there was more to the Soviet Union's foreign policy than an all-consuming communist zeal for propaganda. Even when the Soviet Union was undergoing the immense ideological and institutional upheaval of the 1950s and the 1960s, there was an attempt from nonaligned India, through its foreign policy establishment in Moscow, New Delhi, and, quite significantly, New York to find avenues for collaborative diplomacy. The more the West sought to isolate the communists, the more India pushed for their integration. This was by no means an easy task, and strong personalities from all parts of the political spectrum left it almost impossible for Nehru to affect any stunning shifts. Nevertheless, the Indo-Soviet partnership influenced the course of direct diplomacy as well as diplomacy at the United Nations on questions of import to them both at the time. The eventual collapse of the Soviet Union and the fading away of Indian nonalignment post-Nehru have led to a certain level of triumphalism in Western diplomatic history, propelled as it is by its archive. Arguments emerged in the interim before Russian and Indian materials became more accessible, and it is now possible and necessary that those arguments be examined in the light of new evidence, not only for factual accuracy but also so that global intellectual histories might be written where previously only diplomatic chronicles were possible.

NOTES

1. *Zindabad* is a Hindi expression translated as "long live." Jawaharlal Nehru, Speech at Calcutta Maidan on the occasion of the visits of Soviet leaders Bulganin and Khrushchev to India, 1955, "Visit of the Soviet Leaders," in *Selected Works of Jawaharlal Nehru*, 2nd ser. (hereafter *SWJN*), ed. S. Gopal, 61 vols. to date (New Delhi: Jawaharlal Nehru Memorial Fund, 1984–), vol. 31, 317.

2. For a study of Russia's intellectual changes that affected its relations with the West, see Robert English, *Russia and the Idea of the West* (New York: Columbia University Press, 2000), 256.

3. Indeed, Moscow continually assessed its relations with the Third World in the larger

context of the Cold War. See Andreas Hilger, "Sowjetunion, Realsozialismus und Dritte Welt, 1945–1991, Einleitung," in *Die Sowjetunion und die Dritte Welt: UdSSR, Staatssozialismus und Antikolonialismus im Kalten Krieg, 1945–1991*, ed. Hilger, Schriftenreihe der Vierteljahrshefte für Zeitgeschichte 99 (Munich: Oldenbourg, 2009), 293.

4. For accounts of Moscow's Third World policy, see Roger E. Kanet, ed., *The Soviet Union, Eastern Europe and the Third World* (Cambridge: Cambridge University Press, 1987), 233; Alvin Z. Rubinstein, *Moscow's Third World Strategy* (Princeton, N.J.: Princeton University Press, 1988), 329; and Sobhanlal Datta Gupta, *Comintern and the Destiny of Communism in India, 1919–1943: Dialectics of Real and a Possible History* (Kolkata: Seribaan, 2011), 404. For a comprehensive study of those relations in particular reference to India, see Vojtech Mastny, "The Soviet Union's Partnership with India," *Journal of Cold War Studies* 12, no. 3 (Summer 2010): 50–90.

5. The Geneva Conference, held between April and July 1954, was a major international conference involving the two superpowers, the United Kingdom, France, and China, held to resolve outstanding issues regarding the Korean War and possible peace in Indochina. Other countries, such as India, that had contributed troops or played a mediatory role in the resolution of both crises, were also present at various points during the conference.

6. For a discussion on this, see "Notes on Conversations between the Prime Minister of India and Mr. A. I. Mikoyan, First Deputy Premier of the U.S.S.R., in the Prime Minister's House on March 28, 1956," Subject File No. 19, New Delhi, Subimal Dutt Papers, Nehru Memorial and Museum Library (hereafter NMML), New Delhi, reprinted in *SWJN*, vol. 31, 397–401.

7. "Communists: Lunge to the South," *Time*, 19 December 1955, 24; see also "Route of Conquest: Communists Go by Way of Asia—Africa Next," *Newsweek*, 28 November 1955, 47–48.

8. For the archival documents, see "Documents," in Surjit Mansingh et al., eds., *IndoSoviet Relations in the Nehru Years: The View from India, 1949–1961*, Parallel History Project on Cooperative Security, 2009, accessible at http://www.php.isn.ethz.ch/lory1 .ethz.ch/collections/colltopic1602.html?lng=en&id=56154&nav1=1&nav2=8&nav3=4. See also "Documents: The Stalin Years, 1945–1951," "The Soviet Union and India: The Years of Late Stalinism," "Documents: The Khrushchev Years, 1954–1966," and "The Soviet Union and India: The Khrushchev Era and Its Aftermath until 1966," all in Hilger et al., eds., *IndoSoviet Relations, New Russian and German Evidence*, Parallel History Project on Cooperative Security, 2009, accessible at http://www.php.isn.ethz.ch/lory1.ethz.ch /collections/colltopic1602.html?lng=en&id=56154&nav1=1&nav2=8&nav3=4.

9. See Swapna Kona Nayudu, "The Nehru Years: Indian Non-Alignment as the Critique, Discourse and Practice of Security (1947-1964)" (Ph.D. thesis, King's College London, 2015), chaps. 1, 2.

10. For a discussion of the Third World and the Cold War dominated by the two superpowers, see Odd Arne Westad, *The Global Cold War: Third World Interventions and the Making of Our Times* (Cambridge: Cambridge University Press, 2005), 208–19.

11. Ibid., chap. 3; Rudra Chaudhuri, *Forged in Crisis* (London: Hurst, 2014), 49–80.

12. See "Statement of Molotov, Minister of Foreign Affairs on the Korean Question," 31 March 1953, History and Public Policy Program Digital Archive, AVP RF. F. 3, Op. 65, D. 830, 107–12, obtained by Andrei Mefodievich Ledovskii, https://digitalarchive .wilsoncenter.org/document/117426.

13. For starters, the Soviets attempted a recasting of Mahatma Gandhi in a better light

in their literature; see *Embassy of India, Moscow, The Annual Report on the Soviet Union for 1953*, sent from K. P. S. Menon to the Foreign Secretary R. K. Nehru, 12 February 1953, Ministry of External Affairs (hereafter MEA) File no. R.6/1954, National Archives of India (hereafter NAI), New Delhi.

14. For Madam Pandit's recollections of her time in Moscow, see Vijaya Lakshmi Pandit, *The Scope of Happiness: A Personal Memoir* (New York: Crown, 1979). For a survey of the influence of Indo-Soviet relations on various aspects of the Indian economy, see David C. Engerman, "Solidarity, Development, and Non-Alignment: Foreign Economic Advisors and Indian Planning in the 1950s and 1960s," in *Create One World: Practices of "International Solidarity" and "International Development,"* ed. Berthold Unfried and Eva Himmelstoss, ITH Conference Proceedings, vol. 46 (Leipzig: Akademische Verlaganstalt, 2012); see also Engerman, "The Political Power of Economic Ideas?," in *India in the World since 1947: National and Transnational Perspectives*, ed. Andreas Hilger and Corinna Unger (Frankfurt: Peter Lang, 2012), 384.

15. Professors Mahalanobis, Mukherjee, and Gyan Chand attended the conference that took place in Moscow between 3 and 12 April 1952. See Alec Cairncross, "The Moscow Economic Conference," *Soviet Studies* 4, no. 2 (1952): 114. For a discussion on whether the conference marked a new direction in foreign policy, see Mikahil Lipkin, "La Conférence économique de Moscou: Changement de tactique ou innovation dans la politique extérieure Stalinienne?," *Relations Internationales* 3, no. 147 (2011): 19–33.

16. Gene D. Overstreet and Marshall Windmiller, *Communism in India* (Berkeley: University of California Press, 1959), 603.

17. J. A. Naik, *Russia's Policy towards India: From Stalin to Yeltsin* (Bombay: M. D. Publications, 1995), 152.

18. The exact dates of these meetings were 14 January 1950 and 4 April 1952. For an account of the meetings, see K. P. S. Menon, "Three Conversations of J. V. Stalin and Indian Ambassadors, 1950–1953," *Revolutionary Democracy* 12, no. 1 (April 2006), http://www.revolutionarydemocracy.org/rdv12n1/3convers.htm.

19. Ibid.

20. Ibid.

21. See Yedezad. D. Gundevia, *Outside the Archives* (Hyderabad: Sangam Books, 1987), 93, 344–45.

22. The exact date of this meeting was 18 February 1953. See Menon, "Three Conversations."

23. Ibid.

24. The "Peace Offensive" was originally a Stalinist concept; the phrasing was later appropriated by Khrushchev. For the effect it had on Russian relations with another Asian power, China, see Odd Arne Westad, *Brothers in Arms: The Rise and Fall of the Sino-Soviet Alliance, 1945–1963* (Stanford, Calif.: Stanford University Press, 1998), 22–26.

25. For an interesting note on the perception of V. K. Krishna Menon's appointment to the United Nations and the effect of this on Indian diplomacy in the Cold War, see Vernon M. Hewitt, *The New International Politics of South Asia* (Manchester: Manchester University Press, 1997), 89–90. For suspicions that Menon was a communist, see Sunil Khilnani, "Nehru's Evil Genius," *Outlook* (New Delhi), 19 March 2007.

26. Jawaharlal Nehru, "Letter of 24 May 1953," in Jawaharlal Nehru, *Letters to Chief Ministers, 1947–1964*, ed. G. Parthasarathi, 5 vols. (New Delhi: Jawaharlal Nehru Memorial Fund, 1985–89), vol. 3, 310–11, Point 16.

27. Jawaharlal Nehru, "India's Korean Policy," statement in parliament, 3 August 1950, *SWJN*, vol. 15, 343. See this note for citations from world press.

28. John Lewis Gaddis puts forward an account precisely of how transitory the Americans thought Soviet communism was, and how much they wished it were; see Gaddis, *The Cold War* (New York: Penguin, 2007), viii.

29. *Embassy of India, Moscow, The Annual Report on the Soviet Union for 1953.*

30. Ibid.

31. Ibid.

32. C. D. Jackson, quoted in David C. Engerman, "South Asia and the Cold War," in *The Cold War in the Third World*, ed. Robert J. McMahon (Oxford: Oxford University Press, 2013), 256.

33. Geoffrey Jukes, *The Soviet Union in Asia* (Berkeley: University of California Press), 1973, 304.

34. For all the negotiations to and fro, including those on the inclusion of neutral nations, see "A CWIHP Document Reader compiled for the international conference 'New Evidence on the 1954 Geneva Conference on Indochina,' Washington, D.C., 17–18 February 2006," Cold War International History Project, Wilson Center, https://www .wilsoncenter.org/publication/the-1954-geneva-conference#sthash.9IOBt5wS.dpuf.

35. Jawaharlal Nehru to Vijaya Lakshmi Pandit, "Visit of Soviet Leaders," *SWJN*, vol. 31.

36. For a comprehensive discussion of the Soviet response to the Bandung Conference, see Westad, *Global Cold War*, 99.

37. These responses were noted with satisfaction in Report from Embassy of India, Moscow, "Reactions in the Soviet Press over the Bandung Conference," 31 May 1955, MEA File no. D 886/AAC-55 NAI.

38. "Pravda, 14, 26 and 30 April 1955," quoted in Zafar Imam, "Soviet View of Non-Alignment," *International Studies* 20, no. 1/2 (1981): 445–69. This view had changed in less than a decade. "It is abundantly clear that it [the NAM] can no longer persuade the Soviet Union to give its support or to involve itself merely by highlighting the colonial exploitation of the past or by complaining constantly on the non-conducive nature of world politics." See "Central Committee Reports to the 22nd, 23rd, 24th Congresses of the CPSU, 1961–1971," quoted in ibid., 468.

39. Speech in Dynamo Stadium, Moscow, 21 June 1955, quoted in Subimal Dutt, *With Nehru in the Foreign Office* (Columbia: South Asia Books, 1977), 193.

40. Ibid., 197–98.

41. "Military Blocs Condemned," *Ceylon Daily News*, 16 November 1955.

42. K. P. S. Menon, "Prime Minister's Visit to the Soviet Union," 6 July 1955. See also "Report on Nehru's Visit to the Soviet Union, 6 July 1955"; "Report on Talks between Nehru and Soviet Leaders, 12 July 1955"; and "Reflections on Travelling with Nehru, 29 July 1955," in *The Prime Minister's Visit to the Soviet Union and Other Countries (June–July 1955)*, ed. N. R. Pillai, Secretary General of the Ministry of External Affairs, Subject File No. 16, June–July 1955, New Delhi, Subimal Dutt Collection, NMML.

43. For a record of their talks, see "Record of Nehru's Conversation with Khrushchev and Bulganin, 12 December 1955," in *Selected Works of Jawaharlal Nehru*, 2nd Ser. (Delhi: Jawaharlal Nehru Memorial Fund, 2003), vol. 31, 334–45. For Nehru's talks with Anastas Mikoyan, when Mikoyan visited India in 1956, see "Notes on MikoyanNehru Conversations, 26–28 March 1956," in Subject File No. 19, 1956, Subimal Dutt Papers, NMML, reprinted in *SWJN*, vol. 32, 397–401.

44. "Summary Record of a Talk between Prime Minister of India and Mr NA Bulganin and Mr NS Khrushchev at the Prime Minister's House," 12 December 1955; and "Note by the Prime Minister on the Visit of the Soviet Leaders to India," n.d., Subject File No. 17, Subimal Dutt Papers, NMML.

45. Westad, *Global Cold War*, 67.

46. Escott Reid, *Envoy to Nehru* (New York: Oxford University Press, 1981), 139.

47. Ibid., 134–36.

48. For an enthusiastic Indian perspective, K. P. S. Menon, *The Flying Troika* (London: Oxford University Press, 1963), 18, 110. For a much more muted Russian perspective, see Nikita S. Khrushchev, *Vospominaniya: Vremya, lyudi, vlast'* [Memoirs: Time, people, power], 4 vols. (Moscow: Moskovskie novosti, 1999), vol. 3, 320, 317.

49. Ibid., 68. On the visit, see also Pavel Alekseevich Satiukov, ed., *Missiia druzhby: Prebyvanie N. A. Bulganina i N. S. Khrushcheva v Indii, Birme, Afganistane* [Friendship mission: N. A. Bulganin and N. S. Khrushchev's visit to India, Burma, and Afghanistan], 2 vols. (Moscow: Pravda, 1956).

50. K. P. S. Menon, "Annual Political Report from Moscow, 1955," Moscow, 15 February 1956, MEA File No. D 939 RUI/56, NAI.

51. Ibid.

52. Krishnan Srinivasan, *Diplomatic Channels* (New Delhi: Manohar, 2012), 69.

53. Anastas Mikoyan briefed Nehru on the content of the speech and its aims and objectives when they met soon after in New Delhi. See "Notes on Conversations between the Prime Minister of India and Mr. A. I. Mikoyan, First Deputy Premier of the U.S.S.R., in the Prime Minister's House on March 27, 1956." For a discussion of the speech, see Westad, *Global Cold War*, 68.

54. Nehru, "Letter of 14 October 1956," in Nehru, *Letters to Chief Ministers*, vol. 4, 457–58.

55. Reid, *Envoy to Nehru*, 147.

56. Ibid., 148–49.

57. "Telegram from MEA to Indian Embassy in DC, 30 October 56," in Sarvepalli Gopal, *Jawaharlal Nehru: A Biography*, 3 vols. (London: Jonathan Cape, 1975–84), vol. 2, 291n1.

58. Indeed, some of the criticism came from within the MEA, with Dutt and Reid sharing their concerns; see ibid.

59. *Foreign Relations of the United States*, 1955–57, vol. 25, Eastern Europe, ed. Edward C. Keefer, Ronald D. Landa, and Stanley Shaloff (Washington, D.C.: Government Printing Office, 1990), Document 131.

60. Dutt, *With Nehru in the Foreign Office*, 177. However, this was not only an Indian position—see the U.N. secretary general's assessment of the order of things: "If you disregard all other aspects and look at the time sequence, I think it is perfectly clear to you that Suez had a time priority on the thinking and on the policy making of the main body in the UN." Dag Hammarskjold quoted in Henry P. Van Dusen, *Dag Hammarskjöld: The Statesman and His Faith* (New York: Harper and Row, 1964), 141–42.

61. Vincent Sheean, *Nehru: The Years of Power* (New York: Random House, 1960), 161.

62. In a comprehensively analytical note, Rahman lists the following factors as "instrumental in filling the powder keg": a) Economic deterioration, b) The reign of the Stalinists, c) The rehabilitation, d) Soviet troops, e) Titoism. See "Note from Rahman to the Foreign Secretary, MEA India," in *The Hungarian Revolution 1956—Documents*, vol. 1, pt. 1, 12, MEA Archives, New Delhi.

63. Ibid.

64. Lazslo Borhi, *Hungary in the Cold War, 1945–1956: Between the United States and the Soviet Union* (Budapest: Central European University Press, 2004), 298n181. However, Borhi wrongly lists the Indian ambassador in Moscow as being "Krishna Menon," when it was in actuality K. P. S. Menon.

65. Dutt, *With Nehru in the Foreign Office*, 178.

66. Ibid., 178–79. See Escott Reid, *Hungary and Suez, 1956: A View from Delhi* (Oakville, Ont.: Mosaic Press, 1986), 37, on how Nehru termed the Hungarian Revolution a "civil war" in his speech on 28 October and then again on 9 November.

67. Bekes, "1956 Hungarian Revolution and World Politics." Bekes neglects to mention Indian diplomacy at the United Nations, even in the section titled "The United Nations and the Third World."

68. Reid, *Hungary and Suez 1956*, 41.

69. Reid says that N. R. Pillai sent Nehru a memo warning him against applying double standards to the cases of Suez and Hungary. See Reid, *Envoy to Nehru*, 154.

70. "Cable to KPS Menon," 4 November 1956, *SWJN*, vol. 35, 455.

71. Ibid.

72. Second Emergency Special Session of the UNGA—1004-E.S.(II) ; see also ibid., n3.3.

73. "A cynical and shameful betrayal of the moral unity of the Commonwealth and indeed of all free nations." James Eayrs, quoted in Reid, *Envoy to Nehru*, 162–63.

74. Dutt, *With Nehru in the Foreign Office*, 179–80. However, Krishna Menon's statement at the UNGA clearly states that India "abstained because we agreed with some parts of it but did not agree with others," see "Statement by Krishna Menon at the UNGA on November 8, 1956," in *The Hungarian Revolution 1956—Documents*, vol. 1, pt. 2, 141–45, MEA Archives, New Delhi.

75. "Cable to GL Mehta," 5 November 1956, *SWJN*, vol. 35, 456.

76. Reid, *Envoy to Nehru*, 157.

77. Rahman, *The Hungarian Revolution 1956—Documents*, vol. 1, pt. 1, 36, MEA Archives, New Delhi.

78. Brought on by Lall's comment that he did not know why his country had abstained in the 4 November vote; see *Foreign Relations of the United States, 1955–1957*, vol. 25, *Eastern Europe*, ed. Edward C. Keefer, Ronald D. Landa, and Stanley Shaloff (Washington, D.C.: U.S. Government Printing Office, 1990), Document 171, 103n11.

79. *Paths to Peace: India's Voices in UNESCO, 64 years of UNESCO-India Co-operation* (New Delhi: UNESCO, 2009), 16–17.

80. As Reid puts it, "The United States and India were now the only great powers with clean hands. Only Eisenhower and Nehru could speak for the conscience of mankind"; see Reid, *Envoy to Nehru*, 157.

81. Ibid., 166–67.

82. *Foreign Relations of the United States, 1955–1957*, vol. 25, *Eastern Europe*, Document 175.

83. Ibid.

84. These were U.N. General Assembly Resolution Nos. 1005-(ES II), 1006-(ES II), and 1007-(ES II).

85. "Cable to V K Krishna Menon, 11 November 1956," *SWJN*, vol. 35, 459n2. Brecher is of the view that "on the contrary, when India opposed the proposal to send UN observers

and the call for a UN-controlled election in Hungary, it was clear that Delhi wanted to avoid a precedent for Kashmir." He also says that Nehru's instructions to Menon were that he should abstain, but that Menon voted against it; see Michael Brecher, *Nehru: A Political Biography* (New York: Oxford University Press, 1959), 573. Subimal Dutt says that no instructions were sent to Menon and that he acted of his own accord; see Dutt, *With Nehru in the Foreign Office*, 181.

86. Escott Reid refers to Vijaya Lakshmi Pandit's account of Nehru's telephone conversation with Menon that says Nehru told Menon he should use his own discretion. Reid also discusses Nehru's principal private secretary Mathai's allegation that Nehru had sent Menon a telegram instructing Krishna Menon to abstain in the vote on the resolution and that Menon claimed that the telegram had arrived too late but that this was a lie. See Reid, *Hungary and Suez, 1956*, 106.

87. Ross N. Berkes and Mohinder S. Bedi are of the view that "The total absence of recriminatory clauses in either the preamble or the operative sections of the Austrian resolution was clearly the consideration which won India's support." See Berkes and Bedi, *The Diplomacy of India: Indian Foreign Policy in the United Nations* (Stanford, Calif.: Stanford University Press, 1958), 53.

88. Nikhil Chakrvarty interview, "Rethinking Russia," 80–81, quoted in Sreemati Ganguly, *Indo Russian Relations: Making of a Relationship, 1992–2002* (Delhi: Shipra, 2009), 43n112.

89. "Cable to GL Mehta and Vijaya Lakshmi Pandit," 15 November 1956, *SWJN*, vol. 35, 462.

90. Reid, *Hungary and Suez 1956*, 84.

91. Dutt, *With Nehru in the Foreign Office*, 181.

92. Reid, *Envoy to Nehru*, 177.

93. Mišković says that Nehru saw in Tito "a competent consultant," in Nataša Mišković, "Between Idealism and Pragmatism: Tito, Nehru and the Hungarian Crisis 1956," in *The Non-Aligned Movement and the Cold War: Delhi—Bandung—Belgrade*, ed. Nataša Mišković, Harald Fischer-Tine, and Nada Bodškovska (New York: Routledge, 2014), 250.

94. Mišković, "Between Idealism and Pragmatism," 128.

95. "Cable to V K Krishna Menon," 20 November 1956," *SWJN*, vol. 35, 469–71.

96. Ibid., 472–73.

97. Gopal, *Jawaharlal Nehru*, vol. 2, 297.

98. Nehru quoted in ibid., 296. For the change in Nehru's attitude, see "Letter to CDA Rahman dated November 23, 1956 from New Delhi by the Hungarian Indologist Erwin Baktay," in *The Hungarian Revolution 1956—Documents*, vol. 1, pt. 1, 53–56, MEA Archives, New Delhi.

99. "Cable to V K Krishna Menon," 2 December 1956, *SWJN*, vol. 36, 557–58n5. Yugoslavia had indicated that because diplomatic channels had failed, it would be "compelled to speak out in the UN."

100. "Cable to V K Krishna Menon," 23 November 1956, *SWJN*, vol. 35, 481–82.

101. "Cable to V K Krishna Menon," 2 December 1956, *SWJN*, vol. 36, 557–58.

102. For the correspondence, see *SWJN*, vol. 36, 562–67, 569–70.

103. Dutt, *With Nehru in the Foreign Office*, 184–85.

104. "Cable to V K Krishna Menon," 3 December 1956, *SWJN*, vol. 36, 560.

105. "Cable to V K Krishna Menon," 9 December 1956, *SWJN*, vol. 36, 565–66.

106. See Menon, *Flying Troika*, 171.

107. An often overlooked but well-updated study is Sreemati Ganguli, *Indo-Russian Relations: The Making of a Relationship, 1992–2002* (Delhi: Shipra, 2009), 274.

108. Odd Arne Westad, "Epilogue," in *The Cold War in the Third World*, ed. Robert J McMahon, 217 (Oxford: Oxford University Press, 2013).

109. See, e.g., John Lewis Gaddis, "International Relations Theory and the End of the Cold War," *International Security* 17, no. 3 (Winter 1992/3): 5–58; and Richard Ned Lebow, "The Long Peace, the End of the Cold War, and the Failure of Realism," in *International Relations Theory and the End of the Cold War*, ed. Richard Ned Lebow and Thomas Risse-Kappen (New York: Columbia University Press, 1995), 23–56.

110. J. Nehru, "Cable to Herbert V Evatt," 27 June 1958, and "Cable to KPS Menon," 28 June 1958, *SWJN*, vol. 42, 653–54.

111. Mastny, "Soviet Union's Partnership with India," 56.

Chapter   *Three*

Faiz, Love, and the Fellowship of the Oppressed

SYED AKBAR HYDER

The cultural fronts on which the Cold War was fought are more difficult to discern than the geopolitical ones. These fronts were fortified by historical memories that are mediated much more ambiguously than the seemingly bipolar political ones — through folktales, music, sports, and poetry. Urdu poetry of the Cold War era, popular in both India and Pakistan, challenged neat loyalties to nation-states. In the Cold War context, India's alignment with the Soviet Union and Pakistan's with the United States has persisted as a given. The extent to which citizens of these nations, especially their poets (many of whom remain the prime bastions of resistance to their status quo), fractured these alignments merits discussion. In this chapter I tell a story of one such poet, Faiz Ahmed Faiz (1911–1984). Faiz was a citizen of Pakistan who was equally popular in India; he was a visionary who evoked resistance to oppression by grouping Karl Marx's principles of economic justice with those of the Qur'an and Islamic mysticism; he was a poet who lifted up with gumption a millennium-old genre of Perso-Urdu lyrical poetry, the *ghazal*, on the pillars of concrete sociopolitical struggles around him. A keen observer of nature, Faiz threaded his way across continents, raising awareness of the subaltern plight through his poetry and activism. He called for a collective of witnesses, shorn of vengeance. The story of Faiz's poetry thus brings to the forefront the romance of alternative imaginings of a community in a world devastated by wars, occupations, executions, and poverty. The poetic overtones of this story do not neatly accord with the geopolitical ones to which we are accustomed. The way that Faiz challenges the us-against-them mentality—by anchoring himself in a space that defies any nation-state—highlights the Cold War's intersectionality and a single man's ethical prowess and determination to redress the injustices around him in the language of love. I first discuss how Faiz reframes love in his poetry; I then describe how this reframing alerts us to a vision of an alternative fellowship of citizens and nations that does not sync with the mutually exclusive ideologies that the Cold War posited.

In 1982, the city of Bombay celebrated with pomp the completion of fifty years of sound in Indian films. The occasion was especially uplifted by the presence of Noor Jahan, a singer hailed as the "melody queen" in South Asia, an actor who had played a formidable role in the Indian cinema of the 1940s but who had migrated to Pakistan after that country was created in 1947 and became what might be called one of their national voices. As a gesture of gratitude to an enormous following in India and backed by popular demand, Noor Jahan sang, "Mujh se pahlī sī muḥabbat merī maḥbūb nah māñg" (The love like the former one? Beloved, do not ask of me), a poem that had acquired a legendary status in South Asia:

> Main ne samjhā thā keh tū hai to darakhshāñ hai hayāt
> Terā gham hai to gham-e dahr kā jhagṛā kyā hai
> Terī sūrat se hai 'ālam meñ bahāroñ ko sabāt
> Terī āñkhoñ ke sivā dunyā meñ rakhā kyā hai
> Tū jo mil jāye to taqdīr nigūñ ho jāye
> Yūñ nah thā main ne faqat chāhā thā yūñ ho jāye
> Aur bhī dukh haiñ zamāne meñ muḥabbat ke sivā
> Rāḥateñ aur bhī haiñ vasl kī rāḥat ke sivā
> Anganat sadiyoñ ke tārīk bahīmānah tilism
> Resham o atlast o kimkhāb meñ bunwāye hūe
> Jā bajā bikte hūe kuchah o bāzār men jism
> Khāk meñ lithṛe hūe khūn meñ nahlāye hūe
> Laut jātī hai udhar ko bhī nazar kyā kijiye
> Ab bhī dilkash hai tera husn magar kyā kijiye
> Mujh se pahlī sī muḥabbat merī maḥbūb nah māñg

> I had thought: as long as you remain, life glows
> As long as I pine for you, I need not confront life
> Your form lends permanence to the springs of the world
> Beyond your eyes? Was anything worth my sight!
> When I met up with you, fate surrendered to me—

All of this was not it; I only wished for it.
There are sorrows around us,
apart from the sorrows of love,
other comforts prevail, apart from the comfort of union
Countless, begrimed, brutal spells of centuries
Netted into silk, satin, velvet
Bodies sold everywhere, in the streets, at the markets
Spattered with muck, bathed in blood
My gaze returns to all of that, how can I resist
Your beauty still enchants, yet,
What can be done!
The love like the former one? Beloved! Do not ask from me.[1]

The occasion for this song was Noor Jahan's first visit to the post-1947 India. Noor Jahan's audiences applauded her as a bridge builder, as an artist who rose above parochial geographies and ideologies, much like the poet who had composed the lyrics, Faiz Ahmed Faiz. As the distinguished literary historian Malik Ram contends, Faiz was one of the three most authoritative voices that emerged in twentieth-century Urdu literature of South Asia—the other two being those of Muhammad Iqbal and Josh Malihabadi.[2]

Cultural historians and literary critics laud Faiz's poem "The Love Like the Former One?" that Noor Jahan sang as a "revolutionary" testament of a new vision of love. This poem artfully sets the tone for a love that is not exclusivist and can be read as an allegory of a challenge to unconditional loyalty to any nation-state or superpower. Through this poem Faiz takes Urdu on a voyage that recalibrates the dynamics of traditional love lyrics, the *ghazal*. Whereas the overtures of the *ghazal* were framed by a masochistic lover impressing on his beloved linguistic flair, eloquence, fealty, and resignation, Faiz resorts to a different mode of poetry, the *nazm*, and addresses the beloved with a compassionate indictment of the old ways of love. Arguably, this form of poetry (*nazm*), looser in structure than the *ghazal*, is itself an incrimination of the old form of poetry in which love was dominantly couched.

The *ghazal*, a mono-rhymed multithemed lyrical form of poetry tacks between the *'ishq-e majāzī*, the eros, and *'ishq-e ḥaqīqī*, the agape. The poet of the *ghazal* assumes many personas, at times simultaneously: he is a masochistic forlorn lover who takes pride in emplotting his suffering in ever-new ways; he can be ephemeral or perennial; his poetry testifies to the *takhallus*, the pen-name, he chooses for himself; his gender is in flux even when he speaks in the male voice; the orientation of his love can be homosexual, heterosexual, or pansexual, all categories that arose in the twentieth century and thus cannot be projected on times before that; he knows well that if his art is to see the light of the day, his motifs will be judged according to how well they respond to those of other poets who share not only his region and language but also the multilingual universe in which the idioms of his poetry flourish; his claims can reach the grandiosity of those men and women who confronted the establishment of kings, prophets, and gods; he is a product of long-term evolution and associated with legendary martyrs, lovers, and other poets; he evinces misgivings about the status quo and does not mind the confinement to society's margins; he realizes that the gains he makes through verse can be relinquished under the imperative of prose. While the lover's voice remains dominant in the *ghazal*, the audience also acquires a sense of the beloved: taller than a cypress, prettier than a rose, hotter than a candle's flame, more alluring than Joseph of Canaan, stronger than Moses, God or godlike, and so on and so forth.

I would like to pause on the fact that for Faiz the *ghazal* continues to hold a hegemonic aesthetic status. Unlike many of his contemporaries, many of whom, including Josh Malihabadi, were influenced by the colonially in-flected critique of the *ghazal* by Altaf Husain Hali,[3] Faiz does not castigate the *ghazal* for being bereft of realism or excessively decadent. Instead, he gently nudges the genre out of its complacency the way he nudges his be-loved to defer to love in its pluralistic hues. Acutely aware of how much his audiences rejoiced in the *ghazal* genre, he addresses the beloved in a way that can also be read as an allegorical address to the old genre. As though the lover is professing: I am not quitting you, but neither am I loving you and surrendering to you the way I had once done.

Faiz's most important source of emulation, Muhammad Iqbal (1877–1938), was beholden to the thoughts of the greatest nineteenth-century Urdu poet, Mirza Ghalib, and had already pressed into the service of socioreli-gious reform movements such professions. Iqbal also paid attention to the cultural fallout of British colonialism and fended off attempts to place Mus-lims and their literary traditions as the bane of progress.

The year in which Faiz was born in the Punjab province of British India, into a family of Afghan immigrants, was also the year in which Iqbal launched his impetuous complaint, *Shikwah*, against God, in a poetry assem-bly of Lahore:

Kabhī ham se kabhī ghairoñ se shanāsāī hai
Bāt kahne kī nahīñ tū bhī to harjāī hai

At times you befriend me, at times my rivals,
Pardon my speech: you also are a two-timer

Iqbal was a lawyer by training, and he had received his higher education, including a doctorate, in Europe. To him Islam overlapped with the traditions of the Enlightenment, especially those tied to Immanuel Kant, Friedrich Nietzsche, Henri Bergson, and Karl Marx. Many of Iqbal's poems chart a course of Muslim history that splendidly begins with the community of the Prophet Muhammad and gradually faces decline. Faiz admitted time and again to growing up in Iqbal's shadow, although the forfeiture to Muslim exceptionalism in Faiz's verses separates the two poets.

Legend has it that Muhammad Iqbal was in the audience when Faiz first recited the poem that Noor Jahan so compellingly sang many decades later. When Iqbal heard Faiz in a poetry assembly held at Lahore's Government College in the scorching July of 1936, he in fact predicted that Faiz would go on to become a towering poet in his own right.[4]

The poetry assemblies, *mushā'irahs*, bring together poets and their audiences for an interactive performance. Many of these poetry assemblies, especially in Faiz's time, witnessed the relaying of social concerns relevant to the poets and their mass audiences as much as they witnessed the articulation of verses eliciting aesthetic appreciation based on age-old principles of beauty and creativity. The worldviews expounded in these assemblies are inflected by the agendas of the participating poets and their audience and framed by an array of sentiments, including those of love, religion, patriotism, justice, war, and peace. While the poets angle for a position in the literary pantheon by displaying the ability to outwit those who are their peers as well as their forebears, the crowds enjoy a rapport with the poets by applauding particular verses and calling for encores. These assemblies, especially at moments when the states of Pakistan and India suspended democratic principles, provided an enclave of resistance. Much could be said in these gatherings, and when called for accountability, poets could get away by invoking poetic license. Of course, streams of defiant verses would also churn up the defenders of the state, resulting in the incarceration of the poets. To the poignancy of poetry, incarcerations were a godsend.

With each passing poetry assembly, Faiz's fame grew, and he established a community of devotees who jostled to see him in Lahore as much as they did in London. Faiz's poems circulated widely in India from the 1940s, in their original as well as in translation, as the poet's popularity surged in the 1950s, 1960s, and 1970s in languages other than Urdu. An essay in the *Times of*

India in 1971 aptly summarized the reason behind Faiz's charm: "Even while describing the dark side of life, he holds out great hope for mankind."[5] Perhaps it was for this reason that three of India's prime ministers, Jawaharlal Nehru, Indira Gandhi, and I. K. Gujral, showed stirring admiration for Faiz's words.[6] Gulzar, modern India's renowned poet and filmmaker, reminds his audience of a time when Faiz was stopped at India's eastern border for not carrying with him the required entry documents. Jyoti Basu, the communist chief minister of West Bengal, went to the airport and made sure that Faiz was not detained. The chief minister told the immigration authorities that Faiz belonged to the entire subcontinent and not to any one country. The poet did not need a passport, for his very countenance was his passport.[7] The Indians also knew, at least from the 1950s, that Faiz was triumphing as the poet of conscience in spite of being tormented by the state of Pakistan.

The one seamless historical sequence of British colonialism (in which Faiz was born), nationalism (which Faiz witnessed as an ugly outcome of colonialism just when the poet thought the colonial victims could actually aspire to and attain a just distribution of resources), and authoritarianism (which buoyed the interests of new imperial powers that left the weak as vulnerable as they were during the colonial high noon) branded Faiz's politics from the 1940s. Even though the content of his struggles varied, love remained his matrix. He pursued this love across continents, in wars cold and hot.

When Pakistan came into existence in 1947, instead of celebrating the birth of the nation, Faiz wrote a lament as the earliest entry in the new South Asia's diary:

> Yeh dāgh dāgh ujālā yeh shabgazīdah saḥar
> Voh inteẓār thā jis kā yeh voh saḥar to nahīñ
> Yeh voh saḥar to nahīñ jis kī ārzū le kar
> Chale the yār keh mil jāegī kahīñ nah kahīñ
> Falak ke dasht meñ tāroñ kī ākhirī manzil[8]

> This scarred light, this night-struck dawn
> That for which we waited — this is not that dawn
> This is not the dawn, in the quest of which
> Our comrades had embarked
> Looking for the final destination of the stars
> In the wilderness of the skies

The interplay of light and darkness, the search for roads and destinations, the reassessment of the communities of comrades, friends, rivals, and

Syed Akbar Hyder

lovers—this distinguishes Faiz's poetry from that of his comrades. Much to the dismay of his Soviet-leaning friends, Faiz refuses to sketch the awaited dawn in clear-cut ideological hues.

On multiple occasions the poet took the initiative to blend the horizons of his carnal beloved and the beloved that is his homeland. The word he uses for homeland, *vatan*, itself yields meaning that suggests an expanse beyond the modern nation-state.

The suffering that had set aglow Faiz's imagination when speaking of the beloved's taunts and whims was the same suffering that he underwent when cementing his relationship with his homeland. And just like the traditional *ghazal* lover, the lover-Faiz proudly lacks one attribute, regret:

Is 'ishq nah us 'ishq pe nādim hai magar dil
Har dāgh hai is dil meñ bajuz dāgh-e nidāmat[9]

The heart regrets neither this love nor that one
It has every scar, save that of regret

The late 1940s and early 1950s political climate in which Faiz wrote was tense. His Pakistan had to stand up on its feet with its displaced limbs—the territory of West Pakistan was split from the East by hundreds of miles. How exactly religion (especially Islam) would prefigure the nation's identity was yet to be determined. How severely the future course of the country would be paved by concerns for economic justice was speculative.

Apart from his calling as a poet, Faiz worked in journalism, as the editor of Pakistan's leading newspaper, the *Pakistan Times*. It was during his tenure at this newspaper, in March 1951, that he was accused of conspiring to alter the democratic course of Pakistan in what became known as the Rawalpindi Conspiracy Case. He was not alone. A few of Pakistan's army officers as well as Sajjad Zaheer, the general secretary of the Pakistan Communist Party, also stood accused. One concern that prompted the "conspirators" seemed to be related to the alignment of Pakistan's government with that of the United States—that drawing close to the United States would make Pakistan vulnerable to Cold War violence.[10] The conspiracy, to whatever extent it was one, did not come to a fruition.

However, as a consequence, Pakistan's government tried Faiz and promptly sent him to prison, where he spent the next four years of his life. It was his prison experience that bestowed on South Asia poetry even finer than what he had written as a free man. From the prisons of Pakistan, Faiz wrote of hope:

Yeh gham jo is rāt ne diā hai
Yeh gham saḥar kā yaqīn banā hai
Yaqīn jo gham se karīmtar hai
Saḥar jo shab se 'aẓīmtar hai[11]

The sorrow that the night has bestowed on us
This sorrow has turned into the certainty of the dawn
The certainty that is more merciful than sorrow
The dawn that is mightier than the night

Even though the Perso-Urdu world had encountered the metaphoric prisons in which the lover found himself by the grace of the beloved's sadistic cruelty, Faiz's incarceration at the decree of a modern nation-state and his *ghazals* reflecting the grace with which he was standing his ground endeared him to his devotees even more:

Maqām faiz koī rāh meñ jachā hī nahīñ
Jo kū-e yār se nikle to sū-e dār chale[12]

Faiz, I did not find an apt stopover on the road
When I departed from the beloved's lane,
    I headed straight to the gallows

Faiz did not spare the United States, Pakistan's chief albeit unreliable ally, when speaking of the plight of his birth land. For instance, he protested the execution of Julius and Ethel Rosenberg in 1953 on the charges of espionage for the Soviet Union and expressed solidarity with the executed:

Qatl gāhoñ se chun kar hamāre 'alam
Aur nikleñge 'ushshāq ke qāfile
Jin ki rāh-e ṭalab se hamāre qadam
Mukhtiṣar kar chale dard ke fāsle
Kar chale jin ki khāṭir jahāñgīr ham
Jāñ ganvā kar terī dilbarī kā bharam
Ham jo tārīk rāhoñ men māre gaye[13]

Collecting our battle standards from the slaughterhouses
More caravans of lovers will emerge
The lovers whose desired paths
Have reduced the distance of sorrow for us
The lovers for whose sake:

We lost our lives
And seized the trust of your heart-stealing charm
We who were killed on the dark road

Faiz joined the ranks of those protesting the U.S. intervention in Iran in 1953 that resulted in the overthrow of a democratically elected government and the return of the despotic Shah. Several Iranian students were killed protesting this intervention, and Faiz turned their legacy into the precious jewelry of the queen of life, jewelry that was mercilessly pounded:

Yeh kaun sakhī haiñ
Jin ke lahū kī
Ashrafiyāñ chhan chhan chhan chhan
Dhartī ke paiham pyāse
Kashkol meñ ḍhaltī jātī haiñ
Kashkol ko bhartī jātī haiñ
Yeh kaun javāñ haiñ arz-e ʿajam
Yeh lakh lut
Jin ke jismoñ kī
Bharpūr javānī kā kundan
Yūn khāk meñ rezah rezah hai
Yun kūchah kūchah bikhrā hai
Aye arz-e ʿajam aye arz-e ʿajam[14]

Who are these generous ones
The gold coins of whose precious blood
Jingle by jingle
Fall into the ever-thirsty bowl of the earth
Continue to fill the bowl
Who are these youths, O land of Iran
The extravagance of their bodies
The gold of their wholesome youth
Is shred to pieces in the dust,
Squandered in the streets
O Land of Iran, O Land of Iran

Faiz then turned to Africa for an embrace, to tell the world that he was one with the continent that struggled to be liberated from racist colonial control:

Ā jāo maiñ ne sun lī tere ḍhol ke tirang[15]

Come to me, I've heard the beat of your drums
Come to me, the pulse of my blood is drunk
Come to me, Africa

. . . .

The earth throbs with me, Africa
The seas flutter and the forests chime in
I am Africa: I've taken on your form
I am you, my gait is that of your lion
Come to me, Africa
Come to me, the lion's gait
Come to me, Africa

Annihilation in the love (*fanā fil 'ishq*) had been an age-old desire of
Muslim mystics. Everyone from Mansur al-Hallaj (d. 922) in Iraq to Amir
Khusro (d. 1325) in Delhi had lyricized it. The Qur'anic idea that all of God's
creation comes from Him and ultimately returns to Him had inspired much
of the *fanā* discourse. By giving this poem the title "Africa Come Back," Faiz
suggests that Africa had been temporarily separated from him, just as all of
us are separated from our origin at birth (or, as Jalaluddin Rumi would say,
the reed is separated from the reed bed) and it was high time for this separation to end and for Africa to become one with him.

Prison empowered Faiz the way exile empowered Edward Said's Erich
Auerbach—it forced him to retreat into reflections of his self and society in
the lingering presence of solitude, imagination, and memories. He found his
cell's darkness so seductive that he compared it to the lushest of the rose gar-
dens: "In the prison it was as though one has fallen in love all over again. My
love in prison was with poetry."[16] Rather than considering the prison the bane
of his life, he speaks of its redemptive value—a value that clarifies for him
his unconditional love for the beloved, his resolution, no matter the duress:

When is it that you are not by my side
in my thoughts
When is it that my hand is not in yours
A hundred thanks: among our nights
Not one is that of parting

If the going gets tough there
let's dispose of the heart and give up life

Oh brave souls! In the beloved's lane
Do we not have these options left?

The style with which one walks into the chambers of death
It is that dignity which lives on
This life comes and goes
Its value is not worth a mention

The ground of fealty is no king's court
Who cares here about names and descent
Lover is not a given name, passion is not in one's essence

If the game is that of love
Wage it all, why the fear
If you win, bravo!
If you fail, there is no loss[17]

After his release from the prison, when Faiz was invited to China, he gushed in his versified travelogue at the human collective and its potential to reshape the world that would bring more joy to its underprivileged. He could feel China's millions in his own embrace of love and justice.[18]

And then there was a more instructive journey, to Cuba: when Faiz visited this nation in 1964, he remembered how idealism had also manifested itself in Pakistan's early years. But Cuba had progressed much more than Pakistan had — Cuba did this by curbing U.S. imperialism, creating an egalitarian order that did not foreclose the possibility of a more ideal political system, where the establishment of justice was an ongoing project. Cuba, to Faiz, echoed with music. Our poet was also taken by Cuba's remarkable gender dynamics — Cuba's women could look good as women and wear the uniform of formidable guards protecting the nation's institutions. Faiz in his travelogue addresses several critical points raised by Cuba's adversaries to abrogate the significance of its revolution. To those who say that Cuba opted to take a step back in time by freeing itself of U.S. influence, Faiz reminds them that the United States had worked with Cuba's landlords and other forces of exploitation to shackle the small nation. Faiz in this travelogue ardently defended socialist principles and disavowed any redemptive aspects of capitalism. That Cuba was regressing with its communist form of government made no sense to him. He lends a line from Ghalib's *ghazal* to highlight Cuba's poverty when it existed in the U.S. sphere of exploitation and as his response to socialist Cuba's adversaries:

Ghar meñ thā kyā keh terā gham use ghārat kartā[19]
What was there in the house that would be destroyed by your sorrow

Presumably the lover here is telling the beloved that the latter need not take comfort in bringing about the former's destruction. When Ghalib had become aware of the rumors that the British pillaged Delhi in and after 1857, he apparently responded with this couplet: there was nothing there in the first place to pillage. Faiz shares Ghalib's attitude when it comes to commenting on Cuba's state before it came under the auspices of Fidel Castro and Che Guevara. And Faiz's readers know very well where Ghalib took this line of thinking: the one thing that had been there was a longing for "building," and that longing simply cannot be pillaged (*voh jo rakhte the ham ik hasrat-e t'amīr so hai*). Faiz furnishes this longing as the basis of solidarity with the people of Cuba.

As though to remind his audiences that he was as much of a classical *ghazal* poet as he was a committed socialist and revolutionary, Faiz composed multivocal lines that could be read as the complaint old lovers had of their beloved and the complaint god's creation had against god's inert existence:

Miṭ jāyegī makhlūq to insāf karoge
Munṣif ho to ab ḥashr uṭhā kyūñ nahīñ dete[20]

When the creation will be wiped out, then you will render justice?
If you are the Just One, why do you not summon the doomsday now!

Doomsday in Abrahamic faiths is reserved for the ultimate accountability and justice. The poet in Faiz wonders how such an idea syncs with justice itself—with so much havoc wreaked by exploitation, what is the point of postponing justice to a time that is shrouded in mystery, in uncertainty? He calls on his supporters to take action against injustice and not simply tear up:

Chashm-e nam jān-e shoridah kāfi nahīñ[21]

The tear-filled eyes, the passionate soul—they are not sufficient
Carrying the accusation of a hidden love—this is not enough
Today, walk in fetters through the market
Walk with the stars in your hands, dancing and drunk
With the dust on your head, and blood on your clothes
The entire city of lovers awaits you, get moving

Mansur al-Hallaj (executed in 922 C.E.) went to the gallows at the command of his detractors for claiming oneness with the Truth—*ana'l ḥaq.*

Those who sided with Hallaj's executioners interpreted *ḥaq* to mean God and, consequently, Hallaj's claim as a compromise of God's Oneness. To Iqbal, *ḥaq* meant "Creative Truth," as Salim Akhtar points out,[22] and this is the Truth that is a reflection of constantly unfolding creation and has to be sought out and cultivated by each one of God's creation. Faiz aligns himself with this reading of the Truth and, rather than rendering it esoteric, casts it as broadly inclusive. His most powerful poem in the 1970s, the one that is sung in confrontation to the rise of the brutal Pakistani dictator Zia ul Haq, blends *ana'l ḥaq* with a verse from a powerful Qur'anic chapter, *Raḥmān* (And there will remain the face of Your Lord, Owner of Majesty and Honor), and an American civil rights anthem inspired by the Gospel musical tradition, "We Shall Overcome":

> We will see
> It is for sure that we will see:
> That day which has been promised to us
> That day which has been written on the tablet of eternity
> When the mighty mountains of tyranny and oppression
> Will fly away like the cotton balls
> Under the feet of us, the subjected
> The earths will throb
> Upon the heads of the rulers
> Lightning will roar
> From the Ka'ba of God's earth
> All false idols will be lifted
> We, with the pure souls, we, the outcasts of the holy sanctuaries
> Will be seated with pomp
> All the crowns will be cast to the winds
> All the thrones will be made to fall
> Only Allah's name will remain
> He who is hidden and He who is manifest
> One who is the spectacle and the One who is the spectator
> The cry of "I am the Truth" will rise
> That Truth that is you and that is I
> And God's creation will rule
> The creation that is you and that is I[23]

The poignancy of this anthem should be noted in the context of its popularity throughout South Asia, especially as the United States cozied up to the Pakistani dictator, an intimacy that would eventually push the United States and Pakistan into an ancillary war with the Soviet Union on the doomed fields of Afghanistan.

Faiz knew well that the movement of his pen would be severely bridled if he continued to live in the Pakistan of the late 1970s. He chose exile for himself and, after a brief stint in the Soviet Union and India, ended up in Beirut. He embraced the Palestinian struggle against the Israeli occupation — an occupation that was only bolstered by U.S. support. Faiz protested Palestine's subjugation by writing a variation of his anti-Zia song; this song was redolent with hope:

> We will win
> Verily, we will win
> Ultimately, we will win
> What fear do we have of the enemy's attack
> The chest of every warrior is a shield
> What fear of the blitz of fate
> The souls of martyrs have girded their loins
> What fear
> We will win
> Verily, we will win
> "And say, the Truth has arrived and the Falsehood has vanished"
>   (17:81)
> So says the Greatest of the Lords
> Heaven is under our feet
> And the shadow of mercy upon our heads
> Then why the fear
> We will win
> Verily, we will win
> Ultimately, we will win one day[24]

This "we" in which Faiz spoke rebelled against the territorial nation-state and against neat temporal divisions — Faiz's comrade was the God of the Qur'an who promised vindication for the oppressed as much as he was the tenth-century Iraqi Sufi martyr Mansur al-Hallaj or the twentieth-century communist Turkish poet Nazim Hikmet. The night of oppression in which Faiz writhed was the night that he shared with the old lovers who longed for their beloved, but it was also the night that had sprung from the pain that was much more than that of you and I: *yeh rāt us dard kā shajar hai jo mujh se tujh se 'azīmtar hai.*[25] As the Kashmir-born Agha Shahid Ali, one of Faiz's most

Syed Akbar Hyder

prominent devotees in the world of English poetry, points out: "In Faiz's poetry, suffering is seldom, perhaps never, private (in the sense the suffering of confessional poets). Though deeply personal, it is almost never isolated from a sense of history and injustice."[26] In this vein, Faiz made it clear that unlike Josh Malihabadi's faith in the individual revolutionary taking on the feudal order, Faiz's revolutionary hero is auxiliary to the communities and classes that are fighting for justice. His hero actually embodies a class, not a lone individual.[27] Similarly, the nation is not trammeled by cartography, nor is it beholden to a solidarity other than the one anchored in justice for its most vulnerable members.

In song after song, Faiz clarified how the front lines of fidelity were not the courts of kings where ranks are bestowed on the basis of names and lineages; Lover is not a name with which one is born; and Love is not a birthright[28] — all of this has to be cultivated in response one's context, keeping in mind the privileges that shape us and the silences that serve us.

Though clearly aligned with the grand Marxist aspirations of economic justice, Faiz through his poetry opens up a third front. He joins the Marxists with the intersectional understanding that he would be able to transform the world not simply by joining them but by appreciating culture-specific interpretations and creating a solidarity with them to move forward in a direction that is yet to be determined: "I do not feel socialism is a cure-all, whose recipe is applicable in all places. Every country has its own recipe. The [countries of the world] need to keep in mind their own conditions and traditions . . . socialism is a strategy not faith."[29] He is cautious when it comes to dismissing religion — that which comforts millions. Just as his love calls for more inclusivism, so does his nation-state, his socialism, his Islam.

Even though he did not belong to the Pakistan Communist Party formally, as Faiz's Soviet interpreter and biographer, Ludmila Vassilyeva, points out, during the Cold War, Faiz was rendered into Russian by acclaimed Soviet poets, and he remained one of the most popular South Asian poets there. In 1962 he, along with Pablo Picasso, won the Soviet Union's most acclaimed award reserved for the non-Soviet citizens, the International Lenin Peace Prize. With evident personal enjoyment he spoke of the general Soviet accomplishments glowingly, although he was careful not to sing praises of particular leaders in his poetry. Vassilyeva states: "In spite of his unattained armour for the country, Faiz actually wrote very little on the Soviet subject as opposed to other progressive writers and if you look closely, you will find few poets and writers who have not written stories or poems about Moscow,

Stalin, Lenin and the Red Square. In all of the long years of his association with the Soviet Union, he probably wrote only two poems directly dealing with the system."[30]

To Faiz's left-leaning critics, his ambiguous poetic language was a meager overture that actually muddied the cause of justice. Ali Sardar Jafri, a card-carrying member of the Communist Party of India, struggled to see Faiz's positive intervention in the world of poetry and progress when Faiz, according to Jafri, did not spell out the terms of freedom in his poem "Freedom's Dawn" and simply said that the dawn the subcontinent witnessed after the colonial night was not the awaited dawn. The vagueness of Faiz's verse, compounded by his obsession to couch ideas in idioms of sexual romance, in Jafri's opinion, was an insult to India's freedom fighters, whose "sacrifices were much loftier than sexual deprivations."[31]

To those studying Faiz as a "people's poet," perhaps he seemed overindulgent when he stockpiled his verses with images of precious stones and fabrics that the masses could not even recognize. One of his eloquent Marxist critics, Ralph Russell, writes: "His beloved is not simply a woman; she is a lady—a lady with plenty of money and plenty of leisure to spend on makeup, fine clothes and rare perfume, and it is these, rather than any intrinsic qualities (for he rarely mentions any) that Faiz seems to find attractive."[32]

What Russell does not recognize is that Faiz's verses bespoke his ability to address the beloved with a full recognition of all the capital, the *sarmāya*, that the beloved bore; the fine jewels in which he was bedecked; the lofty mansions he occupied. The lover could claim many shortcomings for himself but not the one of misrecognition. After recognizing the beloved for who he was, the lover invited him into his world to see the price at which luxury came.

The most riveting ideas that well from the tidal waves of Faiz's poetry are those concerning the confluence of people across vast spans, not always acclimatized to the rising and subsiding nation-states, political parties, or movements.

Faiz's lover is a composite of social woes across countries, of many centuries, of many fringe circuits. In several poems, Faiz offers subtitles that suggest a context for the poem; the language of many such poems, however, is void of specificities. In other words, if the readers did not read Faiz's subtitle, they would not know from the verses, for instance, that they were in response to the Rosenberg trial. If fact, this trial is a metonymy for all unjust trials wherein the blind majoritarian system oppresses the minority. So is the case with subtitles referring to Beirut and Bangladesh. This device of distancing and proximating used by Faiz reminds us that it is one moment for which the poem is applicable but it is not limited to that moment since the poem itself has no abiding references to that moment of history. Poetry here becomes universal and timeless. This strategy worked to Faiz's advantage: wherever Urdu was read (and Urdu had more readers in India than it did in Pakistan for the most part of the Cold War years), Faiz became a phenomenon unlike any other poetic one. Singers vied to sing his poems — from Noor Jahan and Begum Akhtar to Mehdi Hassan and Abida Parveen. He never just spoke as a man from Pakistan; his audiences assured his perpetuity in part by raising him above his nation-state. Even if the nation-states vanished, Faiz would remain as a man who made his readers and listeners conjure up a new *vatan*, a new homeland — one that was aspirationally inclusive. Faiz thus poured out his feelings for a land that could not be contained by borders, for a rival who could share the beloved with the lover, for an imagination whose scope could unite the oppressor and the oppressed with the awe of justice:

> Ham se us des kā tum nām o nishāñ pūchte ho
> Jis kī tārīkh nah gughrāfiya ab yād āye
> Aur yād āye to mahbūb-e guzishtah ki tarh
> Rū barū āne se jī ghabrāye[33]

> You ask me about the name and whereabouts of that country,
> The country whose history and geography I do not recall now
> And when I do recall them, then
> Like the bygone beloved, he is frazzled to come face to face with me

These verses appear in a poem dedicated to Andrei Voznesensky (1933–2010), the dynamic Russian poet known for saying, "The students of the world are the best nation."[34]

When reading Faiz closely, there is little doubt that he, like his comrades from Turkey (Nazim Hikmet) and South India (Makhdum Mohiuddin), folded himself into the resistance movements that considered U.S. policies at home and abroad as the scourge of their age; our poet adhered more closely to the Soviet vision of his world. Notwithstanding this empathy for the Soviet Union, Faiz recoiled from an all-out exclusivist embrace of this country and an absolute condemnation of the United States. Mutually exclusive love is antiquated in Faiz. To love one beloved and no one else is a halfway measure at best. Faiz profits from the new love that blurs boundaries, including those created by the Cold War. In Urdu, he gives voice to many poets writing in other languages but showing solidarity with his kind of love. Faiz especially takes a liking to Nazim Hikmet. He translates some of Hikmet's thoughts:

Ham ne ummīd ke sahāre par
Tūt kar yūñ hī zindagī kī hai
Jis tarah tum se 'āshiqī kī hai[35]

Placing my stock in hope
I have thus lived my life, head over heels:
The way I have set my heart on you

Drawing at once on the traditions of classical Persian and Urdu poetry, on the progressive strains of twentieth-century Turkish poetry, and on the resistive tropes of Islamic mysticism, Faiz insists that one's opponent is cast as the beloved to whom the well-disposed lover commits without abandoning the impulses of justice. Faiz's poetry allays any sense of retribution. Weary of sanctimony, he strengthens the resolve to love one's enemies in the lyrical language that tries to diminish a polarized world. He proposes a new collective and alerts us to the limitations of our existing language:

Maiñ kyā likhūñ ki jo merā tumhārā rishtah hai
Voh 'āshiqī kī zabāñ meñ kahīñ bhī darj nahīñ
Likhā gayā hai bahot luṭf-e vasl o dard-e firāq
Magar yeh kaifiyat apnī raqam nahīñ hai kahīñ
Yeh apnā 'ishq ham āghosh jis meñ hijr o visāl
Yeh apnā dard ki hai kab se hamdam-e mah o sāl
Is 'ishq-e khās ko har ek se chhūpāye hūe
Guzar gayā hai zamānah gale lagāe hūe[36]

How shall I write that which binds me to you
It is not listed anywhere in the language of passion
The pleasures of union, the pangs of parting—
    have been written plenty
But this state of ours is not noted anyplace
This passion of ours that embraces parting and union
This pain of ours that's a soulmate to passing times
Hiding this special passion from all
An age has lapsed since I entered your embrace

Syed Akbar Hyder

1. The performance can be viewed at "Noor Jehan Live: Mujhse Pehli Si Mohabbat" (1982), https://www.youtube.com/watch?v=xCJCyZ9yRHw. All English translations of Urdu poetry here are mine. This poem in its entirety appears in the collection of Faiz's poetry: see Faiz Ahmed Faiz, *Nuskhahah-e vafā* (Lahore: Maktabah-e Karvan, n.d.), 61–63.

2. Malik Ram, *Urdu Adab: Faiz Number* 3, 4 (New Delhi: Anjuman-e Taraqqi-e Urdu [Hind], 1985): 11.

3. With the advent of British colonialism in the nineteenth century, many art forms drew colonial ire for not representing the natural world as it really is. The *ghazal* in this discourse stood accused of propagating an imagination that did not correspond to reality, to *nature* as it really is. Many Urdu writers also participated in such modes of criticism and blamed the *ghazal* for holding back the arts of their community. See Frances Pritchett, *Nets of Awareness: Urdu Poetry and Its Critics* (Berkeley: University of California Press, 1994).

4. Nasim Fatimah and Miyan Muhammad Saeed, *Faiz hue hain mar kea mar* (Karachi: Jumbo, 2014), 29.

5. *Times of India*, 28 February 1971, 10.

6. See I. K. Gujral, *Urdu Adab: Faiz Number* 3, 4 (New Delhi: Anjuman-e Taraqqi-e Urdu [Hind], 1985): 76.

7. See "Gulzar: 'Late CM Jyoti Basu Said Poet FAIZ Needed NO PASSPORT!,'" https://www.youtube.com/watch?v=ABjQrhM-TIo.

8. Faiz, *Nuskha*, 116.

9. Ibid., 146.

10. Estelle Dryland, "Faiz Ahmed Faiz and the Rawalpindi Conspiracy Case," *Journal of South Asian Literature* 27, no. 2 (1992): 182.

11. Faiz, *Nushka*, 252.

12. Ibid., 265.

13. Ibid., 268.

14. Ibid., 155–56.

15. Ibid., 278–79.

16. Sayyid Taqi Abidi, *Faiz Fahmī: Taḥqīq o Tanqīd* (Lahore: Multi-Media Affairs, 2011), 590.

17. Faiz, *Nuskha*, 255.

18. Ibid., 320.

19. Faiz Ahmad Faiz, *Safarnāmah-e Cuba* (Lahore: National Publishing House, 1973), 32.

20. Faiz, *Nuskha*, 334.

21. Ibid., 338.

22. Salim Akhtar, *Josh kā Nafsiyāt Muṭāle'a aur dūsre maẓāmīn* (Lahore: Ferozsons, 1987) 28.

23. Faiz, *Nuskha*, 655–56.

24. Ibid., 700–701.

25. Ibid., 248.

26. Agha Shahid Ali, *The Rebel's Silhouette* (New Delhi: Oxford University Press, 1991), preface (n.p.).

27. Taslim Ilahi Zulfi, *Faiz Ahman Faiz in Beirut* (Islamabad: Pakistan Academy of Letters, 2011), 60.

28. Faiz, *Nuskha*, 259.

29. Khalil Ahmad, *Makālimat-e Faiz* (Lahore: Sang-e-Meel Publications), 171.

30. Ludmila Vassilyeva, "Faiz Ahmed Faiz and the Soviet Union," in *Daybreak: Writings on Faiz*, ed. Yasmeen Hameed (Karachi: Oxford University Press, 2013), 194.

31. Bedar Bakht, "Kuch 'ishq kiyā kuch kām kiyā," in *Faiz Fahmī: Taḥqīq o Tanqīd*, ed. Sayyid Taqi Abidi (Lahore: Multi-Media Affairs, 2011), 752.

32. Ralph Russell, "Faiz Ahmed Faiz: Poetry, Politics, and Pakistan," in Hameed, *Daybreak*, 57.

33. Faiz, *Nuskha*, 418.

34. *New York Times*, 22 April 1967.

35. Faiz, *Nuskha*, 694.

36. Sarfaraz Iqbal, "Dāman-e Yūsuf," in *Faiz Ahmad Faiz: Ahvāl o afkār*, ed. Marghub Ali (Delhi: Takhleeqkar, 2013), 501.

Doves of Peace, Dogs of War,
circa 1950–1969

Chapter Four

The Accidental Global Peacekeeper

WAHEGURU PAL SINGH SIDHU

India became a member of the United Nations two years before it was liberated from the colonial yoke, participated in U.N. peace efforts months before gaining independence, and played a defining role in shaping U.N. peacekeeping, owing to a stalemate caused by the U.S.-Soviet Cold War rivalry. Not only has India shaped U.N. peacekeeping and become one of its most vocal advocates, but it has also provided significant leadership and the largest number of peacekeepers both during the Cold War and in the entire history of the United Nations. India's contribution to the practice and theory of U.N. peacekeeping during the Cold War is in contrast to its role as a rule taker — adhering to existing international norms made by others — in almost every other arena. This chapter examines India's important contributions to U.N. peacekeeping.

ORIGINS OF U.N. PEACEKEEPING
AND NORMATIVE DRIVERS

Nowhere in the U.N. Charter is the term *peacekeeping* used. Article 43 of the Charter envisaged a collective security role under the leadership of the five permanent members of the U.N. Security Council.[1] This provision soon fell victim to Cold War rivalries and was never operationalized.[2] Indeed, the only time in its history that the United Nations performed this role was during the 1950 imbroglio on the Korean peninsula under the "Uniting for Peace" resolution, which occurred only because of a Soviet boycott. Instead, the first U.N. secretary-general, Trygve Lie, proposed the establishment of a "small force sufficient to prevent or stop localized outbreaks threatening international peace."[3] This proposal for a so-called U.N. Guard, a modest initial force of eight hundred international volunteers who would serve "as a standing, organic unit of the secretariat, composed of personnel for technical support and for operational duties," also did not come to fruition.[4]

Even so, since 1947 the United Nations has devised and fielded a series of peacekeeping operations that have come to evoke the very raison d'être of the world body. During the Cold War these operations can be divided into two distinct periods. The first efforts, between 1947 and 1955, included missions in Greece (1947–51, to observe border incursions), the Dutch East Indies/Indonesia (1947–51, to ensure the transition from a colonial to a newly independent state), Palestine (from 1947 onward, to observe a cease-fire), and Kashmir (from 1949 onward, to observe a cease-fire). These early missions consisted of unarmed military observers and lightly armed troops with primarily monitoring, reporting, and confidence-building roles. India had no role in these early efforts, apart from serving in the Palestine mission (May–August 1947)[5] and playing a political role in U.N. operations in Korea from 1950 to 1954, examined below.

During the second period, from 1956 until the end of the Cold War (1988–89), the United Nations embarked on a series of operations in Egypt, particularly along the Suez Canal and on the Sinai Peninsula (1956–67), Lebanon (1958), newly independent Congo (1960–64), West New Guinea (1962–63), Yemen (1963–64), Cyprus (ongoing since 1964), India-Pakistan (1965–66), Dominican Republic (1965–66), Egypt-Israel (1973–79), Syria-Israel (ongoing since 1974), and Lebanon (ongoing since 1978). In all, the United Nations conducted sixteen peace operations during the Cold War. It was during the improvised operation in 1956 that Dag Hammarskjöld, who succeeded Lie as secretary-general in April 1953, coined the term *peacekeeping* and "labeled UN peacekeeping operations as 'Chapter Six and a Half' to characterize their tenuous legitimacy under the Charter."[6] In Hammarskjöld's reasoning, peace operations fell "between traditional methods of resolving disputes peacefully, such as negotiation and mediation under Chapter VI, and more forceful action as authorized under Chapter VII."[7] Hammarskjöld elaborated, "Such a military organ of the United Nations, even if . . . it has no military tasks in the conventional sense, can be a decisive factor in preventing hostilities and restoring calm in a troubled area."[8]

Hammarskjöld also enunciated four key U.N. peacekeeping principles: first, that a U.N. force could be deployed only with the consent of the state and would stay only as long as the host state allowed it to remain. Second, the troops deployed were to be neutral or nonaligned both in the global East-West Cold War contest and in the specific conflict at hand. Third, the U.N. forces were to maintain their impartiality and not try to affect a particular political outcome in the conflict. Last, the lightly armed forces were never to use force, except in extreme circumstances for their own self-defense.[9] These principles by and large held during all Cold War U.N. peace operations after 1956, with the exception of the Congo operation, where the United Nations conducted military operations in the name of self-defense.

Hammarskjöld's peacekeeping principles for the United Nations were similar to ideas propounded by the ideological leader of India's freedom movement — Mohandas Karamchand Gandhi. Writing in 1938, Gandhi suggested "the formation of Peace brigades whose members would risk their lives in dealing with riots, especially communal. The idea was that this brigade should substitute for the police and even the military."[10] Although Gandhi proposed the peace brigades only at the domestic or national level, the idea was expanded in 1960 to the international arena by another Gandhian, Jayaprakash Narayan, and the Spanish pacifist and former supporter of the League of Nations, Salvador de Madariaga. In a letter to Hammarskjöld, Narayan and Madariaga underlined the political impossibility of a U.N. armed force and argued that "it follows that an international police should be unarmed. The presence of a body of regular World Guards or Peace Guards, intervening with no weapons whatsoever between two forces combatting or about to combat, might have considerable effect."[11] The letter did not elicit a response, and Narayan later criticized the United Nations for "employing nothing but armed forces to achieve peace."[12] Nonetheless, the concept of U.N. peacekeeping with lightly armed or unarmed peacekeepers clearly resonated with India.

During the Cold War, U.N. peace operations served two objectives. The first was to deal "not primarily with problems of the emerging Cold War but with the parallel post-1945 phenomenon of decolonization." Thus, peace operations, along with facilitating the process of decolonization, "were designed to provide a fire-break around local conflicts to prevent their spread into the larger conflict of the Cold War."[13] Second, as a corollary, these operations were more likely to succeed in their objective if they were conducted primarily by countries not engaged in Cold War rivalry. This also enabled the United Nations to undertake one of its principal charter objectives, that of maintaining international peace and security, which had effectively been blocked by superpower contestation.

Independent India's first prime minister, Jawaharlal Nehru, supported both objectives. He understood the symbiotic relationship between the United Nations and India's policy of non-alignment, and he championed the cause of decolonization. Nehru perceived that for decolonization to succeed, U.N. membership (often in tandem with membership in the non-aligned movement) for newly independent states was crucial, and that for the United Nations to succeed, U.N. peacekeeping was imperative, which could occur only with the support of nonaligned countries like India.

Unsurprisingly then, nonaligned India, along with other select countries (notably the Nordic and other neutral nations), played a key role both in defining the contours of peacekeeping at the U.N. secretariat and in carrying out operations in the field. At U.N. headquarters, Indian leaders and diplomats, especially Major General Indar Jit Rikhye, the first (and last) military adviser to the secretary-general from 1960 to 1968 (when the post was abolished), worked closely with Dag Hammarskjöld and his successor, U Thant, to institutionalize U.N. peacekeeping. Rikhye, who sought to develop a peacekeeping doctrine for the United Nations even after leaving the organization, is regarded as "one of the world's best peacekeepers."[14] On the ground, senior Indian diplomats, military officers, and troops participated in Korea, the first United Nations Emergency Force (UNEF I) in Egypt, the United Nations Observer Group in Lebanon, the United Nations Operations in Congo (ONUC), the United Nations Security Force in West New Guinea, the United Nations Yemen Observation Mission, the United Nations Peacekeeping Force in Cyprus, and the Mission of the Representative of the Secretary-General in the Dominican Republic. In all, India was involved in nine of the sixteen peacekeeping operations in various capacities. However, India's peacekeeping role was often challenged by the superpowers as well as by the affected countries.

HISTORICAL AND MILITARY DRIVERS

At the end of World War II and the beginning of the Cold War, India was one of the few countries among the original fifty-one U.N. members that had the military expeditionary capability to conduct operations well beyond its borders and did not belong to a superpower bloc. This military capability, which India eventually deployed under the U.N. flag to support decolonization, was ironically the result of its colonial legacy.

From the late eighteenth century onward and until India's independence, Indian troops served the cause of the British Empire not only on the subcontinent but in almost every British dominion in Asia and Africa.[15] By the time of World War I, the British Indian Army had swelled to 1.5 million volunteers who fought in foreign lands — from Ypres to Haifa — sustaining more than 70,000 casualties. By World War II, the army had grown to a staggering 2.5 million Indians — the largest voluntary army in history — who fought for the Allies far afield in almost every theater of the global war.[16] The victory of the Allies, particularly in key conflicts in Asia, Africa, the Middle East, and even Europe, was largely determined by the role of Indian soldiers. (Interestingly, some of these World War II sites would become the locale of future U.N. peacekeeping operations.) At the time of India's independence, the military had shrunk to 500,000 soldiers, yet it remained one of the largest forces (outside the Cold War blocs) and one of the few with the experience to deploy globally.

As early as 1946, Jawaharlal Nehru envisaged a continuing global role for India's military: "Whatever the present position of India might be, she is potentially a Great Power. Undoubtedly in the future she will have to play a very great part in security problems of Asia and the Indian Ocean, more especially of the Middle East and South-East Asia."[17] What remained unclear, however, was how India could play this role in a bipolar world without taking sides.

Indeed, it appeared unlikely that independent India's expeditionary capabilities and experience could be used in the Cold War for two reasons. First, India's postcolonial leaders sought to downplay the country's imperial legacy and to bolster its nonaligned credentials by staying out of any partisan Cold War confrontation. Second, before the inception of U.N. peacekeeping in 1956 (and even under United Nations aegis), it was difficult to consider a role for India's military in decolonization, which was essentially seen as a political process.

Yet, while rejecting Cold War power politics, Nehru envisaged carving out an active international role for India and was drawn to the idea of "One World," which had gained momentum during the interwar period.[18] Nehru regarded the United Nations and its central role in ensuring international peace as the Cold War manifestation of the One World concept. In 1948, speaking before the Constituent Assembly in India, he argued that the United Nations "in spite of its failings and weaknesses, is something that is good. It should be encouraged and supported in every way, and should be allowed to develop into some kind of world government or world order."[19] Subsequently, article 51 under the Directive Principles of State Policy section of India's constitution, adopted on 26 January 1950, asserted that India would seek to "promote international peace and security[,] . . . foster respect for international law and treaty obligations," and "encourage settlement of international disputes by arbitration."[20] Although the United Nations is not explicitly mentioned, the world body was clearly the obvious arena for India to manifest article 51. This set the stage for India to play a normative and material role in the evolution of U.N. peacekeeping. Ironically, it was the Cold War paralysis of the Security Council that gave India the opportunity to shape and lead U.N. peacekeeping. Had the Security Council been active during the Cold War—and article 43 of the U.N. Charter, which allows for collective security arrangements, been operational—India might not have been able to perform the starring role in U.N. peacekeeping.

THE KOREAN WAR, 1950–1954

Its normative rationale notwithstanding, India's first U.N. experience during the Korean War was fraught and threatened to drag the new nation into the Cold War conflict. India's involvement began when K. P. S. Menon, independent India's most experienced diplomat, was unanimously elected as the chairman of the U.N. Temporary Commission on Korea in 1948.[21] The commission's mandate was to observe elections following the withdrawal of Soviet and U.S. troops north and south of the 38th parallel and report to the U.N. General Assembly. Under Menon's leadership, the Temporary Commission on Korea pushed for elections in a united Korea on the grounds that "Korea is one and indivisible."[22] However, Soviet intransigence in allowing the commission access to Korea north of the 38th parallel, coupled with the U.S. insistence on holding elections only in the south, led to the failure of the commission's mandate and the de facto division of Korea.

The U.N. General Assembly approved the U.S. draft proposal to hold elections only in the south in February 1948. Curiously, India, which had strongly supported holding elections in a united Korea, voted in favor of the proposal. India justified its vote on the grounds that the elected government of South Korea might be able to establish amicable relations with North Korea, leading to an eventual unification. However, some scholars suspect that India's reversal of position in support of the U.S. proposal was related to its desire for U.S. support in the United Nations following New Delhi's decision to bring the Kashmir issue to the world body in January 1948.[23] The Temporary Commission was replaced by the U.N. Commission on Korea, which also included an Indian representative, with the even more improbable mandate of unifying the two Koreas. Unsurprisingly, the U.N.

Waheguru Pal Singh Sidhu

Commission on Korea collapsed when North Korea invaded South Korea on 25 June 1950.

Nehru and India's U.N. representative, Benegal Rau, initially supported a strong U.N. response to the invasion because they felt that "this was a well-planned aggression that threatened to unravel the fabric of the U.N. if it was not stopped."[24] When the United States sponsored a resolution to permit U.N. troops to cross the 38th parallel, however, India opposed it. As Rau argued: "It would impair faith in the U.N. if we were even to appear to authorize the unification of Korea by the use of force against North Korea, after we had resisted the attempt of North Korea to reunify the country by force against South Korea."[25] And instead of sending troops, India only fielded a 346-man-strong field ambulance unit, which stayed until 1954.

Some scholars have argued that India did not commit forces to the war for at least two other reasons. First, following the 1947–48 war with Pakistan over Kashmir, India did not have enough troops to spare for the Korean conflict. Indian forces, moreover, were still being indigenized and reconstituted, so they were ill prepared to deploy overseas. Second, because India was assiduously trying to court China, it did not want to commit troops against the North Korean and Chinese forces, especially after the U.N. resolution (sponsored by the United States) branded Beijing as an aggressor.[26]

Thus, apart from the services of the 60th Parachute Field Ambulance unit, which received international accolades, India remained out of the conflict until the United States privately asked it to take the lead in formulating an armistice; the Soviets also acquiesced in this request of India.[27] India's U.N. representative V. K. Krishna Menon drafted the resolution, which the first committee of the General Assembly adopted on 1 December 1952. Nonetheless, the resolution was staunchly opposed both by the Soviet Union and China, which suspected India was working at the behest of the United States, and by South Korea, which accused India of being "pro-Communist."[28] Despite making India a scapegoat, however, the parties — failing to find a solution — eventually accepted India's proposed compromise and signed the armistice on 27 July 1953.

India's role in bringing the hostilities to an end was belatedly appreciated by the two warring sides, and both now supported its chairmanship of the Neutral Nations Repatriation Commission (NNRC), which dealt with the exchange of prisoners of war and the delicate issue of thousands of Chinese and North Korean prisoners who "wanted to be free to stay in the South and not go home. The Indians supervised a careful process that ensured they were able to defect, but without too much humiliation for the communist regimes."[29] To support the NNRC, India deployed a 6,000-strong custodian force to manage the prisoners of war and their repatriation. In all, the NNRC and the custodian force managed nearly 23,000 prisoners of war.[30] India's role in the Korean War ended when the NNRC was dissolved on 21 February 1954. For India, the Korean experience was "instrumental in establishing the precedents for her participation in subsequent U.N. operations" and highlighted the perils and rewards of playing on a stage dominated by two superpowers.[31]

UNITED NATIONS EMERGENCY FORCE, 1956–1967

The Suez Crisis of 1956, precipitated by Egypt's decision to nationalize the Suez Canal and the ensuing military response of Israel and two permanent Security Council members, Great Britain and France, posed an unprecedented situation for the United Nations.[32] First, the involvement of two veto-wielding members meant that any peacekeeping response would have to be formulated outside the Security Council. Second, there was recognition that the unarmed peace observation mission already deployed in the area had been unable to prevent conflict and that a similar mission was equally unlikely to succeed.[33] Thus Hammarskjöld, with help from countries like India and Canada, used the 1950 "Uniting for Peace" precedent to call for an emergency session of the General Assembly, which on 4 November 1956 passed Resolution 998, authorizing the secretary-general to set up "an emergency international United Nations Force to secure and supervise the cessation of hostilities."[34]

Hammarskjöld's normative efforts in creating UNEF I—the first full-fledged U.N. peacekeeping operation—were actively supported by Nehru and Krishna Menon.[35] Experts on U.N. peacekeeping noted that "the thinking of most middle powers [like India] on these issues fitted well with the conceptions of the UN's potential value that Hammarskjöld himself began developing after taking office in 1953" and that "he and many middle powers [notably India] drew from a common fund of convictions about the UN's international security responsibilities."[36] Speaking before the General Assembly in December 1956 on events in Egypt and Hungary, Nehru ruminated that "the way of tolerance . . . means something active. It does not mean forgetting any principle that we stand for. . . . It is of the greatest importance that the United Nations . . . should keep in mind the Charter, which is the basis."[37] Nehru went on to acknowledge the dilemma in establishing UNEF I under the shadow of the Cold War. He argued: "It may be that we

Waheguru Pal Singh Sidhu

cannot give effect to the Charter quickly because the world is imperfect. Nevertheless, we should move in that direction step by step. The first thing to remember and to strive for is to avoid a situation getting worse and finally leading to a major conflict, which means the destruction of all the values one holds."[38] Nehru's speech, among others, not only justified the setting up of UNEF I but also paved the way for India to support its mission with men and material. Twenty-four countries offered troops for UNEF I, of which ten — Brazil, Canada, Colombia, Finland, India, Indonesia, Sweden, a mixed contingent from Denmark and Norway, and Yugoslavia — were accepted, and in February 1957, UNEF I reached its maximum strength of six thousand troops. In all, India rotated eleven infantry battalions (thirteen thousand troops) between 15 November 1957 and 19 May 1967, becoming the longest continuously serving contingent in UNEF I.[39] This was both the largest Indian deployment and the biggest U.N. peacekeeping mission during the Cold War.

Before UNEF I forces could be deployed, however, several hurdles needed to be removed. First, both Egypt and Israel were opposed to having U.N. troops deployed on their territory. In addition, nonaligned Egypt opposed accepting troops from Canada, a NATO member closely allied to Britain and France. Through his diplomatic prowess, Krishna Menon convinced a reluctant president Gamal Abdel Nasser to accept the deployment of not only U.N. troops on Egyptian soil but also a Canadian force commander and soldiers.[40]

Significantly, some of the Indian units in UNEF I had served in the Suez during World War II, giving them the advantage of familiarity. In a telling incident of déjà vu, when Rikhye — now a colonel appointed as chief of staff to the UNEF I commander, Canadian lieutenant general E. L. M Burns — was traveling to the headquarters in Gaza, he recalled: "I was returning to this town after 14 years, having last travelled through it in a cattle rail truck with the 8th Indian Division from Damascus to Alexandria en route to Italy in September 1943."[41]

As chief of staff, Rikhye thought that UNEF I was "an odd unit, combining all levels of expertise and none, and with national liaison officers reporting to their own governments."[42] During his tenure as chief of staff, he streamlined the command structure and established the chain of command, with everyone reporting to him. This became standard practice in U.N. peace operations. Rikhye was appointed military adviser to the U.N. secretary-general in 1960 but returned to UNEF I as force commander in 1966, becoming the second Indian to command the operation.[43] It was during his command in 1967 that Egypt (which under Nasser was planning to attack Israel) withdrew its consent for the U.N. presence and asked UNEF I to withdraw. Before the peacekeepers could withdraw, however, war broke out on 5 June and the U.N. headquarters was bombarded, killing many Indian peacekeepers.[44] This abrupt end of the United Nations' first peacekeeping mission had a lasting impact on future missions.

India's contribution was evident in the normative political support that it offered at the highest level to U.N. peacekeeping in general and to UNEF I in particular. This was coupled with India's diplomatic efforts to bring Nasser to accept the presence of UNEF I, plus the men and materiel that India provided for the force. That Indian troops remained part of the mission even through the debacle of the 1962 China-India war and the 1965 India-Pakistan war underlines India's capacity and willingness to support U.N. missions.

UNEF I also established a key U.N. peacekeeping principle: peace operations were likely to work as long as they were insulated from the Cold War and there was no direct interference from the superpowers. As Krishna Menon noted: "We kept the great powers . . . at a distance . . . that was one of the conditions under which we went there."[45]

Perhaps the most significant Indian contribution to UNEF I and U.N. peacekeeping was the "development of operational procedures and wide-ranging techniques for use by multilateral forces, not organized on an international treaty basis but drawn from a world club of national armies, where military experience and professionalism vary to extremes and where the character of the role is based on concepts strange to the ways of soldiers."[46] As noted above, Rikhye, in his role as chief of staff, force commander, and military adviser, was key in developing these U.N. procedures and techniques.

In evaluating India's contribution, M. V. Naidu has argued that the origins of U.N. peacekeeping and UNEF I were the result of "close collaboration between Lester Pearson of Canada, Krishna Menon of India and Dag Hammarskjold. . . . All three individuals accepted that the U.N. can operate only within the parameters permitted by the realities of the Cold War, and only with the constructive cooperation of all groups irrespective of ideologies. . . . This collaboration remains very much unrecognized. Only Pearson's role was recognized through the Nobel Peace Prize."[47]

UNITED NATIONS OPERATIONS IN CONGO, 1960–1964

Barely four years after UNEF I, the United Nations and India were drawn into the first conflict related to decolonization in the Democratic Republic of Congo following its messy independence from Belgium on 30 June 1960. Unlike the relatively peaceful transfer of power of most nations from their former colonial rulers, Congo's experience was chaotic and violent. Postindependence violence prompted Belgium to send troops to protect its interests and citizens, and the resource-rich province of Katanga threatened to secede. Independent Congo was thus born with two existential challenges: an external intervention by its former colonial power and internal secessionist forces who challenged the state's unity. Against this backdrop, the new leaders of Congo appealed to the United Nations for assistance.[48] Complicating matters, the two superpower blocs backed different leadership factions in the newly independent country: the West supported President Joseph Kasavubu, whereas the Soviet bloc backed Prime Minister Patrice Lumumba. This raised the specter that unless the integrity of the nascent nation was preserved, it might suffer a fate similar to that of Korea and Vietnam.

In response, the United Nations, under Hammarskjöld's leadership, launched the United Nations Operations in Congo.[49] Unlike the relatively straightforward mission of UNEF I, ONUC had to deal with an intrastate war—which threatened to escalate into a proxy war between the two superpower blocs—while seeking to preserve Congo's territorial and political integrity and independence. There now emerged an unstated convergence of interests between the United Nations and India. Both wanted to prevent Congo from becoming another divided battlefield in the Cold War and to prove that they could defend decolonization by force, if necessary. For India, keeping Congo united and out of the Cold War arena would not only advance the process of decolonization but also strengthen the nonaligned world.

This convergence was evident in Nehru's U.N. General Assembly speech in October 1960. He posed a rhetorical question to signal his intent: "What is the role of the United Nations in Congo?"

> It is essential to maintain the integrity of the Congo for, if there is disintegration of the State, this is bound to lead to internal civil war on a large scale. There will be no peace in the Congo except on the basis of the integrity of the State. Foreign countries must particularly avoid any interference in these internal affairs or encouragement to one faction against another. . . .
>
> The role of the United Nations is a mediatory one: to reconcile and to help in the proper functioning of the Central government. . . .

There is at present an elected Parliament in the Congo, though it does not appear to be functioning. I think that it should be the function of the United Nations to help this Parliament to meet and function so that, out of its deliberations, the problems of the Congo may be dealt with by the people themselves.[50]

Nehru then emphasized the increasing responsibility and role—including a military presence—of the United Nations in Congo and the need "even within the terms of the Charter, to adapt the United Nations machinery to meet situations as they arise."[51] India backed up this strong political statement with force; from the start of ONUC in July 1960 to its termination in June 1964, India deployed two successive brigades (more than twelve thousand men) and six Canberra bomber aircraft that played a pivotal role in the hazardous operation.[52] India maintained these troops and aircraft even during its traumatic 1962 war with China. ONUC was the United Nations' largest and most robust peace operation during the Cold War, involving nearly twenty thousand personnel at its peak. In all, "over 93,000 men from thirty-five countries served in ONUC."[53]

Indians also held key positions during ONUC's deployment. Rajeshwar Dayal, India's former U.N. permanent representative, was appointed special representative of the secretary-general in Congo,[54] and General Rikhye, who had returned to India in 1960 to command the 114th Infantry Brigade in Ladakh (in anticipation of the coming war with China), was recalled and appointed as military adviser to Hammarskjöld. Both had been involved in earlier U.N. missions and were acutely aware of the world body's desire to support decolonization and prevent the Cold War from spreading.

Two other aspects of India's role in Congo are crucial to appreciate its singular contribution to U.N. peacekeeping in the Cold War. First, India pressured Hammarskjöld to ensure that the resolutions—first from the Security Council and then from the General Assembly (when the two superpowers got involved)—gave ONUC the necessary mandate to operate in a civil war situation. Specifically, they sought a mandate to use ONUC more actively and forcefully to restore law and order, particularly in Katanga, where U.N. forces were constantly attacked, and to ensure the integrity of Congo. As Dayal reasoned, "The UN is here to help but not to intervene, to advise but not to order, to conciliate but not to take sides. . . . But how can the duty of maintaining law and order be discharged without taking specific action when necessary?"[55]

Speaking at the United Nations in December 1960, Krishna Menon was even more assertive. In his characteristic acerbic style, he argued: "If there was no question of using force, why did the Security Council take steps . . . to send 20,000 armed troops to the Congo? They were not going to play in a tournament. If the idea was not to use force then engineers, scientist, parsons and preachers would have gone."[56] To ensure that India did not get roped into the Cold War contest in the Congo, New Delhi stipulated that Indian forces would engage militarily only with troops from renegade armed Congolese units, Belgian military, paramilitary, and other personnel, and other mercenaries.

Second, Hammarskjöld and Dayal (and his predecessor, Ralph Bunche) tried to prevent the superpower conflict becoming a factor in Congo, and they clearly saw this as one of ONUC's purposes.[57] Despite their efforts, both the Soviet Union and the United States stepped up their support of different factions within the Congolese government and turned against ONUC. Washington accused Dayal and Hammarskjöld of supporting the Soviet agenda by protecting Lumumba, and Moscow called for Hammarskjöld's resignation after Lumumba was assassinated at the hands of an alleged U.S.-led conspiracy. Subsequently, Dayal, who was attacked by President Kasavubu and branded a "crypto communist" in Western media, was forced to resign in May 1961.[58] Within months, Hammarskjöld's death, in a mysterious air crash in September 1961 while on a peace mission to Katanga, accentuated the concern that Congo might well end up as another Cold War spoil. Against this backdrop the United Nations was keen to hasten the end of the war.[59]

The Security Council passed two resolutions — 161 and 169 — authorizing ONUC to use force.[60] The second resolution, prompted in part by the tragic death of Hammarskjöld, allowed for unprecedented military response by U.N. forces. Hammarskjöld's successor, U Thant (doubtless on the advice of Rikhye, who was now his military adviser), called for more vigorous military action to ensure the freedom of movement of U.N. troops and to establish law and order in Katanga.

On the ground, Indians troops were at the forefront of ONUC's efforts to enforce peace. Ground forces and aircraft participated in all the key military actions, including Operation Sunflower, Operation Rum Punch, Operation Morthor, and Operation Onukat, aimed at containing the Katanga insurgency and maintaining the territorial integrity of Congo. India sustained 147 casualties, including 39 dead, the highest number the nation suffered in any Cold War U.N. operation.

In one such action in December 1961 to dismantle roadblocks manned by armed Katangan rebels, Captain Gurbachan Singh Salaria and his men were ambushed and outnumbered. Salaria died after successfully leading the charge against the heavily armed rebel position and was awarded the Param Vir Chakra, India's highest military honor.[61]

By January 1962, Indian action had contributed to ONUC regaining control of Katanga. It is evident that whereas India could provide an entire brigade even while facing one of its biggest military threats from China, ONUC could not have survived, let alone achieved its objectives, without the Indian contribution at the U.N. headquarters and on the ground.

India's use of troops in the Congo also provoked both domestic and international criticism, which was a key factor in New Delhi's decision to pull out of ONUC in June 1964.[62] Yet scholars cite evidence to show that had the United Nations not intervened, "the Congo would have become a cauldron into which other African states, the United States, the Soviet Union, and other big powers would have been drawn on one side or the other, and the Congolese . . . would not have the stability on which to build their independent nation-state."[63] This U.N. achievement is due in significant measure to India's role in the Congo crisis.

CONCLUSION

During the Cold War, India became an accidental rule shaper for U.N. peacekeeping. This is not because it needed to but because it could. Although Nehru was keen for independent India to play a leading role in the United Nations, even he did not anticipate that India (along with a few other countries) would be at the forefront of initiating and establishing U.N. peacekeeping. Indeed, had article 43 of the U.N. Charter (which envisaged collective security) come into effect, the five permanent members would have been in the lead of any kind of U.N. operation (as was the case in Korea). However, the Cold War superpower rivalry, especially after 1950, not only thwarted any operations under article 43 but also ruled out a leadership role for the permanent members. This norm took root following the direct involvement of the United States in Korea, of Britain and France in the Suez, and of Russia in Hungary.

As a result, there was a desperate need within the United Nations (identified by Hammarskjöld) to develop a mechanism for keeping the peace, especially given the ongoing decolonization phenomenon under the shadow of the Cold War. Such peacekeeping would require politically acceptable peacekeepers with military skills and "no significant political or economic interests in Third-World arenas of conflict, no prejudicial colonial histories, an identification with active and independent internationalism, and strong support for the United Nations' peace and security functions."[64]

Nehru's internationalism, his perception of the United Nations as a manifestation of his One World vision, his disdain for the Cold War, and his leadership of the nonaligned movement, coupled with his desire to use India's vast expeditionary and constabulary capability and experience beyond its borders, made him and India an ideal partner for Hammarskjöld's vision. It is unsurprising, then, that India, especially under Nehru, answered the United Nations' clarion call and contributed to both building the norms of peacekeeping and the actual operations. Nehru not only encouraged U.N. peacekeeping initiatives in the General Assembly but also supported efforts in the field: for example, he visited an UNEF I observation post of 4 Kumaon in Gaza in May 1960 and addressed the peacekeepers. Nehru also approved additional troops for ONUC and advised Dayal that the United Nations must not be allowed to fail. According to Kabilan Krishnaswamy, India's participation in U.N. peace missions during the Cold War was "disproportionately large" and its participation was "the highest during the period 1956–66," mainly because of the creation and deployment of UNEF I.[65] As Hammarskjöld acknowledged, the "U.N. could not conceive of a single conflict situation without the cooperation from the countries like India."[66]

Several tangible benefits accrued to India from its rule-shaping role. First, U.N. peacekeeping allowed India a high-profile diplomatic and military role (even if not always an appreciated one), which was a significant feat, given that the superpower contest provided very little space for other so-called neutral actors on the global stage. Second, as peacekeeping became linked to decolonization, it increased India's influence in the United Nations when many of the newly independent states became members and looked to India's leadership in the world body. Third, U.N. peacekeeping allowed India's armed forces to retain their global expeditionary capabilities without the country being seen as a threat.

For the United Nations, which had to deal with host countries accepting peacekeepers from only some countries, India was not only the least unacceptable option but also a popular choice for several reasons: "the size and professionalism of its armed forces; the lack of such forces in other developing countries, particularly in the early years after World War II; and India's neutral stance during the cold war."[67] The size of India's forces ensured that it could always contribute troops. According to a 2007 estimate, only 60 units of the Indian army had undertaken U.N. peace operation assignments over the previous fifty years. Thus, "going by the current rate of deployment it would take 250 years for all 360 units to get this opportunity at least once!"[68]

Although India's contribution in the field is well documented, its role in establishing peacekeeping norms was just as crucial. Starting with its support to and adherence of the four basic principles of classic U.N. peacekeeping in UNEF I, India also did not shy away from pushing an ambivalent Hammarskjöld to undertake robust peace enforcement in ONUC. The role of Indian officials, notably Krishna Menon, in contributing to creating these norms and in ensuring their implementation on the ground while navigating the treacherous Cold War currents remains unrecognized.

Similarly, the role of Indar Jit Rikhye remains underappreciated. He was made available to the United Nations on short notice to become the military adviser to the secretary-general in 1960 even though he was commanding a crucial brigade on the border with China; he was instrumental in organizing the chain of command of U.N. operations. In addition to his role in UNEF I and Congo, in his capacity as military adviser to the secretary-general Rikhye was also involved in U.N. peace efforts in Ruanda-Urundi, West Irian, Yemen, Cyprus, Jordan, the Dominican Republic, and Cuba (during the missile crisis, he was the conduit between U Thant and U.S. ambassador Adlai Stevenson and Admiral John McCain, commander-in-chief of the U.S. Eastern Fleet).[69]

Having worked with Hammarskjöld and Thant to launch classic U.N. peacekeeping, Rikhye left in 1969 when the post of military adviser to the U.N. secretary-general was abolished and replaced by a military liaison officer. Although the reason for the abolition was not clear, Rikhye offers a tongue-in-cheek rationale that the downgrading of the post was underlined by the fact that "its holder [Rikhye] was not always available, as he was often given special assignments away from headquarters."[70] After leaving the United Nations, Rikhye established the International Peace Academy in New York, which focused on developing a peacekeeping doctrine for the United Nations and engaged in exercises for peacekeepers.[71]

The Cold War constrained India's actions and in many cases compelled it to follow rules and norms established by others, which were not always in its interests. However, the United Nations in general and U.N. peacekeeping in particular offered an ideal opportunity for India to not only shape rules that advanced New Delhi's strategic interests but also contributed to the global public good and to global governance. As seasoned India observers Howard and Teresita Schaffer have noted: "Indian relished these military

Waheguru Pal Singh Sidhu

and diplomatic opportunities. They demonstrated India's attachment to peace, won it international publicity, and led other countries to take it seriously as a player on the world stage."[72]

However, despite its historical contribution and impressive record as the world's biggest peacekeeping nation, India has not been able to translate its crucial contribution in keeping peace in troubled spots into great-power status either during the Cold War or since. India was unable to use its contributions to U.N. peacekeeping to either secure or further its own economic and political interests or garner greater support for a more prominent global role. Indeed, many countries that benefited from India's peacekeeping contributions remain indifferent or opposed to backing New Delhi's global ambitions. Consequently, India still remains outside the U.N. Security Council and decision-making processes related to international order, particularly international peace and security, and is likely to stay there for the foreseeable future.

NOTES

1. See UN Charter, chapter VII, article 43, http://www.un.org/en/sections/un-charter/chapter-vii/index.html.

2. Larry L. Fabian, *Soldiers without Enemies: Preparing the United Nations for Peacekeeping* (Washington, D.C.: Brookings Institution, 1971), 58–66.

3. United Nations General Assembly, *Twenty-Year Programme for Achieving Peace through the United Nations*, U.N. Doc. A/1304, 26 July 1950, 7. Trygve Lie served as the first U.N. secretary general from 1946 until his resignation in 1952.

4. Fabian, *Soldiers without Enemies*, 74.

5. India was one of eleven "neutral" countries that participated in the United Nations Special Committee on Palestine (UNSCOP), which was given "wide powers to ascertain and record facts, to investigate all questions and issues relevant to the problem of Palestine, and to make recommendations." See https://en.wikipedia.org/wiki/United_Nations_Special_Committee_on_Palestine. Even before independence, Prime-Minister-in-waiting Jawaharlal Nehru was keen that India should be part of UNSCOP and felt that having a neutral stance on the issue might strengthen its chances of being nominated. However, due to the pro-Arab position taken by India's representative to the United Nations, Asaf Ali (much to the chagrin of Nehru), India was not nominated in the first round but was eventually "elected" onto the committee. See P. R. Kumaraswamy, *India's Israel Policy* (New York: Columbia University Press, 2010), 85–107, for a fascinating account of Ali's role in the deliberation leading to the creation of UNSCOP and the role of India's member of UNSCOP, Sir Abdur Rahman, in contradicting New Delhi's position.

6. John F. Hillen III, "UN Collective Security: Chapter Six and Half," *Parameters*, Spring 1994, 28.

7. See *60 Years of UN Peacekeeping*, http://www.unis.unvienna.org/unis/en/60yearsPK/index.html.

8. Dag Hammarskjöld, "Do We Need the United Nations?," Address before the

Students' Association, Copenhagen, 2 May 1959, UN Press Release SG/812, 1 May 1959. Hammarskjöld was the second U.N. secretary-general, serving from 1953 until his death in 1961.

9. James A. Stegenga, "Peacekeeping: Post-Mortems or Previews?," *International Organization*, June 1973, 378. See also *Summary Study of the Experience Derived from the Establishment and Operation of the Force: Report of the Secretary General*, U.N. Doc. A/3942, 9 October 1958, 28–33.

10. M. K. Gandhi, "Qualifications of a Peace Brigade," *Harijan*, 18 June 1938, in *Collected Works of Mahatma Gandhi*, vol. 73, 243–45, available at http://gandhiserve.org/cwmg /VOL073.PDF.

11. Salvador de Madariaga and Jayaprakash Narayan, "Blueprint for a World Commonwealth," in *Perspectives on Peace, 1910–1960* (New York: Carnegie Endowment for International Peace, 1960), 60–63, cited in Gene Keyes, "Peacekeeping by Unarmed Buffer Forces: Precedents and Proposals," *Peace and Change: A Journal of Peace Research* 5, nos. 2 and 3 (Fall 1978): 3–11.

12. Cited in Thomas Weber, *Gandhi's Peace Army: The Shanti Sena and Unarmed Peacekeeping* (Syracuse, N.Y.: Syracuse University Press, 1996), 17.

13. The Editors, "Introduction, Early Experiences: 1948–1963," in *The Oxford Handbook of United Nations Peacekeeping Operations*, ed. Joachim A. Koops, Norrie Macqueen, Thierry Tardy, and Paul Williams (Oxford: Oxford University Press, 2015), 114–15.

14. Obituary, "Indar Jit Rikhye," *Economist*, 7 June 2007.

15. C. Raja Mohan, "India's Military Diplomacy: Legacy of International Peacekeeping," ISAS Working Paper No. 190 (June 2014), 3. See also Srinath Raghavan, *India's War: The Making of Modern South Asia, 1939–1945* (London: Allen Lane, 2016); Yasmin Khan, *India at War: The Subcontinent and the Second World War* (Oxford: Oxford University Press, 2015); and Raghu Karnad, *Farthest Field: An Indian Story of the Second World War* (New York: W. W. Norton, 2015).

16. See Raghavan, *India's War*; Khan, *India at War*; Karnad, *Farthest Field*; and W. P. S. Sidhu, "War, Peace and International Order," *Mint*, 10 November 2014.

17. Quoted in Baldev Raj Nayar and T. V. Paul, *India in the World Order: Searching for Major Power Status* (Cambridge: Cambridge University Press, 2003), 133.

18. Manu Bhagavan, *The Peacemakers: India and the Quest for One World* (New Delhi: HarperCollins, 2012).

19. Quoted in ibid., 121.

20. Constitution of India, part IV, Directive Principles of State Policy, article 51, 24, https://india.gov.in/sites/upload_files/npi/files/coi_part_full.pdf.

21. India was given a slot in the Temporary Commission on Korea and, later, the Commission on Korea "because of its interest in assuming a leading role in Asian politics" and was expected to take an "independent position." See Leon Gordenker, *The United Nations and the Peaceful Unification of Korea: The Politics of Field Operations, 1947–1950* (The Hague: Martinus Nijhoff, 1959), 31.

22. Menon quoted in Kim ChanWahn, "The Role of India in the Korean War," *International Area Review* 13, no. 2 (Summer 2010): 24.

23. Ibid., 25.

24. Richard Gowan and Sushant K. Singh, "India and UN Peacekeeping: The Weight of History and a Lack of Strategy," in *Shaping the Emerging World: India and the Multilateral*

Waheguru Pal Singh Sidhu

Order, ed. Waheguru Pal Singh Sidhu, Pratap Bhanu Mehta, and Bruce Jones (Washington, D.C.: Brookings Institution Press, 2013), 180.

25. Quoted in ChanWahn, "Role of India in the Korean War," 29.

26. Ibid., 27–28, 32.

27. Chester Bowles, *Ambassador's Report* (London: V. Gollancz, 1954), 242. See also *Foreign Relations of the United States, 1952–1954*, vol. 15, pt. 2, *Korea*, ed. Edward C. Keefer (Washington, D.C.: U.S. Government Printing Office, 1994).

28. Central Intelligence Agency, *Issues of the Korean Post-Armistice Political Conference*, Working Draft, 29 July 1953, https://www.cia.gov/library/readingroom/docs/1953-07-29b.pdf.

29. Bruce Riedel, *JFK's Forgotten Crisis: Tibet, the CIA, and the Sino-Indian War* (Washington, D.C.: Brookings Institution Press, 2017), 20–21.

30. Sri Nandan Prasad, *History of the Custodian Force (India) in Korea, 1953–54* (New Delhi: Historical Section, Ministry of Defence, 1976).

31. Alan Bullion, "India and UN Peacekeeping," in *A Future for Peacekeeping*, ed. Edward Moxon-Browne (London: Macmillan, 1998), 61.

32. The 1956 Soviet invasion of Hungary posed an even more formidable challenge for the United Nations, but given the direct involvement of one of the superpowers, there was recognition that the Soviet Union (which had ended its boycott and returned to the Security Council and the General Assembly) was likely to veto any international efforts. In contrast, the Suez Crisis, where the two superpowers were not directly involved, provided some prospect for a U.N. role in ensuring that the crisis did not escalate.

33. Paul F. Diehl, "First United Nations Emergency Force (UNEF I)," in Koops, Macqueen, Tardy, and Williams, *Oxford Handbook of United Nations Peacekeeping Operations*, 145. The unarmed mission was the United Nations Truce Supervision Organization (UNTSO), set up in May 1948 to monitor four armistice agreements between Israel and the four neighboring Arab countries, Egypt, Jordan, Lebanon, and the Syrian Arab Republic.

34. See http://www.un.org/depts/dhl/dag/docs/ares997-998e.pdf. Canada's foreign minister, Lester B. Pearson, translated Hammarskjöld's vision into reality by shepherding the resolution through the General Assembly. His efforts were supported by V. K. Krishna Menon, who played a role in bringing Egypt's Gamal Abdel Nasser to accept the plan for resolution of the conflict. For his efforts Pearson was awarded the 1957 Nobel Peace Prize and is widely regarded as the father of U.N. peacekeeping.

35. India was a member of the seven-nation committee set up to advise Secretary-General Hammarskjöld on the creation and operation of the U.N. peacekeeping force. See Richard Edmund Ward, *India's Pro-Arab Policy: A Study in Continuity* (New York: Praeger, 1992), 56–57.

36. Fabian, *Soldiers without Enemies*, 91.

37. Speech by Prime Minister Jawahar Lal Nehru in the United Nations General Assembly, New York, 20 December 1956, 4, https://pminewyork.org/pdf/uploadpdf/46977lms11.pdf.

38. Ibid.

39. These battalions were from 3 Para regiment, 1 Para regiment, 2 Grenadiers regiment, 4 Kumaon regiment, 4 Rajput regiment, 2 Sikh regiment, 2 Maratha Light Infantry regiment, 9 Dogra regiment, 4 Guards regiment, 3 Punjab regiment, and 1 Sikh Light

Infantry regiment and were among the best troops in the Indian army. See S. K. Sharma, *The Indian Army: United Nations Peacekeeping Operations* (New Delhi: Lancers, 1997), 17.

40. M. V. Naidu, "The Origin of UN Peace-Enforcement and Peacekeeping: Re-Examination of the Crises in Korea (1950), Kashmir (1948) and the Suez (1956)," *Peace Research* 27, no. 1 (February 1995): 19–21.

41. Quoted in Harold A. Gould, "Witness to History," review article, *Economic and Political Weekly*, 24 May 2003, 2040.

42. Obituary, "Indar Jit Rikhye," *Economist*, 7 June 2007.

43. Major General P. S. Gyani replaced Canadian lieutenant general Burns and commanded UNEF I from 1959 to 1964.

44. Adam Bernstein, "I. J. Rikhye; Indian Major General Oversaw U.N. Peacekeeping Efforts," *Washington Post*, 25 May 2007; Gould, "Witness to History," 2042.

45. Quoted in Naidu, "The Origin of UN Peace-Enforcement and Peacekeeping," *Peace Research* 27, no. 1 (February 1995): 15.

46. Indar Jit Rikhye, Michael Harbottle, and Bjørn Egge, *The Thin Blue Line: International Peacekeeping and Its Future* (New Haven, Conn.: Yale University Press, 1974), 70.

47. Naidu, "The Origin of UN Peace-Enforcement and Peacekeeping," *Peace Research* 27, no. 1 (February 1995): 14–15.

48. Jane Boulden, "United Nations Operation in the Congo (ONUC)," in Koops, Macqueen, Tardy, and Williams, *Oxford Handbook of United Nations Peacekeeping Operations*, 160–70.

49. ONUC was established on 14 July 1960 by Security Council resolution 143, which authorized the secretary-general "to take the necessary steps, in consultation with the Government of the Republic of the Congo, to provide the Government with such military assistance as might be necessary until, through that Government's efforts with United Nations technical assistance, the national security forces might be able, in the opinion of the Government, to meet fully their tasks." See http://www.un.org/en/peacekeeping /missions/past/onucM.htm.

50. Statement by Prime Minister Jawaharlal Nehru, 15th Session, 882nd Plenary Meeting, 3 October 1960, 12–13, https://www.pminewyork.org/pdf/uploadpdf/25273lms15.pdf.

51. Ibid.

52. India's 99th Infantry Brigade was deployed, consisting of 1 Dogra regiment, 2 Jat regiment, 3/1 Gorkha rifles regiment, a squadron of the 63rd cavalry, 120 heavy mortar battery, 13 field company, a machine gun company from 4 Mahar, and 95 field ambulance. These units were subsequently rotated. The Canberra bombers were drawn from no. 5 Squadron. See Sharma, *Indian Army*, 27; and Pushpinder Singh, "Canberras in the Congo," *Bharat Rakshak*, 20 July 2009, http://www.bharat-rakshak.com/IAF/History/Congo /1009-Congo01.html.

53. Rikhye, Harbottle, and Egge, *Thin Blue Line*, 71.

54. Rajeshwar Dayal, *Mission for Hammarskjöld: The Congo Crisis* (Oxford: Oxford University Press, 1976).

55. Quoted in Brian Urquhart, "The Tragedy of Lumumba," *New York Review of Books*, 4 October 2001.

56. Krishna Menon quoted in T. Ramakrishna Reddy, *India's Policy in the United Nations* (Rutherford, N.J.: Fairleigh Dickinson University Press, 1968), 97.

57. Urquhart, "Tragedy of Lumumba."

58. Rajeshwar Dayal, *A Life of Our Times* (New Delhi: Orient Longman, 1998), 456.

Waheguru Pal Singh Sidhu

59. Srinath Raghavan, "When Indian Troops Entered the Congo 55 Years Ago," *Mint*, 19 September 2016.

60. Resolution 161 of 21 February 1961 urged the United Nations to "take immediately all appropriate measures to prevent the occurrence of civil war in the Congo, including arrangements for ceasefire, the halting of all military operations, the prevention of clashes, and the use of force, if necessary, in the last resort," whereas Resolution 169 of 24 November 1961 authorized the secretary-general "to take vigorous action, including the use of the requisite measure of force, if necessary, for the immediate apprehension, detention pending legal action and/or deportation of all foreign military and paramilitary personnel and political advisers not under United Nations Command, and mercenaries."

61. Ambassador Samantha Powers, Permanent Representative of the United States to the United Nations, "Remarks on Effective Peacekeeping in the 21st Century," New Delhi, 20 November 2015, 6, https://icwa.in/pdfs/ssreports/2014/LectureSamanthaPower 20112015.pdf.

62. Alan James, "The Congo Controversies," *International Peacekeeping* 1, no. 1 (Spring 1994): 44–58.

63. Rikhye, Harbottle, and Egge, *Thin Blue Line*, 84.

64. Larry L. Fabian, "Some Perspectives on Peacekeeping Institutions," in "The United Nations: Appraisal at 25 Years," special issue, *American Journal of International Law* 64, no. 4 (September 1970): 13.

65. Kabilan Krishnaswamy, "A Case for India's 'Leadership' in United Nations Peacekeeping," *International Studies* 47, 2–4 (2010): 228.

66. Cited in C. S. R. Murthy, "India at UN: From Raj to Rajiv," *World Focus* 6, no. 8 (August 1985): 22.

67. Dipankar Banerjee, "South Asia: Contributors of Global Significance," in *Peace Operations: Trends, Progress, and Prospects*, ed. Donald C. F. Daniel, Patricia Taft, and Sharon Wiharta (Washington, D.C.: Georgetown University Press, 2008), 192.

68. C. S. R. Murthy, "Unintended Consequences of Peace Operations for Troop-Contributing Countries from South Asia," in *Unintended Consequences of Peace Operations*, ed. Chiyuki Aoi, Cedric de Coning, and Ramesh Thakur (Tokyo: United Nations University Press, 2007), 163.

69. Gould, "Witness to History," 2041.

70. Indar Jit Rikhye, *The Theory and Practice of Peacekeeping* (London: C. Hurst, 1984), 207.

71. See, e.g., Henry Wiseman, *Peacekeeping: Appraisals and Proposals* (New York: Pergamon Press for the International Peace Academy, 1983).

72. Teresita C. Schaffer and Howard B. Schaffer, *India at the Global High Table: The Quest for Regional Primacy and Strategic Autonomy* (Washington, D.C.: Brookings Institution Press, 2016).

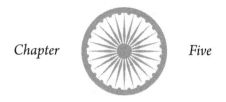

Chapter *Five*

A Missed Opportunity?

The Nehru–Zhou Enlai Summit of 1960

SRINATH RAGHAVAN

Fifty years is a long time, certainly long enough to treat anything of that vintage as nothing but history. But the Sino-Indian crisis and war of 1962 seem to be trapped in a time warp. The events of 1962 have evoked much interest in India following the fiftieth anniversary of the war and the availability of the postwar official inquiry, also known as the "Henderson-Brooks Report." However, much of the recent commentary on the war has been strikingly reminiscent of the post-mortems performed in its immediate aftermath—not least in its continued search for the "guilty men of 1962," to borrow the title of a book by journalist D. R. Mankekar. Jawaharlal Nehru is vilified—especially in the social media—as though he were still the prime minister of a country that had just suffered a humiliating defeat rather than a historical figure that has been dead for more than five decades.

The great German historian Reinhart Koselleck once observed that "in the short run history may be made by the victors. But in the long run the gains in historical understanding have come from the defeated."[1] This has, alas, not been true in India's case with the China crisis. It is a pity that despite the passage of time and the availability of new archival material, we persist in asking the same simplistic questions—and, worse, in insisting on giving the same old answer.

The historiography of the Sino-Indian war of 1962 has passed through two distinct stages. The earliest accounts viewed India as the victim of Chinese betrayal and expansionism. According to these, the Prime Minister Jawaharlal Nehru was credulous and insufficiently alert to Chinese adventurism. This perspective continues to inform public discussions on the subject to

date. More influential in the academia has been the revisionist critique originally advanced by the British journalist and scholar Neville Maxwell in 1970.
Maxwell blamed Nehru for arrogance and obduracy in the face of Chinese
efforts to seek a negotiated solution. Maxwell, however, overreached himself
in attempting to prove that the Nehru government viewed the issue in the
same terms as he saw it later. For an account of Indian decision-making, he
curiously interpreted Delhi's actions almost as Beijing would have viewed
them. In the years since, revisionist scholars have taken little cognizance of
the range of archival materials that have opened up, resorting instead to the
rhetorical trope of denouncing everyone who disagrees with them as by defi-
nition "nationalist."[2]

This chapter aims to move beyond the blame game to focus on a corner-
stone of the revisionist case on Nehru's China policy: the contention that
Nehru rejected the reasonable offer advanced by Premier Zhou Enlai in 1960
because he had already set his mind against any compromise. Such claims
impart a misleading simplicity and fixity to what was a much more nuanced
and shifting position. In particular, perceptions of China's territorial ambitions and of India's relative weakness are crucial to understanding Nehru's
stance. It is crucial to situate the boundary dispute in the wider international
frame of the Cold War as well as the more specific domestic political context of India. The Sino-Indian dispute came to the fore at a time when the
Sino-Soviet relationship was heading toward a sharp deterioration and, in
some ways, acted a catalyst in the subsequent Sino-Soviet split. This Cold
War context is a crucial backdrop to the boundary negotiations. Their failure
set the stage for the Sino-Indian conflict of 1962 and the subsequent turn in
India's nonaligned stance in the Cold War.[3]

EVOLUTION OF INDIA'S BOUNDARY POLICY[4]

The Sino-Indian boundary is usually divided into western, central, and eastern sectors. The western sector encompasses the area of Ladakh, the middle
sector the boundary of Himachal Pradesh and Uttar Pradesh with Tibet,
and the eastern sector the area formerly known as the North East Frontier
Agency, now Arunachal Pradesh. The boundary dispute has spawned a veritable cottage industry of works examining its historical origins.[5] This chapter is agnostic on the merits of either the Indian or the Chinese stand on
the boundary dispute. For our purposes it would suffice to underscore some
salient aspects of the British legacy to independent India.

The status of the boundaries at the time of Indian independence is clear from the maps produced by Delhi as late as 1950. The boundary in the western and middle sectors was marked "undefined." In the western sector, the British had toyed with a variety of boundary alignments in keeping with their perceived security requirements. Thus the Ardagh alignment of 1897 included the Aksai Chin area within the territorial boundaries of India, whereas the MacDonald note of 1899 placed it within China. China's refusal to respond to the MacDonald offer led the British to make further unilateral alterations as mandated by their changing perceptions. The undefined boundary in the western sector reflected the failure of British attempts to secure a frontier agreement with China.

In the eastern sector the boundary was shown as conforming to the alignment formalized between the Indian and Tibetan representatives in the Simla Conference of 1914. The McMahon Line, as it came to be called after the then foreign secretary of India, was defined in a set of notes exchanged between Henry McMahon and the chief Tibetan delegate, Lonchen Shatra, on 24–25 March 1914. Accompanying the notes was a map that delineated the border along the highest line of the Assam Himalaya and that outlined the boundaries and buffer zones between Tibet and China. These were also marked on the map of the draft convention, which was initialed on 27 April 1914 by the Chinese as well as British Indian and Tibetan representatives. The Simla Convention was initialed yet again by the British Indian and Tibetan plenipotentiaries on 3 July 1914. They also signed a joint declaration stating that the convention was binding on both parties, irrespective of Chinese agreement. The Chinese government, however, repudiated the Simla Convention.

Independent India's policy toward Tibet was under sporadic consideration even before the Chinese civil war ended. The contours of official thinking can be discerned from a note prepared in June 1948 by the Indian ambassador in Nanking (Nanjing), K. M. Panikkar. It stated that following British withdrawal, India had become "in law the successor to British rights in Tibet." "The first and most important" of India's interests was the McMahon Line. Panikkar observed that although the Chinese had accepted the Simla Agreement of 1914, they had refused to ratify it. Hence, effective Chinese control over Tibet would mean "the immediate revival of claims against Nepal, Bhutan and Sikkim and also the denunciation of the Macmahon [sic] line."[6] Indeed, the assumption that a strong Chinese government would seize Tibet and advance claims to the region below the McMahon Line appears to have been widely accepted.[7]

No sooner had the communists taken control of China than they announced their intention to "liberate" Tibet. India's policy was to avoid provoking China, but India would not give up its rights in Tibet and would provide moral and material support to the Tibetan government. As the secretary general of the Ministry of External Affairs G. S. Bajpai explained to the British envoy: "Chinese Communists, like any other Communists, reacted well to firmness but would exploit any sign of weakness."[8] This attitude would underpin subsequent Indian policy on the boundary.

After the Chinese invaded Tibet in 1950, the Indian government began seriously considering its boundary policy. Presently, Nehru declared India's stance on the boundary in a statement in parliament. The frontier from Ladakh to Nepal was defined "chiefly by long usage and custom." The frontier in the east was "clearly defined by the McMahon Line which was fixed by the Simla Convention of 1914 . . . that is our boundary—map or no map." This categorical pronouncement was spurred by Delhi's concern to adopt a robust posture in defense of its interests: any sign of weakness, as Bajpai had observed, would be exploited. The emphasis on the McMahon Line stemmed from two considerations. It is evident from Nehru's statement that India was surer of its rights in the eastern sector than in the west. Further, from the standpoint of security, Nehru felt that the "main frontier was the Assam frontier."[9] The importance attached to this sector led to the decision to occupy the town of Tawang in the North East Frontier Agency. As Nehru wrote later, "It was on our side of the McMahon line, but it had not been occupied by us and was practically under Tibetan control till then."[10] On 12 February 1951, a political officer with an armed escort took control of Tawang amid the clamorous ululations of the Tibetans. Beijing, however, did not respond in any fashion.

The Indians felt also that they should try and obtain Beijing's acceptance of the frontier. Bajpai and Foreign Secretary K. P. S. Menon thought that China's recognition of the frontier should form part of an overall settlement on Tibet: India should not withdraw its armed parties from Tibet without securing this. However, Beijing's response was not forthcoming. Menon thought that China's attitude was "cunning." He wondered if the Chinese were "waiting to be free from their preoccupations in the North to be able to enforce a settlement in Tibet after their own hearts?" "Irredentism," wrote Menon, "has always played a part in the policy of the Chinese Government, whether Imperial, Kuomintang or Communists." A former ambassador to China, he recalled "seeing, on the walls of the Military Academy in Chengtu, a map, showing China as it was and ought to be and including large portions of Kashmir and areas to the south of the McMahon Line. This is perhaps the real reason for the Chinese reluctance to discuss the problem of Tibet with us." Menon recommended that "we must firmly adhere to our decision that any such proposal ... can only be considered as part of a general settlement on Tibet."[11]

Following another meeting with Zhou, Panikkar reported that the "question of boundary was not touched and no allusion made to any political problems." Zhou, he argued, knew India's declared position; his persistent silence should, therefore, be treated as acquiescence in — if not acceptance of — India's view. India should stick to the stance that the frontier had been defined and there was nothing to be discussed. Following some debate, Panikkar convinced Nehru of the soundness of his suggestion. The nub of his argument: so long as China was unwilling to rake up the issue, India should use the time to make its position effective in the frontier areas, where its administrative hold was weak and its political position untested.[12]

A key component of India's frontier policy was to adopt a strong stance and eschew any move indicating doubt or weakness. As Nehru explained to his ambassador in Beijing, "If we show weakness advantage will be taken of immediately. This applies to any development that might take place or in reference to our frontier problems. ... In regard to this entire frontier we have to maintain an attitude of firmness."[13] As part of this posture, it was decided in 1953 to publish new official maps that would show the boundary between India and China as unambiguously delimited. The crucial decision, in retrospect, lay in the Ladakh sector. Here the Indian government decided neither on the ambitious Ardagh Line nor on the MacDonald Line but on a "compromise line which had some plausibility."[14] This line placed Aksai Chin within Indian territory. Foreign Secretary R. K. Nehru later recalled that "in 1953, our experts had advised us that our claim to Aksai Chin was not too strong." The prime minister was "agreeable" to adjustments in "Aksai Chin and one or two other places" being made "as part of a satisfactory overall settlement."[15] Thus, during the Sino-Indian talks over Tibet in 1954, Nehru enjoined the Indian delegation to refrain from raising the boundary issue. Importantly, he added that "this will have to be brought in in a larger settlement. In that settlement I should like to make clear our special position in the border States."[16]

Shortly after the 1954 agreement, the two sides began to contest the ownership of a grazing ground called Bara Hoti along the Uttar Pradesh–Tibet border. During his talks with Zhou in Beijing later that year, Nehru referred indirectly to boundary alignment in Chinese maps. Zhou replied that China had been reprinting old maps. They had not undertaken surveys

Srinath Raghavan

or consulted neighboring countries and had no basis for fixing the boundary lines. Nehru replied that he was not worried about these maps: "Our frontiers are clear." Despite the air of nonchalance, Nehru's unease was obvious: "Supposing we publish a map showing Tibet as part of India, how would China feel about it?"[17] Zhou did not raise any question about the new Indian maps, which depicted a firm boundary in all sectors and incorporated Aksai Chin within India.

By early 1956, there were reports that the Chinese were constructing roads on their side of the India-Tibet frontier. The Indian consul general in Tibet wrote that these roads could be used for access to border areas and to take possession of these parts. To counteract this, it was essential to accelerate existing measures to "develope [sic] areas along our border, make roads, educate people and make them conscious of India." The note also called for checkpoints closer to the border and mobile patrols to "ensure that the Chinese will not encroach on our areas."[18]

Nehru's principal concern was with Chinese maps claiming "quite a good part of Assam. . . . Also, a bit of U.P. [Uttar Pradesh]." He was apparently not much bothered about Chinese map lines in the western sector. As noted above, Nehru was amenable to compromise in this sector. He now began to reconsider the wisdom of waiting for China to raise the issue. Zhou had not accepted India's version of the boundary explicitly and had said only that the maps were old. The continued publication of these maps, together with petty border incidents and construction of roads in Tibet, produced "a sense of disquiet." The prime minister felt that "we shall have to take up this matter some time or the other."[19]

During his visit to India in January 1957, Zhou referred to the McMahon Line in the context of the Sino-Burmese boundary. Although the Chinese had never recognized the line, Zhou said, "now that it is an accomplished fact, we should accept it." They had not consulted the Tibetan authorities and would do so. Nehru took this as a clear acceptance of the McMahon Line. He suggested that minor border issues such as Bara Hoti could be settled by discussions among officials. Zhou agreed, but the discussions did not commence until April 1958.[20] Zhou still did not question Indian claims in the western sector even though the Chinese were constructing a highway that linked Xinjiang and Tibet and passed through Aksai Chin. China, of course, regarded Aksai Chin as its territory. But, in retrospect, Zhou's silence on this occasion had deleterious repercussions: it lent credence to Delhi's perception that China had occupied Aksai Chin furtively and treacherously.

In early 1958 an intelligence patrol reported increasing signs of Chinese activity near Aksai Chin. Nehru did not consider it feasible to protest without being much surer about the alignment of the road. As he wrote: "What we might perhaps do is that in some communication with the Chinese government in regard to the points in dispute which have to be decided we should mention the Aksai Chin area."[21] Clearly, Nehru did not believe that Aksai Chin "belonged" to India and was not open to discussion. We may note that he was willing to treat Aksai Chin on a par with other minor areas in dispute like Bara Hoti. On receiving further information about the road in late 1958, India sent notes protesting the road and questioning Chinese maps. China replied that the road ran through its territory. The Indians' response read: "The question whether the particular area is in Indian or Chinese territory is a matter in dispute which has to be dealt with separately. The government of India proposed to do so."[22]

CORRESPONDENCE AND CLASHES

Around this time the Chinese also handed a reply to India's protest about their maps. It reiterated what Zhou had told Nehru in 1954 and added that with the elapse of time and after consultation with neighbors and surveys, a "new way of drawing the boundary" would be decided. In the context of recent developments, Nehru was unwilling to abide with tenuous reassurances, and he decided to write directly to Zhou.

Nehru recalled that Zhou had told him in 1954 that the maps were old. In 1956, Zhou had made it "quite clear" that China proposed to accept the McMahon Line. China had now published a map that depicted "a large part of our North-East Frontier Agency as well as some other parts" as Chinese territory and had given an evasive reply to India's note. He felt "puzzled" because he had thought that there was "no *major* boundary dispute." Nehru made it clear that he would not be satisfied with an assurance that these were old maps. "There can be no question of these *large parts* of India being anything but India" (emphases added). Evidently Nehru was bothered only by the "large" areas shown within China's boundaries south of the McMahon Line. There was no mention of Aksai Chin, for India had already conveyed to China that this area could be resolved through discussions.

In his reply of 23 January 1959, Zhou stated that the entire boundary had never been formally delimited by any treaty or agreement. The matter had not been raised "because conditions were not yet ripe for its settlement and the Chinese side . . . had had no time to study the question." He averred that Aksai Chin had "always been under Chinese jurisdiction"; only recently had

Srinath Raghavan

India laid claim to it. China could not accept the McMahon Line because it was a product of British imperialism and was illegal. Nevertheless, China found it necessary to "take a more or realistic attitude" toward the line, but had to "act with prudence" and needed time. Because the boundary was not delimited, there were bound to be discrepancies in maps. China did "not hold that every portion of this [Chinese] boundary line is drawn on sufficient grounds." For the first time Zhou questioned the Indian map, "particularly its western section." To avoid border incidents Zhou proposed that both sides maintain the status quo.

The Indians were surprised but not alarmed by the letter. Apart from Ladakh, the Chinese had not explicitly claimed any area included in their maps. Yet the letter suggested that the Chinese held that their boundary line was drawn on "sufficient grounds" at least in one sector — probably the western one, where their line ran further to the west of Aksai Chin. Zhou's disavowal of the McMahon Line, coupled with his guarded assurances, might have appeared a slight retraction to Nehru, who believed that Zhou had clearly accepted it in 1956. Most important, the thrust of Zhou's letter was that the entire boundary was undefined and in need of fresh negotiation. The Indians, however, did not think that the boundary drawn by India had no basis at all.

Nehru's response of 22 March 1959 set forth the historical and geographical basis for India's view of the boundary. It is evident from his note that India considered its case for the McMahon Line unassailable and attached greater importance to this sector. In the western sector, a nebulous treaty of 1842 was cited in support of India's claims. On Zhou's suggestion to maintain status quo, Nehru wrote that neither side should take unilateral action in support of its claims: "Further, if any possession has been secured recently, the position should be rectified." Nehru wrote this in connection with Bara Hoti, which he claimed had recently been occupied. The note did not explicitly state that this proposal applied to Aksai Chin, though India would later claim that it did.

In the following months, relations between India and China deteriorated sharply owing to the rebellion in Tibet and India's grant of asylum to the Dalai Lama. In their quest to subdue the Tibetans, the Chinese moved their forces to the frontier with India in the east. The Indians, too, were engaged in fortifying their presence in these parts. By the summer of 1959 the two sides faced each other along a contested border in the North East Frontier Agency. Not surprisingly, clashes occurred. The first of these took place at Longju toward the end of August, with each side accusing the other of provocation. Beijing rightly pointed out that Indian posts at Longju and two other points lay north of the McMahon Line as marked on the original maps of 1914.

The clash at Longju drew the attention of the Soviet Union to the boundary dispute between India and China. On 6 September Beijing briefed the Soviet chargé d'affaires, Sergei Antonov, insisting that the Indians had initiated the clash. The Soviet embassy, however, considered it "logical that the Chinese side had started the skirmishes": Chinese actions during the Taiwan Strait crisis suggested as much.[23] From Moscow's standpoint the incident was most inopportune. Nikita Khrushchev was keenly looking forward to his forthcoming visit to the United States, and the Sino-Indian clash could cast a shadow on his trip. The Soviets realized that if Moscow adopted a pro-China stand, the Eisenhower administration would be cool toward Khrushchev.[24] Further, Khrushchev wished to avoid rupturing ties with India, which had grown strong since his visit to the country in 1955. He believed that Nehru, while not a communist, was a certainly a progressive force in domestic and international politics.[25]

Moscow decided to issue a statement adopting a neutral stance and calling on both sides to resolve the issue peacefully. The Chinese were naturally unhappy with the Soviet decision, while Nehru described it as very fair and unusual. Soon after his American trip, Khrushchev visited Beijing. The Sino-Indian dispute figured prominently in his discussion with the Chinese leadership. Indeed, Moscow's stance opened a crevice in the Sino-Soviet relationship. Khrushchev squarely blamed China for the developments in Tibet: "If you allow him [the Dalai Lama] an opportunity to flee to India, then what had Nehru to do with it?" "The Hindus acted in Tibet as if it belonged to them," retorted Mao. The Chinese leaders accused Khrushchev of opportunism in supporting India: "The Tass announcement made all imperialists happy." Mao, however, told Khrushchev that China would resolve the dispute through negotiations.[26] Even as the Sino-India dispute catalyzed the deterioration of the Sino-Soviet split, this turn in the Cold War would also complicate Sino-Indian relations and the quest for a boundary settlement.

Meanwhile, domestic politics in India also began to impinge on the dispute. When the Longju incident occurred, the Indian government was already being questioned about the frontier on the basis of newspaper reports and leaks. Following a request in parliament, Nehru agreed to consider releasing a White Paper on these issues. He revealed his evolving position on Aksai Chin when he repeatedly stated that the boundary in Ladakh was not sufficiently defined and that Aksai Chin was a disputed area. He described it as a "barren uninhabited region without a vestige of grass," "peculiarly suited" for discussions. The road was admittedly "an important connection" for the Chinese. Ladakh, he declared, was different from the North East Frontier Agency: India would insist on the McMahon Line boundary but would discuss issues of interpretation of the line. In contrast, the dispute over Aksai Chin was a "minor" thing. India was prepared to discuss it on the basis of treaties, maps, usage, and geography.[27]

On 7 September the first White Paper was published. The decision to release it was ostensibly taken to stem the tide of criticism and to demonstrate that the government had not been complacent. This proved a major miscalculation on Nehru's part, for the paper simply inflamed parliamentary and public opinion and brought the government under intense, unremitting pressure. Nehru was pushed to a position where his diplomatic maneuverability was severely curtailed. Henceforth he had to assess constantly what the political marketplace would bear and adopt only those policies that could be conceivably sold to the public.

Nehru's problems were compounded with the receipt of Zhou's letter a day after the White Paper was released. Zhou correctly argued that the boundary in the west had never been formally delimited. But he claimed that the boundary shown by Chinese maps accorded to "a customary line drawn from historical traditions" up to which China exercised administrative control. This last point would be strongly contested by India. Zhou contended that Nehru had misunderstood his statements on the McMahon Line. He had merely stated that Chinese troops would not cross the line in order to maintain amity and facilitate negotiations. He also claimed that the boundary in this sector as shown in Chinese maps was a "true reflection" of the customary boundary before the so-called McMahon Line came up; India had occupied this region only in 1951. Zhou wrote that he sought a settlement that was fair and reasonable to both sides but would not let India impose its one-sided claims on China.

Nehru was taken aback by this letter. He thought that China's claims in the east were "fantastic and absurd" and could never be accepted. Having given evasive answers about maps and assuring him that they accepted the McMahon Line, the leaders in Beijing were not playing fair. The letter produced a "lack of confidence" in China's words and assurances. Indeed, China's claims were still unclear, and the letter left open the possibility of that they would extend them further. On Ladakh, Nehru told parliament on two more occasions that the boundary was unclear. In his reply to Zhou, however, Nehru adopted a firm line. After laying out India's case for a "historical frontier" in all the sectors in considerable detail, he made it obvious that India would not entertain the latest Chinese claims. He also stated that talks could begin only after the Chinese withdrew their posts, "opened in recent months," at Longju, Spanggur, Mandal, and "one or two other places in eastern Ladakh." The letter did not call for a Chinese withdrawal from Aksai Chin.

Nehru's main concern was China's "demand for considerable areas, *more especially in the* NEFA [North East Frontier Agency]." China's claims implied that they wanted to establish presence on the Indian side of the Himalayan barrier. If a foreign power managed to do so, India's "basic security" would be "greatly endangered." Further, the Himalayas were the most "vital part of India's thought and existence." Nehru felt that the Himalayas could not be gifted to the Chinese—a point he had also made in parliament.[28] Nehru's unequivocal rejection of Chinese claims was thus based on considerations of security and nationalism.

Nehru and his advisers thought that Beijing had advanced these claims with the aim of realizing "at least substantial parts of them." Officials in the Ministry of External Affairs confided to the British envoy that Nehru's "uncompromising reply" was actually "a bargaining position." Delhi was willing to make "some adjustments and concessions at various points."[29] Nehru turned down Burmese premier U Nu's offer of good offices on the same grounds: India would not agree to "absurd" Chinese claims and an effort by U Nu might suggest that India was anxious for a settlement thereby hardening China's stance.[30]

Nehru's advisers differed in their assessment of Chinese behavior. Some felt that it arose from events in Tibet: China was behaving "aggressively without any long-term plan of aggression." A majority held a darker view. They feared that this might well be the "first stage in long-term Chinese ambitions to expand south of the Himalayas." These differences apart, Ministry of External Affairs officials were convinced that they had been "wantonly tricked" and that China could "never again be trusted." Any settlement might be temporary, with the Chinese likely to revive their claims when it suited them.[31]

The pessimistic appraisal prevailed after the Kongka Pass incident. On 21 October 1959, an Indian police patrol was apparently ambushed near the pass, leaving five dead, four injured, and ten captured. Delhi's assessment was that the Chinese had crept forward and occupied empty areas in Ladakh (beyond Aksai Chin) over the summer of 1959. Privately, Nehru maintained that this was an "indefinite border." But he was now convinced that India had to face a powerful country bent on spreading out to what it consider its ancient frontiers, and possibly beyond. "The Chinese have always, in their past history, had the notion that any territory which they once occupied in the past necessarily belonged to them subsequently."[32]

Ministry of External Affairs officials thought that the episode demonstrated that Beijing wished to annex areas up to its claim line in the western sector. They doubted that the Chinese would want to "shoot their way through"; it seemed more likely that they would seek to fill any vacuums in Ladakh.[33]

After Kongka Pass, Nehru grew defiant. As he wrote, "We cannot agree to or submit to anything that affects India's honor and self-respect, and our integrity and independence."[34] His attitude also reflected the increasing pressure of public opinion. He wrote to his sister Vijaya Lakshmi Pandit that the leading newspapers were taking advantage of the "high pitch of excitement" on the border issue "to attack all our policies internal and external, and to make me a target of attack." Criticism by erstwhile colleagues Jayaprakash Narayan and Rajagopalachari also stung. Equally troubling was the attitude of some members of the Congress.[35]

On 7 November, Zhou wrote to Nehru that the status quo should be maintained pending delimitation of the border. To obviate further clashes, both sides should withdraw about twelve miles (twenty kilometers) from the McMahon Line in the east, and "the line up to which each side exercises actual control in the west." Zhou also proposed immediate talks at the prime ministerial level. This proposal was unacceptable to India on several grounds. The army argued that pulling back twelve miles from the McMahon Line was "absurd and unrealistic." The Chinese could approach the border by roads, whereas the Indians had to traverse several mountain ridges; pulling back would be tantamount to handing control of the passes over to the Chinese.[36] Delhi also felt that Beijing sought to equate India's possession of the North East Frontier Agency with Chinese control over Ladakh. Delhi believed that the Chinese had come west of the Indian-claimed boundary in Ladakh only between 1956 and 1959. Further, the Chinese had not yet reached the line claimed by their maps. The Chinese idea of a "line of actual control" had no historical basis, nor yet did it accord with on-the-ground reality.[37] Besides, a mere twelve-mile withdrawal would leave the Chinese in effective control of most of the occupied territory.

In response, Nehru suggested that patrolling should be suspended in the North East Frontier Agency. In Ladakh, he proposed that India should withdraw to the west of China's claim line and that China should pull back east of India's claim line. Nehru would meet Zhou only if these measures were implemented. This proposal was unacceptable to Beijing, for it would entail evacuation of nearly twenty thousand square miles and abandonment of the Aksai Chin road, whereas India would have to give up only about fifty square miles. Nehru was aware of the importance of the road to China had thus wanted to couple this proposal with an offer to use the area in Aksai Chin across which the road was built. Owing to opposition from Home Minister G. B. Pant, the offer was withheld.[38] Within a few days, Nehru managed to partially convince his colleagues. In a press conference and in parliament, Nehru stated that as an interim measure India was prepared to allow the use of the Aksai Chin road for civilian traffic.

Nehru's proposals indicated a gradual hardening of India's stance on Aksai Chin. Hitherto, he had voiced his doubts openly about the strength of India's claims. After Kongka Pass, Nehru was disinclined to concede anything to China under duress. Bolstering this attitude was the growing pressure of parliamentary and public opinion, which decried any hint of "surrender" of territory. At this juncture, the director of the Ministry of External Affairs' historical division, Sarvepalli Gopal, returned from London, where he had been studying the basis of India's claims in the National Archives. Gopal thought that India had a sound historical case for Aksai Chin and conveyed it to Nehru; it was only in February 1960, however, that Gopal took Nehru through the evidence and convinced him that India's claims to Aksai Chin were strong.[39] Available evidence suggests that up to this point Nehru was thinking of Aksai Chin as a bargaining counter. As R. K. Nehru recalled, "Until 1960, we ourselves were not sure that the territory belonged to us and we were thinking in terms of giving up our claims as part of a satisfactory settlement." This policy changed after a more thorough examination of India's claims to Aksai Chin.[40]

TOWARD THE SUMMIT

Toward the end of January 1960, Nehru agreed to meet Zhou. The Indians thought that the correspondence was getting nowhere while a thick tension prevailed on the frontiers. As Nehru told Khrushchev, "Although for the moment there is no basis for negotiations, a personal meeting will generally be helpful. . . . It will be unfortunate if tensions were to continue indefinitely."[41] Writing to Zhou, Nehru said there could be no negotiations on the ground that the entire boundary was undelimited: "Such a basis for negotiations would ignore past history, custom, tradition and international agreements."

Underlying this position was the apprehension that if India gave up its stance that the boundary was a traditional one delimited by geography, cus-

Srinath Raghavan

tom, and treaty, the entire border would be up for bargaining. It would open the sluice gates to completely arbitrary and variable Chinese claims all along the frontier. In view of past Chinese conduct Delhi felt that it could ill afford to run the risk.[42] The earlier concerns about China's irredentism were now buttressed by the conviction that the Chinese could not be trusted. Accentuating these perceptions was Nehru's belief that the Chinese leadership had personally deceived him. As Lord Louis Mountbatten observed, Nehru "was greatly shaken by their duplicity."[43]

From the end of 1959, Delhi felt that Beijing would come up with a proposal whereby China would forsake claims south of the McMahon Line in return for India accepting its claims in Ladakh.[44] From the Indian standpoint this would entail giving up not just Aksai Chin but the entire area incorporated by the customary line up to which the Chinese claimed to exercise control. This solution was deemed unacceptable for a host of reasons.

First, public opinion was staunchly opposed to the idea of "barter," as it came to be called. Nehru acknowledged this when he reputedly stated: "If I give them that I shall no longer be Prime Minister of India—I will not do it."[45] It is difficult to judge whether an embattled Nehru was overreacting to public opinion. But we now know that his senior cabinet colleagues and officials also thought that he would be "out of office as Prime Minister" if he ceded territory to the Chinese.[46]

Second, Nehru himself felt that bartering would be incorrect given how the Chinese had used deceit and force to occupy the area. From February 1960 onward, the Indian government was convinced that it had a strong case and saw no reason to relinquish its claims in a deal, particularly when public opinion was "passionate against any concession whatsoever."[47]

Third, in March 1960 the Indian supreme court ruled on the government's boundary agreement with Pakistan over the Berubari enclave, involving transfer of some territory to East Pakistan. According to the ruling, the executive branch lacked the authority to cede or accept territory: it would have to seek an amendment of the constitution on each occasion. Such an amendment would require approval of a two-thirds majority in parliament and at least half of the fourteen state legislatures. Given Nehru's emasculated political position on this issue, securing an amendment would have been very difficult.

Last, and perhaps most important, the Indians had completely lost trust in their Chinese interlocutors. In the run-up to the summit, Zhou Enlai had worked out a draft paper on the approach to the negotiations, wherein he anticipated a limited agreement of some kind.[48] The ambassador in Beijing reported that the Chinese had told other embassies that "we are confident of finding a solution in the forthcoming meeting." His assessment, however, was that "the Chinese will maintain this posture of reasonable trying to make it difficult for us to reject their approach. But we should clearly say 'no' to any attempt to persuade us to accept joint discussions to delimit the entire boundary."[49] The Indians believed that even if they acceded to China's claims in Ladakh, it would not be a "final settlement." The Chinese would only be emboldened to advance additional claims later. The finance minister, Morarji Desai, told the British envoy that Nehru and his colleagues were not prepared to let the Chinese make Ladakh "the thin edge of a wedge."[50]

During this period, the Indians were considering other alternatives, too. These discussions were held very discreetly and were confined to Nehru, his senior cabinet colleagues, and selected officials.[51] The Indians sought to come up with compromise solutions that would not involve formal relinquishment of territory. The outlines of such an idea did not crystallize until a few days before Zhou's arrival on 20 April. As late as 1 April, Vice President Sarvepalli Radhakrishnan told the British high commissioner, Malcolm MacDonald, that there would be "a breakdown" in talks between Nehru and Zhou "on the second day."[52] The internal discussions seemed to have proceeded apace in the next few days. Following a meeting of the cabinet's foreign affairs committee on 5 April, Desai informed MacDonald that the Indian government "fully appreciated" the importance of the Aksai Chin road to the Chinese and were prepared to assure them use of the area. "But this would have to be done without any surrender of Indian sovereignty over the region."[53]

When Radhakrishnan met MacDonald a week later, Nehru's thinking on these lines had evolved further. Radhakrishnan made it clear that Nehru could not cede territory, "if only because Indian public opinion will not tolerate this." India would want China to accept the McMahon Line. In Ladakh, if the Chinese would accept Indian sovereignty "in theory," the Indians would "agree to them remaining in practical occupation of the territory which they now occupied." They realized that the Chinese had established themselves there and were unlikely to get out; hence they had to "face facts." The right solution was thus for "the Chinese to concede to us the shadow while we concede to them the substance" of sovereignty in Ladakh. This was a significant shift in the Indian position. As MacDonald wrote, "This shook me." Asked if India would station any administrative personnel in the area in support of its sovereignty, Radhakrishnan replied in the negative. When MacDonald expressed "great surprise and disappointment" at

Srinath Raghavan

India's changed stance, Radhakrishnan said that the whole idea was a "face saving" one. He reiterated that all faces could be saved if the Chinese yielded the "shadow" while the Indians yielded the "substance." Such an agreement might not be reached at this summit, but the Indians could reach a "tacit understanding" with the Chinese along these lines.[54] The stage was now set for the prime ministerial discussions.

THE OPENING ROUNDS

On 20 April 1960, Zhou Enlai accompanied by Foreign Minister Chen Yi and other officials reached Delhi. The reception was in marked contrast to Zhou's earlier visits. As a junior Indian official noted in his diary, "The welcome was subdued, if not chilly. No 'Hindi-Chini bhai bhai' slogans. The tension was almost visible."[55] The prime ministers held talks over seven sessions in five days. At the outset, it was decided that the prime ministers would meet alone, unaccompanied by ministerial colleagues or officials. Between these discussions, the Chinese leaders met with Nehru's senior cabinet colleagues, including Morarji Desai, G. B. Pant, V. K. Krishna Menon, and Swaran Singh. They also had separate meetings with Radhakrishnan and former ambassador to China R. K. Nehru. In addition, Nehru regularly briefed his colleagues and the foreign affairs committee on his talks with Zhou.

In the opening session, Nehru spoke at length about Indian feelings on the boundary issue. India had no doubts about its own frontiers, which had been "clearly defined on our maps." His earlier discussions with Zhou had led him to believe that there were no major problems between the two sides: only a few minor ones that could be settled by mutual consultations. "What distressed us most was that if the Chinese Government did not agree with us, they should have told us so. But for nine years nothing was said . . . these developments, therefore, came as a great shock." India did not agree with China's claim that the entire frontier was undefined and not delimited. After laying out India's conception of, and basis for, the boundary, Nehru insisted that "the question of demarcation of the entire frontier does not arise."[56]

Zhou responded to Nehru's points at the second session that evening. China had stated that it did not recognize the McMahon Line but was willing to take "a realistic view." Zhou was "shocked and distressed" that the Indian government used the Simla Convention in support of its claims. Interestingly, he clarified that "we only adduced proof that areas south of the McMahon line belonged to Tibet and that there was a customary line which later changed. We did not put forward any territorial claim." China had merely advocated maintenance of the status quo pending negotiations. "There was only a misunderstanding on the part of India." Zhou was evidently suggesting that the position adopted on this sector by Beijing since September 1959 need not be taken at face value. In the western sector, China had "never thought that there was any question on that side." The treaty of 1842 mentioned by India made no specific reference to where the boundary lay. History, administrative records, survey, and maps: all supported China's conception of this boundary. Besides, since 1950 the Chinese had sent had supplies and troops from Xinjiang to Tibet through this area. "It was only last year that the matter was brought up by India and it was a new territorial claim made by India." This muddied the waters, for it led to some confusion among the Indians about what exactly the Chinese premier meant when he referred to territorial claims. On the whole, Zhou averred that "we have made no claims and we have only asked for status quo and negotiations."[57]

Nehru replied that "our interpretation of not only history but facts also differs greatly." Zhou might consider India's position as territorial claims, "but when did we make these claims . . . ? If our maps were wrong, as you hint, surely some idea could have been given to us, when we raised the question on many occasions." The McMahon Line, he emphasized, was based only on a reflection of earlier surveys: "no new line was drawn." On the western sector, Nehru guardedly revealed his approach, stating that the Indians had visited parts of Ladakh that were now occupied by Chinese forces. "I presume, therefore, that this occupation has taken place in the last year or two and is of recent origin." Nehru was more forthright in expressing his domestic constraints: "Boundaries of India are part of the Indian Constitution and we cannot change them without a change in the Constitution itself." This failed to make any impact: the Chinese could not believe that the Indian *political* system could be much different from theirs. For instance, during the meeting with Radhakrishnan, Chen Yi observed that India was not curbing public protests against China's Tibet policy: "There are many people like J. P. Narayan [a prominent activist for Tibet] in China but the Chinese democracy controlled them."[58]

When Zhou repeated that the status quo should be maintained before negotiations, Nehru replied: "The question is what is the status quo? Status quo of today is different from status quo of one or two years ago . . . to maintain a status quo which is a marked change from previous status quo would mean accepting that change. That is the difficulty." Zhou insisted that there had been no such change in the western sector: China had all along controlled the area it claimed. "When we say status quo, we mean status quo prevailing generally after independence."[59] The Indians refused to accept this claim. They held that not only had China sidled westward from the Aksai Chin road over the previous year but that the Chinese still did not control all the areas (beyond Aksai Chin) claimed by them.

The prime ministers continued the exposition of their respective stances the next day. Nehru stated that the western sector was a large area. "I do not know to which part of it your remarks apply. We are quite certain that large areas of it, *if not the entire portion*, were not in Chinese occupation. . . . Apart from the northern tip of the area . . . the Chinese forces seemed to have spread out to other parts . . . only in the last year and a half." He insisted that there was a major dispute in this sector but importantly added: "We must, however, distinguish between eastern Ladakh and certain parts of it."[60] This was consonant with his desire to reach an agreement that would cede to China control of the area around the road the Chinese had built.

Zhou laid out China's case in detail and stated that the areas it claimed had been under Chinese administrative jurisdiction since the eighteenth century. He also pointed that India's control of the eastern sector had been established only in the early 1950s. Nehru said that "apart from minor dents" the eastern sector had never been under Chinese control. India could not give up the watershed as the boundary in this area. The Himalayas were dear to the Indian mind. Besides, if the principle of the watershed as defining the boundary were given up, "the whole country would be at the mercy of the power which controls the mountains and no government can possibly accept it." Reverting to the western sector, he reiterated that he was questioning China's presence not in "the northern tip of this area where the road was made but to the south and south-eastern part" that had come recently into Chinese control.

Seeking a way out of this impasse, Zhou suggested appointing a joint committee to look into the material that both sides possessed and possibly carry out investigations or surveys on the spot to ascertain the facts. Meantime, the status quo should be maintained and troops on both sides pulled back to an agreed distance. Nehru agreed that an examination of the material would be useful. However, he felt that sending teams to the boundaries would be nugatory. The question was not merely geographical but political. The committee could identify areas of divergence for the principals to consider.

On the morning of 22 April, Zhou dealt with the problem in three parts: facts, common ground, and a proposal. After a detailed reprise of Beijing's position, he suggested the following as common ground. First, the boundaries had to be fixed by negotiations. Second, there was a "line of actual control" up to which the administrative personnel as well as patrolling troops of both sides had reached. In the eastern sector, this was the McMahon Line. In the western sector, "the line is the Karakoram [range] and Konka [sic] pass." Third, the watershed was not the only geographical determinant of the boundary: valleys and mountain passes should also count. Fourth, neither side should advance claims to the area no longer under its administrative control. There were "individual places which need to be adjusted individually but that is not a territorial claim." Fifth, like the Indians the Chinese people, too, were emotionally attached to the Himalayas and the Karakoram mountains. Zhou stated that "he had come here mainly for reaching an agreement on principles." He proposed that they set a time limit for the joint committee to submit its report either jointly or separately.[61]

Clearly, Zhou was suggesting that the basis of a final settlement should be China's acceptance of Indian control over the North East Frontier Agency and India's acceptance of China's control over the parts of Ladakh it claimed. The third point indicates that in the western sector, the Chinese sought to press their claims to some areas south of the Karakoram watershed (which ended near Kongka Pass), including the Changchenmo valley, Pangong Lake area, and the Indus valley—areas that they claimed had always been part of Tibet. The third and fourth points together suggested that the Chinese also wished to possess some areas south of the watershed in the eastern sector. This stemmed from two reasons. Having repeatedly and openly denounced the McMahon Line, Beijing could not entirely accept the alignment. As Chen Yi explained to Swaran Singh, "If the Chinese government recognized the Simla Convention and the McMahon Line, there would be an explosion in China and the Chinese people would not agree. Premier Chou has no right to do so."[62] Moreover, doing so would strengthen the Dalai Lama's claim that Tibet had been independent from 1911 until the Chinese invasion. After all, the line had been agreed upon between British Indian and Tibetan representatives. The Chinese might well have sought to acquire pockets of territory—such as Longju—that lay north of the map-marked line but actually ran south of the highest watershed.

At the prime ministers' suggestion, officials from the two sides met that afternoon to clarify their respective positions in detail. Chinese officials, however, told their Indian counterparts that they did not have the requisite documents with them and hence could not provide the precise latitudes and longitudes of their claimed boundary in the western sector. In consequence, there was no detailed exchange of views.

Picking up the discussion the next day, Nehru insisted that it was essential to "know definitely where our differences lie. My idea was that we should take each sector of the border and convince the other side of what it believes to be right."[63] In so doing, Nehru sought to decouple the western and eastern sectors. The Indians had begun to understand that it was by linking these that Zhou strove to obtain concessions from India in the western sector. Following a lengthy recital of India's conception of the boundary in Ladakh, Nehru yet again distinguished between "north Aksai Chin area" and "other parts of eastern Ladakh." Zhou, for his part, insisted that both sectors should be considered together: "When we talk about the western sector of the boundary, we should discuss it in relation to other sectors." After a commensurately detailed rehearsal of China's views on the boundary, he restated the five points set forth the previous day. If Nehru agreed with them, it would facilitate the work of the joint committee and the task of negotiating a settlement.

At the start of the next session, Nehru sought yet again to pin down Zhou on when Chinese forces had moved into different parts of Ladakh. He underscored his oft-repeated distinction between the area adjoining the road and other areas. Zhou retorted that "the case is precisely the same as the eastern sector where India regards the line of actual control as her international boundary." Indian personnel had only reached the Tawang area, for instance, in 1951. "Our position in this area," he reiterated, "is like India's position in the eastern sector." China acknowledged that Indian administration had reached the line that India regarded as its borders. "But, similarly, we think that India should accept that China's administrative personnel has [*sic*] reached the line which it considers to be her border in the western sector."[64] There could little doubt about what the Chinese considered the basis for a settlement.

After further discussion, Nehru conceded that there was yawning gulf between the two sides' positions. He mentioned again that "even the slightest change in our border" would require an amendment of the constitution. He also drew Zhou's attention to the Berubari case and the Indian supreme court's ruling. Nehru agreed with Zhou that it was "very difficult and unlikely for us to find a way of settlement on this occasion." Turning to the five points advanced by Zhou as common ground, he questioned the suggestion that neither side should put forth territorial claims: "Our accepting things as they are would mean that basically there is no dispute and the questions ends there; that we are unable to do." Zhou explained that there should be "no pre-requisites. Neither side should be asked to give up its stand." He also suggested issuing a joint communiqué on the talks.

A couple of hours later, officials from both sides met to draft the communiqué. The Indian draft focused solely on the decision to appointment a joint committee to examine the material held by the countries. The Chinese wanted the draft to include the points of common ground proposed by Zhou. The meeting ended without a communiqué.[65]

At the final prime ministerial session the next morning, Nehru made it clear that points advanced by Zhou were unacceptable and were not to be included in the communiqué. Zhou frankly expressed his disappointment at the draft suggested by Nehru, but eventually he gave in.[66] After five days and nearly twenty hours of discussion, the only point of agreement was on appointing a joint committee.

By the time the summit ended, the Indians clearly understood China's negotiating stance. The foreign secretary informed Indian envoys abroad: "It is quite obvious that the Chinese aim is to make us accept their claim in Ladakh as a price for their recognition of our position in NEFA. Throughout the discussions they have invariably connected Ladakh with NEFA and stressed that the same principles of settling the boundary must govern both these areas. It was also obvious that if we accepted the line claimed by China in Ladakh they would accept the McMahon Line. There might be need for minor frontier rectifications, but that would not create much practical difficulty."[67] Delhi had "of course firmly rejected any such approach."[68] As the secretary general of the Ministry of External Affairs explained to the British high commissioner, public opinion apart, "if they gave way now on this matter, it will only encourage the Chinese to feel that they were weak and to press even more ambitious claims later."[69] Indeed, the Indians were not even sure "whether the Chinese will implement this agreement [to appoint a joint committee] sincerely."[70]

CONCLUSION

The Delhi summit was the last occasion on which the two leaders met to discuss the boundary question. By the time the officials' committees had submitted their reports, events on the ground had over taken meaningful diplomacy. The Cold War context, especially the incipient Sino-Soviet split, which had cast a shadow on the developing dispute, would complicate it further. The "forward policy" adopted by India to prevent the Chinese from occupying territory claimed by them was undertaken in the mistaken belief that Beijing would be cautious in dealing with India owing to Moscow's stance on the dispute and its growing proximity to India. These misjudgments would eventually culminate in India's humiliating defeat in the war of October–November 1962.

The "forward policy" and the defeat against China should not, however, lead to retrospective claims about India's stance on the dispute up to 1960. Nehru's refusal to accept Zhou's suggestions for a solution cannot be attributed simplistically to his intransigence. Indeed, until early 1960, Nehru was open to negotiation and compromise on Aksai Chin, the core Chinese interest. He was unwilling, however, to treat the entire boundary as negotiable. This position stemmed from long-standing apprehensions about China's territorial ambitions. Beijing's handling of the issue bolstered these concerns and convinced Delhi that the Chinese were untrustworthy.

Further, Nehru's willingness to accommodate Chinese interests in Aksai Chin suggests that a solution such as a long-term lease of territory could have been worked out. Here China's unyielding insistence that it had controlled the area for the previous two centuries queered the pitch. In retrospect, this might not seem much of a concession. But given the pressures on Nehru from parliamentary and public opinion, it might well have been the only feasible arrangement.

India's actions reflect what political scientist James Fearon calls the "commitment problem": if I agree now, and I am the weaker party, how can I trust that you as the stronger party will honor whatever agreement we reach?[71] Thus, the Indians felt that if they acceded to Chinese claims in Ladakh, Beijing would simply be emboldened to press for further concessions in the future. Scholars have often claimed that by turning down Zhou's suggestions for a deal Nehru passed up an excellent opportunity to arrive at a settlement, which would have respected both sides' principal interests. Such claims, however, are made in the flat glare of hindsight. More than fifty years on, it is easy to argue that a deal should have been struck with Zhou Enlai on his terms. But opinion within (and outside) the Indian government at the time was overwhelmingly against any such bargain with the Chinese. However appealing in hindsight, the argument fails the test of political plausibility—just as the wider revisionist case fails the test of historical plausibility.

1. Cited in Eric Hobsbawm, *On History* (London: Abacus, 1998), 317–18.

2. See, e.g., the numerous essays on the topic by A. G. Noorani. See also Perry Anderson, *Indian Ideology* (New Delhi: Three Essays Collective, 2013).

3. This chapter draws on official documents and private papers in India and the United Kingdom, as well as on published sources. In particular, it uses the recently available Indian records of the Nehru-Zhou talks. These papers are forthcoming in the *Selected Works of Jawaharlal Nehru*, ably edited by Professor Madhavan Palat.

4. This section draws on the more complete discussion in Srinath Raghavan, *War and Peace in Modern India: A Strategic History of the Nehru Years* (London: Palgrave Macmillan, 2010).

5. Particularly useful are Alastair Lamb's *The China-India Border: The Origins of the Disputed Boundaries* (London: Oxford University Press for R.I.I.A., 1964); *The McMahon Line: A Study in the Relations between India, China and Tibet, 1904 to 1914*, 2 vols. (London: Routledge and Kegan Paul, 1966); and *The Sino-Indian Boundary in Ladakh* (Columbia: University of South Carolina Press, 1975); as well as Parshotam Mehra's *The McMahon Line and After: A Study of the Triangular Contest on India's North-Eastern Frontier between Britain, China, and Tibet, 1904–1947* (Delhi: Macmillan, 1974); and *An "Agreed" Frontier: Ladakh and India's Northernmost Borders, 1846–1947* (New Delhi: Oxford University Press, 1992).

6. Note by K. M. Panikkar, 9 June 1948, FO 371/70042, The National Archives (hereafter TNA), London.

7. See, e.g., British Embassy Nanking to Foreign Office (hereafter FO), 18 August 1948, FO 371/70043, TNA.

8. Report on conversation with G. S. Bajpai, United Kingdom High Commission India (hereafter UKHCI) to Commonwealth Relations Office (hereafter CRO), 2 December 1949, FO 371/76317, TNA.

9. Statement, 20 November 1950, FO 371/76317, TNA, 348; Nehru to B. C. Roy, 15 November 1950, *Selected Works of Jawaharlal Nehru*, 2nd ser. (hereafter *SWJN*), ed. S. Gopal, 61 vols. to date (New Delhi: Jawaharlal Nehru Memorial Fund, 1984–), vol. 15, pt. 2, 341.

10. Note, 27/29 October 1952, *SWJN*, vol. 20, 161.

11. Note by Menon, 11 April 1952, Subject File No. 24, Vijaya Lakshmi Pandit Papers, Nehru Memorial Museum and Library (hereafter NMML), New Delhi.

12. R. K. Nehru, Oral History Transcript (hereafter OHT), 17–18, 31, NMML. R. K. Nehru, a cousin of Jawaharlal, had taken over as foreign secretary in July 1952. He was closely involved with the formulation of the China policy at various points as foreign secretary, ambassador to China, and secretary general of the Ministry of External Affairs. See also Karunakar Gupta, *Sino-Indian Relations, 1948–52: Role of K. M. Panikkar* (Calcutta: Minerva, 1987), 64–65.

13. Cable to N. Raghavan, 10 December 1952, *SWJN*, vol. 20, 488–89.

14. J. S. Mehta, "India-China Relations: Review and Prognosis," in *Indian and Chinese Foreign Policies in Comparative Perspective*, ed. Surjit Mansingh (New Delhi: Radiant, 1998), 468. Mehta was the leader of the Indian team that examined the evidence on the boundary dispute in 1960.

15. Confidential Note, "Our China Policy: A Personal Assessment," 30 July 1968, R. K. Nehru Papers, NMML.

16. Note, 30 August 1953, *SWJN*, vol. 23, 484.

17. Minutes of talk with Zhou En-Lai, 20 October 1954, *SWJN*, vol. 27, 17–20.

18. "Recent Developments in Tibet and Their Effects on the Security of India," by S. L. Chibber, in P. N. Menon to Apa Pant, 3 February 1956, Subject File No. 3, Apa Pant Papers, NMML.

19. Note to Krishna Menon, 6 May 1956; Note to Foreign Secretary and Joint Secretary, 12 May 1956, *SWJN*, vol. 33, 475–78.

20. Record of conversation, 31 December 1956/1 January 1957, *SWJN*, vol. 36, 600–601; Subimal Dutt, *With Nehru in the Foreign Office* (Calcutta: Minerva, 1977), 116–17.

21. Note to Foreign Secretary, 4 February 1958, cited in Sarvepalli Gopal, *Jawaharlal Nehru: A Biography*, 3 vols. (London: Jonathan Cape, 1975–84), vol. 3, 79.

22. *Notes, Memoranda and Letters Exchanged and Agreements Signed between India and China: White Papers*, 8 vols. (New Delhi: Ministry of External Affairs, 1959–66), vol. 1, 26–29. Unless indicated otherwise, all references to official and prime ministerial correspondence henceforth are from these volumes.

23. Alexei Brezhnev, *Kitai* [China] (Moscow: Mezhdunaronye Otnosheniye, 1998), 70.

24. Mikhail Kapitsa, *Na raznykh parallelykh* [At different parallels] (Moscow: Kniga i biznes, 1996), 63–64.

25. Nikita Khrushchev, *Khrushchev Remembers: The Last Testament* (London: Andre Deutsch, 1974), 306.

26. "Memorandum of Conversation, 2 October 1962," *Cold War International History Project Bulletin* 12/13 (Fall–Winter 2001): 266–70.

27. *Prime Minister on Sino-India Relations: Parliament*, 2 vols. (New Delhi: Ministry of External Affairs, 1963), vol. 1, 101–4, 107–9, 123–24.

28. Jawaharlal Nehru, "Letter of 1 October 1959," in Jawaharlal Nehru, *Letters to Chief Ministers, 1947–1964*, ed. G. Parthasarathi, 5 vols. (New Delhi: Jawaharlal Nehru Memorial Fund, 1985–89), vol. 5, 288 (emphasis added).

29. Report of conversations with Secretary-General and Deputy Secretary Eastern Division, 10 October 1959, Dominions Office (hereafter DO) 35/8819, TNA.

30. Nehru to U Nu, 29 September 1959, cited in Gopal, *Jawaharlal Nehru*, vol. 3, 98.

31. "Sino-Indian dispute" by High Commissioner in India, 21 October 1959, FO 371/141272, TNA.

32. Nehru, "Letter of 26 October 1959," in Nehru, *Letters to Chief Ministers*, vol. 5, 303–13.

33. Report of conversations with Secretary-General and Deputy Secretary Eastern Division, UKHCI to CRO, 3 November 1959, FO 371/141273, TNA.

34. Nehru, "Letter of 4 November 1959," in Nehru, *Letters to Chief Ministers*, vol. 5, 322.

35. Nehru to Vijayalakshmi Pandit, 3 and 7 November 1959, Subject File No. 61, Vijayalakshmi Pandit Papers, NMML.

36. Note on conversation with Chief of General Staff, 10 November 1959, DO 35/8820, TNA.

37. Steven Hoffmann, *India and the China Crisis* (Berkeley: University of California Press, 1990), 80–81; Dutt, *With Nehru*, 124–25.

38. Nehru to Pant, 15 November 1959, cited in Gopal, *Jawaharlal Nehru*, vol. 3, 103.

39. Jagat S. Mehta, *Negotiating for India: Resolving Problems through Diplomacy* (New

Delhi: Manohar, 2006), 74. Mehta was the director of China division in the foreign office. See also Hoffmann, *India and the China Crisis*, 82–83.

40. "India & China: Policy Alternatives," n.d., R. K. Nehru Papers, NMML. See also Confidential Note, "Our China Policy: A Personal Assessment," 30 July 1968, ibid.

41. Record of talk between Khrushchev and Nehru (in New Delhi), 12 February 1960, Subject File No. 24, Subimal Dutt Papers, NMML.

42. Dutt, *With Nehru*, 131; Hoffmann, *India and the China Crisis*, 87.

43. Record of talks with Nehru, 13–15 May 1960, DO 35/8822, TNA. See also OHT R. K. Nehru, OHT Kingsley Martin and Dorothy Woodman, NMML.

44. Report of conversation with S. Gopal, 9 January 1960, TNA, UKHCI to CRO, FO 371/150440, TNA.

45. Cited in Maxwell, *India's China War*, 161.

46. Reports of conversations with Secretary General N. R. Pillai, 17 March 1960; Finance Minister Morarji Desai, 5 April 1960, UKHCI to CRO, DO 35/8822, TNA.

47. Reports of conversations with Secretary General N. R. Pillai, 17 March 1960; Finance Minister Morarji Desai, 5 April 1960, UKHCI to CRO, DO 35/8822, TNA. See also N. R. Pillai's views in Hoffmann, *India and the China Crisis*, 86.

48. Niu Jun, "1962: The Eve of the Left Turn in China's Foreign Policy," Cold War International History Project Working Paper No. 48 (October 2005), 11.

49. Ambassador in Beijing to Foreign Secretary, 21 March 1960, Subject File No. 25, P. N. Haksar Papers, NMML.

50. Report of conversation with Desai, 5 April 1960, UKHCI to CRO, DO 35/8822, TNA. See also Dutt, *With Nehru*, 131; and, for Gopal's views, Hoffmann, *India and the China Crisis*, 87.

51. Foreign Secretary to Ambassador in Beijing, 27 March 1960, Subject File No. 25, P. N. Haksar Papers, NMML.

52. Record of conversation with the Vice-President by MacDonald, 1 April 1960, FO 371/150440, TNA.

53. Report of conversation with Desai, 5 April 1960, UKHCI to CRO, DO 35/8822, TNA.

54. It is evident that Radhakrishnan was giving this information after speaking to Nehru. In fact, during the conversation, Radhakrishnan gave MacDonald a gist of the remarks that Nehru would make at the first session of discussions with Zhou. Record of conversation with Radhakrishnan by MacDonald, 12 April 1959, DO 35/8822, TNA.

55. K. Natwar Singh, *My China Dairy, 1956–88* (New Delhi: Rupa, 2008), 87.

56. Record of the talks between PM and Premier Chou En-Lai held on 20th April 1960 at 11am, Subject No. File 24, P. N. Haksar Papers, NMML.

57. Record of the talks between PM and Premier Chou held on 20th April 1960 from 5pm to 7pm, Subject No. File 24, P. N. Haksar Papers, NMML.

58. Record of conversation between the Vice-President and Premier Chou En-Lai, 21 April 1960, Subject File No. 26, P. N. Haksar Papers, NMML.

59. Record of the talks between PM and Premier Chou held on 20th April 1960 from 5pm to 7pm, Subject File No. 24, P. N. Haksar Papers, NMML.

60. Record of the talks between PM and Premier Chou En-Lai held on 21st April 1960 from 4pm to 6.30pm, Subject File No. 26, P. N. Haksar Papers, NMML (emphasis added).

61. Record of talks between PM and Premier Chou En-Lai held on 22nd April 1960 from 10 am to 1.10 pm, Subject File No. 24, P. N. Haksar Papers, NMML.

62. Record of the talks between Swaran Singh and Chen Yi, 23 April 1960, Subject File No. 26, P. N. Haksar Papers, NMML.

63. Record of talks between PM and Premier Chou En-Lai held on 23rd April 1960 from 4.30 pm to 7.45 pm, Subject File No. 26, P. N. Haksar Papers, NMML.

64. Record of talks between PM and Premier Chou En-Lai held on 24th April 1960 from 10.30 am to 1.45 pm, Subject File No. 26, P. N. Haksar Papers, NMML.

65. Verbatim proceedings of the meeting at 4pm, 24 April 1960, Subject File No. 26, P. N. Haksar Papers, NMML.

66. Record of talks between PM and Premier Chou En-Lai held on 26th April 1960 from 11 am to 2.40 pm, Subject File No. 26, P. N. Haksar Papers, NMML.

67. Foreign Secretary to Heads of Mission, 27 April 1960, Subject File No. 25, P. N. Haksar Papers, NMML.

68. Foreign Secretary to Ambassador in Nepal, 25 April 1950, Subject File No. 25, P. N. Haksar Papers, NMML.

69. Report of conversation with N. R. Pillai, 25 April 1960, UKHCI to CRO, FO 371/150440, TNA.

70. Foreign Secretary to Heads of Mission, 27 April 1960, Subject File No. 25, P. N. Haksar Papers, NMML.

71. James D. Fearon, "Rationalist Explanations for War," *International Organization* 49, no. 3 (Summer 1995): 379–414.

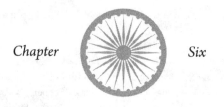

Chapter   *Six*

Nuclear Ambiguity and International Status

India in the Eighteen-Nation Committee on Disarmament, 1962–1969

ROHAN MUKHERJEE

INTRODUCTION

In October 1964, China conducted its first nuclear test, at Lop Nor, in the southeastern region of Xinjiang province. The political fallout occurred more than a thousand miles away, in New Delhi. "China blasted its way into the world's nuclear club today," proclaimed a front-page story in the *Times of India*, a prominent national newspaper.[1] The Indian prime minister, Lal Bahadur Shastri, was alarmed but not surprised by the event — the Indians had known about Beijing's plans since 1960.[2] Memories of a humiliating military defeat at the hands of the Chinese just two years earlier remained fresh in the minds of the Indian elite. "China has been trying to build itself up as a mighty war machine," said Shastri. "The atom bomb is the latest type of weapon which cuts across the general desire of humanity to live in peace."[3] Although many in the government shared Shastri's stance on nuclear weapons, calls for an Indian atomic bomb, louder since the Sino-Indian war of 1962, intensified among political parties and the public.

Despite the dramatically altered security environment and intense public pressure, however, India's political leadership did not opt for a nuclear test in 1964. The next year, Pakistan attacked India and war ensued; yet India's stance on nuclear weapons remained unchanged. In fact, Indian leaders took almost no practical steps toward developing a nuclear device for the next seven years, until Prime Minister Indira Gandhi gave "in principle" support for a nuclear test in late 1971 and official approval a year later.[4]

India's abstinence from nuclear weapons through the 1960s remains a puzzle for political scientists who study the causes of nuclear proliferation and historians who study India's specific path to nuclear weapons. By all accounts, China's first nuclear test coupled with Jawaharlal Nehru's death (in May 1964) should have created the necessary confluence of external and domestic factors for India to embark firmly on the path toward developing nuclear weapons. Yet India's political and bureaucratic elite (excluding the nuclear scientific enclave) remained profoundly ambivalent.

The Argument in Brief

This chapter argues that India's nuclear interregnum of the 1960s is best explained by understanding the status benefits that nuclear ambiguity as a component of a nonaligned foreign policy bestowed on India. India's best response to an external nuclear threat and internal domestic pressure to build the bomb was not to go nuclear but rather to keep the option open publicly while simultaneously pushing for disarmament as a serious foreign policy goal. This strategy—the origins of which can be seen in the 1950s—gave India a special position in the international community as a scientifically advanced and potentially powerful yet essentially peaceful nation. Nowhere was this clearer than in India's contribution to debates in the Eighteen-Nation Committee on Disarmament (ENCD) convened by the United Nations between 1962 and 1969.

Drawing on a growing body of literature on the modern history of nuclear science in India, transcripts of the meetings of the ENCD held over eight years, and primary documents from Indian archives, this chapter demonstrates that as long as the international regime for the control of nuclear weapons remained amorphous and allowed India to retain a nuclear option, India renounced nuclear weapons and pursued genuine attempts at disarmament. Only when the Nuclear Non-Proliferation Treaty (NPT) began to crystallize in the ENCD toward the late 1960s did India see a future in which it would be permanently locked out of the top tier of nuclear powers. This realization strongly influenced India's decision to build the nuclear bomb.

Four explanations, each focusing on internal constraints, are typically offered for India's lack of serious effort toward developing a nuclear arsenal or even assembling a nuclear device in the 1960s. First, given its pressing developmental needs, India could not afford to develop a nuclear arsenal. This line of reasoning—argued by many intellectuals and government officials in the 1960s itself—draws largely from the public statements of Prime Minister Lal Bahadur Shastri, who consistently argued that India "cannot afford to spend millions and millions over nuclear arms when there is poverty and unemployment all around us."[5] Second, India lacked the technological capability to produce nuclear weapons during this period. Specifically, India did not possess plutonium in sufficient quantities to build a nuclear device until 1969,[6] nor were Indian scientists proficient enough to perfect crucial aspects of bomb design until the early 1970s.[7] Third, domestic politics and institutional discontinuities hindered the nuclear program in the 1960s. Nuclear decision-making was largely driven by Jawaharlal Nehru and his chief atomic scientist and technocrat, Homi Bhabha, in the initial years following independence. Nehru's death in 1964, followed by the unexpected deaths of Shastri and Bhabha within a fortnight of each other in 1966 and the ensuing political and institutional instability, dampened progress toward a nuclear weapons capability.[8] Finally, the worldviews of successive Indian prime ministers—Nehru, Shastri, and Indira Gandhi—are cited as evidence of the ingrained "normative aversion" of India's political elite with regard to nuclear weaponry.[9] In constant tension with the security and prestige motives for nuclear weapons acquisition, this factor frequently applied the brakes on the more enthusiastic drive of India's scientific bureaucracy for the bomb.[10]

Evaluating the Explanations

Arguments regarding cost and capability are difficult to evaluate given the thin empirical record. Estimates of the cost of a nuclear warhead diverged greatly in the 1960s, depending on who was making the estimate and for which context.[11] More generally, it was acknowledged globally that some countries (India among them), if they wanted nuclear weapons strongly enough, could muster the resources to build them despite the heavy cost—in other words, cost was not strictly prohibitive.[12] As for technological capability, the jury is divided: although India's Canadian reactor CIRUS began producing plutonium in October 1963 and its reprocessing plant at Trombay, near Mumbai, came online in June 1964 — suggesting that India would have had sufficient plutonium for a nuclear explosion by mid-1965[13] — significant questions remain about the efficiency of these facilities at the time.[14]

Institutional and domestic politics arguments assume an underlying institutional and political desire for nuclear weapons that was halted due to leadership changes. While this was certainly true of the scientific bureaucracy, top decision-makers such as Nehru, Shastri, and even Indira Gandhi made a clear decision that India would not build nuclear weapons. Why they did so becomes important, and this is where the fourth strain of argument — on normative aversion — is relevant. Again, however, the evidence is weak. Indian leaders were not averse to using force in international affairs: Nehru had done so in Kashmir in 1947, in Goa in 1961, and in the conflict with China in 1962; Shastri, even less an adherent of realpolitik than Nehru, did not hesitate to decisively repel an attack by Pakistan in 1965. More important, at no point did Indian leaders *absolutely* renounce nuclear weapons. In all their public speeches and statements, Indian prime ministers were cautious always to leave the door open to potential acquisition of the bomb at a future date if circumstances called for it.

Was Going Nuclear Inevitable?

These four existing strands of reasoning share an underlying assumption that the outcome in the early 1970s was in some sense inevitable or overdetermined due to reasons of external security and domestic pressure for the bomb. Factors such as cost, technology, institutional breaks, and ideology acted only as the viscous medium in which Indian decision-makers had to operate in their inexorable march toward nuclear capability. Recent scholarship has labeled this period as one of "proliferation drift" for Delhi, in which "security motivations mattered substantially" and a host of regional and international threats, coupled with bullying by the United States, gradually drove India to test a nuclear device.[15] There is no doubt that security considerations — which also drove domestic politics on the nuclear question — played an important role in shaping India's nuclear pathway. Absent the ongoing rivalry with Pakistan and the military threat from China, it is unlikely that India would ever have pursued nuclear weapons. However, though a necessary condition for explaining India's nuclear behavior, security is insufficient for explaining the motivation and timing of India's nuclear decision-making.

India's decision to go nuclear was not preordained by security concerns, for two reasons. First, security was not and has never been the only goal of

India's foreign policy. If security was the primary driver of India's so-called proliferation drift in the 1960s, then Delhi should have pursued further steps toward developing nuclear weapons after the first test in 1974. In fact, almost nothing was done on this front until an abortive attempt to test a nuclear device in the early 1980s (the motivations of which are unclear) and eventually a full decision to weaponize in 1989 driven by intelligence about Pakistan's progress toward the bomb. Second, despite a major security threat, we know that top policymakers in Delhi did very little through the 1960s except to sanction theoretical work that might someday result in a nuclear test.[16] It is worth noting that although by 1965 U.S. intelligence estimates had placed the time frame in which India could produce the bomb at anywhere between one and five years,[17] it still took Indian scientists three years to fabricate a device after receiving political approval in 1971, suggesting an extremely low level of preparedness.

NUCLEAR AMBIGUITY AS OPTIMAL STRATEGY

Given the circumstances of the 1960s, India's optimal strategy was neither to pursue nor to renounce nuclear weapons. This strategy is the precursor to what later came to be labeled India's strategy of "nuclear ambiguity," that is, neither expressing nor foreclosing the capacity to build nuclear weapons.[18] It was a two-pronged strategy. First, India consistently pushed for general and complete disarmament in the international system through various conferences and international institutions such as the disarmament conferences at Geneva and the United Nations General Assembly. The 1955 Bandung Conference of African and Asian states, which India had a major role in planning, focused squarely on the issue of "universal disarmament coupled with effective international control," particularly in light of the environmental effects of nuclear testing.[19] In various domestic and international forums through the 1950s and early 1960s, Nehru consistently championed the cause of universal disarmament and called on the great powers to accelerate their efforts toward this end.[20]

Second, Indian leaders consistently kept the nuclear option open, insisting that while they could build nuclear weapons, they chose not to in the interest of international peace and disarmament. India's ambiguous approach to nuclear weapons mirrored the essentially dual nature of atomic power, which Nehru viewed as "Janus-like," facing both "the way of vast destruction and annihilation and the way of great speed in construction and progress."[21] As early as 1948, during the debates of the Constituent Assembly of India, he purported to maintain this ambiguity: "I think we must develop [atomic energy] for the purpose of using it for peaceful purposes. It is in that hope that we should develop this. Of course, if we are compelled as a nation to use it for other purposes, possibly no pious sentiments of any of us will stop the nation from using it that way."[22] Twelve years later, he maintained the same position while discussing the annual report of India's Department of Atomic Energy in parliament: "It is true that in the ultimate analysis a country which has atomic power fully developed can use it for good or evil purposes. And no declaration which I can make today will necessarily bind people in future, but I do hope that we shall create an atmosphere in this country which will bind every Government in future not to use this power for evil purposes."[23] In the following four years, this strategy was challenged by a comprehensive defeat at the hands of the Chinese military and Beijing's first nuclear test. Yet Indian leaders stuck to their ambiguous guns.

Reactions to the Chinese Threat

An examination of Indian reactions and governmental policy in response to the Chinese threat through the 1960s shows that nuclear ambiguity held fast even through this tumultuous period. The primary national concern after 1964 was how to prevent Beijing from engaging in "nuclear blackmail" in future territorial disputes with India.[24] The Indian government faced three alternatives: do nothing, seek security guarantees from the superpowers, or build an independent nuclear deterrent.[25] As mentioned above, Shastri immediately declared that India would not pursue an independent deterrent, primarily for reasons of cost. The argument he and others made was that building and testing one device alone would not amount to a deterrent; rather, in order to credibly deter China, India would need to develop a full-fledged nuclear arsenal with long-range delivery mechanisms to reach Chinese cities.[26] Indira Gandhi later echoed this argument in a parliamentary debate in 1968, by which time China had conducted no fewer than seven nuclear tests: "The choice before us involves not only the question of making a few atom bombs but of engaging in an arms race with sophisticated nuclear warheads and an effective missile delivery system. I do not think that such a course would strengthen national security. On the other hand, it may well endanger our internal security by imposing a very heavy economic burden which would be in addition to the present expenditure on defence."[27]

Those who argued against the bomb offered two other arguments. First, the nuclear threat from China was neither imminent nor credible. Three months after the Chinese test, in reply to a question at a press conference on how his government proposed to meet the challenge of the Chinese bomb, Shastri replied, "The atom bomb is not going to fall on India tomorrow and, therefore, we need not consider this matter." He went on to emphasize that the Chinese threat, if it materialized, would not be nuclear: "There is a greater danger of their using the conventional army and conventional weapons in attacking India. In fact, it is much more important than the use of atom bomb by China."[28] Five months later, in an interview on Canadian television, he argued, "It will take some time for China to develop the deterrent capacity, and to my mind the explosion just at present is with a view to creating a political impression."[29]

The second argument of those against the bomb was that India could rely on security guarantees from the great powers in the event of the threat of a nuclear attack by China. Three days after China's first test, U.S. president Lyndon B. Johnson announced: "Nations that do not seek national nuclear weapons can be sure that if they need our strong support against some threat of nuclear blackmail, then they will have it."[30] Keeping this in mind, H. M. Patel—then recently retired from India's national security bureaucracy—argued that India should arrive at some sort of "arrangement with the West" to guarantee its security.[31] Senior Indian diplomat R. K. Nehru (Jawaharlal Nehru's cousin) argued that an informal guarantee was "good enough," because anything more would mean "a deviation from our basic policy of non-alignment."[32] This tension between non-alignment and the desire for a security guarantee eventually meant that India's efforts on this front went nowhere,[33] though many among the Indian elite doubted the willingness and ability of either superpower to intervene on India's behalf in the face of a Chinese threat in the first place.[34]

Those in favor of an independent Indian deterrent argued primarily against the alleged cost constraint. Subramanian Swamy, then a professor of economics at Harvard University, argued that the opportunity cost of not building a nuclear deterrent was unacceptably high given the Chinese threat.[35] "To me it is inevitable that India produce nuclear weapons, and generally strengthen her defence," he argued. "The logic of cost is quite pedestrian, for it is neither costly nor is it logic."[36] A more moderate stance was taken by those who argued that given the nature of the Chinese threat and given China's capabilities, India should continue investing in its conventional capabilities as it had been doing following the 1962 war *while also keeping the nuclear option open*. P. S. Gyani, a former lieutenant general in the Indian army, argued that "in the Himalayas, we have to fight on a man-to-man basis" but advocated continued improvements in India's ability to manufacture nuclear weapons and delivery systems (which at the time was virtually nonexistent).[37] Shastri himself echoed this opinion. In November 1964, he authorized research on "peaceful nuclear explosions" of the type that the U.S. government's Plowshare program had been advocating for large-scale construction and engineering projects. At a Congress Party conference in January 1965, in a vein similar to Nehru's declarations of ambiguity, he stated, "I cannot say anything about the future, but our present policy is not to manufacture the atom bomb, but to develop nuclear energy for constructive purposes."[38] Later, when questioned further about this statement, he clarified, "When I say for the present, this present is a very long period . . . but I cannot say anything as to what might happen in the distant future."[39]

The Benefits of Nuclear Ambiguity

Despite this diverse range of views and a strong pro-bomb lobby, India's political elite essentially adopted a strategy of nuclear ambiguity through the 1960s. A contemporary analyst summarized India's policy as one of remaining nonaligned, continuing a conventional military buildup, organizing world opinion against China, and refusing publicly to develop nuclear weapons because to do so would be costly, would undermine disarmament, and would increase the overall risk of war in the international system.[40] The two-pronged strategy of promoting disarmament while keeping the nuclear option open was internally reinforcing. So long as international disarmament efforts did not bear fruit, India could retain the future option to build the bomb; and so long as the nuclear option was open, India could legitimately pursue disarmament as part of its foreign policy agenda and strive for its success.

It should be clear, though, that nuclear ambiguity was not optimal from a security perspective. If the China threat was real—and from the perspective of the time, it was, even to those who advocated against the bomb—maintaining the option to build nuclear weapons was a far cry from possessing sufficient nuclear firepower to deter Beijing. Shastri's initial argument that China was still a long way off from possessing a credible deterrent simply deferred the problem. Indeed, China successfully tested a nuclear ballistic missile much sooner than the Indians had expected.[41] Therefore, if nuclear ambiguity didn't serve to enhance India's security, it must have had an alternative purpose, and that purpose was status, or symbolic equality with the great powers.

A small but growing body of political science scholarship relying on insights from social psychology has emphasized the concept of status in understanding the behavior of states with regard to questions of strategic decision-making and war.[42] In a stylized sense, the leaders of country X measure X's status by evaluating what other countries believe about X.[43] Specifically, X's status derives from its leaders' perceptions of how other countries rank X on some dimension of comparison that they value, such as wealth, democracy, or — in the case of rising powers such as India — being a great power. Rising powers are likely to care about *status parity*, or symbolic equality, with the great powers. The policies that emerge from such considerations may not always align with policies that emerge from considerations of security or economic gain, and in fact the pursuit of status — within certain parameters — might trump these other considerations. The key insight that flows from this in the context of nuclear policy is that under certain conditions the pursuit of nuclear weapons might enhance a country's status while at other times the avoidance or renunciation of nuclear weapons might achieve the same outcome.

The desire for status parity with the great powers played an important role in India's foreign policy and, by extension, its nuclear policy in the 1960s. India's first generation of leaders had organized a hugely successful movement of noncooperation against British imperial occupation, winning in some sense a public relations battle by occupying the moral higher ground. They soon realized that status could be earned by injecting moral considerations into the standards by which states are judged globally. Although India did not possess the resources — in the standard sense — to be a competitor for influence in the postwar order, this fact by no means preordained a policy of non-alignment, as some writers have argued.[44] It was entirely possible for India to have sought an alliance with either superpower in an effort to bolster its security and prosperity. However, India chose non-alignment precisely because it bestowed a certain status of being above the fray of Cold War politics. In the words of one analyst, "In the years following independence there was a pervasive sense among many Indians that their nation, though weak in relation to the Great Powers, could still achieve international stature through mediatory efforts and moral suasion."[45]

In the realm of nuclear policy, the strategy of nuclear ambiguity served a similar end. It allowed India to maintain a unique position in the international system as a scientifically advanced and potentially powerful but essentially pacifist country. As a rising power whose nonaligned foreign policy had already won it a considerable degree of international recognition, India valued its position in the international status hierarchy sufficiently to be willing to trade off some amount of short-term security for it. Once we understand India's nuclear policy in these terms, certain counterintuitive behaviors and outcomes such as India's public renunciation of nuclear weapons, its strong support for global disarmament and nonproliferation efforts (before the NPT), the search for security guarantees, and the failure to obtain these guarantees start to make sense.

Investing in Status through Big Science

To understand the role of status in India's nuclear behavior in the 1960s, one has to begin in the late 1940s (at least) with how India's desire for status parity with the great powers drove its efforts in big science, especially atomic energy—the jewel in the crown. Historians of nuclear science and research in India have dealt extensively with how Indian leaders such as Nehru and Bhabha saw in this field the "modernist imperative"[46] of a postcolonial nation and sought constantly to catch up with the great powers.[47] As early as 1945, Bhabha was reported as stating in a speech at the Bombay branch of the Indian Council of World Affairs that "given proper education and facilities for work, the Indian mind was perfectly capable of keeping pace with the other scientifically advanced countries of the West."[48] Nehru highlighted this imperative when introducing the Atomic Energy Bill in the Constituent Assembly of India in 1948: "If we do not set about it now, taking advantage of the processes that go towards the making of atomic energy . . . we will be left behind and we shall possibly only just have the chance to follow in the trail of others. That is not good enough for any country, least of all for a country with the vast potential and strength that India possesses."[49]

Nehru was clear that in order to be an equal of the great powers, India would need to cooperate with them on equal terms and not terms of dependence. He believed that India could develop the human capital necessary to cooperate on equal terms with advanced countries despite a lack of resources in the wider economy. While inaugurating a rare earths factory in Alwaye (Aluva) in Kerala in 1952, he said, "[We] want to do this work ourselves—not to be helpless and dependent upon others, but to cooperate with others in this task. While our financial resources are nowhere near to other countries, we hope certainly to have scientific talent of the first order so that we may go ahead with this by ourselves or in cooperation with others."[50] He believed that, barring the great powers, India in the early 1950s was ahead of the vast majority of the world in the realm of atomic energy.[51] A decade later, Nehru was confident even of outdoing the superpowers in this field. He reminded fellow lawmakers of the need to stay ahead of the technological curve: "We cannot wait for America or Russia or some other country to achieve [technological advancements in nuclear power] and then try to imitate the benefits of that. We have to build up in order to keep in the fore all the time. The moment we give up that effort and wait to take advantage of some further improvement made by a foreign country, we have lost the foothold."[52]

True to Nehru's word, India invested heavily in big science and reaped the status rewards. In 1957, India launched Apsara, a swimming pool reactor that Bhabha and his team had designed using British blueprints and constructed using uranium fuel rods imported from the United Kingdom. At the inauguration, Nehru said, "We are told, and I am prepared to believe it on Dr. Bhabha's word, that this is the first atomic reactor in Asia, except possibly the Soviet areas. In this sense, this represents a certain historic moment in India and in Asia. . . . We are not reluctant in the slightest degree to take advice and help from other countries. . . . But it is to be remembered that this Swimming Pool reactor in front of you is the work, almost entirely, of our young Indian scientists and builders."[53]

By the early 1960s, India had developed research and practical expertise in a number of advanced fields such as atomic energy, oil and gas extraction, geological science, mining, water and power production, and agricultural research.[54] In March 1964, barely two months before Nehru's death and a little over six months before China's first nuclear test, India completed Project Phoenix, its first plutonium separation plant at Trombay. The press release issued by India's Department of Atomic Energy for this event emphasized, "The plant was designed and built entirely by the staff of the Atomic Energy Establishment. . . . [It] is one of the most sophisticated and advanced type of chemical plants, using techniques at the frontiers of chemical technology, and has several unusual features."[55] It went on to add that only four other countries in the world had operating plutonium plants — the United States, the U.S.S.R., Britain, and France — and that the completion of Project Phoenix had placed India "among the first half of a dozen countries in the world in the utilization of atomic energy."[56]

As a self-perceived leading player in the field of atomic energy and nuclear science, India took a strong interest in the international regime set up by the great powers to govern the development and spread of nuclear technology and weapons. In the political science literature, an international regime is defined as the set of "principles, norms, rules, and decision-making procedures around which actor expectations converge in a given issue-area."[57] During the 1960s, the international nuclear regime consisted of an evolving set of principles, norms, and rules centered on disarmament, nonproliferation, and arms control. Being essentially social environments, the international institutions in which these issues were discussed and negotiated offered rising powers such as India a venue in which to attain status. Scholars have largely ignored the role that this broader international regime for the control of nuclear testing and proliferation—the international nuclear regime, for short—played in shaping India's nuclear choices during this period.[58]

As argued above, India's strategy of nuclear ambiguity had two aspects, one of which was to strongly support the international nuclear regime. In April 1964, P. N. Haksar, India's ambassador to Austria, drafted a note presumably intended for his colleagues at the Ministry of External Affairs in New Delhi, requesting that a junior officer from the Department of Atomic Energy be seconded to the office of India's permanent representative to the International Atomic Energy Agency (IAEA), a position held ex officio by Haksar himself. He wrote: "As a permanent member of the Board of Governors of the I.A.E.A., our country occupies a special position. We also occupy a special, even a leading, position among the developing countries." Haksar continued but later crossed out this part: "by reason of the fact that ... we are the most advanced in the field of the development of nuclear energy. Indeed, my impression is that we are quite a leading country, even when compared to some of the West European countries." He went on to argue that given India's position, it should take "detailed interest in the day to day functioning of the Agency [the IAEA]. Our participation should be well informed. We owe this not only to ourselves but to the large number of developing countries who look towards us for guidance and support." Haksar's predecessor Arthur Lall had been largely absent from his Vienna posting, and as a result India had been represented at the IAEA by the chargé d'affaires. Because of this, according to Haksar, "our reputation as effective members of the governing body slumped during this period."[59]

Lall was absent from Vienna because he was involved in the negotiations of the Eighteen-Nation Committee on Disarmament in Geneva, another venue in which India sought to earn considerable status as an active and constructive member. As long as India was able to maintain status parity with the great powers within this institution, Delhi maintained a posture of nuclear ambiguity despite external threats and domestic pressure to develop nuclear weapons after 1962. It was only when the NPT started taking concrete shape that India's thinking on nuclear ambiguity as a source of international status began to change.

The Eighteen-Nation Committee on Disarmament

After years of failed United Nations resolutions, bilateral negotiations, and a single round of multilateral negotiations (in the form of the short-lived Ten Nation Committee on Disarmament), the superpowers came to an agreement via a common declaration on 21 December 1961 to set up the ENCD, which would include five members of the Western bloc (the United States, the United Kingdom, France, Canada, and Italy), five members of the Eastern bloc (the Soviet Union, Czechoslovakia, Poland, Romania, and Bulgaria), and eight nonaligned nations (Brazil, Burma, Ethiopia, India, Mexico, Nigeria, Sweden, and the United Arab Republic). France, from the outset, rejected the ENCD and refused to participate in its official proceedings on the grounds that nuclear disarmament was a matter for the nuclear powers alone and that test bans were ineffectual means of promoting disarmament.[60] The ENCD therefore had seventeen de facto participants, though France did participate unofficially in consultations with the Western bloc at the ENCD.

The United Nations General Assembly initially tasked the ENCD with arriving at a plan for general and complete disarmament. The committee first met on 14 March 1962 and spent the first two years of its existence on this question. Failing to make much headway, committee members decided to focus instead on "partial" disarmament, or goals that were more achievable than general and complete disarmament. These included a ban on nuclear testing, the designation of nuclear-free geographical zones, and nuclear nonproliferation. An early result of these efforts was the 1963 Partial Test Ban Treaty (PTBT), which banned all forms of testing that were relatively easy to detect, that is, in the air, under water, and in space. The harder question of underground testing was put off and remained unresolved.

As for general disarmament, fundamental differences between the positions and proposals of the United States and the Soviet Union precluded agreement. Key issues covered under this rubric at the ENCD included nuclear weapons and other weapons of mass destruction, delivery systems for nuclear weapons, verification and control of disarmament measures, disarmament of conventional forces, and an international military force under U.N. auspices. On nuclear weapons and delivery vehicles, both sides proposed disarmament in stages, except that the United States proposed gradual percentage reductions in each stage whereas the Soviet Union proposed large-scale disarmament in the first stage itself, along with the removal of U.S. forces from Europe and Asia. Each side played to its strength — the United States proposed gradual percentage cuts because in the early 1960s its nuclear warheads and delivery vehicles far outnumbered those of the Soviet Union. In the event, given the basic conflict of interests, the superpowers were unable to agree on a plan for general disarmament.

What did emerge as an area of great power agreement was the need to prevent the spread of nuclear weapons to other countries. In 1960, the National Planning Association in the United States had argued that countering nuclear proliferation was "an opportunity to find at least one common concern which might move the nuclear powers of both the East and of the West to achieve some limited agreements for joint action."[61] In July 1965, the superpowers each introduced a draft nonproliferation treaty. Negotiations over the following three years led to concessions on both sides and eventually agreement on the Treaty on the Non-Proliferation of Nuclear Weapons, or the NPT, which was opened for signature in the United Nations General Assembly on 1 July 1968 and — subject to ratification by the United States, Soviet Union, United Kingdom, and forty other countries — came into force on 5 March 1970. Although the NPT was initially considered a weak treaty with no enforcement mechanisms and boycotted by two nuclear powers, France and China, it has in retrospect been described as "the only important agreement that emerged from the Eighteen-Nation Committee."[62] Just over a year after the NPT was opened for signature, the ENCD held its last and 430th meeting on 26 August 1969. The committee was subsequently expanded into the Conference on the Committee on Disarmament, which eventually became the Conference on Disarmament as it exists today.

The ENCD was the first multilateral institution in which nonaligned states contributed to discussions on nuclear disarmament and nonproliferation alongside the great powers and major powers of both blocs. It was therefore an important venue for a country such as India, which had already earned considerable recognition as being both nonaligned and scientifically advanced relative to other countries of the Third World.

The ENCD's proceedings opened in March 1962 with high-level delegates present from each country. Minister of Defense V. K. Krishna Menon led the Indian delegation in the first six meetings (and would return to Geneva from time to time as required by protocol). Early on in the proceedings, on 20 March 1962, he strongly advocated issues that one would not expect from a country that many suspected was flirting with nuclear weapons. He advocated general disarmament, reminding the committee that this was largely the responsibility of the nuclear powers: "It would be helpful if the sides concerned would take into account the concern of those nations, representing the majority of the peoples of the world, which really cannot put a brake on disarmament—we cannot throw away atomic bombs because we have not got them—all that we can do is to commit ourselves not to make atomic weapons, to the extent we have any capacity to make them."[63] Remarkably, he also pushed for nonproliferation: "We have ourselves advocated for a long time that the spread of these weapons to other countries not only increases the area of danger but also places them . . . in less responsible hands."[64] And finally, he called for a comprehensive test ban and a moratorium on testing as long as the ENCD was in deliberations: "We are in favour of a treaty as sacrosanct as it can be made; we are in favour of any type of arrangements that can be made. But, pending those treaties, we are even more concerned to see to it that even the prospect of such a treaty is not jeopardised by explosions that may take place."[65] Menon's positions on all three issues were unconditional and in stark contrast to positions that India would begin taking in the late 1960s onward.

Of course, it is possible to dismiss his speech as insincere, talk that is essentially cheap for a rising power such as India so long as the great powers are deadlocked on these critical issues. One only has to look at the example of France, however, to see the counterfactual case of a country that deliberately avoided the ENCD because of fears that the superpowers would curb its nascent nuclear weapons program. As noted by one scholar, "Participation in disarmament talks largely beyond its control threatened to ensnare France in a bargaining game whose rules were set by other states, principally the superpowers."[66] India did not suffer from the same fears because at the time, it derived significant status benefits from being an active and constructive member of the ENCD. Menon declared in the committee, "We do not take the view that we have come here as onlookers, merely to bear witness to what has been said and what has not been said, because war and its consequences make no exemptions based on race or creed or geography, or anything of that kind."[67]

Arthur Lall, who led the Indian delegation at the ENCD for the first two years, held similar views of India's role in the committee. Shortly after stepping down from his role, he wrote, in an article in the *Bulletin of the Atomic Scientists*, "In the context of disarmament negotiations one is entitled to ask why the non-aligned nations are there at all." The answer according to him was that "the non-aligned have ... come into a position of quite considerable parliamentary power in world councils to which the major power blocs are sensitive. The political philosophy of non-alignment in international affairs, though no older than about fifteen years, has already won the adherence of some forty-five member states of the United Nations."[68] Lall offered a number of reasons why the nonaligned nations — one can safely infer that he was thinking primarily of India in this context — had gained such influence. These included the increasingly active and successful disarmament-related diplomacy conducted by the nonaligned countries in the United Nations since the mid-1950s; their role in major international peace conferences in Laos, Congo, and the Middle East; the considerable negative security externalities of nuclear weapons for nonnuclear states; "the sterility of the direct confrontation type of negotiations between the two sides"; the fact that some nonnuclear powers such as Sweden and India would soon be able to manufacture nuclear weapons; and the inadvisability of any agreement on general and complete disarmament that might exclude "approximately one-third of the world which chooses to remain outside the power alliances."[69]

Lall viewed the role of India and other nonaligned countries as indispensable to the ENCD's mission. He argued that by 1961, "it was virtually impossible for the two sides to agree to sit down in negotiations without the presence of nonaligned representatives."[70] In a monograph he subsequently produced as a visiting professor of international relations at Cornell University, he noted,

> For the first seven years or so of United Nations history, the non-aligned countries were a small insignificant minority. ... But things suddenly changed. The success of the Indian resolution on Korea altered the status of the nonaligned at the United Nations. ... In April 1954 Prime Minister Jawaharlal Nehru took a step which arose out of this new realization and made the world take note that the nonaligned were no longer going to remain on the side lines. He asked the United Nations to put on its agenda the question of the

cessation of nuclear weapon tests. . . . Thus, it was a nonaligned initiative which brought to the United Nations the issue of nuclear tests.[71]

In April 1962, when American and Soviet negotiators had reached an impasse on the control and verification of nuclear tests largely due to the United States' insistence and the Soviet Union's flat refusal to allow inspections in all environments, the eight nonaligned nations put forward a compromise proposal that would permit inspections only in the case of underground tests. The Soviets accepted this compromise in May and the Americans accepted it in August, introducing two separate treaties, one on underground tests and one on all other environments—the latter became the PTBT. Reflecting on this episode, Lall argued, "The weight of the Eight Nation memorandum . . . increased the standing of the nonaligned at the Geneva Conference as partners in negotiation. The nonaligned, of course, entirely concede the primacy of interest of the nuclear powers in the matter of arms control and disarmament, but they do not at all accept President de Gaulle's view that negotiations should involve nuclear powers alone."[72] Of course, not every effort by India and the nonaligned nations was successful: a similar attempt to break a deadlock on the number of inspections in early 1963 was "stillborn."[73]

India in the ENCD after 1965

From 1965 onward, India's approach to the ENCD underwent a gradual transformation, largely due to the evolution of the nonproliferation issue. Indian leaders had advocated the nondissemination of nuclear weapons and technology to nonnuclear states from an early stage in the ENCD, *as a step toward disarmament*. In July 1962, Krishna Menon said to the committee, "We feel that a simple, but effective, agreement on this matter [that is, nondissemination] could be achieved forthwith if the Governments of the three nuclear Powers here and the Government of France were to declare unilaterally but simultaneously that here and now they will not pass on to any other country or group of countries nuclear weapons or the control of such weapons or the means and knowledge to manufacture them."[74] Vishnu Trivedi, Lall's successor in the ENCD, argued in March 1964 for the nuclear powers to build on the momentum of the PTBT and introduce a similar treaty for nuclear nonproliferation. He stated what he believed to be the basis of an acceptable agreement: "The four nuclear Powers should commit themselves not

Rohan Mukherjee

to transfer nuclear weapons or weapon technology, and the non-nuclear nations should pledge not to manufacture, possess or receive these weapons."[75] Crucially, however, Trivedi argued that nonproliferation was necessary to increase the likelihood of disarmament at a future stage of negotiations—in other words, nonproliferation and disarmament were inextricable from the Indian perspective.

In May 1965, Indian representative B. N. Chakravarty made a speech in the Disarmament Commission in which he outlined a five-point proposal for nonproliferation, which included the nontransfer of nuclear weapons and technology by nuclear powers; the nonuse of nuclear weapons against nonnuclear powers; a United Nations security guarantee for nonnuclear powers threatened by nuclear or potential nuclear powers; tangible progress toward disarmament (including a comprehensive test ban treaty, a freeze on production of weapons and delivery vehicles, and a reduction in existing stocks); and nonacquisition and nonmanufacture of nuclear weapons by nonnuclear powers.[76] Naturally, this was a tall order for the ENCD and the superpowers. In August 1965, the United States and the Soviet Union introduced separate initial drafts of the NPT in which there were no obligations on the nuclear powers to halt the further production of nuclear weapons and delivery vehicles or to reduce existing stocks. Trivedi immediately decried "the unrealistic and irrational proposition that a non-proliferation treaty should impose obligations only on non-nuclear countries, while the nuclear Powers continue to hold on to their privileged status or club membership by retaining and even increasing their deadly stockpiles."[77] Trivedi coined the terms "horizontal" and "vertical" proliferation,[78] as well as "nuclear apartheid,"[79] as a means of criticizing the nuclear powers for engaging in double standards and excluding India from the nuclear club through the NPT. India had publicly renounced nuclear weapons and supported disarmament and nonproliferation in order to maintain status parity with the great powers in the ENCD—the NPT threatened to subvert India's nuclear ambiguity by compelling it to give up the nuclear option while *also* relegating it to second-tier status relative to the great powers.

In November 1966, Lord Chalfont, the British foreign minister, visited India to meet with Indira Gandhi and her top officials to solicit their support for the great-power positions on the NPT. The prime minister did not discuss these matters with her guest, leaving them in the hands of her foreign secretary, C. S. Jha. During his meeting with the latter, Chalfont argued that India's stance on disarmament should not get in the way of a "simple nonproliferation treaty" that did not require inspection and control. He also argued that the nuclear powers should not be expected to relinquish their weapons in the face of "the developing Chinese nuclear threat."[80] Jha explained that India had been in favor of disarmament well before the Chinese nuclear threat had emerged. He was also sanguine in the hope that "with the passage of time, China might adopt a more cooperative attitude to various disarmament proposals particularly after it assumes its place in the United Nations," which Jha himself had lobbied for as permanent representative to the United Nations in 1959. He went on to say that from India's point of view, "it was an unacceptable thesis that China's growing nuclear capability is a sufficient justification for the refusal on the part of the nuclear Powers to agree to disarmament measures. It could in fact be argued that a genuine move in the direction of nuclear disarmament on the part of the nuclear Powers might have a favorable impact on China." Jha also highlighted the growing feeling in India that "disarmament negotiations were being directed towards the preservation of the monopoly of smaller Powers," a direct barb at the British representative.[81] In essence, Jha and his government valued the potential denial of India's status parity with the great powers (via the NPT) more than the potential nuclear threat from China.

Nonetheless, Indira Gandhi desultorily explored security guarantees from the nuclear powers as a way of hedging against the Chinese threat while also pushing for a more balanced NPT. In April 1967, L. K. Jha, principal secretary to the prime minister, visited Moscow, Paris, Washington, and London to discuss the matter of security guarantees for nonnuclear powers in the NPT. In London, along with P. N. Haksar (who was then acting high commissioner), he met with the British prime minister and a handful of his senior ministers and officials, including Lord Chalfont. Aside from stating previously held positions on the proposed security guarantee, the two Indian officials discussed the NPT with Chalfont. In his secret report of this discussion, L. K. Jha recalled telling his interlocutor that "[India] could not sign a treaty which would hamper our potential for developing nuclear technology to the fullest extent. This was one field in which India was not underdeveloped and we proposed not to take a back seat in the advance of nuclear technology."[82] Once again, Indian leaders viewed their country's status in world politics arising from scientific achievements in the field of nuclear technology, yet they were nowhere close to contemplating weaponization — nuclear ambiguity remained Delhi's preferred strategy for attaining status in the eyes of the world.

The NPT, however, denied India its objective and consequently set off the process by which Indian policy-makers arrived at their decision to break with the international nuclear regime. In October 1968, when it was already too late—the treaty was opened for signature in July that year—Indira Gandhi addressed the United Nations General Assembly. On the NPT, she said, "The problems of insecurity cannot be solved by imposing arbitrary restrictions on those who do not possess nuclear weapons, without any corresponding steps to deal with the basic problem of limiting stockpiles in the hands of a few powers. How can the urge to acquire nuclear status be controlled so long as this imbalance persists?"[83] Although India had used its position in the ENCD and General Assembly to get key provisions introduced into the NPT that provided U.N.-backed security guarantees for non-nuclear powers facing nuclear threats and permitted the pursuit of nuclear technology for peaceful purposes (under international supervision),[84] Delhi's main objective—to get the nuclear powers to commit concretely to halting production and reducing stocks of nuclear weapons and delivery vehicles—went unmet. Consequently, India refused to sign the NPT, and its desire for nuclear status began to grow.

CONCLUSION: RECTIFYING THE STATUS IMBALANCE

When the NPT came into force in March 1970, it stated that only countries that possessed nuclear weapons on 1 January 1967 were officially recognized as nuclear powers. There was no clearer demotion of India's status in the international system. The United States, the Soviet Union, and the United Kingdom were official nuclear weapons states. France and China, albeit non-signatories to the NPT, were de facto nuclear powers. India was neither. The carefully crafted strategy of nuclear ambiguity, designed to maximize India's international status, had resulted in disaster. In March 1968, the journalist G. S. Bhargava wrote, "The situation would have been different if two years ago we had gone ahead and launched a peaceful explosion. This would have left us capable of taking the next step [of not signing the NPT] without being immediately committed to making the bomb."[85] In other words, India would now have to demonstrate its nuclear capability. In late 1971, Indira Gandhi gave in principle approval for a test, which India conducted in May 1974.

Three months after the test, Trivedi presented a paper at a meeting in Divonne, France, organized by the Arms Control Association and the Carnegie Endowment for International Peace. In it, he summarized the Indian predicament poignantly: "[India] adopted the Atomic Energy Act in April 1948 and set up its Atomic Energy Commission in August 1948, one year after independence. Indian engineers and scientists designed, built and commissioned the first research reactor in Asia in 1956, built India's own fuel element fabrication plant in 1959 and its first plutonium separation plant in 1964. There was thus nothing to prevent India from exploding a nuclear explosive device before 1 January 1967, the date separating the era of nuclear-weapon powers from the nonnuclear-weapon powers under the Non-Proliferation Treaty."[86] Encapsulated in this statement was everything an observer needed to know about India's desire for status based on nuclear ambiguity in the pre-NPT world, and the sharp jolt that Delhi had received in terms of status demotion that contributed to its subsequent decision for a "peaceful nuclear explosion." The 1974 test truly was the "demonstration" that India's leaders had longed for the world to see.[87] Having restored the status imbalance with the great powers that the NPT had created, India then settled back into a posture of nuclear ambiguity for the next twenty-four years.

NOTES

I am grateful to the Stanton Foundation and the Security Studies Program at the Massachusetts Institute of Technology (MIT) for a nuclear security fellowship that enabled research for this chapter. I am also grateful to two anonymous reviewers and Brendan Green for their comments on a previous draft. Significant portions of this work also appear in Rohan Mukherjee, "Rising Powers and the Quest for Status in International Security Regimes" (Ph.D. diss., Princeton University, 2016).

1. "Solemn Pledge Not to Use It First: Main Aim Is to Break Nuclear Monopoly," *Times of India*, 17 October 1964.

2. Taraknath V. K. Woddi, William S. Charlton, and Paul Nelson, *India's Nuclear Fuel Cycle: Unraveling the Impact of the U.S.-India Nuclear Accord*, e-book (Morgan and Claypool, 2009), 10.

3. "Danger to Peace: P.M.," *Times of India*, 17 October 1964.

4. George Perkovich, *India's Nuclear Bomb: The Impact on Global Proliferation* (New Delhi: Oxford University Press, 2000), 171–72.

5. Lal Bahadur Shastri, *Selected Speeches of Lal Bahadur Shastri (June 11, 1964 to January 10, 1966)* (New Delhi: Ministry of Information and Broadcasting, 1974), 19.

6. Nuclear Weapons Archive, "India's Nuclear Weapons Program," 30 March 2001, http://nuclearweaponarchive.org/India/IndiaWDevelop.html.

7. K. Subrahmanyam, "India's Nuclear Policy, 1964–98 (A Personal Recollection)," in *Nuclear India*, ed. Jasjit Singh (New Delhi: Institute for Defence Studies and Analyses, 1998), 30.

8. Itty Abraham, *The Making of the Indian Atomic Bomb: Science, Secrecy, and the Postcolonial State* (London: Zed Books, 1998), 146.

9. Perkovich, *India's Nuclear Bomb*, 3.

10. On the role of scientists in pushing for the 1974 test, for example, see Raj Chengappa, *Weapons of Peace: The Secret Story of India's Quest to Be a Nuclear Power* (New Delhi: HarperCollins, 2000), 44–58.

11. Bhabha himself cited American experts to argue that a ten-kiloton explosion would

cost $350,000 (Perkovich, *India's Nuclear Bomb*, 67), a figure that included neither expenditure on associated industrial infrastructure in the Indian case nor the additional cost of procuring and fabricating the technology indigenously.

12. National Planning Association, *The Nth Country Problem and Arms Control*, Planning Pamphlet No. 108 (Washington, D.C.: National Planning Association, 1960), viii.

13. Abraham, *Making of the Indian Atomic Bomb*, 123.

14. Nuclear Weapons Archive, "India's Nuclear Weapons Program: On to Weapons Development: 1960–1967," 30 March 2001, http://nuclearweaponarchive.org/India/IndiaWDevelop.html.

15. Jayita Sarkar, "The Making of a Non-Aligned Nuclear Power: India's Proliferation Drift, 1964–8," *International History Review* 37, no. 5 (2015): 934.

16. On 27 November 1964, Shastri informed the Lok Sabha (the lower house of the Indian parliament) that he had sanctioned research toward a Peaceful Nuclear Explosives program, which was modeled on the U.S. Plowshare initiative. See M. V. Ramana, "La Trahison des Clercs: Scientists and India's Nuclear Bomb," in *Prisoners of the Nuclear Dream*, ed. M. V. Ramana and C. Rammanohar Reddy (New Delhi: Orient Longman, 2003), 225.

17. For the one-year estimate, see *Foreign Relations of the United States, 1964–1968*, vol. 25, *South Asia*, ed. Gabrielle S. Mallon and Louis J. Smith (Washington, D.C.: U.S. Government Printing Office, 2000), Document 237. For other estimates, see Scott D. Sagan, "Why Do States Build Nuclear Weapons? Three Models in Search of a Bomb," *International Security* 21, no. 3 (Winter 1996–97): n. 22.

18. Ashley J. Tellis, *India's Emerging Nuclear Posture: Between Recessed Deterrent and Ready Arsenal* (Santa Monica, Calif.: RAND, 2001), 10.

19. A. Appadorai, "The Bandung Conference," *India Quarterly* 11, no. 3 (1955): 227.

20. See Jawaharlal Nehru, *Jawaharlal Nehru's Speeches: September 1957–April 1963*, vol. 4 (New Delhi: Ministry of Information and Broadcasting, 1964), 309, 318, 362–63, 394.

21. Ibid., 436.

22. Constituent Assembly of India Debates (Proceedings), vol. 5, 3323, cited in Perkovich, *India's Nuclear Bomb*, 20.

23. Nehru, *Jawaharlal Nehru's Speeches*, 436.

24. Raj Krishna, "A Limited Programme," *Seminar*, no. 65 (January 1965): 21.

25. Ibid., 22.

26. H. M. Patel, "Arrangement with the West," *Seminar*, no. 65 (January 1965): 19. See also Romesh Thapar, "To Be or Not to Be," ibid., 34; and R. K. Nehru, "Control and Disarm," ibid., 39.

27. Indira Gandhi, *Selected Speeches of Indira Gandhi, January 1966—August 1969* (New Delhi: Ministry of Information and Broadcasting, 1971), 372.

28. Shastri, *Selected Speeches*, 25–26.

29. Ibid., 41.

30. "Text of Johnson's Address," *New York Times*, 19 October 1964.

31. Patel, "Arrangement with the West."

32. R. K. Nehru, "The Challenge of the Chinese Bomb," *India Quarterly* 21, no. 1 (1965): 10–11.

33. E. L. M. Burns, "Can the Spread of Nuclear Weapons Be Stopped?," *International Organization* 19, no. 4 (1965): 215.

34. See A. D. Moddie, "What Difference Lop Nor?," *Seminar*, no. 65 (January 1965):

14–15; Krishna, "Limited Programme," 21–22; Sisir Gupta, "Break with the Past," ibid., 30; and H. R. Vohra, "U.S. Intrigued at Indian Desire: A-Guarantees," *Times of India*, 4 June 1966.

35. Subramanian Swamy, "Systems Analysis of Strategic Defence Needs," *Economic and Political Weekly* 4, no. 8 (22 February 1969): 405.

36. Subramanian Swamy, "Foreword," in R. L. M. Patil, *India—Nuclear Weapons and International Politics* (Delhi: National, 1969), vii.

37. P. S. Gyani, "India's Military Strategy," *India Quarterly* 23, no. 1 (1967): 26.

38. Quoted in W. P. S. Sidhu and Jing-dong Yuan, *China and India: Cooperation or Conflict?* (Boulder, Colo.: Lynne Rienner, 2003), 27.

39. Shastri, *Selected Speeches*, 24.

40. Raj Krishna, "India and the Bomb," *India Quarterly* 21, no. 2 (1965): 129.

41. Writing in 1965, R. K. Nehru ("Control and Disarm," 39–40) stated, "The explosion of a few bombs does not make a country a nuclear power. The country must build an arsenal of nuclear weapons and an effective delivery system. It took the UK, with its highly developed industrial base, 13 years to attain its present position of what has been described as 'comparatively modest nuclear strength.'" By this reasoning, he expected, "there does not seem to be much prospect . . . of China becoming a major nuclear power in the foreseeable future."

42. See Richard Ned Lebow, *A Cultural Theory of International Relations* (Cambridge: Cambridge University Press, 2008); William C. Wohlforth, "Unipolarity, Status Competition, and Great Power War," *World Politics* 61, no. 1 (2009): 28–57; Deborah W. Larson and Alexei Shevchenko, "Status Seekers: Chinese and Russian Responses to U.S. Primacy," *International Security* 34, no. 4 (2010): 63–95; and T. V. Paul, Deborah W. Larson, and William C. Wohlforth, eds., *Status in World Politics* (New York: Cambridge University Press, 2014).

43. Allan Dafoe, Jonathan Renshon, and Paul Huth, "Reputation and Status as Motives for War," *Annual Review of Political Science*, no. 17 (2014): 375–76.

44. Taya Zinkin, "Indian Foreign Policy: An Interpretation of Attitudes," *World Politics* 7, no. 2 (January 1955): 181.

45. Stanley J. Heginbotham, "In the Wake of Bangla Desh: A New Role for India in Asia?" *Pacific Affairs* 45, no. 3 (Autumn 1972): 374.

46. Jahnavi Phalkey, *Atomic State: Big Science in Twentieth-Century India* (Ranikhet: Permanent Black, 2013), 11–12.

47. Abraham, *Making of the Indian Atomic Bomb*, 19–34.

48. "Keeping Abreast of Scientific World: Dr. Bhabha Stresses Need for India," *Times of India*, 28 August 1945, 4.

49. Jawaharlal Nehru, *Pandit Jawaharlal Nehru on Atomic Energy* (Bombay: Bhabha Atomic Research Centre, 1989), 8.

50. Ibid., 21.

51. Ibid., 47–48.

52. Nehru, *Jawaharlal Nehru's Speeches*, vol. 4, 439.

53. Itty Abraham, "Contra-Proliferation: Interpreting the Meanings of India's Nuclear Tests in 1974 and 1998," in *Inside Nuclear South Asia*, ed. Scott D. Sagan (Stanford, Calif.: Stanford University Press, 2009), 110.

54. See M. S. Thacker, "Scientific Research: Progress in India since Independence," *India Quarterly* 13, no. 4 (1957): 287–307.

55. Department of State, "Inauguration of Indian Plutonium Separation Plant," Telegram from American Consul in Bombay, Ref. A-249, 29 April 1964, National Security Archive, http://nsarchive.gwu.edu/NSAEBB/NSAEBB187/IN03.pdf, 2. In fact, like the Apsara reactor, this plant was also built with significant foreign assistance (see Perkovich, *India's Nuclear Bomb*, 64).

56. Department of State, "Inauguration," 4.

57. Stephen D. Krasner, "Structural Causes and Regime Consequences: Regimes as Intervening Variables," *International Organization* 36, no. 2 (Spring 1982): 1.

58. One exception is A. Vinod Kumar, *India and the Nuclear Non-Proliferation Regime: The Perennial Outlier* (Delhi: Cambridge University Press, 2014), though this work focuses more on recent and contemporary dynamics.

59. P. N. Haksar, Untitled draft note (dated 1 April 1964), 19–21, available in Subject Files, S. No. 27, P. N. Haksar Papers, Installments I and II, Nehru Memorial Museum and Library (hereafter NMML), New Delhi. The final version of this draft was not available.

60. Arthur S. Lall, *Negotiating Disarmament: The Eighteen Nation Disarmament Conference: The First Two Years, 1962–64* (Ithaca, N.Y.: Center for International Studies, Cornell University, 1964), 7.

61. National Planning Association, "The Nth Country," xi.

62. Albert Legault and Michel Fortmann, *A Diplomacy of Hope: Canada and Disarmament, 1945–1988*, trans. Derek Ellington (Montreal: McGill-Queen's University Press, 1992), 198.

63. Eighteen Nation Committee on Disarmament (henceforth ENCD), Fifth Meeting, 32, available at http://quod.lib.umich.edu/e/endc/.

64. Ibid., 35.

65. Ibid., 37.

66. Edward A. Kolodziej, "French Disarmament and Arms Control Policy: The Gaullist Heritage in Question," in *The Fifth Republic at Twenty*, ed. William G. Andrews and Stanley Hoffmann (Albany: State University of New York Press, 1981), 413.

67. ENCD, Fifth Meeting, 42.

68. Arthur S. Lall, "The Nonaligned in Disarmament Negotiations," *Bulletin of the Atomic Scientists*, May 1964, 17.

69. Ibid., 18–19.

70. Ibid., 18.

71. Lall, *Negotiating Disarmament*, 2.

72. Ibid., 23.

73. Ibid., 25.

74. "No Supply of A-Arms to Others: Menon Asks Big Powers to Act," *Times of India*, 25 July 1962. The proceedings of this meeting are missing from the online ENCD archive.

75. ENCD, 174th Meeting, 17.

76. Burns, "Can the Spread of Nuclear Weapons Be Stopped?," 862.

77. ENCD, 223rd Meeting, 13.

78. E. L. M. Burns, *A Seat at the Table: The Struggle for Disarmament* (Toronto: Clarke, Irwin, 1972), 216.

79. ENCD, 298th Meeting, 10. See also Perkovich, *India's Nuclear Bomb*, 138.

80. Ministry of External Affairs, "Summary Record of Discussions between Lord Chalfont, British Minister of State for Foreign Affairs and Prime Minister, Minister of State, Foreign Secretary and Chairman, Atomic Energy Commission," Secret Document,

8 November 1966, 45, in Subject Files, S. No. 28, P. N. Haksar Papers, Installments I and II, NMML.

81. Ibid., 46.

82. L. K. Jha, "Summary of Discussions in London," Secret Memorandum, Copy no. 7, 5 May 1967, 26–27, available in Subject Files, S. No. 110, P. N. Haksar Papers, Installment III, NMML.

83. Gandhi, *Selected Speeches*, 359–60.

84. George Bunn, "The Nuclear Nonproliferation Treaty," *Wisconsin Law Review* no. 3 (1968): 772–76.

85. G. S. Bhargava, "A Non-Policy on Non-Proliferation," *Economic and Political Weekly* 3, no. 12 (23 March 1968): 483.

86. Vishnu C. Trivedi, "India's Approach towards Nuclear Energy and Non-Proliferation of Nuclear Weapons," Working Paper presented at the Divonne meeting, 9–11 September 1974, organized by the Arms Control Association and the Carnegie Endowment for International Peace, http://meaindia.nic.in/cdgeneva/?pdf0592?000.

87. Abraham, "Contra-Proliferation," 118–19.

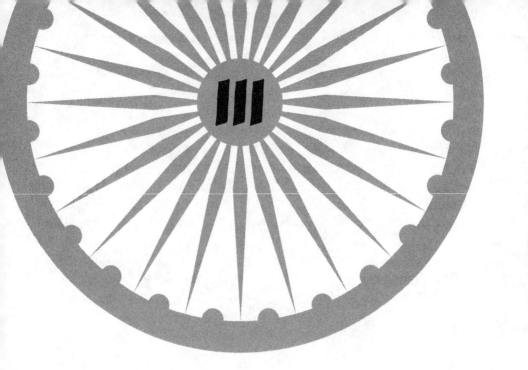

The Development of
Imagination, circa 1950–1980

Promoting Development without Struggle

Sino-Indian Relations in the 1950s

ANTON HARDER

INTRODUCTION

The global Cold War was a phenomenon in which competing superpower intrusions into Third World modernization, manifested as the promotion of either the Soviet or American model of development, became entangled with local efforts to manipulate, resist, or collaborate with these interventions.[1] This perspective has seen development, by which is meant the means of pursuing modernity, become a major concern of historians of Cold War foreign policy, particularly those studying U.S. diplomacy.[2] Scholars are now exploring how Third World actors manipulated external developmental resources, be that material or ideological, to advance their own visions of national modernity, as well as how encounters with the Third World influenced development thinking in superpower capitals.[3] Clearly, development is now at the center of historians' efforts to understand how states in Asia and Africa functioned within the Cold War international system.

Historians of Nehru's India have highlighted the practical relationship between development and his foreign policy of non-alignment in the Cold War. Several, for instance, have referred to Polish economist Michal Kalecki's metaphor for a nonaligned state's promiscuous approach to overseas aid as "the calf that suckled two cows."[4] Sunil Khilnani echoes this pragmatic perspective, noting that Nehru was basically a social democrat and his interest in the Soviets' model was chiefly for their expertise in planning and industry.[5] Others have shown that Nehru saw development as a unifying national endeavor that would overcome India's many caste, class, and ethnolinguistic divisions.[6] And indeed, Ramachandra Guha has underlined that there was a consensus in favor of planning in Nehru's India.[7] Francine Frankel has emphasized the novelty of Nehru's hybrid model and stressed that it was not simply a case that foreign policy served domestic needs, à la Kalecki's greedy calf, but that domestic policy was also a tool of diplomacy. Frankel argues that Nehru's "third way" sought a revolutionary improvement in average living standards through peaceful means, what she describes as the "paradox of accommodative politics and radical social change," but which was also regarded by Nehru as a "model" for the postcolonial world.[8] Partha Chatterjee and Benjamin Zachariah have both contended that Nehru sought to depoliticize development, making it simply a technical process, and so cast the Indian National Congress government as the mediator between labor and capital.[9] Recently scholars have agreed that Nehru believed India's approach to the countryside was not only "revolutionary" but a key part of the model that Delhi could promote in other developing countries.[10] So, Indian development was not just subject to external forces but was also regarded as something that should have influence overseas. And David Engerman has shown that encounters with India even led to significant changes within attitudes to development in the Soviet Union.[11]

Accounts of Nehruvian India's foreign relations in the early Cold War have not fully explored how attitudes toward development related to diplomacy and have focused chiefly on the United States and debating the balance of idealism and national interest within a policy of non-alignment.[12] The latest studies of Indian diplomacy, such as Rudra Chaudhuri's account of Indian relations with the United States, go beyond the debate over the morality or pragmatism of non-alignment, arguing rather that Nehru saw these as complementary motives. But these have not considered how Nehru linked development and foreign policy or how other states' perceptions of Indian development affected relations.[13] Engerman's work, mentioned above, and Dennis Merrill's early study of Indo-US relations are notable exceptions to this shortfall.[14] In addition, Manu Bhagavan's study of Delhi's efforts to promote some form of supranational authority under the "One World" banner does link internal and external policy. Bhagavan argues that the Nehruvian proponents of an international regime of human rights believed that independent India could be a model for the world, in terms of its domestic and foreign policy. India's example would show the common ground that was available between the Cold War blocs.[15]

Development has not featured as a key concern in the major accounts of Sino-Indian relations during the Nehru era, which have continued to focus mainly on the 1962 border war and its causes in a putative clash of imperial ambition in the Himalayas.[16] Some recent short studies have been excellent exceptions and highlighted the cooperation and development exchanges that occurred despite the underlying territorial suspicions.[17] This chapter adds to these recent accounts and shows that development was a dynamic factor at the heart of Sino-Indian relations in the early Cold War.

Nehru had long emphasized the importance for Asia and the world of China's recovery from its humiliation by imperial powers over the previous century.[18] By 1949, however, it became clear that the Chinese Communist Party (CCP) and its chairman, Mao Zedong, were going to defeat Nehru's friend Jiang Jieshi, the leader of China's governing nationalist party, the Guomindang, and establish a state ideologically aligned to Josef Stalin's Soviet Union. It seemed that the Cold War would now spread to Asia, and Nehru feared the consequences. Despite his misgivings and for a variety of reasons, the Indian prime minister decided to engage the new revolutionary state, the People's Republic of China (PRC). One practical benefit which Nehru expected was that friendly relations between New Delhi and Beijing would incline China to respect a degree of autonomy for Tibet, thus minimizing the security threat to India from that region. But Nehru also expected that Chinese nationalism would prove an antidote to an isolated overdependence on an alliance with the Soviet Union, and he believed that Indian cooperation with Beijing would encourage that effect. In the late 1940s and early 1950s, Nehru was deeply skeptical of Stalin's U.S.S.R.[19] But he also believed in principle that alliances destabilized international politics. Furthermore, if, as Pallavi Raghavan argues elsewhere in this volume, India and Pakistan saw the Cold War as an opportunity to establish their international personalities, then a key benefit of engaging communist China was to burnish India's non-alignment and independence of action. Finally, Nehru's desire to prevent the isolation of the PRC must be seen in the context of the broad One World agenda, to buttress the legitimacy and viability of the United Nations as the necessary condition for a genuinely global system of human rights.[20] If Nehru's motives were clear, so too were his means. Just as Nehru believed that development could rally Indians together, so did he also often claim that a common aspiration for development could bring some unity across

Asia.[21] He imagined that India's hybrid development model mirrored his non-alignment as an example of the harmony that was possible despite the Cold War. An important implication was that Nehru would have to prove that his model was progressive to win Beijing's trust.

Although the PRC initially adhered to Stalin's dismissal of Nehruvian India as barely independent and viewed its prospects of genuine development as deluded, Beijing desired Delhi's cooperation regarding Tibet and came to regard Nehru as a useful mediator in international affairs. In 1953, with Stalin dead and the Korean War winding down, prospects for Nehru's efforts to engage revolutionary China grew, given also Moscow's new enthusiasm for India, outlined by Swapna Kona Nayudu in this volume. As the PRC presented a new moderate face to the world, Sino-Indian relations became warmer and exchanges grew. It appeared that Beijing agreed with Moscow that both nations should end their support for overseas revolution and engage more actively with Third World nationalist leaders like Nehru.[22] However, although he initially thought that development would afford a means for Delhi to draw the Chinese away from Moscow, as the 1950s progressed, Nehru instead came to feel closer to the Soviets than to China. This change was compounded by Mao's turn from the Soviets' development model and ideas about moderation. In 1956, while Soviet premier Nikita Khrushchev was proposing his new theories of "peaceful coexistence" and "peaceful transition," canonizing his political commitment to moderation, Mao began to think that absolute adherence to peaceful methods disarmed the socialist bloc and communist parties in face of inevitable counterrevolutionary attack. Mao began to warn communist comrades in countries like India of his misgivings. Most important, from 1957, Chinese analyses of Indian economic policy and domestic politics started to corroborate Mao's view. On the vast canvas of Indian politics, Chinese analysts, armed with their simplifying theories of class conflict, confidently identified an array of culprits who not only hobbled Indian development but sought closer relations with the United States and enmity with the PRC. Increasingly, Beijing regarded India as evidence that Soviet ideas about the Third World were deeply misguided and that the theory of peaceful transition, which claimed that a state could evolve to socialism peacefully without violent revolutionary action, was blind folly. As a result, despite Nehru's hopes of using his development model to bridge the gap with China, the model instead became a subject that poisoned Chinese attitudes toward both India and the Soviet Union.

This chapter's focus on attitudes toward development contributes to new assessments of the causes of the Sino-Indian border war of 1962, Sino-

Indian relations in general, and the Sino-Soviet split. Srinath Raghavan, in this volume, identifies Chinese intransigence as an underappreciated cause of the failure of the April 1960 border talks between Beijing and Delhi. This chapter reveals that Beijing sought confrontation with Delhi after 1959 due to the perception that the politics of development in India revealed the growing power of reactionary groups hostile to China and its revolution. Priya Chacko shows in this volume how important U.S. influence over Indian development was over many decades, not least for supporting the Nehruvian consensus, before it broke down in the mid-1960s. But this chapter also demonstrates the importance of the Chinese conviction that Nehru's model was failing in the late 1950s. While Nehru sought to advance radical social and economic progress through peaceful means, promoting development without struggle, the Chinese increasingly believed this to be an oxymoronic proposition. This perspective gives India more prominence in the history of the Sino-Soviet split, revealing how important Soviet sympathy for India's development policy was to the growing differences within the communist bloc.[23] Indian economic policy can therefore be seen to have had profound meaning for the international history of the early Cold War, even beyond its immediate impact on the hundreds of millions of individuals seeking a better life within its borders.

FIRST ENCOUNTERS

The idea of economic development was at the heart of Nehru's strategy to socialize communist China. The "third way" development model girded India's claim of independence and non-alignment and served its broader One World agenda, indicated by Nehru's explanation that India sought to "harmonize" the "two prevailing tendencies of the age," which separately extolled "democratic freedom" and "social justice."[24] In addition, the prime minister had also long believed that a concern for development created an affinity among Asians. He had therefore regularly emphasized the moderate, agrarian, and nationalist character of Mao's revolution as a symbol of Asian resurgence, rather than its communism and ties to Moscow.[25] Following the founding of the PRC in October 1949 and the signing of the Sino-Soviet Treaty of Friendship in early 1950, however, Nehru acknowledged that China's future direction was uncertain.[26]

Nehru therefore sought to cultivate Beijing's moderation and independence from Moscow. As India's first ambassador to the PRC, K. M. Panikkar, wrote in retrospect, "It was my mission, as I saw it, to prove it to him [Chairman Mao Zedong] that a neutral position was also possible."[27] The Indian government was learning from its own encounter with a domestic communist insurgency that underdevelopment could spawn radical threats.[28] In 1949, Panikkar himself had proposed to Commonwealth colleagues that the communist danger in Southeast Asia could be contained through a program of economic aid.[29] Nehru believed that, just as economic development would defuse domestic communist threats, a shared aspiration to wrestle with underdevelopment would give Beijing and Delhi common ground and dilute Beijing's emphasis on relations with the radicals in Moscow. Nehru's concern was far less to do with communism per se than with the destabilizing impact on international politics of a growing alliance of communist states.[30] Hence, he wanted to encourage the PRC to assert an independent international position. The prime minister was so keen to recognize the PRC as a major power and integrate it into the international system that he dismissed the U.S. idea that India might replace China as the fifth permanent member of the U.N. Security Council.[31] Nehru also hoped that a less fearful Beijing would be more likely to preserve Tibetan autonomy. So Delhi sought to use its development model to prove its independence and establish a dialogue with Beijing to cultivate trust.

Although the first discussions between Ambassador Panikkar and the PRC's leaders, in May 1950, appeared to the Indians to confirm the potential for using the issue of economic development to find common ground, these exchanges obscured vastly different approaches. Panikkar's talks with the Chinese premier and foreign minister Zhou Enlai overwhelmingly focused on shared economic issues and the rural challenges both countries faced. Zhou stressed in particular, "There is something else that is also similar, that is that the agricultural products of our two countries are controlled by imperialism."[32] When Panikkar met Chairman Mao, he was also encouraged to think that Beijing shared Indian views about the importance of economic development for Asian independence: "We talked about Asia in general and about the withdrawal of Europeans from the continent, but he said more than once that as long as European economic power was entrenched in Asia the freedom was not complete."[33]

But Panikkar did not grasp the extent to which Chinese and Indian approaches to critical development issues like land reform differed. He and Zhou had discussed India's system of landholding and its imposition by the British, a link between domestic reaction and foreign oppression that Zhou would have appreciated, and the limited success of reform efforts so far in India.[34] The Chinese premier must have thought that India's approach to land reform and development in general would necessarily be limited by the distaste for violence. Indeed, in 1950 the Chinese Communist Party was extending what historian Hua-yu Li calls "brutal" land reform across China. The "cruelty" of these appropriations with mass meetings and the humiliation of landlords contrasted with the more administrative approach across much of Eastern Europe.[35] Chinese leaders wanted to replicate the forced industrialization and collectivization of agriculture achieved by Stalin in the 1920s and 1930s and sought Soviet guidance on establishing a gulag labor system, among other things.[36] Mao's emphasis on the withdrawal of European economic influence from Asia glossed over the Soviet assistance and radical economic transformation that Beijing foresaw. The reality was that whereas Nehru's whole approach sought to remove the friction from economic policy, for the CCP, genuine development could not be separated from conflict or Soviet support.

The Chinese used discussions of economic development to encourage Delhi to believe in the possibility of a cooperative relationship, disguising their disdain for India's model and the fact that it was actually regarded as a target for revolution. After all, shortly after the People's Republic of China was founded, the CCP had sent a note to the leaders of the Communist Party of India (CPI) predicting India's eventual liberation from the "yoke of imperialism and its collaborators."[37] Furthermore, the Chinese leadership had chosen to ally with the Soviet Union partly to underline to its own population that no alternative development model was available.[38] Beijing's challenge was to use conventional diplomacy to serve revolutionary ends.[39] As Zhou Enlai told his staff in March 1950, "Being sent to India to work is a big task, if done well then there are 900 million [people] united together."[40] In line with this ambition, Mao made an unprecedented appearance at a party hosted by Panikkar in January 1951 and proposed an alliance between India and the Soviets and Chinese.[41] In a period when Beijing followed Moscow's diplomatic lead, Mao shared Stalin's view that friendship with India was tactically useful for securing Beijing's position in Tibet.[42] Indeed, despite its suspicion of Indian ambitions for Tibet, Beijing urged Delhi to assist with the "peaceful liberation" of that region and encourage the Tibetan leader the Dalai Lama to negotiate with the CCP rather than flee.[43] The Chinese also exploited U.S. insensitivity toward Indian famine conditions by sending to India several grain shipments, as well as cultural delegations, through 1951.[44] Beijing's increasingly friendly diplomacy belied, however, a fundamental distrust of the Indian government as an ally of imperialism and oppressor of the Indian population.

Despite the positive image Beijing sought to establish, more intimate contact with the PRC made Delhi increasingly aware of both Chinese skepticism of India and the strength of Sino-Soviet bonds. Nehru had to strive to demonstrate that his government was progressive and independent of the United States. In January 1952, Shiv Shastri, an Indian diplomat in Beijing, reported, from his "ideological prison," that Delhi's hopes that China would diverge from Moscow might be exaggerated. Crucially, he underlined that the Chinese firmly agreed with Moscow that India was still "semi-colonial" and "not really independent."[45] Such reservations were augmented by the Indian Intelligence Bureau's suspicion that a Chinese cultural delegation had been providing money and guidance to branches of the Indian Communist Party.[46] In spring 1952, the Indian prime minister sent his sister, Vijaya Lakshmi Pandit, who had formerly served as ambassador in both Moscow and Washington, to Beijing. One goal for Pandit related to Indian mediation between the different parties in the Korean War.[47] However, Pandit was also tasked to counter the negative characterization of Indian development efforts in the Chinese media. Armed with sheets of statistics, she was to explain that Delhi was successfully reducing the influence of foreign capital in India. Furthermore, she was to defend the reputation of Indian democracy. The CPI had recently intensified its attacks on India's electoral system as a charade, and Delhi believed Beijing and Moscow were behind these public criticisms. Pandit was to point out that "several Ministers" had lost their seats recently. Finally, she was to reject the slanderous rumor that India was supplying strategic materials to the United States.[48] Delhi was seeking to demonstrate that a hybrid economic policy was possible and complemented the practice of a genuine nonaligned foreign policy.

Change, when it came, was less to do with Delhi's efforts than with wider shifts in the international scene. As the Korean War wound down in 1953, the atmosphere became more conducive to a Sino-Indian relationship emphasizing shared economic challenges. Under the post-Stalin Soviet "Peace Offensive," discussed in this volume by Swapna Kona Nayudu, Moscow and Beijing began using the phrase "peaceful coexistence" to define a newly moderate foreign policy. Shelving general support for revolutionary action overseas, Beijing was now less interested in the immediate details of Indian development politics and its implications for making revolution there. In 1954, China and India would agree to base their bilateral relations on the "Five Principles of Peaceful Coexistence" (Panchsheel), and they appeared to settle their differences over Tibet.[49] Beijing's desire for a new moderate foreign policy that minimized conflict and overseas commitments was in no small way born of the need to revive the economy.[50] Furthermore, a key aspect of the moderate image and, its corollary, an Asian identity, which Beijing began to assert, included an emphasis on the common underdevelopment and agricultural character of the region's economies.[51] Beijing now seemed to accept Nehru's notion that warm diplomatic relations could be fostered around shared challenges of economic development.

THE SOVIET UNION AND PEACEFUL TRANSITION

Attitudes toward development were at the heart of changes in the triangular relations between the PRC, U.S.S.R., and India through the 1950s. While Indian and Soviet thinking converged to a degree, differences began to emerge between Moscow and Beijing. Nehru had thought that a shared aspiration for economic progress would foster ties with Beijing and facilitate his effort to socialize China and weaken its bonds to Moscow. From 1953, with the First Five-Year Plan experiencing difficulties, Nehru had steered Indian planning in a more Soviet direction, emphasizing heavy industry and the public sector.[52] And at the same time, the Soviets had sought to nourish Indian industrial development,[53] a shift welcomed by Indian diplomats, who saw an opportunity to balance support received from the United States.[54] Following his visit to the Soviet Union in 1955, Nehru began revising his view that it was the Chinese, rather than the Soviets, who would be more inclined to moderation. It seemed to Nehru that whereas revolution and fear had retreated in the Soviet Union, Beijing was willing to risk millions of lives to recover Guomindang-occupied Taiwan.[55] Moscow's increasingly positive interpretation of Indian development contrasted with the view of Chinese Foreign Ministry analysts who regarded the Indian model as deeply flawed.[56] Mao believed that it was the PRC that was pioneering Asian modernity.[57]

But the central problem would be the Soviet idea of peaceful transition. In February 1956, Soviet premier Nikita Khrushchev sought to reinforce the new era of foreign policy moderation by formalizing this concept, along with peaceful coexistence and "peaceful competition," as a major theoretical innovation for the nuclear age. Peaceful transition posited that a state could realize socialism through nonviolent means and implied that nongoverning communist parties, such as the Communist Party of India, could adopt parliamentary methods to achieve its goals.[58] But more than this, peaceful transition also seemed an endorsement of Nehru's hybrid model, characterized by Frankel as "accommodative politics and radical social change." Khrushchev's theory suggested that vested interests, the "feudal forces" and "capitalists" of Marxist rhetoric, would acquiesce in the piecemeal erosion of their privileges. However, despite Mao's reservations related to the Soviets' unexpected launch of de-Stalinization,[59] and the applicability of Panchsheel to the United States and socialist bloc, the Chinese Communist Party's Eighth Congress, in autumn 1956, endorsed Khrushchev's new ideas.[60] Beijing also declared that class conflict was no longer a major concern in China, given the successful completion of the socialist transformation of private ownership. Mao's confidence in moderate methods was so firm that in April 1956 he had invited nonparty critics to offer evaluations of the CCP's record in a movement known as the "Hundred Flowers."[61] But Mao's views would change quickly, with dramatic consequences.

Events soon led Mao to take a far more critical view of Khrushchev's theoretical justification of absolute commitment to peaceful means. Turbulence in Eastern Europe, climaxing with Moscow's invasion of Hungary in October 1956 to safeguard pro-Soviet communist rule, major instability in outlying areas of Tibet caused by resistance to the CCP, and the unexpected bitterness of the Hundred Flowers led Mao to query Moscow's new theories.[62] Mao interpreted the problems in Hungary, in Tibet, and with the Hundred Flowers as demonstrating that a moderate policy, which avoided violence, allowed the survival and even renewal of counterrevolutionary enemies. The failure to eradicate such potential opposition was compounded by the danger of transnational class alliances, demonstrated by the Hungary and Tibet cases, where overseas support had bolstered local opposition to communist party rule. Mao's skepticism of moderate methods was revealed by his mocking of the comrades in Eastern Europe for their failure to kill sufficient counterrevolutionaries.[63] And the chairman's sense of the risks for China's own revolution were clear from his speculation as to whether the Hundred Flowers critics of the CCP actually desired a revival of the old order.[64]

With Mao now profoundly skeptical of Khrushchev's theories of peaceful means, India became something of a laboratory for testing these ideological differences. Although in late 1956 Mao wrote a long article publicly backing Moscow on an array of issues, the omission of any reference to peaceful transition hinted at his real feelings.[65] To senior party cadres he privately revealed his philosophical misgivings about Soviet ideas on war and peace.[66] The Communist Party of India was the lab rat in this doctrinal dispute because its success would measure the feasibility of peaceful transition. And indeed, electoral victory in the Indian state of Kerala in 1957 convinced the CPI to embrace peaceful transition.[67] In December 1957, at the Moscow

conference of communist parties, the Soviets and Chinese themselves compromised on the question, with Beijing acknowledging that the Kerala case
might prove that peaceful transition worked and the Soviets accepting that
the theory might not be universally applicable.[68] Mao nevertheless privately
tried to persuade the Indian communists that peaceful transition could only
be tactical.[69] In 1958, however, the Indian communists unilaterally upheld
the Soviet doctrine as formal policy, disregarding the Moscow conference
compromise, because they felt that their party's continued success in Kerala
merited no change. And the Soviets made no attempt to hold the party to the
agreement reached with Beijing.[70]

China's own official studies of India increasingly corroborated Mao's
skepticism of peaceful transition, suggesting that its economic model could
not work, that class contradictions were intensifying, and that Indian reactionaries were forcing a closer relationship with the United States. By
summer 1957, China's Central Investigation Department (CID) reported on
food riots and starvation in India. The Chinese believed that intrinsic constraints on Indian development stemmed from the power of the capitalist
class, which undermined the financing of the Five-Year Plan, and of "feudal"
forces that, allied to parts of the Congress Party, blocked land reform.[71] In
April 1958, the CID claimed that Nehru's "middle ground" was narrowing,
pressured on one side by the Communist Party of India, which was winning
elections and growing in membership, and on the other side by the Congress Party's right wing and India's "big capitalists." The latter, the analysts
wrote, were "colluding" with U.S. capital to secure their interests. The Tata
Group was cited as an example, having won loans from the World Bank and
United States totaling $116.8 million. Efforts to squeeze Nehru's allies, such
as the defense minister V. K. Krishna Menon, out of the cabinet were seen
as evidence of political struggle, as were comments by some newspapers that
G. B. Pant, union home minister and "one of the right-wing chiefs," should be
made deputy prime minister. Therefore, it was claimed, Nehru's concessions
to the right were growing and restrictions on private and foreign capital were
being eased.[72] In addition, Chinese analysts highlighted the confrontation
in Kerala, where the governing communist party's opponents used "legal
and illegal" means to subvert it. The Chinese believed that this instability
might spread as the party expanded from its core areas in the states of Kerala,
Andhra, and West Bengal into Bihar and Uttar Pradesh.[73]

Just as Mao had perceived the danger posed by class enemies in Hungary
and Tibet to be compounded by their alliance with reactionary forces overseas, so did Chinese analysts now highlight the coagulation of cooperation

between Indian reactionaries with the United States. Officials in the Chinese Foreign Ministry concluded that India's economic problems would increase India's dependence on the United States.[74] But continued faith in peaceful transition seemed particularly naive to Chinese analysts, given their perception of warming ties between the Indian and U.S. militaries. The Indian chief of the general staff General K. S. Thimayya appeared a particular target for American courtship because, like Finance Minister Morarji Desai, he was an opponent of "progressive forces" and politically had "wild ambitions."[75] Furthermore, the Chinese believed that Desai was seeking U.S. support in his struggle with Krishna Menon over the balance of public and private involvement in the defense industry.[76]

Historian Liu Xiaoyuan has suggested that the Chinese perception that Indo-U.S. relations were dramatically improving at this time contradicted Chairman Mao's overall assessment of the Cold War environment as now favoring the socialist bloc, articulated in his claim in Moscow in November 1957 that the "East Wind" prevailed.[77] But official Chinese perceptions of both a growing intimacy in Indo-U.S. relations and of the growth of political confrontation in India would all have added to Mao's surging confidence by confirming his theoretical conviction that peaceful transition was folly. Having purged all ideological opposition in China with the antirightist campaign, Mao was on a roll, and preparing to break with the Soviet development model through his utopian Great Leap Forward.[78] More broadly, Mao's advice to the many Third World delegations he now received made clear his doubts about both India and Moscow: nationalism and peaceful transition were both insufficient to realize genuine independence. Mao confidently explained that domestic class enemies must be eradicated or else they would continue to offer a channel for imperialist meddling.[79] Mao even cast his bombardment of the Guomindang-controlled offshore islands of the Taiwan Strait in 1958 as an act aimed to inspire global revolution and opposition to the United States,[80] action which so shocked Khrushchev that he curtailed nuclear aid to China.[81] Despite this, Beijing also seemed to gain ground in its contest with Moscow as some CPI figures began advocating a line closer to the CCP's rural and conflict-based strategies.[82] Furthermore, Moscow now joined in Beijing's criticism of Indian development, with Soviet ambassador to China Pavel Yudin ridiculing in print Indian claims that land reform could proceed nonviolently.[83]

Chinese perceptions of a growing polarization of Indian politics were not entirely misguided. Nehru's response to the political disturbances demonstrates how he linked his defense of the domestic middle ground to his international strategy, as well as what historian Rudra Chaudhuri shows to be his careful balancing of ideals and practical concerns in the diplomatic sphere. Steep falls in agricultural production in 1957 led to a conflict between the Planning Commission, with its preference for state trading and price controls in the rural sector, and the food minister A. P. Jain and many state government leaders, who preferred the introduction of incentives and new technologies.[84] Nehru contended with an intensifying confrontation between left and right: on the one hand, he ridiculed communists' criticisms that India's economic problems were due to "monopoly capitalists";[85] and on the other, he dismissed fears that the country faced collapse without Western aid and that revolution would sweep Moscow and Beijing's influence to the heart of India.[86] The corollary to this was the defense of non-alignment, under threat from Western aid.[87] Throughout 1957, Nehru continued to deny that India was closer to the United States than it appeared, that non-alignment was under threat, and that the Congress government was retreating from socialism.[88]

Although Chaudhuri has analyzed Nehru's management of non-alignment and material needs in the context of Indo-U.S. relations and Manu Bhagavan has related Nehru's domestic politics to his effort to bring Washington and Moscow closer over human rights, less has been said about how Nehru related Indian politics to the socialist bloc. It is the link between domestic gradualism and his international ambitions that made Nehru more than a Fabian socialist, seeking social progress through incremental means. For Nehru, his hybrid economic model also continued to have the specific importance of encouraging Sino-Soviet moderation. His effort now to fortify the middle ground was related to his sense that the political confrontations within India, not least in Kerala, where the communist government was in acute conflict with an array of religious and conservative groups, was linked to a new hard line from the Soviets and China. He had observed, in May 1958, that Moscow and Beijing had turned on Yugoslavia once more, attacking its moderate policies and reducing their own recent emphasis on different roads to socialism. Nehru remarked that the Hundred Flowers had "become weeds to be pulled out" and the CPI had been caught out by the reversal of policy.[89] As a result, Nehru sought reassurances that Kerala's communist government would uphold the constitution and would give no special role to Moscow.[90] Meanwhile, clashes between supporters and opponents of the CPI government continued to grow in July.[91]

Because Nehru believed that his development model and international strategy were interlinked, when sharp domestic disputes emerged in 1957 and 1958, he acted to reinvigorate his middle way. Nehru genuinely drew inspiration from both sides of the Cold War. He admired, for example, the apparent relationship between social reform in China and increased rural production.[92] And yet, he wanted India to study the U.S. ability to use productivity growth to offset social inequality.[93] As a result, beginning in 1957, and leading to the resolution at the Nagpur Congress in January 1959, Nehru found himself persuaded by arguments proposing that only significant reorganization of the rural scene could salvage Indian development plans.[94] Nehru backed the idea of a unique Indian form of rural cooperative, which he labeled "joint-farming." He imagined that India could reproduce the apparent dynamism of Soviet and Chinese cooperatives without the coercion involved in those states. Thus, India would demonstrate a peaceful, democratic route to a classless society, dissolving the need for class confrontation. A "new spirit" in the Indian peasantry would stimulate a revival in agricultural production.[95] The success of such an approach would of course prove the validity of Khrushchev's theory of peaceful transition. However, Nehru's insistence that peasants were not to be coerced and that the "service cooperatives" were entirely voluntary could not disguise the obvious contradictions.[96] On the one hand, he claimed there would be no real change of land ownership, but on the other, Nehru roamed philosophically across the face of a future scientific society of "abundance" and common ownership.[97] It was all too easy for his critics on the right wing of Congress and elsewhere to hurl dire warnings of Soviet-style collectivization and violence at his plans.[98]

Although Nehru may not have persuaded all his opponents within India, it is possible that his attempt to renew his syncretic model helped disrupt the renewed, albeit brief, Sino-Soviet consensus against Indian development. Despite Yudin's earlier lambasting of Delhi's economic policies, Nehru and Khrushchev corresponded warmly in February 1959 about a high-powered Soviet planning delegation due in India, and Nehru thanked the Soviets for an offer of long-term credit.[99] Whether Moscow was encouraged by the Nagpur proposals or else simply saw warmer ties with India as a condition of detente with the United States, this Soviet support for Indian development was viewed with deep suspicion by the Chinese. For instance, by May, Beijing's diplomats in Delhi were dismayed that India seemed to be successfully manipulating the Soviets to secure growing quantities of economic aid and trade.[100] But Beijing's concern with Moscow's India policy was more profound than that. Nehru's ideas of democratic socialism and non-alignment implied the possibility of domestic and international class harmony. If these concepts proved successful, they would add luster to Khrushchev's claim that peaceful coexistence and peaceful transition were viable. To Beijing, the Soviets appeared oblivious to the revolutionary possibilities emerging in the crucible of Indian class confrontation.

The increasingly broad territorial dispute that emerged in the late 1950s must be seen in the context of the general distrust that had developed. Beijing's reticence, which Delhi interpreted as hostility, arose from the perception that its enemies both within India and abroad wanted to create a territorial dispute to disrupt Sino-Indian relations. Delhi's increasing concern that China harbored significant claims on Indian territory, which Srinath Raghavan elucidates in this volume, was compounded by the sense that Beijing was retreating from moderation in general. As 1958 ended, alarmed by Beijing's harsh treatment of an Indian patrol seized in the disputed territory of Aksai Chin, in Ladakh, where a Chinese road had been discovered,[101] Nehru sent a note directly to Zhou complaining about major errors in the delineation of the Sino-Indian border on Chinese maps.[102]

Throughout 1958, Beijing had been growing far more cautious about cooperating with India. In July, for instance, Mao canceled a prior invitation for Nehru to tour Tibet with Zhou. No doubt the chairman wanted to screen the instability in Tibet from Nehru, but Beijing was also aggravated by the collaboration of Indian figures with Tibetan rebels, the hostility of certain officials and media toward Chinese rule in Tibet, and transgressions of Panchsheel, such as the smuggling of a radio to the Indian consulate in Lhasa. Nehru himself had even publicly sympathized with attacks on China by J. B. Kripalani, an advocate for Tibet's independence. Furthermore, the government of India had shown a worrying tolerance of anti-PRC activities by Chinese residents of Calcutta sympathetic to Jiang Jieshi's Guomindang.[103] Beijing was concerned that the emerging territorial dispute was related to these efforts to wreck relations between China and India. The Chinese embassy in Delhi interpreted a recent U.S. success in mediating a breakthrough in Indo-Pakistan negotiations, on an array of contentious issues, as simply a scheme to reduce the Indian public's fixation with Pakistani offenses and transfer this attention instead to problems with China. The Chinese diplomats ruminated that the U.S. calculation was that a territorial dispute between Delhi and Beijing would stimulate a sustained anti-China mood in India, which would serve the long-term anticommunist struggle in South Asia.[104] By the end of 1958, Beijing's analysts were clear that the map dispute was entangled with India's internal struggle: those like Krishna Menon, who advocated distance from the United States, dismissed as "nonsense" the claims of a territorial dispute.[105] It was only at this point, in January 1959, that Beijing finally replied to Delhi's notes about the maps explaining that the border had never been delimited, that disputes certainly existed, but that each side should respect the status quo while they considered a temporary solution.[106]

So by early 1959, Beijing believed that its enemies in the United States and India sought to destabilize Sino-Indian relations and that Moscow was shockingly complacent on this issue. In this context, Mao regarded the Lhasa rebellion, which exploded in March, as offering various opportunities. First, the implacable hostility of the CCP's class enemies in Tibet was confirmed, thus justifying ruthless suppression.[107] Second, certain of Indian malfeasance in Tibet, Chinese leaders also now welcomed the chance to test Delhi's real character.[108] Mao believed that a key CCP strength had been its historical success in identifying "comprador" capitalists, those elite collaborators with foreign imperialism.[109] Delhi's actions now would indicate the level of comprador influence over Nehru's government. At the end of 1958, Chinese analysts had observed that Nehru was under huge pressure to crush the Indian Communist Party.[110] Crisis in Tibet would only intensify Nehru's dilemma, forcing him, like the Dalai Lama and everyone else, to take sides. Finally, Mao also believed that the rebellion in Lhasa favored his argument with Moscow. He explained to visiting Italian communists that the problem in Tibet now was "to take the arms from the shoulders of the serf-owners and give them to the laborers. This problem leads to a theoretical problem, namely class struggle in the end always needs a war, to transition peacefully is very difficult."[111] Launching class struggle in Tibet and ending its autonomy forced the Tibetan elite, Delhi, and Moscow all to show their hand.

As Mao had expected, Nehru's political opponents used the Tibet crisis to launch a comprehensive attack on the prime minister. Nehru reacted by appealing to Moscow and Beijing for support. He had recently welcomed the domestic debate that had arisen in response to the renewed rhetoric of land reform at the Congress Party's annual session at Nagpur.[112] However, because the end of Tibet's autonomy seemed to be a major failure for Nehru's China policy, the whole package of related domestic and international policies could now be challenged. Nehru tried to contain the fallout by limiting the Dalai Lama's activities and calming Indian passions about Tibet.[113] This pressure combined with continuing assaults on his economic policy to trap Nehru between the left and the right.[114] But the prime minister defied the Cold War within India. He dismissed the fear that land reform and cooperatives meant "red ruin" for India and complained that some feared India would be swallowed by U.S. imperialism and others by China. Nehru countered: "No country, great or small, is going to swallow India. If it attempted to do so, it would have most violent indigestion."[115] But this confidence was belied by Delhi's secret appeals for Chinese understanding, warning that non-alignment would fall with Nehru.[116]

Beijing rejected these appeals for sympathy and instead adopted diplomacy as a form of struggle, an intervention in Indian politics on the side of those battling reactionary forces.[117] Mao was convinced that Nehru's whole politics, his hybrid development model and nonaligned foreign policy, obstructed the revolutionary resolution of class contradictions in India and beyond. Mao thus publicly attacked Nehru in an article published on 6 May 1959, titled "The Revolution in Tibet and Nehru's Philosophy." Mao wanted to highlight Nehru's obstruction of reform in Tibet, his territorial ambitions, and his confused desire that Tibet be a buffer.[118] The critique underlined that reactionary forces in India blocked more progressive economic and foreign policy. Chinese diplomats were clear that the root of the Tibet problem was that Indian elites feared that China's success in that region would whet the appetite of their own population for a more revolutionary development model.[119] Mao still sought friendship with India.[120] But friendship was sought along class lines. The polemical attack on Nehru was the Leninist pursuit of unity through struggle.[121] Zhou and Mao themselves told a Soviet delegation that they wanted to demonstrate to the people of the world the links between some of India's "big capitalists" and the Tibetan rebels and that, because Nehru was left some "leeway," relations with India would be friendly again since there was no argument with the Indian people as a whole.[122] China's new foreign minister, Chen Yi, and Ambassador Yudin agreed that Nehru wanted help fending off the "right-wing attacks," but Chen explained that the Chinese were not inclined to do so.[123] The difference was clear: Beijing wanted Nehru to choose sides in the crucible of Indian, and world, politics, whereas the Soviets did not—they were content with Nehru, his non-alignment, and his hybrid economics.

CONCLUSION

Nehru had a strategy for socializing the People's Republic of China. In his mind, a sense of the common challenge of underdevelopment would complement Delhi's non-alignment to provide a foundation for Sino-Indian relations, thus integrating China into the international system and reducing Beijing's reliance on Moscow. Delhi set out to persuade Beijing that its own mixed-development model was capable of relieving the poverty of the Indian masses and securing India's independence, proving Indian "neutrality," as Panikkar put it in 1950. But this mission soon encountered obstacles. Moscow's post-Stalin peace offensive confounded Nehru's expectation that it was the Chinese who were bound to set aside disruptive radicalism more quickly. In fact, although Nehru had thought economic development would provide a sphere of trust between Beijing and Delhi, instead it was Moscow and Delhi that soon grew closer on this issue, as Khrushchev began giving substantial economic support to India. Subsequently, Indian development became a major source of contention in Sino-Soviet relations. In late 1956, Chairman Mao began to question the equanimity that had settled over the socialist bloc with regard to class-based threats, indicated by the new theories of peaceful coexistence and peaceful transition. Mao decided that instability in Eastern Europe and across broad Tibetan areas of China, as well as the virulent dissent in China sparked by the Hundred Flowers, all indicated that continued moderation of international and domestic policy permitted the proliferation of counterrevolutionary enemies, doubly dangerous because of their ability to form transnational alliances. Chinese analysis of economic and political conditions in India suggested to Beijing that peaceful transition was indeed a naive strategy. Chinese officials thought that Nehru's mixed-development model was doomed due to the opposition of varied reactionary groups and individuals and that these same people were also seeking to deepen ties with the United States. In Beijing, this was all related to the general shift rightward of India's foreign policy. The intensifying territorial dispute and flagrant support for the Tibet rebels in 1959 merely confirmed in Beijing's eyes how successful certain forces in India were in dragging Delhi into an anti-China position. For Beijing, these developments underscored how deluded the Soviets were to believe that the strategy of peaceful transition could realize socialist transformation and indicated the futility of Soviet endorsement of India's bankrupt economic strategy. David Engerman has shown that Soviet encounters with India led to a more tolerant approach to Third World development strategies in Moscow. However, the opposite occurred with China, as Beijing decided that the Indian case demonstrated the need for more radical methods.

Beijing's intransigence at the April 1960 territorial talks, which Srinath Raghavan demonstrates, therefore needs to be seen in this light. Specifically, given the perception in Beijing that India's posture was taken under the influence of the Indian reactionaries, Mao would have considered any concession to Nehru simply a reward for those anti-China forces within India. Furthermore, convinced of Moscow's ideological corruption, Mao would rather have seen the political confrontation swirling around Nehru continue to intensify, because it proved to a global audience that the Soviet assessment of India was utterly incorrect. Nehru had thought that economic development would serve as a bridge between Delhi and Beijing, but instead, from the Chinese point of view, it served as a barometer of the dangerous nature of the Indian state.

NOTES

1. Odd Arne Westad, *The Global Cold War: Third World Interventions and the Making of Our Times* (Cambridge: Cambridge University Press, 2005), 3.

2. Nick Cullather, *The Hungry World: America's Cold War Battle against Poverty in Asia* (Cambridge, Mass.: Harvard University Press, 2010); Michael E. Latham, *The Right Kind of Revolution: Modernization, Development, and U.S. Foreign Policy from the Cold War to the Present* (Ithaca, N.Y.: Cornell University Press, 2011); David Ekbladh, *The Great American Mission: Modernization and the Construction of an American World Order* (Princeton, N.J.: Princeton University Press, 2010).

3. On the first point, see David C. Engerman, "Development Politics and the Cold War," *Diplomatic History* 41, no. 1 (2017): 1–19; and on the second point, see Engerman, "Learning from the East: Soviet Experts and India in the Era of Competitive Coexistence," *Comparative Studies of South Asia, Africa and the Middle East* 33, no. 2 (2013): 227–38.

4. Benjamin Zachariah, *Nehru* (London: Routledge, 2004), 157; Engerman, "Development Politics," 4.

5. Sunail Khilnani, *The Idea of India* (London: Penguin, 2003), 76–80.

6. Benjamin Zachariah, "The 'Nehruvian' State, Developmental Imagination, Nationalism and the Government," in *Political Transition and Development Imperatives*, ed. Ranabir Samaddar and Suhit K. Sen (New Delhi: Routledge, 2012), 77.

7. Ramachandra Guha, *India after Gandhi: The History of the World's Largest Democracy* (London: Macmillan, 2007), chap. 10.

8. Francine R. Frankel, *India's Political Economy, 1947–2004: The Gradual Revolution*, 2nd ed. (New Delhi: Oxford University Press, 2005), 3.

9. Partha Chatterjee, "Development Planning and the Indian State," in *State and Politics in India*, ed. Partha Chatterjee (Delhi: Oxford University Press, 1997), 271–97; Zachariah, "'Nehruvian' State," 72.

10. See Daniel Immerwahr, *Thinking Small: The United States and the Lure of Community Development* (Cambridge, Mass.: Harvard University Press, 2015), 9–11, chap. 3; Nicole Sackley, "Village Models: Etawah, India, and the Making and Remaking of Development in the Early Cold War," *Diplomatic History* 37, no. 4 (2013): 749–78.

11. Engerman, "Learning from the East."

12. Dennis Kux, *Estranged Democracies: India and the United States, 1941–91* (New Delhi: Sage, 1994); H. W. Brands, *India and the United States: The Cold Peace* (Boston: Twayne, 1990).

13. Rudra Chaudhuri, *Forged in Crisis: India and the United States since 1947* (New York: Oxford University Press, 2014); see also Srinath Raghavan, *War and Peace in Modern India* (Basingstoke, U.K.: Palgrave Macmillan, 2010).

14. Dennis Merrill, *Bread and the Ballot: The United States and India's Economic Development, 1947–1963* (Chapel Hill: University of North Carolina Press, 1990).

15. Manu Bhagavan, *India and the Quest for One World: The Peacemakers* (Basingstoke, U.K.: Palgrave Macmillan, 2013), 3, 11–13, 53.

16. Neville Maxwell, *India's China War* (London: Cape, 1970); John W. Garver, *Protracted Contest: Sino-Indian Rivalry in the Twentieth Century* (Seattle: University of Washington Press, 2001); Bérénice Guyot-Réchard, *Shadow States: India, China and the Himalayas, 1910–1962* (Cambridge: Cambridge University Press, 2016).

17. Sulmaan Wasif Khan, "Cold War Co-Operation: New Chinese Evidence on Jawaharlal Nehru's 1954 Visit to Beijing," *Cold War History* 11, no. 2 (2011): 197–222; Arunab Ghosh, "Accepting Difference, Seeking Common Ground: Sino-Indian Statistical Exchanges 1951–1959," *BJHS Themes* 1 (2016): 61–82.

18. Guha, *India after Gandhi*, 152–54.

19. Chaudhuri, *Forged in Crisis*, 28; see also the chapter by Swapna Kona Nayudu in this volume.

20. See Bhagavan, *India and the Quest for One World*.

21. For example, "Our Objectives," speech delivered at the Indian Council of World Affairs, New Delhi, 22 March 1949, *Jawaharlal Nehru's Speeches* (hereafter *JNS*), vol. 1, *September 1946–May 1949* (Calcutta: Ministry of Information and Broadcasting, 1958), 233.

22. Odd Arne Westad, *Restless Empire: China and the World since 1750* (London: Bodley Head, 2012), 320–22.

23. The historical literature on the Sino-Soviet split has given the Sino-Indian border dispute a prominent role but has barely discussed the impact of China's views about Soviet attitudes toward Indian development. Much of the literature on the split can be divided in terms of the debate over the relative importance of national interest, security, and culture versus ideological differences. For a recent example of the former, see Zhihua Shen and Yafeng Xia, *Mao and the Sino-Soviet Partnership, 1945–1959: A New History* (Lanham, Md.: Lexington Books, 2015); and for the latter, see Jeremy Scott Friedman, *Shadow Cold War: The Sino-Soviet Split and the Third World* (Chapel Hill: University of North Carolina Press, 2015).

24. "15 July 1950," Jawaharlal Nehru, *Letters to Chief Ministers, 1947–1964*, 5 vols. (New Delhi: Jawaharlal Nehru Memorial Fund, 1985–89), vol. 2, 142.

25. For Asian affinities, see "Meeting Ground of East and West, 8 March 1949," *Nehru's Speeches*, 233. For views on the CCP, see "23 December 1948," Nehru, *Letters to Chief Ministers*, vol. 1, 249; see also "4 June 1949," ibid., 368.

26. "18 January 1950" and "16 February 1950," Nehru, *Letters to Chief Ministers*, vol. 2, 5, 29.

27. K. M. Panikkar, *In Two Chinas: Memoirs of a Diplomat* (London: Allen and Unwin, 1955), 73.

28. Taylor C. Sherman, "The Integration of the Princely State of Hyderabad and the Making of the Postcolonial State in India, 1948–56," *Indian Economic and Social History Review* 44, no. 4 (2007): 505.

29. Panikkar, *In Two Chinas*, 55.

30. Nehru often expressed his sense that alliances and pacts between states were

fundamentally destabilizing for the international system. See, e.g., "5 August 1949," Nehru, *Letters to Chief Ministers*, vol. 1, 433.

31. Anton Harder, "Not at the Cost of China: New Evidence Regarding US Proposals to Nehru for Joining the United Nations Security Council," Cold War International History Project Working Paper no. 76 (11 March 2015); see also Nabarun Roy, "In the Shadow of Great Power Politics: Why Nehru Supported PRC's Admission to the Security Council," *International History Review* 40, no. 2 (2018): 376–96.

32. "Zhou enlai zongli chuci jiejian yindu dashi pannijia de tanhua jilu" [Memorandum of Conversation of Premier Zhou Enlai's First Meeting with Indian Ambassador Panikkar], 17 May 1950, 105-00009-02, Chinese Ministry of Foreign Affairs Archive (hereafter CMFA), 1.

33. Panikkar, *In Two Chinas*, 80.

34. "Zhou enlai zongli," 105-00009-02, CMFA, 1.

35. Hua-yu Li, *Mao and the Economic Stalinization of China, 1948–1953* (Lanham, Md.: Rowman and Littlefield, 2006), 15–16.

36. Deborah Kaple, "Agents of Change: Soviet Advisers and High Stalinist Management in China, 1949–1960," *Journal of Cold War Studies* 18, no. 1 (Winter 2016): 7–15.

37. Hemen Ray, *Peking and the Indian Communists: The Strategy and Tactics of the CCP toward the Indian Communist Movement in the Evolution of Sino-Indian and Sino-Soviet Conflicts* (Bombay: Jaico, 1980), 17.

38. Guangzhang Shu, "The Sino-Soviet Alliance and the Cold War in Asia, 1954–1962," in *The Cambridge History of the Cold War*, vol. 1, ed. Melvyn P. Leffler and Odd Arne Westad (Cambridge: Cambridge University Press, 2010), 353.

39. Yang Kuisong, "The Theory and Implementation of the People's Republic of China's Revolutionary Diplomacy," *Journal of Modern Chinese History* 3, no. 2 (2009): 135.

40. Liao Xinwen, "Ershi shiji wushi niandai Mao Zedong deng dapo xifang fengsuo he baowei de juece licheng" [The Decision-Making of Mao etc. in Breaking Down the West's Blockade and Encirclement of China in the 1950s], *Dangde Wenxian* 4 (2008): 15.

41. "Mao zedong zhuxi chuxi yindu guoqing zhaodaihui yu yindu dashi pannijia tanhua (character unclear) yao deng" [Chairman Mao Conversation with Indian Ambassador Panikkar when Attending Indian National Day Reception], 26 January 1951, 105-00016-01, CMFA.

42. "Record of a conversation between Stalin and representatives of the Indian Communist Party," 9 February 1951, History and Public Policy Program Digital Archive, Russian State Archive of Socio-Political History [RGASPI], fond 558, opis 11, delo 310, listy 71–86, translated for the Cold War International History Project, Wilson Center, by Gary Goldberg, http://digitalarchive.wilsoncenter.org/document/113938.

43. "Guanyu yindu ganshe wo jiefang xizang shi de waijiao tongbao" [Diplomatic Bulletin Regarding Indian Interference in the Liberation of Tibet], 24 November 1950, 105-00011-02, CMFA; "Zhou enlai zongli jiu dalai yu li xizang shi tong yindu dashi pannijia de tanhua jilu ji yinfang biaotai" [Memorandum of Conversation and Indian Reaction to Premier Zhou Enlai's Discussion with Indian Ambassador Panikkar regarding the Dalai Lama's Desire to Leave Tibet], 21–26 March 1950, 105-00010-04, CMFA.

44. Andrew Jon Rotter, *Comrades at Odds: The United States and India, 1947–1964* (Ithaca, N.Y.: Cornell University Press, 2000), 260, 270–71; "Zhongguo tong yindu ji bajisitan guanxi de youguan cailiao" [Materials Related to China's Relations with India and Pakistan], 1–17, 1–31 October 1955, 203-00180-03, CMFA.

45. "Telegram to Pandit," 14 January 1952, Subject File No. 24, Vijaya Lakshmi Pandit Papers, Installment II, Nehru Memorial Museum and Library (hereafter NMML), New Delhi.

46. "A Brief review of the activities of the Chinese Cultural Delegation in India (1951) Secret" (sent to H. V. R. Iyengar and K. P. S. Menon on 3 January 1952 by Assistant Director of Intelligence Bureau A. Jayaram), in *Exchange of goodwill missions between India and China*, 786-CJK/50, Ministry of External Affairs (hereafter MEA), CJK Branch, National Archives of India (hereafter NAI), New Delhi.

47. Chaudhuri, *Forged in Crisis*, 70.

48. "Ministry of External Affairs, XP Division S Sen," 24 April 1952 [contains a note on "Communist Propaganda in India"], *1952 Notes/correspondence with K. M. Panikkar, K. P. S. Menon, Y. D. Gundevia regarding V. L. Pandit's visit as a cultural delegate to China, includes extracts of her speeches, etc.*, Subject File 24, Pandit Papers, Installment II, NMML, 47.

49. *Panchsheel* is a Sanskrit term adopted by Nehru meaning "Five Principles."

50. Guangzhang Shu, "Constructing 'Peaceful Coexistence': China's Diplomacy toward the Geneva and Bandung Conferences, 1954–55," *Cold War History* 7, no. 4 (2007): 510; Yang Kuisong, "Mao Zedong and the Indochina Wars," in *Behind the Bamboo Curtain: China, Vietnam, and the World beyond Asia*, ed. Priscilla Roberts (Stanford, Calif.: Stanford University Press, 2006), 64–65.

51. Niu Jun, "Chongjian 'zhongjiandidai': zhongguo yazhou zhengce de qiyuan, 1949–1955," in *Lengzhan yu zhongguo waijiao zhengce* ["Reconstructing the 'Intermediate Zone': The Origins of China's Asia Policy, 1949–1955," in *The Cold War and China's Diplomatic Policy*] (Beijing: Jiuzhou chubanshe, 2012), 253; See also Shu, "Constructing 'Peaceful Coexistence,'" 513.

52. Frankel, *India's Political Economy*, 94, 114–18; Guha, *India after Gandhi*, 206–7.

53. Brands, *India and the United States*, 65, 80–86; David C. Engerman, "The Romance of Economic Development and New Histories of the Cold War," *Diplomatic History* 28, no. 1 (2004): 37–39.

54. Vojtech Mastny, "The Soviet Union's Partnership with India," *Journal of Cold War Studies* 12, no. 3 (2010): 52.

55. "Nehru Talks to Heads of Mission in Europe . . . , 28–30th June, 1955," in *Selected Works of Jawaharlal Nehru*, 2nd ser. (hereafter *SWJN*), ed. S. Gopal, 61 vols. to date (New Delhi: Jawaharlal Nehru Memorial Fund, 1984–), vol. 29, 242–57; see also 20 July 1955, Nehru, *Letters to Chief Ministers*, vol. 4, 192.

56. Xiaoyuan Liu, "Friend or Foe: India as Perceived by Beijing's Foreign Policy Analysts in the 1950s," *China Review* 15, no. 1 (2015): 125–26.

57. "Zai zhongguo gongchandang quanguo daibiao huiyi kaimuci" [Opening Address at the Chinese Communist Party National Congress], 21 March 1955, in *Jianguo yilai mao zedong wengao (JGYLMZDWG)* [Collected Documents of Mao Zedong since the Founding of the People's Republic of China], 8 vols., digital ed. (Beijing: Zhongyang wenxian), vol. 5, 59.

58. Shen Zhihua, *Chuzai shizi lukou de xuanze: 1956–1957 nian de zhongguo* [At the Crossroads: China in 1956–1957] (N.p.: Guangdong renmin, 2013), 55.

59. Ibid., 84–89, 100–102.

60. Ibid., 133–39.

61. Wennan Liu, "Studying the Chinese Communist Party in Historical Context: An

Interview with Yang Kuisong, October 17, 2015," *Journal of Modern Chinese History* 10, no. 1 (2016): 81–82.

62. Shen, *Chuzai shizi lukou de xuanze*, 277–88.

63. Ibid., 284.

64. Ibid., 296–309.

65. Ibid., 293.

66. "Zhanzheng yu heping ji huxiang paichi you huxiang lianjie" [War and Peace are Mutually Exclusive and Mutually Interrelated], 27 January 1957, in *Jianguo yilai mao zedong junshi wengao* (*JGYLMZDJSWG*) [Collected Military Documents of Mao Zedong since the Founding of the People's Republic of China], 3 vols. (Beijing: Zhongyang wenxian, 2010), vol. 3, 338.

67. Georges Kristoffel Lieten, "China and the Undivided Communist Party of India," *Social Scientist* 3, no. 12 (July 1975): 5; see also Victor M. Fic, *Peaceful Transition to Communism in India: Strategy of the Communist Party* (Bombay: Nachiketa, 1969), 232, 287.

68. Fic, *Peaceful Transition to Communism in India*, 329–30; see also Shen, *Chuzai shizi lukou de xuanze*, 8, 80–84, 349–97.

69. "Geming de fazhan zongshi jingguo yuhui daolu zhubu shangsheng" [The Development of Revolution Always Proceeds Torturously and through Gradual Advance], 16 November 1957, in *JGYLMZDJSWG*, vol. 3, 355.

70. Fic, *Peaceful Transition to Communism in India*, 363–64.

71. "Yindu jingji muqian fasheng yanzhong kunnan de yuanyin he yindu zhengfu de duice" [The Causes of the Serious Problems Currently Occuring in the Indian Economy and the Indian Government's Countermeasures], 25 July 1957, 105-00835-01, CMFA.

72. "Muqian yindu guonei zhengzhi douzheng de xinghshi jiqi yingxiang" [The State and Impact of India's Current Domestic Political Struggle], 26 April 1958, 105-00891-10, CMFA.

73. "Cong nihelu muqian de kumen kan yindu zhengju" [Considering India's Political Situation from Nehru's Current Dejection], 9 December 1958, 105-00891-09, CMFA.

74. "Yindu jingji qingkuang" [India's Economic Situation], 5 September 1958, 105-00891-01, CMFA.

75. "Yindu meiguo guanxi" [India's Relations with America], 31 March–14 November 1958, 105-00892-02, CMFA, 5–16.

76. "Yindu guodadang neibu maodun he douzheng" [Contradictions and Struggle within the Indian National Congress], 5 November 1958–19 January 1959, 105-00891-07, CMFA.

77. Liu, "Friend or Foe," 132–35.

78. Shen, *Chuzai shizi lukou de xuanze*, 1–9. See also Liu, "Friend or Foe," 130; and Chen Jian and Yang Kuisong, "Chinese Politics and the Collapse of the Sino-Soviet Alliance," in *Brothers in Arms: The Rise and Fall of the Sino-Soviet Alliance, 1945–1963*, ed. Odd Arne Westad (Washington, D.C.: Woodrow Wilson Center, 1998), 267.

79. "Dui diguozhuyi de 'wenming' yao pochu mixin" [We Must Eliminate Blind Faith in the "Civilisation" of Imperialism], 12 July 1958, *Mao zedong waijiao wenxuan* (*MZDWJWX*) [Selected Diplomatic Documents of Mao Zedong] (Beijing: Zhongyang wenxian), 319; "Liangci shibai shi women xuehuile dazhang" [We Learnt How to Make War after Two Defeats], 1 February 1959, in *MZDJGYLJSWG*, vol. 3, 5; "Feizhou de renwu shi fandui diguozhuyi" [Africans Oppose Imperialism], 21 February 1959, in *MZDWJWX*, 369.

80. "Mei diguozhuyi yi bei ziji zhizao de jiaosuo taozhu" [American Imperialism Is Already Trapped in Its Own Noose], 8 September 1958, in *MZDWJWX*, 348; "Ba zhanzheng wenti xiangtou jiu bu haipa zhanzheng" [With a Thorough Understanding of War One Does Not Fear War], 13 March 1959, in *JGYLMZDJSWG*, vol. 3, 16.

81. Shu, "Sino-Soviet Alliance," 363–64.

82. "Yindu jingji qingkuang" [India's Economic Situation], 5 September 1958, 105-00891-01, CMFA.

83. "Cong nihelu muqian de kumen kan yindu zhengju" [Considering India's Political Situation from Nehru's Current Dejection], 9 December 1958, 105-00891-09, CMFA; "Yudin's Article," 26 December 1958, in *SWJN*, vol. 45, 722.

84. Frankel, *India's Political Economy*, 143–55.

85. "The Difficulties of Advancing Economy," 20 November 1957, in *SWJN*, vol. 40, 69.

86. "Cable to TT Krishnamachari," 23 September 1957, in *SWJN*, vol. 39, 115.

87. "US Foreign Aid Policy," 18 March 1957, in *SWJN*, vol. 37, 560.

88. "National and International Issues," 21 October 1957, in *SWJN*, vol. 39, 768.

89. "The Indian Path to Socialism," 12 May 1958, in *SWJN*, vol. 42, 525.

90. "To EMS Namboodiripad," 30 June 1958, in *SWJN*, vol. 42, 397. See also "To EMS Namboodiripad," 15 June 1958, in ibid., 394.

91. See *SWJN*, vol. 43, 329–40, for documents related to the growing tension in Kerala.

92. "Tribute to DK Karve," 18 April 1958, in *SWJN*, vol. 42, 850.

93. "To PCC Officials: Speech—II," 19 March 1959, in *SWJN*, vol. 47, 181.

94. Frankel, *India's Political Economy*, 153–61.

95. See "Community Development Schemes," 27 April 1957, in *SWJN*, vol. 37, 195; "Cooperative and Scientific Farming," 29 April 1957, in ibid., 202; "3 September 1957," Nehru, *Letters to Chief Ministers*, vol. 4, 554; "23–24 January 1958," Nehru, *Letters to Chief Ministers*, vol. 5, 9; and "Village Cooperatives of Landless Labourers," 10 January 19598, in *SWJN*, vol. 46, 227.

96. "In the Lok Sabha," 19 February 1959, in *SWJN*, vol. 46, 72.

97. "To CPP," 16 March 1959, in *SWJN*, vol. 47, 167.

98. "In the Lok Sabha," 19 February 1959, in *SWJN*, vol. 46, 72.

99. "To NS Khrushchev," 5 April 1959, in *SWJN*, vol. 48, 539.

100. "Zhi waijiaobu, Beijing" [To the Foreign Ministry, Beijing], 5 May 1959, *Yindu sulian guanxi* [Indo-Soviet Relations], 105-00946-04, CMFA.

101. "4 November 1958," in *SWJN*, vol. 45, 697.

102. "14 December 1958," in ibid., 702–5.

103. "Yin guanfang he baojie dui wo bu youhao de yanlun huiji" [Compilation of Unfriendly Statements by Indian Officialdom and Media], 17 July 1958, 105-00590-01, CMFA; "Youguan qita yindu fanhua an" [Regarding Other Anti-China Cases in India], 22 April–28 June 1958, 105-00590-05, CMFA.

104. "Yindu, bajisitan zongli guanyu bianjie wenti de huitan" [Premiers of India and Pakistan Negotiations on Border Problem], 22 September 1958, 105-00836-02, CMFA.

105. "Meinong yu desai zhijian de maodun fazhan qingkuang" [The Development of Contradictions between Menon and Desai], 20 November 1958, in *Yindu guodadang neibu maodun he douzheng* [Contradictions and Struggle within the Indian National Congress], 5 November 1958–19 January 1959, 105-00891-07, CMFA.

106. "22 January 1959" in *Zhou enlai nianpu, 1949–1976* (ZELNP) [Zhou Enlai Almanac, 1949–1976], digital ed. (Beijing: Zhongyang wenxian).

107. "17 March 1959" in ibid.; Chen Jian, "The Tibetan Rebellion of 1959 and China's Changing Relations with India and the Soviet Union," *Journal of Cold War Studies* 8, no. 3 (2006): 72–78.

108. "17 March 1959" in ZELNP. Zhou Enlai had pointed out that events in Lhasa were related to the Indian authorities; Chen, "Tibetan Rebellion," 85–86.

109. "Liangci shibai shi women xuehuile dazhang" [We Learnt How to Make War after Two Defeats], 1 February 1959, in *JGYLMZDJSWG*, vol. 3, 8.

110. "Cong nihelu muqian de kumen kan yindu zhengju" [Considering India's Political Situation from Nehru's Current Dejection], 9 December 1958, 105-00891-09, CMFA.

111. "Guangda de xizang qunzhong yu jiefangjun zhanzai yiqi" [The Great Tibetan Masses Stand Together with the People's Liberation Army], 19 April 1959, in *JGYLMZDJSWG*, vol. 3, 31.

112. "Implement Congress Policies," 24 February 1959, in *SWJN*, vol. 46, 295; see also "25 March 1959," in Nehru, *Letters to Chief Ministers*, vol. 5, 218.

113. "To Subimal Dutt: No Political Activity by the Dalai Lama," 9 May 1959, in *SWJN*, vol. 49, 569; "To G Parthasarathi: China Policy," 10 May 1959, in ibid., 571.

114. "At Delhi: Press Conference," 14 May 1959, in *SWJN*, vol. 46, 183.

115. "Public Meeting: Cooperative Farming, Rajaji's New Party," 1 June 1959, in *SWJN*, vol. 49, 41.

116. "Wo zhu aiji dashi chen jiakang yu yindu zhu gaiguo dashi xiao nihelu tan xizang wenti" [Our Ambassador in Egypt Chen Jiakang Discusses the Tibet Problem with India's Ambassador in This Country "Little" Nehru], 23 April 1959, 105-00656-01, CMFA; "Bocailuobu zhi keliukefu han: guanyu Zhongyin guanxi wenti" [Podtserov to Kryuchkov: On Problems with Sino-Indian Relations], 6 May 1959, in *Guanyu zhongyin bianjie chongtu de e'guo dang'an (GZBCED)* [Soviet documents on the Sino-Indian boundary conflict], ed. Shen Zhihua, unpublished Chinese translations.

117. I am indebted to a conversation with Lorenz Luthi for the origin of the idea of diplomacy as struggle. He had suggested that in this period, and maybe others, Beijing conducted diplomacy as if it was holding a struggle session with a reformable class enemy.

118. Chen, "Tibetan Rebellion," 86–88.

119. "Xizang panluanfenzi zai yindu de huodong qingkuang" [On the Activities of Tibetan Rebels in India], 27 May 1959, 105-00944-01, CMFA; "Puzhannuofu yu qiao shaoguang huitan jiyao: Xizang pingpan yu zhongyin guanxi" [Summary of Talks between Puzanov and Qiao Shaoguang: Pacification of Tibet and Sino-Indian Relations], 7 May 1959, in *GZBCED*.

120. Chen, "Tibetan Rebellion," 86–88.

121. "Yindu fuzongtong dengren tong sulian dashi tan xizang wenti" [India's Vice President and Others Discuss the Tibet Problem with the Soviet Ambassador], 105-00657-03, CMFA, 9–12; Chen, "Tibetan Rebellion," 87.

122. "6 May 1959" in ZELNP.

123. "Chen yi fuzongli jiejian sulian zhuhua dashi yujin" [Vice Premier Chen Yi Meets Soviet Ambassador to China Yudin], 8 May 1959, 105-00657-03, CMFA.

Chapter **Eight**

Indira Gandhi, the "Long 1970s," and the Cold War

PRIYA CHACKO

INTRODUCTION

The ideological conflict that underpinned the Cold War pitted the Soviet Union and the United States against each other as the successors to European modernity. This conflict manifested in their need to prove the universal applicability of their competing ideas through interventions in the Third World.[1] These interventions were undertaken through military means, covert political operations, and overt attempts to shape the economic trajectories of countries through foreign aid, technology transfers, and multilateral institutions. This chapter explores the consequences of Cold War economic statecraft—defined as the use of economic inducements or coercion to achieve foreign policy goals—on India's political and economic development. The chapter focuses specifically on attempts by the United States to influence India's economic policy in the late 1960s. The United States often used economic statecraft in a bid to spread American ideals of the free market and integrate its allies and nonaligned states, like India, into a U.S.-dominated global economic system.[2] The Marshall Plan, for instance, aimed to rebuild Europe in ways that would bring it in line with American economic and labor practices, and it served as the blueprint for the American approach in Asia.[3] Although Cold War competition had less extensive and destructive effects in India than in other countries, it still had significant consequences for India's political and economic development.

The argument presented here follows Peter Gourevitch's approach to understanding the relationship between international and domestic politics, which he called the "second image reversed," in his classic 1978 article. The "second image reversed" refers to the demarcation in international relations of the individual, the state, and the international system as the first, second, and third "image," respectively.[4] Critiquing the tendency in much of international relations and comparative politics at the time to treat the second image of domestic structure as an independent, intervening, or irrelevant variable in explanations of foreign policy, Gourevitch pointed to the rich tradition of scholarship including that of, among others, Alexander Gerschenkron and Immanuel Wallerstein that highlighted the impact of the international system on domestic political structures. Gourevitch's focus was the influence of the international distribution of power and the international economy, or what he termed "war and trade." Specifically, Gourevitch argued that external economic and military pressures help to shape, rather than determine, domestic policy making and politics. They do so, first, by influencing cleavages on policy questions, since international pressures require policy responses that result in mobilizing particular constituencies. Second, international pressures can influence institutional development, since different policy responses have specific institutional consequences.[5] There has been a rapid proliferation of literature taking a second image reversed perspective since the 1990s because of growing trade and production linkages, the expansion of international organizations and regimes, and the growing focus on issues of transnational concern, such as climate change. Yet the current concern with transnational flows should not obscure the interpenetrated nature of international relations and domestic politics in other periods such as the Cold War.

This chapter seeks to bring to the fore the role that American economic statecraft, as a contributing factor, played in domestic political and economic change in India during the Cold War. It begins by examining the impact of American Cold War economic statecraft in the 1950s and early 1960s. American assistance was used by India to consolidate an urban, industrial model of economic development that ultimately proved unsustainable. In the late 1960s, the consensus on India's economic direction broke down both internationally and domestically. These years of upheaval, from the late 1960s to the early 1980s, can be termed the "long 1970s," a period that is increasingly being recognized as a pivotal time of global crisis and reform.[6] China's reforms and improved relations with the United States during these years, for instance, put it on its path to becoming the "factory of the world."[7] Declining economic growth and rising inflation in the West resulted in a crisis in the postwar settlement of democratic capitalism and the introduction of "neoliberal" policies of monetary stabilization, restricted wage growth, privatization, deregulation, and trade liberalization.[8] Global human rights and environmental movements emerged in the 1970s owing to a variety of factors such as ecological and humanitarian disasters and technological change but, above all, as Samuel Moyn has suggested, "the collapse of other, prior utopias, both state-based and internationalist."[9] The long 1970s in India were similarly a period in which the collapsed utopias of earlier eras had created the space for the rise of new social forces, political actors, and ideas amid economic discontent and political flux. Although the erosion of the domestic political settlement had its own dynamics, it took place against a backdrop of Cold War politics that shaped such key domestic developments as Indira Gandhi's agrarian populism, economic nationalism, and, later, authoritarianism and probusiness economic policies. External factors contributed to domestic change in two central ways. First, pressure from the United States and multilateral agencies to liberalize the Indian economy empowered a preexisting pro–economic reform constituency and resulted in short-term policy shifts. These changes, however, could not be sustained because of the small size of the pro-reform faction and the nature of the consequences of the reforms that were undertaken, which were perceived to have compromised rather than bolstered India's autonomy. Second, these short-term developments would nonetheless have important consequences by contributing to institutional shifts within two dominant domestic actors, the Congress Party and the Planning Commission. These shifts induced significant long-term changes — namely, the circumvention of the liberalization of India's economy and modifications in agricultural policy.

The institutional and political outcomes of these domestic developments laid the path for the turn to the particular model of state capitalism that exists in India today. The 1970s were thus a critical juncture in India's political and economic development. In historical institutionalist analysis, a "critical juncture" is a period in which domestic structures — economic, cultural, ideological, and organizational — weaken for a period of time, thereby expanding the range of policy possibilities. A critical juncture is not necessarily a period of radical change. Rather, its significance lies in the creation of new or deeper political cleavages and in the reshaping of institutional arrangements in ways that have significant long-term consequences by triggering path-dependent processes that place constraints on future choices.[10]

Postindependence India's primary challenge was dealing with the legacies of the colonial encounter amid budding Cold War conflict and within an international system that emerged in the eras of colonialism and imperialism. Influenced by a number of intellectual currents including Fabian socialism, British liberalism, Gandhian nationalism, and Tagorean cosmopolitanism, the postindependence government embarked on what was famously described by Jawaharlal Nehru as "a third way which takes the best from all existing systems—the Russian, the American and others—and seeks to create something suited to one's own history and philosophy."[11] This model of democratic socialism was to be built by establishing a centrally planned economy based on import-substituting industrialization with state-owned enterprises and a tightly regulated private sector. It also incorporated a federal political structure with independent institutions, a free press and civil society, redistributive policies, and a state-mediated class compromise between labor and capital.[12] A focus on domestic savings, limited reliance on foreign aid, and food imports was to ensure India's autonomy. The government's approach to agriculture emphasized institutional changes in the form of land reforms, cooperatives, and the establishment of local government bodies. The main thrust of the economic model, however, was urban, industrial growth that would sustain and fund social transformation and poverty eradication through long-term modernization and urbanization rather than immediate wealth redistribution through expansive social policies or welfare programs.[13]

Nehru's third way included his policy of non-alignment, which meant that aid and technology could be obtained from both the Soviet Union and the United States. Despite the country's commitment to self-reliance, India's weak economy following colonial rule led its leadership to request economic assistance, especially from the United States, given its economic strength. American economic statecraft during the Cold War took form through direct government-to-government assistance, the Bretton Woods Institutions, and private U.S. foundations such as the Ford and Rockefeller Foundations. Although these organizations cannot be seen simply as agents of the American state, the United States was the dominant actor in the World Bank and International Monetary Fund (IMF), and private foundations worked closely with the U.S. government.[14] These organizations, moreover, were committed to the promotion of the basic tenets of the U.S. Cold

War ideology of capitalist growth and the defeat of communism.[15] Nelson Rockefeller, for instance, sought to convince Congress to finance the Tata Iron and Steel Corporation's expansion of its operations. He argued that "India's strategic importance to the United States in Southeast Asia" made it worthwhile to get a privately owned U.S.-built steel mill in operation before a Soviet-built mill was completed, as this would "provide a very interesting and important comparison in many aspects of U.S. versus U.S.S.R. enterprise and achievement."[16] Likewise, successive presidents of the World Bank, George Woods, an American banker, and Robert McNamara, a former U.S. secretary of defense, were driven to fund educational facilities and programs in India, despite these initially being seen as outside the bank's remit, in order to counter the successful mass literacy campaigns of socialist countries and what McNamara, in particular, saw as the clear link between poverty and communism.[17] Indian officials appealed directly to Cold War competition and the threat posed by communist China to India in their requests to the Truman administration for steel, food, and other commodities.[18] Yet the focus on Europe and the Marshall Plan, India's marginal place in the U.S. Cold War strategy, the scale of India's resource needs, and India's policy of non-alignment meant that these appeals for direct government-to-government aid amounted to little.[19] Instead, India was encouraged to seek support from the World Bank while the Ford and Rockefeller Foundations contributed to funding and implementing the government's Community Development Programs for the establishment of local government bodies and agricultural cooperatives.[20]

The distribution of government-to-government aid became a key part of U.S. Cold War strategy from the 1950s only when concerns about the communist threat moved from Europe to Asia following the Chinese Revolution and North Korea's attack on the South. American concerns about India centered on the growing influence of the Soviet Union in the country and fears that India's economic failure would undermine the democratic path to development, particularly given the emergence of China and its rival communist model.[21] In 1951 an American loan supplied two million tons of wheat to India, and in 1952 the two governments signed the Indo-American Technical Agreement. India soon became the major beneficiary of the 1954 Public Law 480 Act (PL-480), which authorized the export of surplus grain and other commodities produced by the price supports given to U.S. farmers through concessional sales to countries experiencing food shortages. This was because even though food grain production in India grew steadily in the 1950s after the expansion of irrigation and fertilizer use, the government's Second

Five-Year Plan in 1956 decreased the funds available for agriculture in order to place emphasis on the industrial sector. Moreover, major institutional reforms like land reform were not successfully implemented. Subsequently, and due also to the failure of monsoon rains, agricultural production fell, shortages of some commodities began to appear in urban areas, and agricultural prices fluctuated.[22]

Aside from government-to-government assistance, in 1958 an Aid India Consortium was set up by the World Bank, with the United States as its driving force.[23] The broad goal of U.S. economic statecraft was to restructure the societies of recipient countries to allow market access, the export of profits, and the exclusion of communists and socialists from political leadership.[24] With regard to India specifically, the U.S. government was focused on agricultural development, and in this it was assisted by the Ford and Rockefeller Foundations. This reflected the emerging place of both India and Pakistan as frontline states in the Cold War in the minds of U.S. military strategists. The Truman administration regarded India as key to South Asian stability, and an economic aid program was thought necessary to ensure its stability, promote its orientation to the West, and provide raw materials and manpower for the United States' national defense.[25]

American aid to India, however, achieved none of these aims, as the Indian government persisted with plans for industrialization and urban modernization while remaining nonaligned. American imports were a relatively small, though significant, proportion of India's overall food stocks, peaking at 15 percent in 1966.[26] Specifically, during the 1950s and 1960s, concessional food imports from the United States were used to underwrite India's urban, industrial model of planned economic development, and as Nick Cullather notes, they had the effect of changing consumption and production patterns in ways that increased India's food dependence on the United States.[27] American wheat, in particular, stocked the fair-price shops that sold subsidized food commodities to consumers under the government's food welfare program, the Public Distribution System (PDS). American wheat facilitated the expansion of the PDS between 1957 and 1965, but this expansion was designed to further industrial growth by keeping food prices and wages low for urban workers rather than for the rural poor.[28] Cold War U.S. economic statecraft thus helped to sustain rather than challenge or undermine the urban, industrial-focused mixed-economy model preferred by the Indian leadership. When the legitimacy of this model was called into question in the late 1960s, however, the United States was able to take advantage of the weakening of domestic policy consensus to attempt to reshape the nature of

India's political economy in accordance with U.S. preferences using more coercive tools of economic statecraft.

THE EROSION OF THE "NEHRUVIAN CONSENSUS": INTERNATIONAL PRESSURES AND DOMESTIC RESPONSES

The legitimacy of the "Nehruvian consensus" of democratic socialism through urban, industrial modernization and a planned economy had begun to erode by the mid-1960s, both domestically and internationally. Domestically, although India had experienced steady, if modest, industrial and economic growth during the Nehru era, the benefits of this growth were unevenly spread, and the projected targets for India's public-sector programs were not met. The compromise envisaged between labor and capital in 1947 had failed to materialize. The national Congress leadership focused instead on a development policy premised on a partnership between the state and business with labor accommodated within this system.[29] Although this move increased the power of the state with respect to labor, Vivek Chibber argues that its compromise with capital left it unable to impose the disciplinary state apparatus necessary to create a developmental state that could facilitate social transformation.[30] The resistance of the rural elite and the reliance of the Congress's regional leaders on their support stymied agricultural reforms.[31] In addition, as mentioned above, the failure of monsoon rains contributed to a 17 percent decline in food production between 1964 and 1966, with a resulting rise in food prices. Increased defense expenditure due to wars with China and Pakistan also put stress on India's foreign exchange reserves.[32]

Major changes in economic policy making, however, became possible only after Nehru's death in 1964 and the elevation of the comparatively weak leader Lal Bahadur Shastri, who lacked a power base or strong ideological beliefs and preferred consultative, consensual economic decision-making. In addition, the failure of the government's food policies and an increasingly vocal business community, which was critical of planning and the neglect of consumer industries and agriculture, also created a domestic push for policy change.[33] At the same time, India's dependence on the United States, the World Bank, and the IMF to deal with its food and foreign exchange shortfalls gave these external actors a level of influence to press the government for reforms that they had not previously had. This heightened ability to influence Indian policy coincided with political changes in the United States following the election of Lyndon Johnson and the evolution of the World Bank as a financial institution. Elected in 1963, Johnson promoted a distinctive agenda that he called the Great Society. This involved a domestic reform program aimed at putting "an end to poverty and racial injustice" through social welfare schemes and investments in education and health care, as well as a foreign policy agenda that would make it "possible for all nations to live in enduring peace."[34] Johnson often remarked that his foreign policy was based on the export of his Great Society reforms, and democratic India became key to his vision.[35]

By 1963, under the presidency of Woods, the World Bank began to move away from its role as a commercial bank concerned mainly with project loans for investments in infrastructure and physical assets toward a focus on influencing the economic policies of its loan recipients, particularly in the area of agricultural policy.[36] The consensus of the 1940s and 1950s among such leading development economists as Walt Rostow, Raul Prebisch, and P. C. Mahalanobis that industry rather than agriculture was the engine of economic growth broke down in the 1960s. So too did the idea that import substitution could be used in conjunction with export promotion to facilitate rapid industrialization.[37] India's economic policies came in for particular criticism from 1958, as the failure of land reforms to take place was judged to show that agricultural policy based on institutional reform was unrealistic. The inability of India's public sector undertakings to meet targets was also taken to indicate that a greater role was needed for the Indian private sector and foreign private capital.[38] In the 1960s, the World Bank and the U.S. government pressed for the devaluation of the Indian rupee and changes in agricultural policy. The coercive ways in which this external pressure was applied, and the consequences of their adoption, shaped policy cleavages in India in ways that would reinforce anti-reform positions in relation to the liberalization of industrial policy while strengthening pro-reform constituencies in relation to agricultural policy.

International Pressures: The "Short-Tether" Strategy and the Suspension of Aid

The recommendation to devalue the Indian rupee was raised in the World Bank's Bell Mission report, named after Bernard Bell, who led the team tasked with evaluating India's Third Five-Year Plan in 1965. The major themes of the Bell report were the need for India to reorient its public investment to agriculture, move toward import liberalization, and establish export-oriented industries. The report's first recommendation was to devalue the Indian currency because the overvalued exchange rate reduced India's economic competitiveness by making its exports comparatively more expensive. In exchange for adopting these reforms, the World Bank promised substantial increases in foreign assistance to India from the Aid India Consortium, and in 1966, the IMF made the issuance of further loans conditional on currency devaluation.[39]

In 1965, the U.S. government adopted a more coercive form of economic statecraft, the "short-tether" policy, which released food grain in short-term rather than multiyear shipments and tied the continued supply of grain to the requirement that recipient nations, including India, undertake reforms toward food self-sufficiency. As Kristin L. Ahlberg has shown, this change in policy was Johnson's attempt to internationalize his Great Society vision through what he described in his 1966 State of the Union address as a "worldwide attack on hunger and disease and ignorance."[40] His focus on India reflected the belief that, as his adviser Robert Komer put it, the country was "essential to our Asian containment strategy of boxing in Red China."[41] The short-tether strategy aimed to restructure India's agricultural policy using American "know-how" under a revitalized PL-480 program, renamed Food for Peace. Such an initiative, according to Orville Freeman, the secretary of agriculture, "would capture the imagination of people from palaces to palisades, to slums, to mud huts all over the world."[42] In addition, the short-tether strategy was aimed at moderating India's criticisms of the Vietnam War while diverting funds from defense spending into agriculture, thereby lowering the chance of war with Pakistan and preventing India from developing a nuclear deterrent against China.[43]

To strengthen its argument for economic policy reform, the U.S. government highlighted a new type of statistical modeling to predict global food needs. The development of this new tool was prompted by the growing panic about global population growth and the Cold War context in which mass starvation in places like China and Ukraine was interpreted as indicating the failure of communism.[44] Regarding India, the modeling assessments predicted food deficits of various extents. The U.S. Department of Agriculture, for instance, predicted a calamity several times more serious than the devastating Bengal famine of 1943, which killed millions.[45] The short-tether strategy, however, failed to prevent the outbreak of the 1965 India-Pakistan War, following which the United States suspended aid altogether and made its resumption conditional on broader changes to economic policy that were in line with the Bell Mission's recommendations.[46]

A domestic constituency that was in favor of reform used the World Bank's intervention, the U.S. government's statistical modeling, and the short-tether policy to strengthen its position against opponents of reform, such as Finance Minister T. T. Krishnamachari and members of the Planning Commission. A major pro-reform advocate was C. Subramaniam, whom Shastri had appointed to the Agriculture Ministry and the Planning Commission to break down its opposition to agricultural reforms. Another key advocate of reform was L. K. Jha, a former finance secretary whom Shastri had appointed to the prime minister's Secretariat, which emerged as an alternative source of policy advice. Asoka Mehta, the deputy chairman of the Planning Commission, and several state chief ministers had also changed their positions to favor the introduction of price incentives for farmers, modern technology to boost agricultural production, and greater reliance on private investment.[47] The reforms they sought were broadly in line with those being pushed by the World Bank, the Ford Foundation, and U.S. advisers and included a mixture of currency devaluation, the use of high-yielding seed varieties, fertilizers, and price incentives for farmers, and a population control program.[48]

The pro-reform constituency gained traction in 1966 when the suspension of U.S. aid and the unwillingness of the IMF to issue further loans deepened India's foreign exchange crisis. Indira Gandhi, who had succeeded Shastri as prime minister after his death in 1965, tasked a new committee with considering economic reforms.[49] The committee consisted of advocates of currency devaluation and agricultural reform, including Mehta, Subramaniam, the new finance minister Sachin Chaudhuri, and L. K. Jha, all of whom viewed devaluation as the only way of regaining access to foreign aid.[50] Subramaniam had received assurances in 1965 that the government's agricultural reforms, which had already begun to be implemented, would result in the resumption of U.S. food shipments. Moreover, after the government's decision to devalue the rupee in January 1966 was relayed to the IMF, the organization approved a line of credit for $187 million.[51] Chaudhuri announced the 37 percent currency devaluation in June 1966 and introduced other reforms, including lower import duties, tax credits, and the opening of state industries, such as fertilizer production, to foreign investors. The reforms had their desired effect on the U.S. government, which resumed its aid almost immediately but maintained the short-tether strategy of monthly shipments of grain.[52]

The domestic reaction to the currency devaluation, however, was vociferously negative, and this sentiment crossed ideological lines. Expressions of dismay came from the conservative Swatantra Party, the Hindu nationalist Jana Sangh, and the Communist Party of India, which accused the Bretton Woods Institutions and the U.S. government of forcing India "down to her knees" and the Congress Party of the "greatest betrayal of national interest since Independence."[53] There was discontent too from within the Congress Party, particularly owing to the exclusion of senior party leaders such as party president K. Kamaraj from the decision-making process.[54] In general, the business community had gone along with the currency devaluation as a temporary measure owing to the shortfall of foreign exchange but had sought greater export assistance from the government.[55] The decision to expand the use of chemical fertilizers with U.S. assistance and the reliance on foreign aid, more generally, also generated protest from the left, while the continued use of the short-tether strategy by the U.S. government provoked resentment, anxiety, and anger among the public and Congress rank and file owing to the perception that India was losing its independence in foreign policy making.[56]

Political and Policy Flux

This opposition reinvigorated the Planning Commission, which released a Draft Outline of the Fourth Plan that sought to reverse the government's liberalizing reforms while marginally lowering spending on agriculture. The plan argued against reliance on production increases in agriculture and placed the focus back on public sector industrial production.[57] Yet although the Draft Outline addressed concerns about economic liberalization, it faced extensive criticism from within the Congress, the chief ministers of state governments, the opposition, and the business community for its treatment of agriculture and the continuing dependence on foreign aid. The Planning Commission had misinterpreted the opposition to liberalization as support for a return to the status quo in agricultural policy. Subsequently, Indira Gandhi abandoned the Draft Outline while disbanding the Planning Commission and reconstituting its membership.

The impact of currency devaluation turned out to be far less favorable to India's trade balance than expected, and the Aid India Consortium did not deliver on its promised increases in aid, in large part because of U.S. congressional cuts to the foreign aid budget.[58] Moreover, in the wake of the currency devaluation, Indira Gandhi's government suffered shock losses in the 1967 election at both the national and state levels, while food shortages intensi-

Priya Chacko

fied and inflation rose, causing deaths in Bihar and triggering riots in Kerala and West Bengal. These events meant that when a new Draft Outline of the Fourth Five-Year Plan was finally handed down in 1969, agricultural reform received priority, with the achievement of national food self-sufficiency as the ultimate goal. With the diversion of funds to agriculture, greater reliance was placed on the private sector to stimulate growth in industrial production through the relaxation of controls on industrial licensing.[59] The aftermath of the currency devaluation also heightened tensions within the Congress Party between senior party leaders, collectively known as the Syndicate, and an increasingly assertive Indira Gandhi.

Political and Policy Outcomes

External pressure from Cold War U.S. economic statecraft thus contributed to exposing and deepening political cleavages within the previously Congress-dominated polity and within the Congress Party itself. This had several major political and policy outcomes. The tensions within the Congress Party came to a head after Gandhi moved to nationalize commercial banks in 1969. This was the beginning of a populist turn designed to establish her dominance over policy making in the party while building a popular support base through the cultivation of an antagonism between a loosely defined "rural poor" and "urban rich."[60] Major institutional change ensued with the breakup of the Congress Party in 1969 into the Congress (O) (Organisation) of the Syndicate and Indira Gandhi's Congress (R) (Requisition). This in turn led to long-term policy change because, in attempting to consolidate her power following the split in the Congress Party, Indira Gandhi initiated a so-called socialist turn in economic policy. The final version of the Fourth-Year Plan, released in 1970, reversed the loosening of industrial licensing requirements in the 1969 Draft Outline of the Fourth Plan, established a new bureaucratic apparatus to regulate the private sector, placed new restrictions on big industrial houses, and introduced a Foreign Exchange Regulation Act to limit inflows of foreign capital.[61]

The diminished influence of the Planning Commission in economic policy making was another long-term institutional shift that would have important policy consequences. Initially established as a central actor in a national planning process, the Planning Commission was now an advisory body to the national and state leaderships and subordinate to the ministries. The reduced power of the Planning Commission removed a key barrier against a pivotal shift in agricultural policy away from an institutional approach that aimed at fundamental social change to one based on price incentives and technology. The most significant outcome of this shift was the Green Revolution — a set of agricultural policies that included the use of high-yielding seed varieties, higher fertilizer use, the expansion of irrigation, and the use of incentives such as price supports for farmers and subsidies for water and irrigation.

THE LONG 1970S AS A CRITICAL JUNCTURE

The political cleavages and institutional changes that emerged in the late 1960s became further entrenched during the 1970s, producing path-dependent processes that would have a long-term impact on India's political economy. For instance, the implementation of Green Revolution agricultural reforms boosted wheat production and created a class of large and middling capitalist farmers in the wheat-growing areas of northern India. The more serious problems of inequality in land distribution and land tenure, however, meant that the yields of rice, India's most extensively grown crop showed little improvement.[62] The empowerment of surplus-producing farmers in the northern Indian states of Punjab, Haryana, and western Uttar Pradesh, led to the emergence of an "oppositional populism" by farmers' movements, and eventually political parties, that advanced critiques of the "urban bias" in the dominant development regime.[63] This shifted the power dynamic in the dominant class coalition by expanding the ranks of the rural elite and entrenched a system of agricultural subsidies that persists today.[64] Partha Chatterjee argues that since economic liberalization in the 1990s, the dominant class coalition now consists of a corporate capitalist class, landed elite, and managerial-bureaucratic class and that, within this coalition, the corporate capitalist class is in the ascendant.[65] However, as the failed attempt to alter the Land Acquisition Act to make it more business friendly indicates, farmers' organizations remain potent policy actors.[66] Aside from the political interests created by the Green Revolution, as a study on the persistence of electricity and fertilizer subsidies has shown, proponents of ongoing subsidies have successfully linked them to the goal of food self-sufficiency, which became paramount in the late 1960s, in large part, because of the coercive economic statecraft employed by the United States.[67] Food self-sufficiency remains a key political goal and source of political legitimacy for policy makers across the spectrum, against the arguments of advocates of economic reform that global food markets are now sufficient to ensure food security.

In early 1970, following the Congress Party split, Indira Gandhi dissolved parliament and called an early election. Her sweeping election victory launched a spate of new redistributive programs with a rural focus, such as the Small Farmer's Development Agency and the Drought-Prone Areas Program, which provided subsidized loans and public employment to increase the income and consumption of the rural poor. Where the Nehruvian state emphasized industrial growth with redistribution and welfare as a secondary priority, Gandhi's government highlighted redistribution in its own right. This agenda positioned the poor as an antagonistic force against the landlords and urban elite who were the core constituencies and allies of her political opponents in the Congress (O). The emergence of rural welfare programs represented a major change in the dominant model of development, in the basis of political legitimacy, and in the political expectations of the rural poor. The model of social transformation through state-led growth, modernization, and urbanization that had underpinned the Nehruvian state was replaced with a twin-track strategy of growth produced through private incentives in combination with schemes for poverty alleviation. Appeals to growth alongside social justice have since become a staple of the election campaigns and policy platforms of the two major political parties, the Congress and the Bharatiya Janata Party.[68]

Finally, a business-state alliance has emerged as a core part of India's model of state capitalism, the origins of which are usually traced to the 1980s. Key changes toward business and industrial policy, however, began to appear in the mid-1970s.[69] This was the outcome of reforms to agriculture and industrial policy, the continued failures of implementation by an increasingly deinstitutionalized Congress Party, and the spike in international oil prices that together revealed the limitations of the path chosen in 1970. Agricultural reforms, as noted above, worked to increase rural inequality, while social welfare schemes failed to improve these inequities in any substantial way. The agrarian welfare programs of the 1970s changed state-society and intrasocietal relationships to the extent that, at least in some areas, the state was seen as more accountable to lower-caste rural laborers, which in turn lessened the ability of the landed elite to underpay or threaten violence against these groups.[70] However, in the absence of a concerted, grass-roots organizational effort at the state and local level to challenge the power of landed elites, poverty alleviation programs had a limited impact.[71] By 1972–73, the Green Revolution's limitations were also becoming clear as wheat production started to fall due to depleted soil fertility, inadequate electricity supplies, and fertilizer shortages. The approach taken to agriculture and welfare, therefore, was not able to facilitate the creation of the strong domestic market necessary for a successful import-substituting industrialization strategy.[72] The decline in food production, the center's inability to widen the tax base, a sharp rise in international oil prices, and the financial burden of the war with Pakistan in 1971 all contributed to rising inflation, labor unrest—as workers' real wages fell—and a perilous balance of payments situation. Moreover, the tightening of industrial licensing, the limitations on external investment, and the threat of nationalization meant that the private sector remained stagnant.[73] In 1973, an attempt to take over the private wheat trade imperiled the food welfare scheme, the PDS, by reducing rations and raising prices. This was caused by resistance from private traders, who continued to trade illegally, and state government workers, who abetted them.[74]

The threat posed by inflation to economic development and social stability, in particular, prompted Indira Gandhi to seek out new ideas and advisers on economic policy, such as Manmohan Singh, who later presided over India's liberalization. She also approached the World Bank and IMF for loans to shore up India's balance of payments.[75] Unlike in 1966, however, changes in Cold War politics and the consequences of the short-tether policy and currency devaluation meant that external pressure on India to reform was largely absent. Although some senior World Bank officials made calls for greater oversight of India's economic policies in exchange for loans, the experience of 1966 meant that the bank had since sought to avoid macro-conditionality with India and was wary of giving the impression of complicity with U.S. economic statecraft.[76] The United States also had little role in shaping policy cleavages during this economic shift. This was caused by Indian criticisms of U.S. foreign policy, India's reluctance to succumb again to aid dependence on the United States, and the deterioration of India-U.S. relations following American arms sales to Pakistan, which had become an important Cold War ally.[77]

Among the early pro-business changes made in the mid-1970s, before and during the period of authoritarian rule known as the Emergency, were a wage freeze, the loosening of industrial licensing to boost production and increase exports, automatic approval of import licenses, and pegging the rupee to the pound sterling, thereby indirectly devaluing the currency. A particular target of the reforms to licensing and import restrictions was export-oriented engineering industries.[78] These reforms were consolidated after Indira Gandhi returned to power in 1980. Following another spike in oil prices and a major drought, Gandhi introduced a range of policies, such as the reduction of corporate taxes and restraining labor, to support big capital in the interests of prioritizing economic growth.[79]

Priya Chacko

CONCLUSION

In the history of India's political economy, the 1970s are usually seen as a period of socialist radicalism that India had to cast off to achieve high growth rates and a liberal economy. In fact, however, the central character-istics of the model of state capitalism that exists today had their origins in what many have called the long 1970s. This chapter highlights the role that Cold War economic statecraft played in creating these path-dependent char-acteristics. For much of the 1950s and 1960s, the Indian leadership used U.S. economic assistance to bolster its chosen economic path of urban, indus-trial modernization through import substitution. This reflected the U.S. lack of interest in using coercive economic statecraft to change India's behavior and the consensus on India's development strategy until the late 1950s in the Bretton Woods Institutions and among American philanthropic bodies. At the end of the 1960s, a distinctive set of circumstances, including domestic political and economic change in the United States and India, drought, and war, created a context in which the United States, the World Bank, and the IMF sought to deploy coercive economic statecraft to bring about changes in agricultural and economic policy. This economic statecraft was not di-rectly responsible for the policy changes that eventuated but rather, helped to influence the process by exposing and deepening policy cleavages. This, in turn, induced long-term institutional changes. When another window for reform opened in the mid-1970s, however, further changes in Cold War poli-tics meant that neither the United States nor the World Bank could greatly influence the process of economic reform, which proceeded in ways that would consolidate an indigenous business-state alliance. In these ways, the twists and turns of the Cold War played an important role in the evolu-tion of India's political economy and its current model of state-permeated capitalism.

NOTES

1. Odd Arne Westad, *The Global Cold War: Third World Interventions and the Making of Our Times* (Cambridge: Cambridge University Press, 2005), 5.

2. Jamey Essex, *Development, Security, and Aid: Geopolitics and Geoeconomics at the U.S. Agency for International Development* (Athens: University of Georgia Press, 2013), 557.

3. Michael Cox, "From the Truman Doctrine to the Second Superpower Detente: The Rise and Fall of the Cold War," *Journal of Peace Research* 27, no. 1 (1990): 6.

4. Peter Gourevitch, "The Second Image Reversed: The International Sources of Domestic Politics," *International Organization* 32, no. 4 (1978): 419–38. This "images" or levels of analysis approach derives from the work of Kenneth Waltz. See Kenneth N. Waltz,

Man, the State, and War: A Theoretical Analysis (New York: Columbia University Press, 1959).

5. Peter Gourevitch, "Reinventing the American State: Political Dynamics in the Cold War Era," in *Shaped by War and Trade*, ed. Ira Katznelson and Martin Shefter (Princeton, N.J.: Princeton University Press, 2002), 303–4.

6. Niall Ferguson et al., eds., *The Shock of the Global: The 1970s in Perspective* (Cambridge, Mass.: Belnap Press of Harvard University Press, 2010); Jan Eckel and Samuel Moyn, eds., *The Breakthrough: Human Rights in the 1970s* (Philadelphia: University of Pennsylvania Press, 2013); Samuel Moyn, *Human Rights and the Uses of History* (London: Verso, 2014); Daniel J. Sargent, *A Superpower Transformed: The Remaking of American Foreign Relations in the 1970s* (Oxford: Oxford University Press, 2015).

7. Odd Arne Westad, "The Great Transformation: China in the Long 1970s," in Ferguson, *Shock of the Global*.

8. Wolfgang Streeck, "The Crises of Democratic Capitalism," *New Left Review*, no. 71 (2011): 5–29; David Harvey, *A Brief History of Neoliberalism* (Oxford: Oxford University Press, 2005).

9. J. R. McNeill, "The Environment, Environmentalism and International Society in the Long 1970s," in Ferguson, *Shock of the Global*; Samuel Moyn, *The Last Utopia: Human Rights in History* (Cambridge, Mass.: Belknap Press of Harvard University Press, 2010), 8. Moyn makes this comment in relation to the human rights movement, but it applies equally to global environmentalism.

10. Giovanni Capoccia and R. Daniel Kelemen, "The Study of Critical Junctures: Theory, Narrative, and Counterfactuals in Historical Institutionalism," *World Politics* 59, no. 3 (2007): 348.

11. R. K. Karanjia, *The Mind of Mr Nehru: An Interview* (London: Allen and Unwin, 1960), 100–101.

12. Vivek Chibber, "From Class Compromise to Class Accommodation: Labour's Incorporation into the Indian Political Economy," in *Social Movements in India: Poverty, Power, and Politics*, ed. Raka Ray and Mary Fainsod Katzenstein (Lanham, Md.: Rowman and Littlefield, 2005); Atul Kohli, *State-Directed Development: Political Power and Industrialisation in the Global Periphery* (Cambridge: Cambridge University Press, 2004).

13. Ashutosh Varshney, "Ideas, Interest and Institutions in Policy Change: Transformation of India's Agricultural Strategy in the Mid-1960s," *Policy Sciences* 22, no. 3–4 (1989): 292.

14. Corinna R. Unger, "Towards Global Equilibrium: American Foundations and Indian Modernization, 1950s to 1970s," *Journal of Global History* 6, no. 1 (2011): 121–42; Westad, *Global Cold War*, 153.

15. Arturo Escobar, *Encountering Development: The Making and Unmaking of the Third World* (Princeton, N.J.: Princeton University Press, 1995).

16. Cited in Dennis Merrill, *Bread and the Ballot: The United States and India's Economic Development* (Chapel Hill: University of North Carolina Press, 1990), 120.

17. Charles Dorn and Kristen Ghodsee, "The Cold War Politicization of Literacy: Communism, UNESCO, and the World Bank," *Diplomatic History* 36, no. 2 (2012): 394–95.

18. R. J. McMahon, *The Cold War on the Periphery: The United States, India, and Pakistan* (New York: Columbia University Press, 1994), 47.

19. Ibid., 49, 59.

20. Merrill, *Bread and the Ballot*, 120–22.

21. Nick Cullather, "Hunger and Containment: How India Became 'Important' in U.S. Cold War Strategy," *India Review* 6, no. 2 (2007): 64.

22. Francine R. Frankel, *India's Political Economy: 1947–2004*, 2nd ed. (New Delhi: Oxford University Press, 2005), 137–42.

23. Jason A. Kirk, *India and the World Bank: The Politics of Aid and Influence* (London: Anthem, 2011), 12.

24. Westad, *Global Cold War*, 31.

25. Richard P. Dauer, *A North-South Mind in an East-West World: Chester Bowles and the Making of United States Cold War Foreign Policy, 1951–1969* (Westport, Conn.: Praeger, 2005), 49–50; Cullather, "Hunger and Containment," 63.

26. Varshney, "Ideas, Interest and Institutions in Policy Change," 212.

27. Cullather, "Hunger and Containment," 70–71.

28. Jos Mooij, "Food Policy and Politics: The Political Economy of the Public Distribution System in India," *Journal of Peasant Studies* 25, no. 2 (1998): 83.

29. Chibber, "From Class Compromise to Class Accomodation."

30. Vivek Chibber, *Locked in Place: State-Building and Late Industrialization in India* (Princeton, N.J.: Princeton University Press, 2003).

31. Frankel, *India's Political Economy*, 183–84.

32. Rahul Mukherji, *Globalization and Deregulation: Ideas, Interests, and Institutional Change in India* (New Delhi: Oxford University Press, 2014), 42.

33. Frankel, *India's Political Economy*, 246–52.

34. Lyndon B. Johnson, "The Great Society," *Michigan Quarterly Review* 66, no. 2 (Fall 1964): 230.

35. Kristin L. Ahlberg, "'Machiavelli with a Heart': The Johnson Administration's Food for Peace Program in India, 1965–1966," *Diplomatic History* 31, no. 4 (2007): 672.

36. Devesh Kapur, John Prior Lewis, and Richard Charles Webb, *The World Bank: History*, vol. 1 (Washington, D.C.: Brookings Institution Press, 1997), 382.

37. Ibid., 381.

38. Frankel, *India's Political Economy*, 269.

39. Ibid., 271, 296.

40. Ahlberg, "'Machiavelli with a Heart,'" 687.

41. Ibid.

42. Cited in ibid., 677.

43. Ibid., 674.

44. Nick Cullather, *The Hungry World: America's Cold War Battle against Poverty in Asia* (Cambridge, Mass.: Harvard University Press, 2010), 218–19.

45. Ibid., 221.

46. Varshney, "Ideas, Interest and Institutions in Policy Change," 312–13.

47. Mukherji, *Globalization and Deregulation*, 5; Frankel, *India's Political Economy*, 251–59.

48. Cullather, *Hungry World*, 208.

49. Frankel, *India's Political Economy*, 296.

50. Ibid., 288, 29; Mukherji, *Globalization and Deregulation*, 54.

51. Frankel, *India's Political Economy*, 286, 297.

52. Ibid., 29; Varshney, "Ideas, Interest and Institutions in Policy Change," 313.

53. Cited in Mukherji, *Globalization and Deregulation*, 5; cited in Frankel, *India's Political Economy*, 300.

54. Rajni Kothari, "India: The Congress System on Trial," *Asian Survey* 7, no. 2 (1967): 87.

55. Mukherji, *Globalization and Deregulation*, 55–58.

56. Kothari, "India: The Congress System on Trial," 8; Varshney, "Ideas, Interest and Institutions in Policy Change," 313–14.

57. Frankel, *India's Political Economy*, 301–2.

58. Ibid., 322.

59. Ibid., 314–15.

60. Akhil Gupta, *Postcolonial Developments: Agriculture in the Making of Modern India* (Durham, N.C.: Duke University Press, 1998), 78–79.

61. Frankel, *India's Political Economy*, 437–38.

62. Ibid., 559.

63. Gupta, *Postcolonial Developments*, 74–75.

64. Pranab K. Bardhan, *The Political Economy of Development in India* (Oxford: B. Blackwell, 1984).

65. Partha Chatterjee, "Democracy and Economic Transformation in India," *Economic and Political Weekly* 43, no. 16 (2008): 56–57.

66. Pradeep Kaushal and Ruhi Tewari, "Land Bill: Modi Govt Gives In, Agrees to Bring Back UPA's Key Provisions," *Indian Express*, 4 August 2015.

67. Regina Birner, Surupa Gupta, and Neeru Sharma, *The Political Economy of Agricultural Policy Reform in India: Fertilizers and Electricity for Irrigation* (Washington, D.C.: International Food Policy Research Institute, 2011), 189.

68. Bharatiya Janata Party, "Election Manifesto 2014," Bharatiya Janata Party, http://www.bjp.org/manifesto2014; Indian National Congress, "An Expanding Economy — A Just Society — Freedom from Hunger and Unemployment," All India Congress, http://allindiacongress.com/admin/upload/pdf/Economic%20Agenda%202004.pdf (website no longer operational).

69. Atul Kohli, "Politics of Economic Growth in India, 1980–2005: Part I: The 1980s," *Economic and Political Weekly* 41, no. 13 (2006): 125; Srinath Raghavan, "Indira Gandhi: India and the World in Transition," in *Makers of Modern Asia*, ed. Ramachandra Guha (Cambridge, Mass.: Belknap Press of Harvard University Press, 2014), 234–35.

70. Gupta, *Postcolonial Developments*, 71–73.

71. Frankel, *India's Political Economy*, 507.

72. Ibid., 584.

73. Ibid., 510–13.

74. Ibid., 507–8.

75. Baldev Raj Nayar, *Globalization and Nationalism: The Changing Balance in India's Economic Policy, 1950–2000* (Thousand Oaks, Calif.: Sage, 2001), 11; Raghavan, "Indira Gandhi," 233.

76. Kirk, *India and the World Bank*, 22–24.

77. See *Foreign Relations of the United States, 1969–1976*, vol. E-8, *Documents on South Asia, 1973–1976*, ed. Paul J. Hibbeln and Peter A. Kraemer (Washington, D.C.: U.S. Government Printing Office, 2007), chaps. 4, 5.

78. Raghavan, "Indira Gandhi," 235–36.

79. Kohli, "Politics of Economic Growth in India, 1980–2005: Part I: The 1980s," 1256.

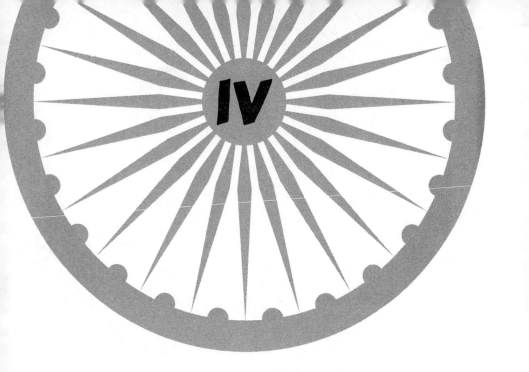

Epilogue

Chapter   Nine

Bertrand Russell in Bollyworld

Film, the Cold War, and a Postmortem on Peace

RAMINDER KAUR

In 1967 British philosopher-mathematician and social critic Bertrand Russell made a cameo appearance in a Hindi popular film, *Aman* (Peace, directed by Mohan Kumar). At the frail age of ninety-four, such a remarkable performance was not to be repeated, and neither has it merited scholarly attention. Russell's Indian movie debut is not in any stereotypical convention for the representation of white men in South Asia—the colonial officer lording it over others or the licentious cigarette-toting Westerner, as is often played out in the melodramatic idiom of mid-twentieth-century cinema. Nor does his appearance merely signal an early gesture at cinematic cosmopolitanism, as has become increasingly common in neoliberal cinema from the 1990s. Rather, a slight, bespectacled man sits on a flowery armchair wearing a taupe-colored three-piece suit set off with a pair of bright red slippers. Representative of a "guru of peace," he is in conversation with an overseas Indian student, Gautam Das, played by the renowned actor Rajendra Kumar. They talk about the iniquity of nuclear weapons and the need to help the people who were irradiated after bombs were dropped on two Japanese cities in August 1945.

How can we make sense of such an audiovisual excerpt inserted in an "epic melodrama," to use Ashis Rajadhyaksha's term to describe Indian popular cinema?[1] Melodrama is characterized by multiple plots, a drive toward excess, the sensational and spectacular, affective intensities and sensory overload, recourse to coincidences and reversals, and the significance of familial structures.[2] The scene with Russell seems to run counter to the ex-

Bertrand Russell meets Gautam Das. (*Aman* [1967])

pectations of this kind of Indian cinema as it does to expectations of a British philosopher and mathematician. Nevertheless, his appearance imbues a certain gravitas to the masala aesthetic that makes Russell both culturally and politically relevant to the film, and to an analysis of the larger Cold War context of the 1960s through the film.

Including a real-life and scripted character, the excerpt is not simply a documentary or a drama, yet it is a document and drama of the era — a period in which India's stance against the nuclear bomb, epitomized by the views of its first prime minister, Jawaharlal Nehru, was beginning to show signs of change. Even though the statesman had died three years before the film's release, Russell was present in the film to keep the Nehruvian vision alive. Containing elements of historical document and (melo)drama, the excerpt is an interpenetrative assemblage of the real and fictional that I call "docu-drama-ment" to distinguish it from its nearest cousin, docudrama or "true story" cinema.[3]

With a consideration of wider political currents that extend from the United States to Japan, this chapter places Indian cinema in the flows and counterflows of world history, lifting it from its national parameters.[4] Accordingly, the use of the term *Bollyworld* in the title ironically plays with the colloquial, sometimes controversial term *Bollywood* but also puts its nation-limited parameters under erasure.[5] In the case of *Aman*, the outer-national counter/flows are primarily to do with the horror of the United States' atomic attacks on Hiroshima and Nagasaki, the proliferation of atomic tests

Raminder Kaur

and weapons, a critique of imperialism, the international peace movement, and the postwar rise of Japan—this is in a period during the mid-twentieth century when the U.S.S.R. played a game of nuclear chess with China and, like their opponent, the United States, tried to court Indian officials who were manifestly committed to a policy of non-alignment during the peak of the Cold War era.[6]

THE MEETING OF MINDS

To return to the meeting of Russell with the medical expert in *Aman*, we have a variation of what Beatriz Jaguaribe calls the "shock of the real" to refer to graphic representations of urban violence in contemporary realist Brazilian film.[7] With this excerpt in the film, we have an instance of what might appear to be "the surprise of the real."[8] It is a surprise in that this particular encounter shakes our understanding of Indian mass entertainment as much as it does of a British rationalist philosopher and campaigner. A filmic convention overly tied to the effusive is pried open to make space for a foreign person discussing a topic of solemn sobriety. A priori categories to do with film, culture, and nation are disturbed as we try to work out why a philosopher-mathematician associated with the highbrow world of intellectualism and campaigns for world peace has presented himself in a cultural vehicle associated with the vernacular, and that too of a far removed national-cultural tenor.

But what to the Eurocentric "cognitive style" of decoding imagery is the "surprise of the real" may well be, to an audience acquainted with the popular film format, a "pedagogy of the real"—where the appearance of a distinguished British philosopher overlaid with the authorial voice of a narrator adds weight to the film medium as socially relevant pedagogy, a predominant theme in postindependent Indian cinema.[9]

Gautam Das is a recent graduate in medicine at a British university. His valorization of science reflects the postindependent stress on science and technology as a tool to uplift Indian society that Nehru wholly endorsed. Gautam has resolved to research a remedy for those people who were harmed by the atomic attacks in Hiroshima and Nagasaki. This is despite the fact that his mother was killed in the Japanese bombings of Burma during World War II. His medical mission is a consuming passion to show solidarity with the victims of war, no matter their nationality. His dedication to his work in some ways acts as a salve for his inability to save his mother's life as she died in his arms.

In a letter, Russell agrees to grant the young medic an interview. De-

A medical graduate, Gautam Das (played by Rajendra Kumar), venerates a photograph of Bertrand Russell in his room in London. (*Aman* [1967])

scribed as a *mahapurush* (literally a holy or great man), he is treated as a venerated sage. Gautam excitedly tells his friend:

> *Gautam*: I had never imagined that before leaving England I would be able to perform this pilgrimage too.
> *Friend*: Wow! A letter from Lord Bertrand Russell. He has called you for an interview, Khoka [a pet name for Gautam]!
> *Gautam*: Yes Panchu! Yes. For two years, I had been trying to get an audience with this great man.
> *Friend*: This great man is the only hope of the world. He is like the sun god in [a world of] darkness. What an honor![10]

Simultaneously overjoyed and humbled, Gautam walks up to Russell's portrait hanging on the wall of his residence and salutes it, saying, "Thank you very much sir." The stage is set to introduce to the film's audience, "the only hope of the world" for peace — the only hope because India's renowned ambassadors of peace, Mohandas Karamchand [Mahatma] Gandhi and Nehru, were no longer alive at the time of the film's release.

Dressed in his best, Gautam attends the meeting and sits opposite Russell in his armchair. He explains to Russell that he has made a decision to help and find a remedy for radiation overexposure: "I have been a medical student, here in England, for the last four years. And all these years, I've been going through your teachings, statements and writings on world peace and against atomic war. And, in fact, your thoughts have shaped the philosophy

Raminder Kaur

of my life, sir. . . . Before embarking on my plans, I want to have your guidance." As Gautam speaks in English, a narrator's voice glides in, explaining the scene in Hindi to the film spectator.

> *Narrator*: Young Dr. Gautam told Lord Russell that he was very
> impressed by reading and listening to his views against the
> atom bomb and in favor of peace in the world. That is why he
> had decided not to go back to his country, but instead to go to
> Japan and serve those thousands of unfortunate patients who,
> as victims of the atom bomb, are stricken with incurable and
> dangerous illnesses.
> *Gautam continues in English*: I will consider myself very fortunate
> if I will be able to do anything for them. And before I take this
> project on my shoulders, I want your blessings.

The voiceover moves beyond the diegetic interpersonal between men of learning, one actual (Bertrand), another fictional (Gautam), and assumes a superindividuated register as a voice of learning directly addressed to the audience before returning to the men in the film.

The film is also notable for its invocations and phantasms of Nehru.[11] It begins with a portrait of India's late prime minister with the statement, "This motion picture is humbly dedicated to the esteemed memory of Pandit Jawaharlal Nehru, apostle of peace." It ends with allegorical reference to Nehru's stately funeral procession in 1964 when the film commemorates Gautam's death in a public display on the streets of Delhi. In between, Gautam's encounter with Russell itself raises a Nehruvian phantasm as they exchange views endorsed by the late statesman — a commitment to promoting a peaceful and nonnuclear world and the development of science in the service of society.[12]

Radiation concerns also bring together the three personas — phantasmal, actual, and fictional. Nehru was in fact one of the first statesmen to warn against the dangers of nuclear radiation. He had commissioned a survey on the effects of nuclear explosions as they began to be conducted with increasing regularity by the United States, the U.S.S.R., and the United Kingdom.[13] The decision to undertake the survey was made after a 1955 visit to London in which he had met Russell. Both were against the atomic bomb and the need for "neutral nations" such as India in a period of increasing antagonism between superpowers as Cold War tensions mounted.[14] Gautam is of a similar persuasion. He is vehemently against nuclear bombs, decrying their proponents as *shaitan* (devils). Equally, he is a firm believer in the constructive use of science for people's benefit. Russell recognizes these chords in Gautam, and responds: "I do most profoundly hope that you will succeed in finding a cure which medical men hitherto have not succeeded in. . . . Your work is of great importance. . . . And I consider that all nations should help you in this difficult work." The narrator reiterates in Hindi, underlining the importance of Gautam's work for the world: "And the leader of peace, Lord Russell, while giving his blessings, told Dr. Gautam that 'my well wishes are with you. This problem is the problem of the whole world and I hope that you will be successful in this endeavor. I respect your views. Your work is of great importance and I hope that all the countries of the world would appreciate your work.'"

With Russell's blessings, Gautam is "honored and encouraged" to pursue his medical research, and instead of staying in India with his father, he relocates to Japan. He embarks on what others might see as an impossible task—finding a "cure" for radiation-related illnesses. He begins work in the Michiko Nuclear Diseases Memorial Hospital, a center that takes care of atomic bomb victim-survivors, more on which will follow after a theoretical consideration of the filmic assemblage and its interpretations in vastly different historical and political contexts.

DRAMATIC DOCUMENTS

The epic melodrama of popular cinema is very distinct from realist cinema that, in India, pertains more to the "art cinema" associated with Satyajit Ray from the 1960s and the "parallel cinema" that emerged during the 1970s. While the former catered to the national mainstream, the latter was addressed to relatively limited audiences in India—mainly the urban, often English-educated middle class and elites conscious of international standards set in cinema.[15] Multiple artistic and cultural traditions that informed the development of Indian popular cinema mean that the film refuses a linear narrational track. As well as its masala aesthetic, there is always something beyond the frame that animates the screen, be it godly, mythical, miraculous, or, increasingly after India's independence in 1947, allegories of the modern nation. In the film, Russell assumes a saintly role in the age-old tradition of the student-teacher relation, *guru-shishya*. His photo is approached as if it were a modern-day deity, Gautam goes to him for his blessings as he might his guru, and the graduate listens with intent and delight when he goes to meet him to approve his project.[16] However idiosyncratic Russell might ap-

Raminder Kaur

pear, what could be described as the "foreign particle" is couched in familiar cultural and filmic conventions of the epic melodrama.

The excerpt is not in the conventional sense of *dramatized reenactments* of actual events that happened, as might occur in a docudrama or true story cinema.[17] These are characterized by the use of literary and narrative techniques to flesh out the known "facts" of a series of events with which creative license is taken for the sake of enhancing the story. In the process, *reality effects* are created that may appeal to the affective register of suspense, terror, happiness, or sadness, which the lean and cold vehicle of documentary may not be able to accomplish on its own. But we cannot say that this encounter with Russell and an Indian medical student actually happened. Nor does docudrama or true story cinema combine fictional with real-life characters in the same mise-en-scène.

Neither is *Aman* a variation on the theme of docufiction, a recording of contemporary lives as with direct cinema or *cinema verité*, where the camera is used to provoke a certain kind of spontaneous reaction or fictional situation.[18] Rather it is something else, something to do with a film that tries to capture the particularities and urgencies of the historical moment with living, absent, and fictional characters. Like trying to catch theoretical butterflies, nomenclature simply fails the object of description. This is where the term *docu-drama-ment* is of potential use to view the overlaps between the real and the fictional, the present and the absent, in *Aman*.

Conventionally, the documentary and drama, like their homologies, fact/nonfiction and fiction, are seen as distinct from each other. But this view overlooks the constructed nature of the documentary and its monopoly on representing truth. Throughout its historical development, the camera, whether it be still or moving, has had a commanding claim on veracity and evidence. Such imaging technologies hold the status of mirrors to the lived world.[19] While fictional films revel in their contrived constructions, documentaries that claim to represent the real conceal their constructed nature, created as they are out of various entities such as photographs, interviews, tape recordings of sounds, and the influence of directors, editors, and narrators. In all cases, the real is being selected and represented and is thus never equal to the raw reality it pertains to represent. Theorists have pointed out that having any filmic recording of an event is a "text." Film footage is necessarily an imprint from a particular angle and thus an incomplete representation of any event. As Vietnamese filmmaker and theorist Trinh T. Minh-ha argues: "There is no such thing as a documentary—whether the term designates a category of material, a genre, an approach, or a set of techniques."[20] What we call a documentary is actually part and parcel of a documentary effect—a reality created by the synchronization of sound and twenty-four images over one second that we have come to accept as natural, along with the use of such other conventions as grainy and sometimes handheld shaky newsreel, talking heads speaking to the camera, and/or a person off-center addressing the subject to convey the apparently unadulterated delivery of information to the viewer.

So although docudrama implies the conjunction of documentary and drama in which the former pertains to an actuality and the latter a fiction, I too propose that the documentary is a textual construct: hence the destabilizing of the two categories with the double-sutured term *docu-drama-ment*.[21] Documentary is as much a fiction as drama is an allusion to the real. The term *drama*, in the case of *Aman*, necessarily assumes a melodramatic form as an emotionally intensified, family-orientated spectacular as described above.

Fiction, therefore, is entangled in a cat's cradle with realist narrative, the nonreferential with the referential, and the fanciful with the apparent document in *Aman*. The cine-territory indicates less an *insertion* of a document into the fictional or vice versa, and more of an *interpenetration*. The melodramatic fictional is lent transnational gravitas while the textual basis of the documentary conventionally associated with evidential status and authentic presence is affectively intensified by being placed in the epic arc of Indian cinema. By reconceptualizing film in terms of a mélange of reality effects, we can begin to level the field between a real-life Russell in a fictional frame in conversation with a scripted character who himself also alludes to actual individuals and events.

With the ever-expanding varieties of documentaries that are now being produced in the contemporary era, there has been a turn to a "post-documentary culture."[22] Media scholar Keith Beattie critiques the "exclusion and marginalisation, and the restricted range of formal processes endorsed within the existing documentary canon."[23] With his notion of "documentary display," Beattie is able to consider optimal interpretations of "scopic practices," including "exhibitionistic, expressionistic and excessive attractions" operating through various different combinations of the screened imagery and its exhibition and reception.[24] By addressing the more open term of "documentary display," Beattie proposes that we move beyond "telling," "exposition," and the image as "visible evidence," as is characteristic of conventional documentary, toward "showing" and "evocation, sensory affect, or 'poetic' allusion."[25]

There is a certain degree of correspondence with "documentary display" and aspects of the docu-drama-ment, fully appreciating that, when considering *Aman*, we need to bear in mind different cultural-epistemological and temporal contexts that precede the latter-day post-documentary turn. Docu-drama-ment takes these insights on the evocative and sensorial on board but also modifies them for the specificities of Indian epic melodrama. It is this docu-drama-ment display that has something fascinating to add to the historical currents of Cold War realpolitik that have been recorded in the written archives (themselves following their own representational conventions).[26]

Aman captures various moodscapes of 1960s India and geopolitics, but not in a linear series of correspondences between text and context. Political moodscapes allude to a constellation of events from which we get *a sense of history* (as with the inclusion of Russell in the film, Gautam as an ersatz Nehru, and other themes explored below). These audiovisual moodscapes are not intended as a reflection of political ideology or events. Nor is knowledge to be reduced to cognitive or factual information. Rather the film encourages both an informed and an engaged sensory and imaginative experience — in Beattie's words, "subjective, affective, visceral and sensuous."[27] A political moodscape, then, conveys a sensory perception of history rather than a cognitive one that relies on the obstinacy of facts. This proposal is not one about oppositions where sensory is counterposed against cognition but rather one of emphases.[28]

These political moodscapes are conspicuous at various points in the 152-minute narrative of *Aman* that encourages us to conduct a postmortem on India's position with respect to the politics of the nuclear bomb in former decades. First, as noted, they are evident in the film's pitch for a socially beneficial science and embrace of world peace. Second, the film portrays a vivid disapproval of imperialism and, in the aftermath of the 1952 Treaty of Peace between Japan and India when U.S.-led occupational forces had left Japan, growing admiration for Japan's economic reconstruction and rapid growth while demonstrating synergies with Asian cultures.[29] Third, in the film's condemnation of nuclear proliferation in a context of Cold War repercussions, there is an emergent thread that impugns not just the established nuclear superpowers, the United States and U.S.S.R., but also emerging nuclear weapons states such as France and China. In this matrix, India is celebrated as a country that represents a nonaligned and third way to Cold War bipolar tensions. Fourth, there is the Nehruvian political legacy that by the time this film was released in 1967 was threatened by reactionary populism in view of domestic pressures and ascendant geopolitical tensions between India and its neighbors China and Pakistan.

Now on to an exploration of some of these political moodscapes that affected the making of the film: arguably, 1960s India represented a watershed moment from the euphoria of independence and the possibility of a nonaligned alliance of decolonized nations to one of political pragmatism, increasing jingoism, and a concern about national security in a period that saw former friends turn foe and vice versa. The border conflict with China in 1962 that ended in India's defeat is often portrayed as destroying Nehru's resolve and his cherished ideals of Asian socialist solidarity.[30] The conflict represented the final floundering of the Panchsheel Agreement, the Five Principles of Peaceful Coexistence, first formalized between China and India in 1954.[31] Soured relations between the two countries had in fact surfaced in the 1950s, anticipated by China's presence in Tibet, India granting safe haven to the Dalai Lama in 1959, and China's alliance with Pakistan. Most troublesome was the British colonial legacy of the McMahon Line, which India had come to accept by the time of independence but which China could not, claiming that it was made when the country was under severe duress and could not present a delegation.[32]

With notable exceptions discussed below, Japan had been sidelined by many Indians from the period of World War II for its imperialist ambitions and then, after its defeat, for being under the wings of the U.S.-led occupation forces. But a new perspective began to be cemented in the 1960s, one that embraced Japan while it repudiated China.[33] In fact, the 1964 Olympic Games held in Tokyo lent much to the fetishization of this Far Eastern mecca of modernity, as is also clear in the film released a year before *Aman, Love in Tokyo* (directed by Pramod Chakravorty, 1966).

While these leanings toward Japan reached their fruition in the 1960s, they had in fact been anticipated earlier in the century, most controversially by the nationalist Subhas Chandra Bose in the 1940s. With the formation of the Indian National Army, Bose swore to the maxim that "an enemy's enemy is your friend" and went out of his way to befriend the Axis powers against the colonial British. However, Bose's strategic orientation and his violent tactics were not ones that Nehru endorsed. Nevertheless, shortly after the Hiroshima and Nagasaki bombings of 1945 that ended the theater of world war in the East, Nehru entertained ideals of a nonaligned movement that included Japan.

Indeed, Nehru's empathy for Japan has received little commentary in the scholarly literature on India's relations with countries to the east. This matter has been eclipsed by India's relationship with China. As is often cited, before the dispute over India-China boundaries emerged in the late 1950s, Nehru was of the view that China was characterized by an ancient civilization, with freedom fighters who fought defiantly against oppression and now aspired to pursue their vision of socialist-style modernization very much like India. He had made his sentiments clear in his 1935 work, *Glimpses of World History*, and, later, in *The Discovery of India*, first published in 1946.[34] He went on to become an ardent advocate for the People's Republic of China's membership in the United Nations. In *The Discovery of India* he had also chastised Japan for their imperialist ambitions and aggressive militarism in China.

But elsewhere he had expressed hope that Japan's reputation could be redeemed as part of a broad Asian alliance as he began to sow the seeds of what was to become the checkered path of non-alignment and peaceful coexistence. Ever the idealist, Nehru's opinion on Japan was that it could abandon its imperialistic ambitions and help foster a pan-Asian solidarity not only between India and Japan but even between the rivals Japan and China. In an article entitled "Mr Nehru's Advice to Japan: 'Reject Imperialism'" that appeared in the *Times of India* on 12 October 1945, Nehru critiqued Japan's imperialist ambitions and the invasion of China, yet held on to a distinct hope for the country:

> Japan has caused deep injury to China, both material and spiritual, and therefore Japan's special task must be to gain the goodwill of the Chinese people. Ultimately the peace of the Far East depends on the co-operation of the Chinese and the Japanese, and such co-operation can only be based on freedom. If this policy is followed by Japan, she will not only gradually heal the deep scars of war but will also cure the deeper spiritual injuries caused to herself and to others to bridge the gulf which now separates men from other nations. India and the other countries of Asia will outlive yesterday's anger and resentment and join hands with Japan in the furtherance of Asiatic freedom and co-operation within the larger framework of world peace.[35]

Mutual experiences of suffering could be the way to start afresh, despite holding Japan to account as one of the hawkish perpetrators of war. The force of the atomic bomb not only created ground zeros out of two cities, Hiroshima and Nagasaki, but also enabled a zero point from which to reenvisage Japan moving away from an aggressor to a country that could potentially develop a creed of international pacifism and pan-Asian camaraderie. This larger political context is clear in the film *Aman* with Gautam's decision to express his solidarity with victim-survivors in Japan even though his mother had been killed by Japanese bombs in Burma.

The postindependent Indian solution to nuclear proliferation was to mobilize the Gandhian notion of nonviolence, or *ahimsa*—*ahimsa* that in the light of the atom bomb was given a global spin and rearticulated as world peace, an alternative to the way of the atom bomb orchestrated by powers to the west.[36] Greater international cooperation was seen as the way forward to establish a One World movement that could counter predatory national-nuclear interests.[37] When optimistic hopes for a world government floundered, Nehru was even more eager to navigate a third way through a sea of belligerent bipolarity. This included Asia-Africa alliances as epitomized by the 1955 Bandung Conference, and pan-Asian solidarity that could act as a counterpoint to the powers of Britain, the United States, and U.S.S.R.[38] Nehru's intention was made clear very early at the Asian Relations Conference in Delhi in March–April 1947.[39] At this event in India's capital, thirty-two leaders of independence movements from as far afield as Egypt, Iran, Turkey, Mongolia, China, Tibet, and Indonesia gathered for what were avowedly nonpolitical agendas. They were united in their stance against imperialism and the goal of world peace. With statements such as "Asia, after a long period of quiescence, has suddenly become important again in world affairs," Nehru declared the significance of inclusive internationalism based on common bonds of struggles against oppression and a shared future looking toward peace, equality, and progress.[40] While denouncing colonialism as well as isolationism, or what he described as "narrow nationalism," Nehru elaborated, "The West has . . . driven us into wars and conflicts without number and even now, the day after a terrible war, there is talk of further wars in the atomic age that is upon us. In this atomic age, Asia will have to function effectively in the maintenance of peace."[41]

Combating the proliferation of nuclear weapons was a key part in the drive toward world peace. With the atomic bomb attacks in Hiroshima and Nagasaki, Nehru believed that Japan too had fallen prey to the brutality of Western colonialism and thus, along with other countries in Asia, remained a potential partner with which to rally against belligerent powers toward the west.[42] Yet these ambitions had to be thwarted in the immediate sense by post–World War II reconstruction that meant Japan, first, remained under the thumb of the Allied forces and then, later in the 1950s, became an ally of the United States. At the Asian Relations Conference, Japan was conspicuous by its absence.

Despite such drawbacks, racist animosity against the Japanese was less prevalent in India than in the United States, which reached its height following Japan's attack on Pearl Harbor in 1941.[43] As is clear with Gautam's conviction of character in the film, Indian sympathies lay predominantly with the Japanese victims. Japanese leaders may have nursed imperialist ambitions, but the Japanese people themselves, by the war's end, were reassessed as innocent Asians in a conceptual field where Western powers were held most suspect for their track record of oppression and hypocrisy. The prevailing public mood in India could be summed up with disapproval of Japanese imperialist politics but empathy for the victims of atomization in the East. As an unnamed writer in the Marathi newspaper *Nav Kal* wrote in 1946:

> The inhuman destruction of Hiroshima brought about by the atomic bomb is fresh in everyone's memory. . . . The reality of this city is stranger than the imaginary wonders of Aladdin's lamp! The dreadful and fearful scenario prevalent in Hiroshima is such that it has far surpassed any horror movie [*bhayaanak chitrapat*]. . . .
>
> The shadow of a bridge that no more exists is seen on the road. Elsewhere, there falls the shadow of a bullock-cart and a cart-driver. In another place, there is the shadow of a 10–12 year old schoolgirl with a bundle of books tucked in her arms.[44]

A graveyard city locked in the shadowlands of nightmares: a repeat of such prospects had to be avoided at all costs. This moodscape seeps into *Aman* as well. At one point the daughter of the hospital's director, Meloda (played by the well-known actor Saira Banu), shows Gautam the sights of Japan. The couple visit the Hiroshima Peace Memorial Museum. As soon as they get to the door of the museum, a haunting track begins. There is no conversation, no dubs or voiceovers, only the doleful singing in Hindi by the playback singer Mohammad Rafi.

> See the image of a Hiroshima destroyed.
> The world's worst human transgression
> We are the first target of the atom menace
> Everything was like the color of spring, now we have been burnt into
>   dust

Gautam and Meloda (played by Saira Banu) in the
Hiroshima Memorial Museum. (*Aman* [1967])

With this sin of humanity, even the sky bent down [with the burden
   of shame]

The time stopped where it was
These hands cut up, legs cut up, and hanging body parts
Around these bodies, human lives like ours were built
Mothers' smiling laps [with babies] became empty
I have heard that even the full moon night became dark
The situation of Hiroshima calls out and says, "Don't travel the way I
   have had to journey."

The song is a tribute to those who lived in Hiroshima while also interpel-
lating the viewers into empathizing with their fate through the use of the lyrical "we" accompanied by visual and visceral registers such as mannequins in
the shape of deformed bodies and photographs of empty ruins. Time stood
still at Hiroshima—exactly at 8:16 in the morning when the atom bomb exploded, emphasized by a chilling focus on clocks retrieved from the debris.
Correspondingly, there is a slow pace to the representations of image and
sound as Gautam tries to take everything in. He sighs and gulps when the
force of the displays becomes too much for him to digest. Toward the end of
the song, disquiet comes to a head when images repeat themselves in quick
succession. This is in tune to a cascade of soprano chants and discordant
violin and atonal piano sounds. Images and sounds reach a disorientating
crescendo: the doctor is shot on the diagonal, he looks on with tearful eyes,

Raminder Kaur

Clocks at the Hiroshima Peace Memorial Museum stopped at 8:16 A.M., the time when the American B-29 bomber the *Enola Gay* dropped an atomic bomb on the city. (*Aman* [1967])

cannot take it anymore, wipes his head with his hand, and to a dramatic end, runs out of the museum, leaving Meloda in self-absorbed mourning before she too follows suit.[45]

After the visit to the Hiroshima Memorial Museum, Meloda takes Gautam to the old house where she used to live when the bomb was dropped. As a young girl, Meloda was outside learning to play golf with her father at the time of the atomic attack. But her mother was not so fortunate and died on that day. Meloda recalls her mother's memory as she lays a wreath at her former home, which now lies in ruins. As she recounts her personal history, we see what appear to be docu-reels of the Hiroshima bomb blast and the ferocious effects on its residents. In actuality, they are insertions of footage from other Japanese films on the Hiroshima bomb attack, such as *The Bells of Nagasaki* (directed by Hideo Oba, 1950), the film based on Takashi Nagai's book (1949, *Nagasaki no kane*). Nagai was a radiologist who died of radiation sickness six years after the bombing—the consequences of having been present on the perimeters of the atomic attack.[46] What appears to be documentary inserts to establish historical or factual representation led to other fictionalized film in yet another vindication of the unsteady grounds of the docu-drama-ment. The episode brings to mind the American anthropologist Clifford Geertz's anecdote of an Indian story where he recounts interminable unfolding: "There is an Indian story—at least I heard it as an Indian story—about an Englishman who, having been told that the world

Meloda shows Gautam the ruins of her former home, destroyed by the atomic blast in 1945, and lays a wreath with a dove looking on. (*Aman* [1967])

Meloda recalls the day of the atomic attack against its reproduction from a Japanese film. (*Aman* [1967])

rested on a platform which rested on the back of an elephant which rested in turn on the back of a turtle, asked (perhaps he was an ethnographer; it is the way they behave), what did the turtle rest on? Another turtle. And that turtle? 'Ah, Sahib, after that it is turtles all the way down.'"[47]

While Geertz's point is about the intrinsic incompletion of analyses, mine is to address the difficulty if not impossibility of getting to the "real" through the reel. In this spiraling turtle scenario, we can at best aim for an affective sense of the real.

Raminder Kaur

When Japan's national sovereignty had been established, postwar diplomatic relations between Japan and India commenced. In the Treaty of Peace between Japan and India, concluded in 1952, India waived reparation claims against Japan in its bid to restore relations between the two countries. In 1957, Prime Minister Nobusuke Kishi visited India, the first visit made by a leading Japanese statesman to the postcolonial nation. Subsequently, Nehru traveled to Japan with his daughter, Indira, at which point a visit to Hiroshima was also made.[48] Renowned for his anti–atom bomb stance, Nehru was greeted very warmly, especially in Hiroshima.

Culturally, too, films began to be exchanged between the two countries. Some years after their release in India in 1954, *Chandralekha* (directed by S. S. Vasan, 1948) and *Aan* (Pride, directed by Mehboob Khan, 1952) were released in Japan. Nor is it a coincidence that Raj Kapoor's popular film, *Shri 420*, from 1955, has him singing his signature tune, *Mera juta hai Japani* (My shoes are Japanese), underlining this recent fetishization of a modern yet Eastern country. This is a sentiment that stretched from the affluent cosmopolites to more vernacular and subaltern contingents when consumer goods from postwar Japan became widely affordable in India.[49] As well as Japanese shoes, the song included reference to communist affiliations with a nod to the red Russian hat and a token of mimicry to colonial vestiges with his "Englistani trousers" over his essentially "Indian heart" — a performative modernity that was at once avant-garde, socialist, hybrid, and patriotic.[50]

The film *Aman* is yet another outcome of this cultural-political turn toward another Eastern power where the "Indian heart" could feel modern without having to directly cast its anchor to the west. Japan provides a sleek paean to a pinnacle of Eastern modernity, with its bullet trains, high rises, pristine highways and byways, stylish cars and houses, and helicopters that are deployed by the main protagonists in later scenes. Replete throughout these icons of modernity is a civic emphasis on cleanliness, organization, and efficiency. Despite continuing alliances with the United States, Japan represented a parallel site of modernity that had not sold out to the ideological baggage and homogeneity implied by processes of Westernization.[51] Accordingly, Japan was portrayed as modern yet distinguished by a cultural and dignified difference evident through its distinctive music, language, religion, dress, art, and architecture.[52]

This is as evident in *Aman* as it is in *Love in Tokyo*: both films highlight the Tokyo Tower, the city's communications and observation tower, standing tall and erect as if it was an Eiffel Tower, with its superlative connotations of Eastern prowess, cosmopolitanism, and romance.[53] It is here that Gautam goes with his Japanese love interest, Meloda. In fact, the transcultural romance leads to their betrothal in the film. The love marriage between Gautam and Meloda is sanctioned by both their fathers, the embodiment of the established laws of the land. With a celebratory note, newspaper headlines also decree: "Indian doctor to wed Japanese heiress."

Interleaved throughout the film are other signifiers of Asian convergence such as earlier artistic and cultural liaisons forged by the poet Rabindranath Tagore. The Bengali writer elaborated on his views in the compilation *Japanyatri* (A Sojourn to Japan), based on his four-month stay in the country in 1916–17.[54] A large portrait of Tagore painted by Meloda, who herself had studied in Tagore's institution in Bengal, Shantiniketan, hangs over their lounge in *Aman*, in homage to a pan-Asian creative tour de force.[55]

Nor does the regionally shared veneration of the Buddha go amiss, indicating the forging of ancient commonalities between the two countries. It is not accidental that the main protagonist's name, Gautam, recalls the name of the Buddha, Siddhartha Gautam. The point is reiterated by one of the blind patients in the hospital who notes that just like the Buddha, this medical Gautam will lift people's pains and give peace to their souls through his dedicated research. With fervent conviction, he states: "My heart believes that from these [Gautam's] hands, a new life will begin."

RUSSELL AND NEHRU

To return to the unlikely Hindi film star philosopher: Why would Russell appear in the film with the ersatz Nehru in the shape of Gautam Das? I have not come across any archival material on Russell's decision to be in *Aman*, but we can look to the available evidence that can help us understand his position. It is well known that Russell was involved in a number of national and international campaigns against nuclear weapons, fascism, and imperialism. With his advocacy in international peace and denuclearization, Russell instigated and served as the president of the Pugwash Conferences on nuclear weapons and the Campaign for Nuclear Disarmament from the 1950s. His outspoken views led him to be derided, even imprisoned for his pacifism during World War I and for inciting civil disobedience in 1961, proving that even at the age of eighty-nine, one can still be a rebel. Simultaneously, Russell was widely respected: he received the Order of Merit and several prestigious awards, including the Nobel Prize for Literature, and was made an honorary fellow of the British Academy in 1949. In 1963, appalled by the hegemonic bias of the United Nations against China's membership as well as the war crimes committed by U.S. forces in the Vietnam War, Russell set up the Bertrand Russell Peace Foundation and enjoined several distinguished leaders, including Nehru, to support and fund it.[56]

For the most part, Nehru had shared a mutual appreciation club with Russell from an early age. When in Europe in the 1920s, Nehru read books by Russell and was deeply impressed by his rationalism.[57] Both had been educated at the University of Cambridge, although Nehru was of a younger cohort. They shared common friends and a similar rationalist outlook tempered with the mission of world peace and unilateral nuclear disarmament. Russell was president of the Indian League and had long favored the country's independence, calling himself "a life-time friend of India."[58] There was even an instance in which Russell was one of the key backers (along with Lord Louis Mountbatten and the author E. M. Forster) to nominate Nehru for the position of university chancellor.[59] Even though Nehru felt honored to be put forward, he eventually persuaded his supporters to withdraw his candidature, stating that he was too busy being India's prime minister.

This mutual respect is not to assume that Russell and Nehru were not without their thorny disagreements. One notable case was their difference in views over the Sino-Indian border conflict, where Nehru felt affronted while Russell preferred negotiations and eventually concurred that China's case for territory was greater than that of India.[60]

Aggrieved by the Sino-Indian conflict between what he had thought of as cultural and ideological partners, Nehru was famously despondent.[61] In broader political terms, a marked shift to the right appeared in the subcontinent as a consequence of India's border defeat to China.[62] This debacle exposed the intrinsic weakness of the Indian left, who continued to show ideological affinity with China and, as a result, lost national popularity. The political position of the Indian army was also sharply changed, almost reversed, and thereafter civilian interference in internal army matters was to be quelled. In fact, in a letter to Russell after the 1962 war, Nehru referred to "the danger of the military mentality spreading in India, and the power of the Army increasing."[63]

Despite and perhaps because of Nehru's death three years before *Aman* was released, respect lingered for the statesman's role as an antinuclear mediator of international repute. With the subcontinental beacon of peace and hope no more, and in the face of increasing threats of nuclear proliferation and warfare, Russell appears in a Hindi film as a last-ditch attempt to resuscitate the Nehruvian vision and legacy of a peaceful, nonisolationist, and nuclear weapons–free world. The impact of the Chinese nuclear tests in 1964 in the same year of Nehru's death cannot be overlooked when considering Russell's concerns that India not "go nuclear" as well.[64] Despite his criticism of India's conduct over the Sino-Indian conflict, Russell wanted to demonstrate that he remained sympathetic and continued to encourage India to remain nonaligned and nonnuclear. Disturbed by nuclear proliferation in a larger Cold War context marred by U.S.-U.S.S.R. political shenanigans, Russell maintained that "Nehru stood for sanity and peace . . . perhaps it will be he who will lead us out of the dark night of fear into a happy day."[65] He continued: "Had India foregone non-alignment, it is seriously doubtful that other nations can seriously maintain it," and "Non-alignment prevented war on more than one occasion."[66] This view eastward was also made urgent by U.S. and French nuclear testing in the Pacific and the brutality of U.S. bombings and use of chemical weapons in Vietnam.[67]

Throughout his campaigning, Russell had become an avid exploiter of media to communicate with the general populace. He pioneered the role of "media philosopher" as he stepped up his appearances in several radio and television programs through his many contacts in the arts, media, and theater world to spread his anti-imperial and antinuclear message as well as solicit support for his foundation.[68] His appearance in *Aman* is yet another token of his appreciation for the communicative potential of mainstream media to spread his views, this time in the East.

In *Aman*, Gautam does indeed go on to find a "radiation cure," after which news about Gautam's success spreads widely. In a display of Indian pride, one news headline in the film reads: "Indian Doctor Achieves Probable Breakthrough in Radiation Cure." But later in the film, Gautam dies of radiation overexposure when trying to rescue fishermen from French nuclear tests in the Pacific Ocean. This is not before Gautam makes an impassioned speech on his hospital bed in front of an international coterie of reporters, telling the world to stop developing the atomic bomb. Gautam dies on the devotional words, *He Ram, he Ram, he Ram*—a cry back to the assassination of the paramount paragon of peace, Mahatma Gandhi, whose last few words invoking the Hindu god Ram were emblazoned in the memories of virtually all Indians.

After his death, Gautam's body is taken back to India and paraded in central Delhi as a tribute to his selfless research for society. The scenes of the procession to the pyre on the Yamuna River are combined again with mellifluous lyrics à la Mohammad Rafi singing, *Aman ka Farishta, kaha ja raha*

Gautam's body on the way to the funeral pyre in the center of New Delhi, his death caused by irradiation while trying to save fishermen near thermonuclear tests in the Pacific Ocean. (*Aman* [1967])

hai? (The Angel of Peace, where is it going?). Reminiscent of actual events when Nehru's body was conveyed to his cremation a few years earlier, the ersatz Nehru merges with the ghost of Nehru. Crowds gather in the heart of Delhi's political center to see Gautam off as if they were attending the state funeral of a dignitary. His demure father sits in a military jeep with a mournful Meloda dressed in a white sari, signifying her status now as an Indian widow. Their car follows a red tractor that pulls Gautam's corpse on another vehicle.[69]

Even as *Aman* becomes a commemoration of Nehru's life, vision, and death, it is also a lament about the fate of humanity under the threat of nuclear bomb proliferation while valorizing socially beneficial science to remedy the world's wrongs. The funeral parade could be seen as marking the end of one episode of the atomic age in India that professed to support only the "peaceful" development of atomic science. Behind the scenes, as came to light in 1974, the development of an Indian nuclear bomb was under serious consideration under a new political leadership at the behest of Indira Gandhi. Political realism may not be alien to or separate from idealism among earlier Indian politicians, but the "peaceful nuclear explosive"—as the 1974 test in the deserts of Pokhran was called—heralded not just a scientific achievement but an era awakened to the possibilities of the nuclear bomb and political pragmatism.[70]

Jawaharlal Nehru's funeral procession through the capital city of New Delhi.
(Hulton Archive Collection, courtesy of Getty Images)

Gautam's funeral procession through the capital city of New Delhi. (*Aman* [1967])

At least four points, or perhaps promontories, from the flat screen of entertainment in *Aman* lift this film from just being a source of cinematic dis-
traction to being a rare entry point into the twilight years of 1960s national,
regional, and transnational politics. I have focused on the more prominent
film excerpts and simultaneously painted several canvasses with which to
begin to appreciate the spiral of meanings between film text and sociopolitical realities at the time of its production and release.

In the filmic assemblage, we first considered the meeting with Bertrand Russell where reality idioms of the actual (cameo appearance) were
interlaced with the dramatis persona of Dr. Gautam Das. Second, we encountered the visit to the Hiroshima Peace Memorial Museum, where two
fictional characters, Gautam and Meloda, respond to the residual objects,
traces, and memories of the Hiroshima attack, memorialized in a museum
that exhibits grainy pictures, simulated mannequins, and atomic blast rem-
nants, such as the clocks scarred with the death of time at 8:16 A.M. Then we
moved on to family reminiscences of the Hiroshima blast through the character of Meloda, where we saw the intervallic editing of what appear to be
newsreel clips of the atomic blasts but are in effect footage from other films
combined with reconstructed studio settings. Last, we focused on the death
of the main protagonist when Gautam's irradiated body is paraded through
the political heart of Delhi. The scenes evoke the ghosts of Gandhi and especially Nehru, whose state funeral procession was filmed three years earlier. In
view of larger currents, the funeral parade, both filmic and allusively actual,
appears to signal the end of an era with reference to India's official stance
with respect to the nuclear bomb.

With all of these excerpts, there is a deconstruction of the idea that
documentary pertains to the evidential and factual and the dramatic/melo-
dramatic pertains to the fanciful and fantastic. Instead, there are different
contours and combinations of reality effects that can encompass the historical, the nonfictional, the phantasmal, the performative, the spectacular, and
the emotive.

Altogether, *Aman* becomes a unique and affective register of political
moodscapes of 1960s Cold War from the point of view of India and its relations to countries farther east. As Nehru stated at the Asian Relations Conference in 1947: "Strong winds are blowing all over Asia. Let us not be afraid
of them but rather welcome them for only with their help can we build the

new Asia of our dreams."[71] These strong winds have not abated in the current era, and along with other countries India, too, has succumbed to them. They carry vastly different reverberations when "the new Asia of our dreams" is built on the affective intensities of neoliberalism and the proliferation of nuclear arms. The lessons embodied in the film are yet to be taken to heart.

NOTES

Versions of this chapter were presented at the South Asia Center at Yale University, New York University, the India Centre at Kings College London, and the University of Oxford. My thanks to the organizers, especially Kalyanakrishnan Sivaramakrishnan, Arvind Rajagopal, Kriti Kapila, Iain Morley, and Morgan Clarke, and to those who engaged with the paper in its fledgling days, especially Saif Eqbal and Rea Amit. Thanks also to Manu Bhagavan for his editorial insights, and to Nicholas Griffin from the official Russell Archive at McMaster University in Canada and Tony Simpson from the Bertrand Russell Peace Foundation in Britain for providing further details about Russell's work. Some of the historical research for this article was conducted earlier at the British Library with support from the Economic and Social Research Council (RES-000-23-1312, 2006–8) and the Arts and Humanities Research Council (AH/HOO/3304/1, 2009–10).

1. Ashish Rajadhyaksha, "The Epic Melodrama: Themes of Nationality in Indian Cinema," *Journal of Arts and Ideas* (1994): 25–26, 55–70.

2. See Rosie Thomas, "Melodrama and the Negotiation of Morality in Mainstream Hindi Film," in *Consuming Modernity: Public Culture in a South Asian World*, ed. Carol A. Breckenridge (Minneapolis: University of Minnesota Press, 1995), 157–82; and Ravi Vasudevan, *The Melodramatic Public: Film Form and Spectatorship in Indian Cinema* (London: Palgrave Macmillan, 2011).

3. See Richard Rushton, *The Reality of Film: Theories of Filmic Reality* (Manchester: Manchester University Press, 2011).

4. Eric Wolf, *Europe and the People without History* (Berkeley: University of California Press, 1982).

5. Raminder Kaur and Ajay Sinha, eds., *Bollyworld: Popular Indian Cinema through a Transnational Lens* (New Delhi: Sage, 2005).

6. As Manu Bhagavan elaborates, India's nonaligned policy was less about "neutrality" and more "a proactive Gandhian means of equal engagement with two, opposed warring factions." Manu Bhagavan, *India and the Quest for One World: The Peacemakers* (New Delhi: HarperCollins, 2012), xi.

7. Beatriz Jaguaribe, "The Shock of the Real: Realist Aesthetics and the Urban Experience," *Space and Culture* 8 (2005): 66–83.

8. "The surprise of the real" as proposed here is distinct from the experience of film that Tom Gunning describes as the "aesthetic of astonishment." The former entails a familiarity with the filmic medium but an unfamiliarity with what appears to be an intervention of the realist-prosaic into a culturally distinct melodramatic form. Tom Gunning, "An Aesthetic of Astonishment: Early Film and the [In]Credulous Spectator," in *Viewing Positions*, ed. Linda Williams (New Brunswick, N.J.: Rutgers University Press, 1995). Even though, as Rick Altman proposes, genre-mixing is commonplace in film to give audiences the sense that they are watching something new, some inclusions may appear more startling than

Raminder Kaur

others, a point I return to below. See Rick Altman, *Film/Genre* (London: British Film Institute, 1999).

9. Such experiences could be felt simultaneously and compared with the metaphor of the compound lens. A compound lens is a collection of simple lenses of different shapes and made of materials of different refractive indices, arranged one after the other (or even juxtaposed in front of each other) with a common axis. As such, it can enable a plurality of scopic styles — a differentiated ocular experience transmitted through learned codes and cultural meanings that the viewer brings to the film content and interprets accordingly. The viewing of the film is both discrepant and intensively affective. Up to a certain threshold, the more discrepant the representation, the more it shakes our orientation. The more effective and affective this is, the more real it becomes. On cognitive style, see Andrea Barbosa, "Meaning and Sense in Images and Texts," *Visual Anthropology* 23 (2010): 299–310, 301. On "scopic regimes" in differing historical contexts, see Martin Jay, "Scopic Regimes of Modernity," in *Vision and Visuality*, ed. Hal Foster (San Francisco: Bay Press, 1988). On the "reflexive spectatorship" of Hindi popular film in the diasporic context, see Raminder Kaur, "Cruising on the *Vilayeti* Bandwagon: Diasporic Representations and Reception of Popular Indian Movies," in Kaur and Sinha, *Bollyworld*.

10. Translated from the Hindi. https://www.youtube.com/watch?v=nf7jBGH4V30.

11. There is a comparison to note with Laura Mulvey's notion of the screen presence of the star. In this case, we have the star personas, although differentially conceived, of Russell and Kumar that override their pivotal position in the plot cloaked in the reverential light of Nehru's status and memory. Laura Mulvey, *Visual and Other Pleasures: Theories of Representation and Difference* (Bloomington: Indiana University Press, 1989).

12. This is to acknowledge that Nehru had hinted at nuclear weapons as an optional by-product from the constructive and "peaceful" development of nuclear science should it be needed, a path that India had been following since independence. Dorothy Norman, cited in M. V. Ramana (n.d.), "Nehru, Science and Secrecy," http://www.geocities.ws/m_v _ramana/nucleararticles/Nehru.pdf. See also Rohan Mukherjee's chapter in this volume; and Itty Abraham, *The Making of the Indian Atomic Bomb* (London: Zed Books, 1998).

13. D. S. Kothari, *Nuclear Explosions and Their Effects*, with a foreword by Nehru (New Delhi: Ministry of Information and Broadcasting, 1958). In the wake of more above-ground nuclear tests, the issue of radiation dangers was taken up widely from the mid-1950s. The World Health Organization produced its report in 1957, *Effect of Radiation on Human Heredity: Report of a Study Group Convened by WHO together with Papers Presented by Various Members of the Group* (Geneva: World Health Organization, 1957), available at http://apps.who.int/iris/handle/10665/40094; and in 1958, the United Nations Scientific Committee produced its report, *Report of the United Nations Scientific Committee on the Effects of Atomic Radiation*, General Assembly, Official Records: Thirteenth Session Supplement no. 17 (A/3838), available at http://www.unscear.org/unscear/en/publications /1958.html.

14. Nicholas Griffin, *The Selected Letters of Bertrand Russell*, vol. 2, *Public Years, 1914–1970* (London: Routledge, 2001), 399–490.

15. Ashis Nandy, "National Identity and the Realist Aesthetic," in *National Identity in Indian Popular Cinema, 1947–1987*, ed. Sumitra S. Chakravarty (Austin: University of Texas Press, 1993), 85.

16. Thanks to Brian Larkin for highlighting this point.

17. Derek Paget, *No Other Way to Tell It: Dramadoc/Docudrama on Television*

(Manchester: Manchester University Press, 1998); Alan Rosenthal, *Why Docudrama? Fact-Fiction on Film and Television* (Carbondale: Southern Illinois University Press, 1999); Steven N. Lipkin, *Real Emotional Logic: Film and Television Docudrama as Persuasive Practice* (Carbondale: Southern Illinois University Press, 2002).

18. On cinema verité, see Paul Stoller, *The Cinematic Griot: The Ethnography of Jean Rouch* (Chicago: University of Chicago Press, 1982); Jean Rouch, "The Camera and Man," in *Principles of Visual Anthropology*, ed. Paul Hockings (New York: Mouton de Gruyter, 2003); and Paul Henley, *The Adventure of the Real: Jean Rouch and the Craft of Ethnographic Cinema* (Chicago: University of Chicago Press, 2009).

19. See Richard Rorty, *Philosophy and the Mirror of Nature* (Princeton, N.J.: Princeton University Press, 1979).

20. Trinh T. Minh-ha, "The Totalizing Quest of Meaning," in *Theorizing Documentary*, ed. Michael Renov (New York: Routledge, 2012), 29.

21. There is scope for this conceptualization to be applied to other films in their aesthetic, historical, and cultural particularities, as with the composite film *The Battle of Algiers* (directed by Gillo Pontecorvo, 1966), which looks as if it contains documentary footage that is in effect all reconstructed; and *Forrest Gump* (directed by Robert Zemeckis, 1994), with its fictional character digitally integrated with archived and re-created footage. Other Indian films could include what might be described as sport cinema, where the lives of world champions are dramatized, cut through with actual footage from tournaments, as in *Bhaag Milkha Bhaag!* (Run Milkha run!), directed by Rakeysh Omprakash Mehra, 2013), *M. S. Dhoni: The Untold Story* (directed by Neeraj Pandey, 2016), and *Dangal* (Wrestling competition, directed by Nitesh Tiwari, 2016). But these are more in the tenor of true-life stories treated with much artistic license rather than a docu-drama-ment as invoked here.

22. See Thomas Austin and Wilma de Jong, eds., *Rethinking Documentary: New Perspectives, New Practices* (New York: McGraw-Hill/Open University Press, 2008). John Corner, "Performing the Real: Documentary Diversions," *Television and New Media* 3, no. 3 (2002): 255–69.

23. Keith Beattie, *Documentary Display: Re-Viewing Nonfiction Film and Video* (London: Wallflower, 2008), 1.

24. Ibid., 4. In each filmic assemblage under focus, the terms of the debate need finer contextualization. As to its relation with the signified, the docu-drama-ment is a film under erasure but one that nevertheless *evokes* rather than *invokes* something outside of the diegetic frame that alludes to historical and culturally mediated phenomena. The notion of the docu-drama-ment impels a deconstruction before it can be reconstructed as a filmic assemblage for analysis. On the one hand, docu-drama-ment throws the gauntlet at expressions of the real or the realist-prosaic aesthetic as a somewhat higher avenue to a truth or the actual facts. On the other, it encapsulates and alludes to various political moodscapes tempered by recognizable historical incidents channeled through the fictional idiom of popular cinema.

25. Beattie, *Documentary Display*, 5.

26. See Sudipta Kaviraj, *The Unhappy Consciousness: Bankimchandra Chattopadhyay and the Formation of Nationalist Discourse in India* (Delhi: Oxford University Press, 1998), 107–57.

27. Beattie, *Documentary Display*, 16.

28. A parallel might be noted in cognitive theory that is largely based on sensory or

Raminder Kaur

visceral effects of the film-watching experience: see, e.g., Noel Carroll, *Theorizing the Moving Image* (Cambridge: Cambridge University Press, 1996); and Carl R. Platinga and Greg M. Smith, *Passionate Views: Film, Cognition, and Emotion* (Baltimore: John Hopkins University Press, 1999). Thanks to Rea Amit for this point.

29. India also played a part in this reconstruction in becoming the major resource for iron ore once trade resumed between the two countries. See http://www.india-center.org /content/history.php.

30. P. K. Banerjee, *My Peking Memoirs of the Chinese Invasion of India* (Delhi: Clarion, 1990).

31. The Panchseel Agreement rested on five principles: (1) mutual respect for each other's territorial integrity and sovereignty; (2) mutual nonaggression; (3) mutual noninterference in each other's internal affairs; (4) equality and mutual benefit; and (5) peaceful coexistence between India and China. See "'No. 4307. Agreement' between the Republic of India and the People's Republic of India on Trade and Intercourse between Tibet Region of China and India. Signed at Peking, on 29 April 1954," in *Treaties and International Agreements Registered or Filed and Recorded with the Secretariat of the United Nations*, vol. 299 (1958), I. Nos. 4303–25, 70, available at https://treaties.un.org /doc/publication/unts/volume%20299/v299.pdf.

32. Alastair Lamb, *The China-India Border: The Origins of the Disputed Boundaries* (Oxford: Oxford University Press, 1964). Neville Maxwell, *India's China War* (New York: Pantheon Books, 1971). See also chapters by Rohan Mukherjee and Pallavi Raghavan in this volume.

33. See, e.g., the film *Prem Pujari* (directed by Dev Anand, 1970), whose plot centers on aggression with, and suspicions cast on, the Chinese.

34. Jawaharlal Nehru, *Glimpses of World History* (1934–35; reprint, New Delhi: Penguin, 2004); and Nehru, *The Discovery of India* (1946; reprint, New Delhi: Penguin, 2004).

35. "Mr Nehru's Advice to Japan: 'Reject Imperialism,'" *Times of India*, 12 October 1945.

36. See Raminder Kaur, *Atomic Mumbai: Living with the Radiance of a Thousand Suns* (New Delhi: Routledge, 2013). *Ahimsa* (roughly translated as nonviolence) was an integral part of Gandhi's notion of *satyagraha* (truth-force). For a more complete exposition of these concepts, see Gita Dharampal Frick, Monica Kirloskar-Steinbach, Rachel Dwyer, and Jahnavi Phalkey, *Key Concepts in Modern Indian Studies* (New York: Routledge, 2015); and Raminder Kaur, *Performative Politics and the Cultures of Hinduism: Public Uses of Religion in Western India* (New Delhi: Permanent Black, 2003), 199.

37. See Bhagavan, *India and the Quest for One World*; and the chapter by Waheguru Pal Singh Sidhu in this volume.

38. See the chapter by Rohan Mukherjee in this volume.

39. This was a transnational sentiment that was to be revived in the mid-1950s, particularly after the Suez Crisis and the Hungarian Revolution that was crushed by the U.S.S.R. See the chapter by Waheguru Pal Singh Sidhu in this volume. On pan-Asianism in Japan, see Cemil Aydin, "Japan's Pan-Asianism and the Legitimacy of Imperial World Order, 1931–1945," *Asia Pacific Journal* 6, no. 3 (2008): 1–32.

40. Jawaharlal Nehru, speech at Asian Relations Conference, 24 March 1947, in Jawaharlal Nehru, *India's Foreign Policy: Selected Speeches, September 1946–April 1961* (1961; reprint, New Delhi: Ministry of Information and Broadcasting, 1971), 249–53.

41. "Asian Conference 'To Promote Peace and Progress,'" *Times of India*, 24 March 1947.

42. As early as 1949, when Nehru learned of children's hopes to bring an elephant to

Ueno Zoo in Japan, he presented the zoo with an elephant named after his daughter, Indira. In a letter he sent to the children of Tokyo, Prime Minister Nehru said, "I hope that when the children of India and the children of Japan will grow up, they will serve not only their great countries, but also the cause of peace and cooperation all over Asia and the world. So you must look upon this elephant, Indira by name, as a messenger of affection and goodwill from the children of India." *The Japan Forum*, http://www.tjf.or.jp/eng /content/japaneseculture/37giftsfromanimals.htm.

43. John W. Dower, *War without Mercy: Race and Power in the Pacific West* (New York: Pantheon, 1986); Eqbal Ahmad, "Racism and the State: The Coming Crisis of U.S.-Japanese Relations," in *Japan in the World*, ed. Masao Miyoshi and Harry Harootunian (Durham, N.C.: Duke University Press, 1993); Tetsuden Kashima, *Judgement without Trial: Japanese American Imprisonment during World War II* (Seattle: University of Washington Press, 2004).

44. "Hiroshima: The Fearsome City," *Nav Shakti* (Bombay), 17 March 1946 (emphasis in the original).

45. Elsewhere, I discuss such moments as an example of "atomic schizophrenia." Building on Kantian notions of the sublime, I note how the schizophrenic condition constitutes a breakdown of temporality and language, therefore an inability to enter the Symbolic order and thus consequent attempts to reappropriate it through a navigation of what Jacques Lacan described as the Symbolic, or, in other words, culture. These attempts at recuperation can never be fully realized, which is essentially how the schizophrenia differs for the experience of the sublime, according to Immanuel Kant. The effect is rather like a hole that is created by the signifier of the atom bomb into which meanings pour only to disappear. In this case, the experience does not reach resolution but opens up a series of wounds that propel Gautam further to find a cure for radiation-inflicted diseases. Immanuel Kant, *Critique of Judgment*, trans. John Henry Bernard (New York: Barnes and Noble, 2005); Jacques Lacan, *Écrits: A Selection and the Seminars*, trans. Alan Sheridan (London: Tavistock, 1977); Raminder Kaur, "Atomic Schizophrenia: Indian Reception of the Bombings of Hiroshima and Nagasaki, 1945," *Cultural Critique*, no. 84 (Spring 2013): 70–100. On the nuclear uncanny and nuclear sublime, see Joseph Masco, *The Nuclear Borderlands: The Manhattan Project in Post–Cold War New Mexico* (Princeton, N.J.: Princeton University Press, 2006); and Rob Wilson, *The Nuclear Sublime: The Genealogy of a Poetic Genre* (Madison: University of Wisconsin Press, 1991).

46. In their particular ways, what MGM's *The Beginning or the End* (1947, directed by Normal Taurog), with its footage of docu-reels on the atomic blast, was to the history of U.S. film-making, *Aman* was to the history of Indian film-making on the atomic theme.

47. Clifford Geertz, *The Interpretation of Culture: Selected Essays* (New York: Basic Books, 1977), 29.

48. See "Dated October 11, 1957: Nehru's Visit to Hiroshima," *The Hindu*, http://www .hindu.com/2007/10/11/stories/2007101155510901.htm; and "From the *Stars and Stripes* Archives: Nehru Arrives in Japan on Goodwill Visit," *Stars and Stripes*, August 12, 1976, http://www.stripes.com/news/nehru-arrives-in-japan-on-goodwill-visit-1.41661.

49. The idea of Japan's distinct modernity stretches back to the early twentieth century, particularly after the Japanese victory in the Russo-Japanese War (1904–5). In comparison with the West, modernity in Japan was seen to be rooted in a genuine rapprochement with cultural and everyday life rather than a discontinuous discrepancy with it. See Harry Haratoonian, *Overcome by Modernity: History, Culture, and Community in Interwar Japan*

(Princeton, N.J.: Princeton University Press, 2002); and Manu Bhagavan, *Sovereign Spheres: Princes, Education, and Empire in Colonial India* (New Delhi: Oxford University Press, 2003).

50. See Kaur and Sinha, *Bollyworld*, 11–12. On hybridity, see Homi Bhabha, *The Location of Culture* (London: Routledge, 1993). The attraction to Indian movies in Japan is marked by the fêting of art-house movies epitomized by Satyajit Ray films that ruled the roost from 1966, when his *Apu Trilogy* was released in the country. Popular movies received little attention in Japan until the runaway success of the Tamil film *Muthu* (directed by K. S. Ravikumar, 1996), the first Indian film dubbed directly into Japanese for distribution in the country from 1998 translated as *Muto: odoru maharaja. Muthu* was picked up by a Japanese film critic visiting Singapore. Amid the decline of Hong Kong cinema after its reunion with China, certain kinds of Indian popular films, such as action-packed and comic capers, saw a new lease of life in Japan. Rajnikanth's *Robot* (directed by S. Shankar, 2010) was also very successful in Japan.

51. See Brian Larkin, "Indian Films and Nigerian Lovers: Media and the Creation of Parallel Modernities," *Africa* 67, no. 3 (1997): 406–40.

52. American occupation continued in the Ryukyu Islands after Japan's independence in 1952, including Iwo Jima and Okinawa, which remained under occupation until 1968; U.S. military personnel stayed in Japan at the invitation of the Japanese government under the 1960 Treaty of Mutual Cooperation and Security between the two countries.

53. The scenes recall the film *Sangam* (Confluence, directed by Raj Kapoor, 1964), which shows a honeymooning couple touring iconic sites in Europe.

54. On the impact of pan-Asian and anti-Westernism in the arts in the early twentieth century, see Partha Mitter, *Art and Nationalism in Colonial India, 1850–1922: Occidental Orientations* (Cambridge: Cambridge University Press, 1994).

55. An early expression of this anticolonial pan-Asian movement is evident in the establishment of the Oriental Youngmen's Association in Japan in 1900. See Poomagame Anantharamaiah Narasimha Murthy, *India and Japan: Dimensions of Their Relations: Historical and Political* (Delhi: ABC, 1986).

56. Brian Carr, *Bertrand Russell, an Introduction: Edited Selections from His Writings* (London: Allen and Unwin, 1975), 21; Griffin, *Selected Letters of Russell*, 568.

57. Sankar Ghose, *Jawaharlal Nehru: A Biography* (Mumbai: Allied Publishers, 1993), 47.

58. Bertrand Russell, *Selected Letters* (London: Allen and Unwin, 1962), 557.

59. Ghose, *Jawaharlal Nehru*, 279. See also "When Nehru Almost Became Chancellor of Cambridge," *Firstpost*, October 14, 2011, http://www.firstpost.com/world/when-nehru-almost-became-chancellor-of-cambridge-108281.html.

60. Griffin, *Selected Letters of Russell*, 559.

61. Banerjee, *My Peking Memoirs*.

62. After his volte face on developing the bomb, the nuclear scientist J. Robert Oppenheimer became another admirer of Nehru. Oppenheimer even wrote to Nehru urging him not to sell thorium to the United States in case it would be used for destructive ends. Nayantara Sahgal, *Jawaharlal Nehru: Civilizing a Savage World* (New Delhi: Viking/ Penguin, 2010).

63. Bertrand Russell, *Autobiography*, 627.

64. See the chapter by Rohan Mukherjee in this volume.

65. Ghose, *Jawaharlal Nehru*, 279.

66. Ibid., 297.

67. Bertrand Russell, *War Crimes in Vietnam* (London: Allen and Unwin, 1967).

68. Bertrand Russell, *The Autobiography of Bertrand Russell*, vol. 3, *1944–1967* (London: Allen and Unwin, 1969), 160–61, 163. See also "Bertrand Russell: The First Media Academic?," *BBC Radio 4, Archive on 4*, http://www.bbc.co.uk/programmes/b019dzpp. A number of film projects were discussed, but little documentation exists and few materialized; one even included a film with the Beatles spearheaded by Paul McCartney to establish his credentials alongside John Lennon as a political voice in the group. In 1966, under the heading, *Beatles and Vietnam*, there is an "outline of a documentary film" running to five pages. Meetings were held and a director lined up who later pulled out under the impression that he would not get his due credit if he was to work with the world-famous Beatles. Thanks to Nicholas Griffin and Tony Simpson for this information. The fact that the Beatles film was also intended as a "documentary film" is pertinent to Russell's aims to use a popular fiction format to relay messages about global politics as it is to the aims of this chapter to explore the terrain of fiction and nonfiction. Russell's media interests even included his efforts to get the U.S. television company CBS into North Vietnam to document U.S. war crimes. Griffin, *Selected Letters of Russell*, 597.

69. Stills and docu-reel of Nehru's death procession are also evident in the film *Naunihaal* (directed by Rah Marbros, 1967), about a child's wish to meet the leader; see http://www.youtube.com/watch?v=S13F_KeGFLE. A motor vehicle was used in Nehru's procession. In *Aman*, a tractor is used to pull Gautam's body — underlining the narrative of all-embracing modernization to develop India including its rural communities.

70. George Perkovich, *India's Nuclear Bomb: The Impact on Global Proliferation* (New Delhi: Oxford University Press, 1999). On realism and idealism in Indian politics, see Bhagavan, *India and the Quest for One World*.

71. Nehru, speech at Asian Relations Conference, 24 March 1947.

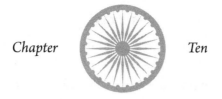

Chapter   Ten

Hindu Nationalists and the Cold War

RAHUL SAGAR

It is generally accepted that during the Cold War divergences between "hope and reality" rendered India and America "estranged democracies."[1] The precise nature of the Indo-American relationship during these decades remains a subject of fruitful study. For instance, Rudra Chaudhuri has argued that the Cold War's many crises actually prompted India and the United States to "forge" a more nuanced relationship than scholars have realized.[2] This chapter does not join this discussion. It examines a different side of the story. Rather than study the workings of the Congress Party–affiliated political and bureaucratic elite in power during the Cold War, it focuses on the principal Opposition—the ideas and policies of the Hindu Mahasabha, the Jan Sangh, and the Bharatiya Janata Party (BJP), which have championed the cause of Hindu nationalism. The Cold War–era policies of these parties have not been studied carefully thus far. A common assumption is that these parties had little to say about international affairs or that, to the extent that they had something to say, their outlook was resolutely militant. This chapter corrects this misperception. It shows that these parties' policies alternated between being attracted to and being repulsed by the West. Distaste for communism and commitment to democracy drove them to seek friendship with the West, while resentment at U.S. efforts to contain India as well as fears about materialism and Westernization prompted them to demand that the West be kept at a safe distance.

Surprisingly little has been written about the diversity of Indian views on international relations in the Cold War era. The conventional view is that there was at the start of the Cold War a "Nehruvian consensus" on the ends and means of Indian diplomacy.[3] This consensus, ostensibly crafted by Jawaharlal Nehru, committed India to furthering peaceful coexistence by means of anti-imperialism, nuclear disarmament, and above all non-alignment. These means, the former president of the Congress Party J. B. Kripalani declared in 1959, were "generally accepted by the country and are in keeping with the genius of our people."[4]

However, as Ankit Panda and I have shown, there was little consensus on this front—not even within the Congress.[5] For instance, when the Constituent Assembly considered whether India ought to remain in the Commonwealth, a number of important figures insisted that India ought to side with the West. This stance owed partly to the belief that such an alliance would be profitable. For example, Kameshwar Singh, the ruler of Darbhanga and a long-serving member of the Council of State, argued that India could only "ensure the peace of the world" if the country became militarily and economically "strong." "She can be made so," he asserted, "by the co-operation of the Commonwealth countries and America."[6] Others voiced a more fundamental objection. Balkrishna Sharma, a leading member of the Congress Party's conservative wing, spoke for many when he forcefully declared that "going Red" was not in India's interest because it was self-evident that in the communist bloc "before the Ogre of the State the individual is being sacrificed every minute of his existence."[7]

A more sustained critique came from outside the Congress, initially from the Hindu Mahasabha and later the Jan Sangh, which quickly emerged as the principal Opposition. Cold War–era observers typically overlooked this critique. They claimed that because internal problems were "overwhelming" during the Cold War years, opposition parties devoted "rather little attention to matters of foreign policy."[8] To the extent that observers considered the role cultural values played in shaping public policy, they took seriously the view, popularized by Mahatma Gandhi, that India's religious heritage counseled nonviolence. So when discussing "a renewed interest in the value of Hindu philosophy as a guide to the formulation of national policies," the example that observers often cited was Nehru's proto-Buddhist Panchsheel doctrine of peaceful coexistence.[9]

More recently, the BJP's post–Cold War rise has motivated scholars to take the Hindu nationalist worldview more seriously.[10] Unfortunately, this worldview has all too often been described in dire terms.[11] Chris Ogden, for example, characterizes it as embodying a "strong, assertive, and militaristic nationalism" that seeks to challenge "effeminate idealism and morality."[12] Similarly, Kanti Bajpai claims that Hindu nationalists subscribe to a "hard-bitten" ethic.[13] For instance, whereas "nuclear weapons are seen by many Westerners as a tragic necessity," he writes, "political Hinduism embraces them."[14] The implication here is that Hindu nationalists' "stance on international relations and the use of violence is not a particularly prudential one."[15]

Such claims seriously misjudge Hindu nationalism, especially as it took shape in the Cold War period. In particular, they overlook its moral dimension, represented most visibly by the doctrine of integral humanism, which still constitutes the BJP's "basic philosophy."[16] Coined by Deendayal Upadhyaya, the Jan Sangh's foremost intellectual, this doctrine expresses a holistic worldview stemming from the late nineteenth-century Hindu renaissance. As we shall see, in the Cold War era this doctrine led Hindu nationalists to champion a number of idealistic foreign and economic policies at some remove from the militant image typically ascribed to them. Some of these policies—such as a commitment to religious freedom—prompted them to call for closer relations with the West, while others—such as their skepticism about the market economy—brought them into deep conflict with it. This complicated history casts grave doubt on contemporary rhetoric about India and the United States being "natural allies."[17] Before discussing these policies, let me briefly outline the worldviews that informed Hindu nationalism during this period.

BEFORE INDEPENDENCE

In the latter half of the nineteenth century, socially prominent Hindus made two divergent discoveries: the profusion of Orientalist scholarship brought their past grandeur into focus, while the post-1857 consolidation of British rule exposed their present weakness. This embarrassing contrast spurred reform movements centered on Bengal, Bombay, and the Punjab. These movements took the view that India's subjection owed to cultural perversions such as the caste system that had undermined the unity and vitality of Hindu society. A return to purer forms of Hinduism described in the ancient scriptures would, they argued, unify and uplift Hindu society.

A key example here is Raj Narain Bose's *The Superiority of Hinduism to Other Existing Religions* (1882). The name "Hindu," Bose counseled, "possesses magical power" because "by means of this name all Hindus will be bound by the tie of brotherhood." And when "the aspirations of all will be the same," he continued, "they will all make united effort for the attainment of all kinds of freedom." For Bose, unity was desirable because it would allow Hindus to defend their civilization and advance humanity more generally—power and riches were not the objective. "Religious and moral civilization is true civilization," Bose argued, but "that civilization has not yet dawned upon the earth." However, one could "reasonably hope that the Hindu nation, by re-attaining its ancient religious and moral civilization . . . will stand as the best and the foremost of all nations on the earth."[18]

A contrasting view came from Bankim Chandra Chatterji. Chatterji rejected the idea that "true" Hinduism was "rooted in the Hindu scriptures."[19] In his view, much of what these scriptures prescribed was outmoded or inconclusive.[20] Sorely needed, then, was a basis on which Hindus could evaluate their scriptures and customs. This basis, he thought, ought to be social utility. In his words: "That which protects people and contributes to human welfare is *dharma*."[21] Chatterji was well aware of how radical this claim was. "Some are likely to consider this," he acknowledged, "an extremely utilitarian reading of *dharma*."[22] It certainly seemed so to Bose, who declared Chatterji's "New Religious Opinion" the work of "an atheist."[23]

Chatterji agreed with his contemporaries that India's "long servitude" owed to a "lack of a sense of nationalism."[24] Hence, in his view, *dharma* commanded fostering a culture of patriotism. But Chatterji discerned that patriotism had to have a martial aspect because "[a] strong people is always ready to fall upon the weaker ones."[25] Hence, whereas reformers like Bose expected a reinvigorated Hindu nation to be a beacon of spirituality, Chatterji counseled Hindus to also cultivate their physical faculties—for instance, they ought to learn to wrestle and swim, to use weapons and withstand the cold, and to drink wine and eat beef.[26] Chatterji did not glorify violence, though. Only a defensive form of patriotism is justified, he argued, because Hinduism enjoins loving the world.[27]

By the close of the nineteenth century, then, there were at least two distinct accounts of the Hindu nation in circulation—one oriented toward moral exceptionalism, the other toward political necessity. These differences sharpened at the turn of the twentieth century, as Hindu nationalists were either repelled or impressed by muscular forms of nationalism emerging in Europe and Asia (in Japan and China in particular).

The former view was championed most notably by Narendranath Datta—better known as Swami Vivekananda. Europe, Vivekananda observed at the turn of the twentieth century, was trying to understand "how much more power a man can possess by hook or by crook." But this approach was flawed because history showed "nations rising and falling almost every century—starting up from nothingness, making vicious play for a few days, and then melting."[28] Far preferable, then, were "mildness, gentleness, forbearance, toleration, sympathy, and brotherhood," as these qualities would permit national differences to be worked out peacefully.[29] But these qualities could only come to the fore, Vivekananda emphasized, if nations learnt to renounce. "Giving up the senses," he asserted, is what "makes a nation survive."[30] And this was where Hinduism excelled: "The cause of India's greatness," he declared, was that "we have never conquered. That is our glory."[31] As a consequence of its unique history, Vivekananda argued, it became India's duty to "spiritualize" the world by spreading the message of love and unworldliness. "Let foreigners come and flood the land with their armies, never mind," he told his listeners, "up, India, and conquer the world with your spirituality."[32]

Chatterji's realism was championed most notably by Aurobindo Ghosh. Ghosh urged his countrymen to meditate on Japan's modernization, which had "enabled the little island empire to wield the stupendous weapons of western knowledge and science."[33] A "nation must develop military and political greatness and activity, intellectual and aesthetic greatness and activity, commercial greatness and activity, moral sanity and vigour," he warned, for "it cannot sacrifice any of these functions of the organism without making itself unfit for the struggle for life and finally succumbing and perishing under the pressure of more highly organised nations."[34] This was the lesson of history, which showed that "purely aesthetic and intellectual state[s] like the Greek colonies in Italy . . . are blotted out of existence in the clash with ruder but more vigorous and many-sided organisms."[35]

Ghosh was also clear about religion's role in cultivating such power. Chatterji, he noted, had discerned that the "moral strength" needed to undergird "physical strength" could come only from "the religion of patriotism"—or "the infusion of religious feeling into patriotic work."[36] Consequently, Ghosh followed Chatterji in seeking to convince Hindus that their religion did not condemn violence. "A certain class of minds shrink from aggressiveness as if it were a sin," he wrote in "The Morality of Boycott." Their cry is to "heal hate by love" and to "slay sin by righteousness." But political action, he argued, ought to be governed not by "the Brahmanical duty of saintly sufferance" but rather by the "morality of the Kshatriya."[37]

In the decades before 1947, the worldviews described above resonated in the speeches and writings of Mahatma Gandhi and Vinayak Savarkar, respectively. Gandhi challenged the view that Hindus had been subdued due to their failure to distinguish between personal and political morality. "There seems to be no historical warrant for the belief," he declared in his famous essay "Ahimsa," "that an exaggerated practice of *ahimsa* synchronized with our becoming bereft of manly virtues."[38] On the contrary, "our civilization tells us with daring certainty that a proper and perfect cultivation of the quality of *ahimsa*, which in its active form means purest love and pity, brings the whole world to our feet."[39] Hence, calls for the use of violence were actually "a foreign growth" since Hinduism enjoined "abstention from *himsa*."[40] And so, "to arm India on a large scale," he said, would be to "Europeanise it."[41]

Equally vigorous was Gandhi's assault on elements of modernity that militant Hindu nationalists viewed as essential for national power. "Modern civilization," Gandhi famously argued, "occupies itself in the investigation of the laws of matter and employs the human ingenuity in inventing or discovering means of production and weapons of destruction." Hindu civilization, by contrast, had historically been "chiefly occupied in exploring spiritual laws."[42] The latter called for the "limitation of activities promoting wealth" because "economic progress" was invariably "antagonistic to real progress."[43] This was borne out, Gandhi argued, by the ill effects of mechanization, which rendered workers dependent on employers and encouraged consumers to chase artificial desires.[44] Europe's various social stresses revealed that modern "civilisation is such that one has only to be patient and it will be self-destroyed."[45]

On the opposite side stood Savarkar. Savarkar thought—in large part because of the horrors of World War I—that political life was scarred by a "terrible struggle for existence" that made "survival of the fittest . . . the rule."[46] Hence, like Chatterji and Ghosh, he advocated for a corporate identity that would motivate Hindus to rally in opposition to external aggression. "As long as other communities . . . are busy in organizing offensive and defensive alliances and combinations on entirely narrow racial or religious or national basis," he warned Hindus, "strengthen . . . those subtle bonds that like nerve threads bind you in one organic social being."[47]

The same concern for survival also led Savarkar to advocate a martial ethic. "We denounce your doctrine of absolute non-violence not because we are less saintly but because we are more sensible than you are," he thundered in response to Gandhi.[48] Equally important, in his view, was pragmatism in international relations. "The sanest policy for us," he asserted, "is to befriend those who are likely to serve our country's interests in spite of any 'ism' they follow for themselves and to befriend only so long as it serves our purpose."[49]

Like Ghosh, Savarkar appreciated the link between political power and material capability. History's lesson, he observed, is "that nations which, other things equal, are superior in military strength are bound to survive, flourish and dominate while those which are militarily weak shall be politically subjected or cease to exist at all."[50] Thus, in deliberate contrast to Gandhi, Savarkar insisted that "national production" ought to be on "the biggest possible machine scale" because the world was now in "a Machine age."[51]

AFTER INDEPENDENCE

We have seen that between the late nineteenth century and the mid-twentieth century, two views of the Hindu nation took shape — one oriented toward moral exceptionalism, the other toward political necessity. The Cold War–era policies of the Hindu Mahasabha, the Jan Sangh, and the BJP can be traced to the commingling of these streams.

A central figure in this story is Syama Prasad Mookherjee, who succeeded Savarkar as president of the Hindu Mahasabha before breaking away to form the Jan Sangh. Mookherjee carried into the new era three of Savarkar's core beliefs. First, foreign policy must be "realistic" — in other words, "every country must settle its attitude towards . . . other nations primarily in relation to its own problems and interests."[52] Second, military capabilities are irreplaceable because "in the modern age freedom cannot be maintained by any nation even for a single day unless there is an adequate armed strength available at its disposal."[53] Third, the importance of industrial capability for defense made it essential "to guard against . . . the future economic penetration of India by any foreign country."[54] At the same time, unlike the resolutely tough-minded Savarkar, Mookherjee voiced support for an idea hitherto championed by Vivekananda and Gandhi, to wit, that the West's "failure of spirit," as evidenced by the cataclysmic wars of the twentieth century, implied that India's "spiritual fervour" made it uniquely qualified to guide efforts to establish a "permanent peace in the world."[55]

The commingling took on a further dimension over the following decade. Key here is K. R. Malkani's visionary 1951 pamphlet *Principles for a New Political Party*, for which Mookherjee wrote a glowing introduction. Malkani, then the editor of *Organiser*, the influential weekly affiliated with the Rashtriya Swayamsevak Sangh (RSS), and later a key figure in the BJP, underscored Savarkar's continuing influence when he declared that since the world "is ruled by the law of jungle," India's foreign policy ought to be "wise, not philosophic."[56] In the context of the Cold War this implied that non-alignment, though useful because it kept India out of "the fray," was ultimately insufficient because "strength" was required to "persevere in the policy of peace."[57] And here, Malkani declared, "the failure of the government to build up the industrial potential—the only source of military might—of the country stands out as gross error of omission."[58]

But having said this, Malkani then turned around to adopt a Gandhian perspective on the question of industrialization. In his view, an appropriate economic policy—a *Bharatiya*, or social economics—was one centered on social and human well-being.[59] In his words: "Industry must not dwarf man. Machine must not be allowed to master Man. It must not dehumanise him."[60] A parallel contradiction arose on the question of foreign economic relations. On one hand, Malkani welcomed foreign capital as helpful to industrialization; on the other, he recommended autarky so as to lessen India's "dependence on foreign countries."[61] What Malkani left unanswered was how India might develop military power without large-scale industrialization and how large-scale industrialization could occur in a poor country without foreign investment.

Malkani's fellow travelers only muddied the waters. A crucial figure in these decades was Madhav Sadashiv Golwalkar, the long-serving leader of the RSS. Golwalkar reaffirmed Savarkar's focus on social cohesiveness: Europe's strength stemmed, he insisted, from its cherishing and fostering of "correct national consciousness."[62] Golwalkar was equally clear about the nature of international relations: "friendship or hostility between nations," he commented, "is decided according as their national interests coalesce or clash with one another."[63] Hence, he supported, albeit somewhat reluctantly, the acquisition of nuclear weapons. At the same time, like Malkani, Golwalkar questioned the value of industrialization. "The Western theory of creating multiplicity of wants, more machinery to meet them," he emphasized, "will only result in making man the slave of machine."[64] Far preferable, in his view, were decentralized "small scale and home industries."[65]

The aforementioned commingling reached its apogee in the thought of Deendayal Upadhyaya, who moved from the RSS to become the general secretary (and subsequently president) of the Jan Sangh. Like his contemporaries, Upadhyaya underscored the importance of interests and capabilities in the conduct of international relations. "The foreign policy of a country," he declared, "should be framed with the sole objective of securing the en-

Rahul Sagar

lightened self-interests of the nation. It has to be realistic and should take into account the mundane nature of the world."[66] At the same time, those who assumed that India "can be defended simply by clever manipulations of foreign policy" were "living in a world of unreality." If "the government continues to neglect the military build-up of the country can any one," he asked, "assure that there would be no aggression, or if there is one, it would be successfully repelled?"[67]

These pragmatic statements were accompanied, however, by deep concern for the upholding of an authentic Hindu morality. Upadhyaya voiced dismay at contemporary India's "thoughtless imitation of the West."[68] The West had, to be sure, birthed a number of "good ideals," including nationalism, democracy, socialism, and pacifism.[69] But modern history showed that the West had repeatedly failed to reconcile these ideals, invariably pursuing one or the other to an inhumane extreme. This meant that the West was in no position to offer others guidance on how to live well. The question worth pondering was whether India could "contribute something" to the ethical dilemma confronting the world—to wit, the dilemma of pluralism or the challenge of reconciling conflicting human needs and aspirations.[70]

What Hinduism brought to the table, Upadhyaya contended, was its ability to synthesize. Its accumulated wisdom taught that the good life is the "integrated life"—a life that fulfills the plurality of human needs and aspirations.[71] From this perspective, the prevalence of unhappiness in a materialistic, consumerist West was not surprising—it owed to the failure to appreciate humankind's spiritual needs. Seeking to avoid replicating such an unhealthy imbalance, Upadhyaya called for an economic system "which does not make us slaves of its own grinding wheels" but instead "helps in the development of our humane qualities."[72] This recommended an economic policy centered on, among other things, ecological preservation, basic social protection, guaranteed employment, and decentralized industry featuring limited mechanization. In his words: "Our machines must not only be tailored for our specific economic needs, but also must, at least, avoid conflict with our sociopolitical and cultural objectives."[73]

THE HINDU MAHASABHA

Having briefly surveyed the worldviews that informed Hindu nationalism during the Cold War period, we are now in a better position to analyze and appreciate the policies of the Hindu Mahasabha, the Jan Sangh, and the BJP. What we will see is that their policies featured paradoxical elements, veering between shrewd pragmatism and high idealism. This is hardly surprising, since these policies stemmed from a commingling of otherwise opposed worldviews.

In the period immediately following independence, the principal Hindu nationalist organization remained the Mahasabha. Contrary to what Cold War–era observers claimed, the Mahasabha did in fact have fairly worked-out positions of foreign policy. For instance, its leaders expressed hostility to foreign interference with respect to Kashmir on the grounds of national sovereignty as well as skepticism about the United Nations' impartiality.[74] They also expressed strong support for Israel. This stance owed both to their admiration for the Jewish people's "tenacious" struggle and to their dislike for what they saw as the Arab states' religiously motivated support for Pakistan.[75] The Mahasabha consistently expressed support for persons of Indian origin, especially those subject to racial discrimination, with South Africa being a particular cause of concern.[76] It also called for closer ties with East and Southeast Asia, built on the "tremendous amount of good-will" generated by the fact that these countries looked on India as their "cultural and spiritual home-land."[77]

The Mahasabha had even more to say about relations with the United States and the Soviet Union. Here the Mahasabha encountered a serious difficulty: it strongly desired closer relations between India and the West because it opposed communism, which it saw as collectivist, materialist, and irreligious. But in practice, it was confronted with growing estrangement between India and the West (for reasons outlined at the start of this chapter).

The Mahasabha's response was two-pronged. It criticized non-alignment as ineffectual, especially in view of the paucity of support at the United Nations for India's position on Kashmir. It was, as N. B. Khare, the president of the Mahasabha, declared in 1951, "high time that India realises that international affinities and hostilities do not come about by mere pious wishes, but are dependent upon our inner strength and needs of the countries concerned." At the same time, Khare criticized the United States for allying with Pakistan, claiming that the "interests of the democracies demand that India with its vast resources in men and materials should be with them in the world politics."[78]

What explained this preference for the United States? N. C. Chatterjee's 1954 presidential address provides the clearest exposition. Responding to widespread revulsion at the United States' recently announced defense pact with Pakistan, Chatterjee called for a "sober and balanced perspective," warning that those "who in anger and passion of the moment call for alliance with the Soviet Bloc and call for Military aid from Moscow should realise the price that India may have to pay—the ultimate destruction of the heritage, culture and religion of India and the installation of a system which will lead to the regimentation of life and the suppression of the individual."[79]

As a result, Chatterjee persisted in the strategy of appealing to the West. "We warn the United States of America," he thundered, "that this unstatesmanlike act on their part in giving aid to a country whose leaders have hostile designs on India is bound to weaken the cause of democracy in the world" because "India may be ultimately driven to accept help for the sake of her self-preservation from those very forces which the United States is anxious to combat by giving aid to Pakistan."[80]

Even as Chatterjee was voicing this angst, he was simultaneously stressing the idea that Hinduism rather than the West had a distinctive answer to the question of the good life. Quoting Vivekananda, Chatterjee called on the Mahasabha to take abroad the "certain eternal truths for which India has stood."[81] The flip side of this pride in Indian culture was concern about the role of foreign missionaries, which was soon to become a recurring theme and a cause of increasing anxiety about the religious and social impact of deepening relations with the West.[82]

Toward the end of the 1950s, the Mahasabha turned a corner. It continued to complain about India's growing proximity to the Soviet Union, which was evidenced by the country's reserved stance on events in Hungary.[83] But now, disillusioned by the United States' continued support for Pakistan, the Mahasabha's 1957 manifesto reemphasized Savarkar's message about the importance of capabilities: "The Mahasabha had always stood for the principle—the Militarisation of the Indian Nation. The world will laugh at us if we base our foreign policy on mere idealism. . . . [We must provide] our Army, Navy and Air Forces with the latest equipment capable of resisting attack and aggression from any quarter and then only Panch-Shila will work and India shall command respect and prestige in the comity of nations."[84]

By the end of the decade, with China now firmly ensconced in Tibet, the Mahasabha adopted a starker position. Ram Singh, the president at the 1959 annual meeting, warned that "strict neutrality is an impossibility in this closely knit present world" because "whatever act you do is bound to have an effect on the other nations of the world."[85] This implied that "there is no such thing as foreign policy, as [a] strong military is the only guarantee of a respectable position of a nation among the comity of nations." And on this front, he continued, "Are we so silly that we cannot hope to make [a] hydrogen bomb some day? Where there is will, there is way."[86]

Yet even as the Mahasabha was arguing for greater realism on matters of foreign and defense policy, its economic policies evidenced a lack of realism about how the country might secure the requisite means. A good example is V. G. Deshpande's RSS-inspired call in his 1960 presidential address for the pursuit of "Hindu Socialism," a doctrine of anti-Marxist "spiritualistic collectivism" that cashed out as proposals for collective farming, a planned economy, and market intervention "to suppress with iron hand the profiteering and exploiting tendencies of the capitalists."[87] How an economy organized along these lines would generate the "thousands of crores" Deshpande wanted to spend on militarization was left unexplained.[88]

THE JAN SANGH

By the close of the decade, the Hindu Mahasabha was a spent force, having been rapidly overtaken by the Jan Sangh. Established in 1951 by Mookherjee in conjunction with the RSS, the Jan Sangh early on adopted positions that bore some resemblance to the Mahasabha's. For instance, like the Mahasabha, the Jan Sangh questioned the United Nations' legitimacy, called for "special attention" to be given to the countries of Southeast Asia,[89] and criticized Nehru's "callous policy of indifference" toward Indians abroad, especially in Ceylon, Burma, and South Africa.[90] The Jan Sangh also quickly made clear its distaste for communism, declaring in 1952 that "the spirit of India is fundamentally opposed to totalitarianism" and that India must therefore "stand for the development of freedom and democracy in the world."[91]

The above notwithstanding, the Jan Sangh went its own way in two important respects. First, it called for non-alignment to be understood as "neutrality" and "non-involvement."[92] India's objective, it declared, "should be to avoid involvement in the power-blocs"[93] lest the country become a "cockpit."[94] Equally, India should "try to win friends and cooperation of all countries by avoiding involvements in such international conflicts and issues as do not directly concern India."[95] Nehru had failed on both counts, the Jan Sangh alleged, because by leaning toward the Soviet bloc and by involving India in arbitrating the Korean conflict, he had needlessly strained relations with the West.

Second, in contrast to the Mahasabha's more militant tone, the Jan Sangh followed Mookherjee in stressing that "true to traditions of *Bharat*," it will "work for the maintenance of world peace and mutual understanding."[96] Here the Jan Sangh's operating premise was that "world peace cannot be permanently assured so long as political subjugation, economic exploitation, and prejudices based on colour continue in the world."[97] From this premise flowed three major commitments—anticolonialism, hostility to foreign interference, and universal nuclear disarmament—that, contrary to the Jan Sangh's calls for India to exhibit "aloofness," actually led it in practice to rail against the superpowers (for instance, against U.S. intervention in Cambodia and Vietnam and against Soviet intervention in Eastern Europe).[98]

At the start of the next decade, however, the Jan Sangh's posture underwent a noticeable transformation. In the face of the long-drawn-out border tensions with China, its outlook became more confrontational. It fiercely criticized Nehru for being "indifferent to the imperative concomitant ... of non-alignment, namely, the building up of adequate military strength."[99] An immediate policy implication was that though the Jan Sangh had previously called for universal nuclear disarmament to save the world from "catastrophe,"[100] from 1963 onward it began to demand, ever more stridently, that India develop a nuclear deterrent to counter China.[101]

Before long, the Jan Sangh was questioning non-alignment itself. China's actions revealed, it argued, that the world was now multipolar rather than bipolar. In the event, the "forging of a new alignment aimed at containing and rolling back Peking's threat has become imperative," it declared in 1963.[102] To this end, the Jan Sangh now urged closer relations with countries in Southeast Asia, Israel, Australia, Japan, and the United States in particular.[103]

By the middle of the 1960s, influenced by its new president, the arch-realist Balraj Madhok, the Jan Sangh stepped up the assault on the status quo. Continued U.S. and British support for Pakistan during the 1965 Indo-Pakistan War was "sorely disappointing," the Jan Sangh said.[104] Enough "with platitudes like world-peace and coexistence and with clichés and catchwords like non-alignment"[105] that had "ceased to be relevant."[106] Henceforth India's foreign policy ought to be "independent" and based on "reciprocity."[107]

Over the following decade, the Jan Sangh had a number of opportunities to translate this principle into policy, starting with the 1971 Indo-Pakistan war. Confronted with U.S. support for West Pakistan in spite of its genocidal behavior in East Pakistan, and with U.S. "gun-boat-diplomacy" in the form of the U.S.S. *Enterprise*,[108] the Jan Sangh strongly condemned the United States, observing that its actions "clearly proved that there is no place for any principles, charity or morality in international relations."[109] At the same time, it criticized the 1971 Indo-Soviet Treaty for effectively allying India with the Soviet bloc. A more appropriate policy, it argued, would be to "broad-base" India's diplomacy by signing such "friendship treaties" with multiple countries, including Indonesia and Japan.[110]

The advent of the Non-Proliferation Treaty (NPT) provided another opportunity to showcase what an independent stance implied in practice. "It is obvious," the Jan Sangh's response went, that neither the United States nor the Soviet Union "wishes to see us come up." Their objective in pushing India to accede to the treaty was to ensure that it could be "blackmailed and brow-beaten" at a later date in order to secure their interests.[111] Under such circumstances, it declared, India ought to go nuclear "without delay" and its defense strength ought to be "doubled"[112] with a view to allowing the country to become an "independent power centre."[113]

The most important opportunity the Jan Sangh received to elaborate its worldview was when it briefly came to power in 1977 as part of the social-ist Janata Party, allowing Atal Bihari Vajpayee to become foreign minister. Though observers expected the Jan Sangh, on the basis of Hindu nationalists' long-standing hostility toward communism, to push for a closer relationship with the United States, Vajpayee pursued "genuine non-alignment," which translated into only "downgrading" Indira Gandhi's perceived "tilt" toward the Soviet Union.[114] Beyond this, however, Vajpayee chose not to follow the Jan Sangh's script. Instead of pursuing an activist foreign policy directed at building a coalition against China and Pakistan, he trumpeted India's civili-zational commitment to "genuine co-existence."[115] This became the basis for his efforts to normalize relations with India's neighbors by making conces-sions that his colleagues in the Jan Sangh had previously criticized as naive— for instance, visiting China in spite of the ongoing border dispute and re-nouncing the development of nuclear weapons.[116] These moves surprised contemporary observers, who had failed to discern that Mookherjee's suc-cessors were influenced not only by the tough-minded realism promoted by Savarkar but also by civilizational ideals of mutual accommodation emanat-ing from Vivekananda.

Gandhi's influence, meanwhile, was apparent in the economic sphere. Though the Jan Sangh claimed it wanted to make India an "independent power centre,"[117] and hence called for 10 percent growth, its economic phi-losophy—summarized as "growth in production, equity in distribution, and restraint in consumption"—prioritized social and moral objectives.[118] For example, given its discomfort with "conspicuous consumption,"[119] the Jan Sangh proposed reducing income inequality by capping maximum expend-able income to ten times the minimum income.[120] Given its fixation on de-veloping "technology to suit Indian conditions,"[121] it proposed to achieve self-sufficiency in consumer goods through decentralization and reservation of production to village and small-scale industries, and the imposition of controls on the import and consumption of consumer goods.[122] Given its emphasis on national control, it proposed to "revive the spirit of *Swadeshi*," by seeking to "discourage the use of foreign goods" and challenging foreign ownership of industries, promising to "progressively Indianise them in their capital, ownership and personnel."[123] Like Malkani and Golwalkar before it, the Jan Sangh failed to explain (or perhaps even to consider) how such economic policies would permit India to generate the surpluses needed to pursue a truly independent foreign policy.

THE BHARATIYA JANATA PARTY

In 1980, with the Janata Party experiment having failed, members of the erstwhile Jan Sangh formed the BJP. Led by Vajpayee, the BJP started out advocating the less militant of the Jan Sangh's ideals. Recall that although the Jan Sangh had declared non-alignment irrelevant, Vajpayee had deviated from the script by calling for "genuine" non-alignment. The BJP now ratified Vajpayee's position, affirming non-alignment's continued "relevance."[124] The immediate motive was countering Indira Gandhi's "tilt" toward the Soviet Union, whose intervention in Afghanistan the BJP denounced. But the BJP was also genuinely concerned about U.S. intentions—the American presence in Diego Garcia, for instance, was viewed as militarizing the Indian Ocean.

Having affirmed non-alignment, the BJP spent the 1980s elaborating the concept's "moral content." At heart, it declared, the concept emerged from "the rejection of domination in all its forms."[125] This insight prompted the adoption of four key policies. First, the BJP stressed the importance of being a "good neighbour" so as to deny the superpowers an opportunity to interfere in the South (or at least in South Asia).[126] Second, it took up the cause of inequality, calling for "a more equitable world order," through "South-South cooperation" if necessary.[127] On this front, it vigorously challenged the West-sponsored emergent global trading order and demanded instead the creation of a "new international economic order."[128] Third, it championed the cause of regional peace, calling for the transformation of South Asia into a "zone of peace" and for the normalization of relations with Pakistan and China.[129] It followed the early Jan Sangh in calling for universal nuclear disarmament. Contrast present assertions about the BJP's "militarism" with this 1981 declaration: "The search for mutually assured destruction leads the world towards nuclear holocaust. This mad race for armaments makes the world spend over 150 million dollars daily on armaments whilst the majority of mankind goes hungry, shelterless and deprived of other essentials. A search for a more equitable world order becomes meaningless in the face of larger and more potent instruments of death."[130] Fourth, the BJP became far more vocal about "foreign domination,"[131] stressing the "inviolability of the sovereignty and territory of nations."[132] Here it announced its "rejection of the self-adopted role as a 'world policeman' by the U.S.A."[133] Even long-admired Israel did not escape criticism: "Israel certainly has a right to exist," the BJP declared, "but not as an expanding regional power, with freedom to define its own concept of secure frontiers."[134]

Not unlike how the 1962 war had prompted the Jan Sangh to move in a more realist direction, the end of the Cold War prompted the BJP to revise its worldview. The impetus was fear of American hegemony. As the BJP explained in 1992:

> The post–cold war world lacks a balanced power structure. This is inherently bad for the world because untrammelled power in the hands of one country or a group of countries with ideological similarity would inevitably lead to a resurgence of hegemonic attitudes. Even today hegemonistic [sic] tendencies abound. The treatment meted out to the countries of the Third World by a group of powerful countries clearly violates a fundamental principle of international relations viz. the principle of sovereign equality of nations. They exert pressure openly on the countries of the third world to follow their philosophy and their political and economic models.[135]

The BJP responded to this threat in a number of ways. First, it revived the Jan Sangh's policy of "active" bilateralism and "strict reciprocity,"[136] calling on the Rajiv Gandhi government to "maximise the number of our friends abroad," encouraging it to deepen ties with Israel and Japan in particular.[137] Having deemed the nonaligned movement "the foundation" of its "policy plank" as recently as 1984,[138] the BJP now declared in 1991 that nonalignment had "lost its relevance."[139] Second, having previously been vocal on nuclear disarmament, it now wheeled around to demand that, in view of American unilateralism in the Persian Gulf and continued U.S. and Chinese support for Pakistani nuclear proliferation, India must give its defense forces "Nuclear Teeth."[140] Confronted subsequently with pressure for India to accede to the "discriminatory" Comprehensive Test Ban Treaty (CTBT) and the NPT, the BJP urged that the country "immediately manufacture and deploy" nuclear weapons.[141] Third, in view of the growing threat of external intervention, and seeking to make India an "autonomous power center," it called for the United Nations to be reformed and for India to be accorded a seat at the Security Council.[142]

So far, we have seen that in foreign policy the BJP made much the same somersault that the Jan Sangh did—initially calling for non-alignment or aloofness from power politics and then subsequently, in the face of setbacks, emphasizing bilateralism and reciprocity. In the economic sphere, however, the BJP remained fully wedded to the Jan Sangh's call for nationalism and humanism. These commitments remained in place even after the end of the Cold War, only evolving in the mid-1990s. Strikingly, not once during this period did the BJP openly question whether its idiosyncratic combination of Gandhian socialism, austerity, and autarky might conflict with its desire to see India become one of the poles of a multipolar system.

In the first half of the 1980s, the BJP focused its attention on India's growing balance of payments problem, which had prompted Indira Gandhi, under pressure from the International Monetary Fund, to take small steps toward liberalizing the economy. The BJP viewed these steps—which included de-reserving the small-scale sector and permitting technological imports—as "detrimental" and "humiliating" because they detracted from "self-reliance"[143] and caused "distortion in favour of exports and large industrial units."[144] Subsequent measures—which included devaluation of the rupee, efforts to attract foreign investment, and the raising of dollar loans— were described as a "wilful surrender to international economic imperialism"[145] and the start of a slide into "a veritable death-trap of international financial barons."[146] The path to true economic recovery, the BJP claimed in 1984, was not to import "fancy equipment" and to permit foreign funds to "take over well run industries in India" but instead to revive the "spirit of 'swadeshi'" and to direct scarce credit toward agriculture and small and cottage industries.[147]

In the second half of the 1980s, the BJP targeted Rajiv Gandhi's New Economic Policy, which emphasized technological advance. If the country was to escape its "dependence on foreign . . . know how and the strangle hold" of multinational corporations, the BJP argued, it needed to "evolve a technology appropriate" to its needs and resources because "high technology is not an unmixed boon."[148] So opposed was the BJP to the policy of "the computer boys"[149] that by the late 1980s it was calling on the government to halt "indiscriminate computerisation," arguing that such technologies would increase unemployment and hence should be used only "where they are extremely necessary."[150]

Following the end of the Cold War, the BJP redoubled its opposition to foreign investment. In 1990, it resolved that though "the total reversal of the axioms underlying the economic model of the socialist block" necessitated a rethink of India's economic policy, "technology should [nonetheless] not be allowed to degrade man and reduce him to being just another input in the Gross National Product. Man must be the focus of our developmental policies."[151] Even as late as 1992, it continued to express preference for "import substitution in every possible sphere" and fiercely questioned the utility of foreign investment,[152] especially in consumer industries. "We need modern technology urgently but not in the production of Pepsi Cola, Potato chips, soaps and Talcum powders,"[153] the BJP claimed, as this would render India's cooperatives "sick."[154]

CONCLUSION

This chapter has traced how the Hindu Mahasabha, the Jan Sangh, and the BJP reacted to the Cold War and to the United States in particular. Contrary to the widely held belief that these parties either had little to say about international affairs or that what they had to say was resolutely militant in nature, we have seen that Hindu nationalists initially expressed a clear preference for the West. But over time this became a guarded preference because Hindu nationalists came to doubt U.S. willingness to countenance India's rise and because they fretted about the consequences of materialism and Westernization. The end of the Cold War, we have seen, brought this subterranean anxiety to the surface.

The foregoing analysis reveals a deep dilemma at the heart of Cold War–era Hindu nationalism. Hindu nationalists understood that weakness invites aggression, and they recognized that strength depends on modernization. Yet because they worried about the moral and cultural consequences of modernization, they were unwilling to commit to this project, even though they considered it essential. And so it came to be that, because they commingled realist and humanist traditions, the Hindu nationalists' pursuit of interests and capabilities confounded, and was confounded by, their desire to realize certain values and morals. Fortunately for them, because they were in the Opposition for nearly the entire Cold War period, they were never really compelled to address this awkward tension between interests and values — that is, they were never actually forced to choose between security and modernization on one hand and moral and cultural integrity on the other.

Rahul Sagar

1. Harold A. Gould and Sumit Ganguly, eds., *The Hope and the Reality: U.S.-Indian Relations from Roosevelt to Reagan* (Boulder, Colo.: Westview Press, 1992); Dennis Kux, *India and the United States: Estranged Democracies, 1941–1991* (Washington, D.C.: National Defense University Press, 1992). Other important surveys include Nathan Glazer and Sulochana R. Glazer, eds., *Conflicting Images: India and the United States* (Glenn Dale, Md.: Riverdale, 1990); and A. P. Rana, ed., *Four Decades of Indo-US Relations: A Commemorative Retrospective* (New Delhi: Har-Anand, 1994).

2. Rudra Chaudhuri, *Forged in Crisis: India and the United States since 1947* (New York: Oxford University Press, 2014).

3. See, e.g., Stephen P. Cohen, *India: Emerging Power* (Washington, D.C.: Brookings Institution Press, 2002), 37.

4. J. B. Kripalani, "For Principled Neutrality," *Foreign Affairs* 38, no. 1 (1959): 60. See also Robert L. Hardgrave Jr., "Linkage Politics in India: The Relationship of Domestic Politics to Foreign Policy," in *Asia and the Major Powers: Domestic Politics and Foreign Policy*, ed. Robert A. Scalapino (Berkeley, Calif.: Institute of East Asian Studies, 1988), 308.

5. Rahul Sagar and Ankit Panda, "Pledges and Pious Wishes: The Constituent Assembly Debates and the Myth of a 'Nehruvian Consensus,'" *India Review* 14, no. 2 (2015): 203–20.

6. Constituent Assembly Debates: Official Report (Tuesday, 17th May 1949): Resolution re Ratification of Commonwealth Decision–(contd.), 60.

7. Ibid., 39.

8. Werner Levi, *Free India in Asia* (Minneapolis: University of Minnesota Press, 1952), 7–9; Richard M. Fontera, "Anti-Colonialism as a Basic Indian Foreign Policy," *Western Political Quarterly* 13, no. 2 (1960): 425. See also Asoka Mehta, "The Political Mind of India," *Foreign Affairs* 35, no. 4 (1957): 686. A rare exception is Donald E. Smith, *India as a Secular State* (Princeton, N.J.: Princeton University Press, 1963), 472.

9. L. F. Rushbrook Williams, "Hindu Nationalism Today," *Spectator*, 17 August 1956, 226. The classic essay here is Angadipuram Appadorai, "Traditional Indian Values in the Direction of Peace," in *Essays in Politics and International Relations* (New Delhi: Asia Publishing House, 1969), 151–65.

10. Kanti Bajpai, "Indian Conceptions of Order and Justice: Nehruvian, Gandhian, Hindutva, and Neo-Liberal," in *Order and Justice in International Relations*, ed. Rosemary Foot, John Gaddis, and Andrew Hurrell (Oxford: Oxford University Press, 2003), 248–53.

11. On this, see Rahul Sagar, "'Jiski Lathi, Uski Bhains': The Hindu Nationalist View of International Politics," in *India's Grand Strategy: History, Theory, Cases*, ed. Kanti Bajpai (New Delhi: Routledge, 2014), 234–57.

12. Chris Ogden, *Hindu Nationalism and the Evolution of Contemporary Indian Security: Portents of Power* (Oxford: Oxford University Press, 2014), 68–69. See also B. L. Maheshwari, "Foreign Policy of Jan Sangh," *Economic and Political Weekly* 3, no. 35 (1968): 1334–35.

13. Kanti Bajpai, "Hinduism and Weapons of Mass Destruction: Pacifist, Prudential, and Political," in *Ethics and Weapons of Mass Destruction*, ed. Sohail Hashmi and Steven P. Lee (New York: Cambridge University Press, 2004), 313.

14. Ibid., 317–18.

15. Ibid., 317.

16. L. K. Advani, *My Country, My Life* (New Delhi: Rupa, 2008), 153.

17. Rahul Sagar, "What's in a Name?," *Survival* 46, no. 3 (2004): 115–36.

18. Raj Narain Bose, "Superiority of Hinduism to Other Existing Religions: As Viewed from the Standpoint of Theism," *Theosophist* 4, no. 2 (1882): 35.

19. Bankim Chandra Chattopadhyay, "Hinduism Revisited," in *Bankim's Hinduism*, ed. Amiya P. Sen (New Delhi: Permanent Black, 2011), 136.

20. Ibid., 139; Bankim Chandra Chattopadhyay, "The Utilitarian Basis of Hindu Dharma," in Sen, *Bankim's Hinduism*, 142, 144.

21. Bankim Chandra Chattopadhyay, "The Essence of Dharma — in Krishna's Words," in Sen, *Bankim's Hinduism*, 167. See also Chattopadhyay, "Utilitarian Basis of Hindu Dharma," 144.

22. Chattopadhyay, "Essence of Dharma," 167.

23. Raj Narain Bose, "Nutan Dharmamat" [New religious opinion], *Tattwabodhini Patrika*, August–September 1884 (Bhadra 1806 Shak.).

24. Bankim Chandra Chattopadhyay, "Bharat Kalanka" [Bharat's Shame], in *Rachanabali*, vol. 2, available at https://archive.org/details/in.ernet.dli.2015.354975.

25. Bankim Chandra Chatterji, *Essentials of Dharma*, trans. Manomohan Ghosh (Calcutta: Sribhumi, 1977), 52.

26. Ibid., 53–54.

27. Ibid., 137.

28. Swami Vivekananda, "Reply to the Address of Welcome at Madras," in Vivekananda, *Complete Works*, vol. 3, *Lectures and Discourses*, available at https://archive.org/details/SWAMIVIVEKANANDACOMPLETEWORKSVol3.

29. Swami Vivekananda, "First Public Lecture in the East," in ibid.

30. Vivekananda, "Reply to the Address of Welcome at Madras."

31. Swami Vivekananda, "The Work before Us," in Vivekananda, *Complete Works*, vol. 3. See also Swami Vivekananda, "History of the Aryan Race," in Vivekananda, *Complete Works*, vol. 9, *Letters — Fifth Series*, available at https://archive.org/details/SWAMIVIVEKANANDACOMPLETEWORKSVol9_201711. Vivekananda declared there that it was a "glorious thing" that India was "the only nation that never went beyond its frontiers to cut the throats of its neighbours."

32. Vivekananda, "Work before Us."

33. Aurobindo Ghosh, "Bhawani Mandir," in Aurobindo Ghosh, *Bande Mataram* (Pondicherry: Sri Aurobindo Ashram Trust, 2002), 86. See also Aurobindo Ghosh, "The Progress of China," in Aurobindo Ghosh, *Karmayogin* (Pondicherry: Sri Aurobindo Ashram Trust, 1997), 265–66; and Aurobindo Ghosh, "The Growth of Turkey," in Ghosh, *Karmayogin*, 289–90.

34. Aurobindo Ghosh, "National Development and Foreign Rule," in Ghosh, *Bande Mataram*, 363.

35. Ibid., 364.

36. Aurobindo Ghosh, "Rishi Bankimchandra," in Ghosh, *Bande Mataram*, 318.

37. Aurobindo Ghosh, "The Morality of Boycott," in Ghosh, *Bande Mataram*, 1118. Also see Aurobindo Ghosh, "Khulna Speech," in Ghosh, *Karmayogin*, 48–53.

38. Mohandas K. Gandhi, "Ahimsa," in Mohandas K. Gandhi, *Speeches and Writings of M. K. Gandhi* (Madras: Natesan, 1922), 282.

39. Mohandas K. Gandhi, "The Gurukula," in Gandhi, *Speeches and Writings*, 268–69.

40. Mohandas K. Gandhi, "On Anarchical Crimes," in Gandhi, *Speeches and Writings*, 230–31.

41. Mohandas K. Gandhi, *Hind Swaraj or Indian Home Rule* (Madras: Natesan, 1921), 63.

42. Gandhi, "Gurukula," 268.

43. Mohandas K. Gandhi, "Economic vs. Moral Progress," in Gandhi, *Speeches and Writings*, 290.

44. Gandhi, *Hind Swaraj*, 95–99.

45. Ibid., 24.

46. Vinayak D. Savarkar, *Hindu Rashtra Darshan* (Poona: Maharashtra Prantik Hindusabha, 1964), 15.

47. Vinayak D. Savarkar, *Essentials of Hindutva* (Delhi: Bharati Sahitya Sadan, 2003), 141.

48. Savarkar, *Hindu Rashtra Darshan*, 85.

49. Ibid., 81.

50. Ibid., 84.

51. Ibid., 61.

52. Syama Prasad Mookherjee, *Presidential Address at the 26th Session of the All India Hindu Mahasabha, 24th December 1944* (New Delhi: All India Hindu Mahasabha, 1944), 12.

53. Ibid., 13.

54. Ibid., 18.

55. Ibid., 24–25.

56. K. R. Malkani, *Principles for a New Political Party* (Delhi: Vijay Pustak Bhandar, 1951), 42–43.

57. Ibid., 42, 45.

58. Ibid., 44.

59. Ibid., 9, 12–13.

60. Ibid., 29.

61. Ibid., 33, 37–38.

62. Madhav Sadashiv Golwalkar, *We or Our Nationhood Defined* (Nagpur: Bharat, 1939), 62.

63. Madhav Sadashiv Golwalkar, *Nation at War* (Bangalore: Prakashan Vibbhag, 1966), 13.

64. Rashtriya Swayamsevak Sangh, *Spotlights: Guruji Answers* (Bangalore: Sahitya Sindhu, 1974), 12.

65. Ibid., 7.

66. Deendayal Upadhyaya, *Political Diary* (Bombay: Jaico, 1968), 51; see also 83–84.

67. Ibid., 51–52.

68. Deendayal Upadhyaya, "Our Direction," in Deendayal Upadhyaya, Shri Guruji, and Shri D. B. Thengdi, *The Integral Approach* (New Delhi: Deendayal Research Institute, 1979), 8.

69. Ibid., 11.

70. Ibid., 12.

71. Deendayal Upadhyaya, "Integral Humanism," in Upadhyaya, Guruji, and Thengdi, *Integral Approach*, 23; see also 18–19.

72. Deendayal Upadhyaya, "Economic Structure Suited to National Genius," in Upadhyaya, Guruji, and Thengdi, *Integral Approach*, 59.

73. Upadhyaya, "Economic Structure Suited to National Genius," 67; see also 63–69, 73–74.

74. All India Hindu Mahasabha, *Full Text of the Resolutions Adopted by the Working Committee on 10th and 11th September 1949* (New Delhi: All India Hindu Mahasabha,

1949), 5; N. B. Khare, *Presidential Address at the Special Session of the All India Hindu Mahasabha, 28th April 1951* (Jaipur: Hindu Mahasabha, 1951), 15–16.

75. All India Hindu Mahasabha, *Full Text of the Resolutions Adopted by the Working Committee*, 6–7.

76. N. C. Chatterjee, *Presidential Address at the 30th Annual Session of the All India Hindu Mahasabha, 28th December 1952* (New Delhi: All India Hindu Mahasabha, 1952), 7–8.

77. Akhil Bharat Hindu Mahasabha, *Full Text of Resolutions at the 30th Annual Session, 28th, 29th and 30th December 1952* (New Delhi: Hindu Mahasabha Bhawan, 1953), 9.

78. Khare, *Presidential Address*, 16–17.

79. N. C. Chatterjee, *Presidential Address at the 31st Annual Session of the All India Hindu Mahasabha, 7th May 1954* (New Delhi: All India Hindu Mahasabha, 1954), 16.

80. Ibid., 25.

81. Ibid., 13.

82. Ibid., 21.

83. Akhil Bharat Hindu Mahasabha, *Election Manifesto 1957* (New Delhi: Akhil Bharat Hindu Mahasabha, 1957), 10.

84. Ibid., 11.

85. Ram Singh, *Presidential Address at the 44th Annual Session of the All India Hindu Mahasabha, 20th February 1959* (New Delhi: Akhil Bharat Hindu Mahasabha, 1959), 11.

86. Ibid., 13.

87. V. G. Deshpande, *Presidential Address at the 45th Annual Session of the Akhil Bharat Hindu Mahasabha, 29th May 1960* (New Delhi: Akhil Bharat Hindu Mahasabha, 1960), 7–8.

88. Ibid., 16.

89. "Foreign Policy, January 1, 1955, Jodhpur, III. All India Session," in Bharatiya Jana Sangh, *Party Documents, 1951–72*, vol. 3, *Resolutions on Defence and External Affairs* (New Delhi: Bharatiya Jana Sangh, 1973), 35. See also "Foreign Policy, June 14, 1952, Delhi, Central Working Committee," in Bharatiya Jana Sangh, *Party Documents, 1951–72*, 21.

90. "Plight of Overseas Indians, December 30, 1963, Ahmedabad, XI. All India Session," in Bharatiya Jana Sangh, *Party Documents, 1951–72*, 104. See also "South Africa's Apartheid Policy, December 31, 1952, Kanpur, I. All India Session," in ibid., 22; "Indian Settlers in Ceylon, August 28, 1955, Calcutta, All India General Council," in ibid., 39; "Indian Settlers in Ceylon and Burma, November 24, 1957, Hyderabad, Central Working Committee," in ibid., 50–51; "'Stateless' Overseas Indians, December 28, 1958, Bangalore, VII. All India Session," in ibid., 62–63; and "Plight of Indians in Burma, December 30, 1963, Ahmedabad, XI. All India Session," in ibid., 103.

91. "Foreign Policy, June 14, 1952, Delhi, Central Working Committee," 21.

92. "Unrealistic Foreign Policy, November 24, 1957, Hyderabad, Central Working Committee," in Bharatiya Jana Sangh, *Party Documents, 1951–72*, 52–53.

93. "Foreign Policy, June 14, 1952, Delhi, Central Working Committee," 21.

94. "Foreign Policy, January 1, 1955, Jodhpur, III. All India Session," 34.

95. "Unrealistic Foreign Policy, November 24, 1957, Hyderabad, Central Working Committee," 52.

96. "1951 Manifesto," in Bharatiya Jana Sangh, *Policies and Manifestoes*, vol. 1 (New Delhi: Bharatiya Janata Party, 2005), 291.

97. "Desirable Summit Meet, January 25, 1960, Nagpur, VIII. All India Session," in Bharatiya Jana Sangh, *Party Documents 1951–72*, 72–73.

Rahul Sagar

98. Ibid., 73; "More Meaningful UNO, January 1, 1961, Lucknow, IX. All India Session," in Bharatiya Jana Sangh, *Party Documents, 1951–72*, 85.

99. "Revise and Reorientate Foreign Policy, December 30, 1962, Bhopal, X. All India Session," in Bharatiya Jana Sangh, *Party Documents, 1951–72*, 93.

100. "Summit Conference Failure, June 1, 1960, Delhi, Central Working Committee," in Bharatiya Jana Sangh, *Party Documents, 1951–72*, 79.

101. "Nuclear Deterrent Necessary, December 4, 1964, Patna, Central Working Committee," in Bharatiya Jana Sangh, *Party Documents, 1951–72*, 7–8; "Pindi-Peking Axis, May 1, 1966, Jullundur, XIII. All India Session," in ibid., 10; "Beware of Non-Proliferation Treaty, March 22, 1968, Bhopal, Central Working Committee," in ibid., 12; "Effective and Massive Deterrence, April 6, 1963, Delhi, Central Working Committee," in ibid., 95–96; "Foreign Policy Statement, January 24, 1965, Vijayawada, XII. All India Session," in ibid., 122.

102. "Effective and Massive Deterrence, April 6, 1963, Delhi, Central Working Committee," 96.

103. "Revise and Reorientate Foreign Policy, December 30, 1963, Ahmedabad, XI. All India Session," in Bharatiya Jana Sangh, *Party Documents, 1951–72*, 102–3.

104. "War with Pakistan, September 27, 1965, Delhi, Central Working Committee," in Bharatiya Jana Sangh, *Party Documents, 1951–72*, 131.

105. "Foreign Policy Statement, January 24, 1965, Vijayawada, XII. All India Session," 121.

106. "Revise and Reorientate Foreign Policy, April 26, 1969, Bombay, XV. All India Session," in Bharatiya Jana Sangh, *Party Documents, 1951–72*, 147.

107. "Joint Committee for Defence and Foreign Policy, December 26, 1967, Calicut, XIV. All India Session," in Bharatiya Jana Sangh, *Party Documents, 1951–72*, 140. Here see Balraj Madhok, "India's Foreign Policy: The Jana Sangh View," *India Quarterly* 23, no. 1 (1967): 3–7; and esp. Balraj Madhok, *What Jana Sangh Stands For* (Ahmedabad: Ahmedabad Junior Chamber, 1966), 8–21. Another important document is M. L. Sondhi, *Non Appeasement: A New Direction for Indian Foreign Policy* (New Delhi: Abhinav, 1972).

108. "Statement on the Indian Ocean, Passed by the All India Working Committee, 5–7 April, 1974, Ujjain," in Bharatiya Jana Sangh, *Defence and External Affairs: Party Documents*, vol. 3, *1952–1980* (New Delhi: Bharatiya Janata Party, 2005), 6.

109. "Recognise Swadhin Bangladesh, July 2, 1971, Udaipur, XVII. All India Session," in Bharatiya Jana Sangh, *Party Documents, 1951–72*, 156. See also "Hungarian and Suez Crisis, 30 December, 1956, Delhi, V. All India Session," in Bharatiya Jana Sangh, *Defence and External Affairs*, 192–93.

110. "Indo-Soviet Treaty, August 13, 1971, Delhi, Central Working Committee," in Bharatiya Jana Sangh, *Party Documents, 1951–72*, 158–59.

111. "Statement on Foreign Policy, As Adopted by All India Working Committee, 9–11 February, 1973, Kanpur," in Bharatiya Jana Sangh, *Defence and External Affairs*, 38.

112. "National Security, 27 November, 1971, Ghaziabad, All India General Council," in Bharatiya Jana Sangh, *Defence and External Affairs*, 16.

113. "Statement on Foreign Policy, as Adopted by All India Working Committee, 9–11 February, 1973, Kanpur," 38.

114. Atal Behari Vajpayee, "India and the Changing International Order," in K. P. Misra, *Janata's Foreign Policy* (New Delhi: Vikas, 1979), 9; A. G. Noorani, "Foreign Policy of the Janata Party Government," *Asian Affairs* 5, no. 4 (1978): 225; M. S. Rajan, "India's Foreign Policy: Problems and Perspectives," in Misra, *Janata's Foreign Policy*, 20.

115. Vajpayee, "India and the Changing International Order," 4.

116. Ibid., 7–8. See also Noorani, "Foreign Policy," 226; Rajan, "India's Foreign Policy," 23–25; and Margaret Alva, "Janata's Foreign Policy: A Critique," in Misra, *Janata's Foreign Policy*, 12–17.

117. "Statement on Foreign Policy, as Adopted by All India Working Committee, 9–11 February, 1973, Kanpur," 38.

118. Atal Behari Vajpayee, "Foreword," in Bharatiya Jana Sangh, *Party Documents, 1951–1972*, vol. 2, *Resolutions on Economic Affairs* (New Delhi: Bharatiya Jana Sangh, 1973), iv. An important influence during this period was one of Upadhyaya's comrades, Dattopant B. Thengadi; see D. B. Thengadi, *The Perspective* (Bangalore: Sahitya Sindhu, 1971), chap. 17.

119. "Planning," in Bharatiya Jana Sangh, *Party Documents, 1951–1972*, vol. 2, 3.

120. Vajpayee, "Foreword," vii.

121. Ibid., vii.

122. "1951 Manifesto," 286–90.

123. "1954 Manifesto," in Bharatiya Jana Sangh, *Policies and Manifestoes*, 272–74.

124. "Resolution Adopted at the National Executive Meeting Held at Cochin on April 23, 1981," in Bharatiya Janata Party, *Foreign Policy Resolutions and Statements, 1980–1999* (New Delhi: Bharatiya Janata Party, 1999), 5.

125. Ibid., 5.

126. "Resolution Adopted at the National Executive Meeting Held at New Delhi on September 5, 1980," in Bharatiya Janata Party, *Foreign Policy Resolutions and Statements*, 3.

127. "Resolution Adopted at the National Executive Meeting Held at New Delhi on April 13–14, 1981," in Bharatiya Janata Party, *Foreign Policy Resolutions and Statements*, 12.

128. "Election Manifesto 1984," in Bharatiya Janata Party, *Election Manifestoes: Party Documents*, vol. 1 (New Delhi: Bharatiya Janata Party, 2005), 417.

129. "Resolution Adopted at the National Executive Meeting Held at New Delhi on April 13–14, 1981," 13–14.

130. Ibid., 11.

131. Ibid., 15.

132. "Resolution Adopted at the National Executive Meeting Held at New Delhi on September 5, 1980," 4.

133. "Resolution Adopted at the National Executive Meeting Held at Cochin on April 23, 1981," 5.

134. "Resolution Adopted at the National Executive Meeting Held at New Delhi on April 13–14, 1981," 15.

135. "Resolution Adopted at the National Council Meeting Held at Gandhinagar on June 2, 1992," in Bharatiya Janata Party, *Foreign Policy Resolutions and Statements*, 34.

136. "Resolution Adopted at the National Executive Meeting Held at Bhuvaneshwar on November 7, 1992," in Bharatiya Janata Party, *Foreign Policy Resolutions and Statements*, 48.

137. "Resolution Adopted at the National Executive Meeting Held at Thiruvananthapuram on September 30, 1991," in Bharatiya Janata Party, *Foreign Policy Resolutions and Statements*, 31–33.

138. "Election Manifesto 1984," 416.

139. "Foreign Affairs Section of BJP's Election Manifesto 1991," in Bharatiya Janata Party, *Foreign Policy Resolutions and Statements*, 25.

140. "Election Manifesto 1991," in Bharatiya Janata Party, *Election Manifestoes*, 352.

141. "Resolution Adopted at the National Executive Meeting Held at Bhuvaneshwar

on November 7, 1992," 46–47. See also "Resolution Adopted at the National Executive Meeting Held at Vadodra on June 9, 1994," in Bharatiya Janata Party, *Foreign Policy Resolutions and Statements*, 51–52.

142. "Foreign Affairs Section of BJP's Election Manifesto 1991," 27.

143. "Resolution of the National Executive, New Delhi, 4–6 Dec 1981," in Bharatiya Janata Party, *BJP Resolutions: Economic, 1980–1999* (New Delhi: Bharatiya Janata Party, 1999), 9–10; see also 8.

144. "Resolution of the National Executive, Bhubaneshwar, 12–14 Feb 1982," in Bharatiya Janata Party, *BJP Resolutions*, 14; see also 13, 15.

145. "Resolution of the National Council, Surat, 4–6 Jun 1982," in Bharatiya Janata Party, *BJP Resolutions*, 17, see also 19.

146. "Resolution of the National Executive, Bangalore, 28–30.08.1982," in Bharatiya Janata Party, *BJP Resolutions*, 21. See also "Resolution of the National Council, New Delhi, 15–17 Apr 1983," in ibid., 27; "Resolution of the National Executive, Lucknow, 21–23 Oct 1983," in ibid., 36.

147. "Resolution of the National Executive, Indore, 6–8 Jan 1984," in Bharatiya Janata Party, *BJP Resolutions*, 47–48. See also "Resolution of the National Council, Pune, 1–4 Oct 1984," in ibid., 57–59.

148. "Resolution of the National Executive, Bhopal, 19–21 Jul 1985," in Bharatiya Janata Party, *BJP Resolutions*, 60.

149. "Resolution of the National Executive, Bhopal, 19–21 July, 1985," in Bharatiya Janata Party, *Economic Resolutions: Party Document*, vol. 6, *1980–2005* (New Delhi: Bharatiya Janata Party, 2005), 276.

150. "Resolution of the National Executive, Jamshedpur, 01–03 July, 1988," in Bharatiya Janata Party, *Economic Resolutions: Party Document*, 230. See also D. B. Thengadi, *Our National Renaissance: Its Directions and Destination* (Bangalore: Sahitya Sindhu, 1980), 9–12, 18–20.

151. "Resolution of the National Executive, Madras, 21–23 July, 1990," in Bharatiya Janata Party, *Economic Resolutions: Party Document*, 208.

152. "Resolution of the National Executive, Ernakulam, 1–3 January, 1988," in Bharatiya Janata Party, *Economic Resolutions: Party Document*, 223.

153. "Resolution of the National Executive, Madras, 21–23 July, 1990," 209.

154. "Resolution of the National Executive, Ahmedabad, 07–09 October, 1988," in Bharatiya Janata Party, *Economic Resolutions: Party Document*, 233.

Contributors

MANU BHAGAVAN is professor of history and human rights at Hunter College and the Graduate Center–The City University of New York and senior fellow at the Ralph Bunche Institute. He is the author of *The Peacemakers* (2012, 2013) and *Sovereign Spheres* (2003) and the editor or coeditor of four other books. He is currently writing a biography of Madam Vijaya Lakshmi Pandit, the first woman in the world to become a global celebrity diplomat. His *Quartz* essay on global authoritarianism went viral internationally and was translated into German as the cover article of *Berliner Republik* (May 2016). He is the recipient of a 2006 fellowship from the American Council of Learned Societies. He regularly appears in the media to comment on global affairs.

PRIYA CHACKO is senior lecturer in international politics in the Department of Politics and International Studies at the University of Adelaide. She is the author of *Indian Foreign Policy: The Politics of Postcolonial Identity from 1947 to 2004* (2011) and the editor of *New Regional Geopolitics in the Indo-Pacific* (2016). Her current research projects focus on the rise of authoritarian populism in India and the economics-security nexus in the Indo-Pacific region, and she has published on these topics in the *Journal of Contemporary Asia* and the *European Journal of International Relations*.

ANTON HARDER completed his Ph.D. at the London School of Economics in September 2016 with a thesis on Sino-Indian relations between 1949 and 1962. He has previously published on Nehru's policy toward China's seat at the United Nations. He is now working on a book project based on his thesis and a number of articles on Beijing's changing views of India and the Third World in the late 1950s. He is currently a teaching associate in modern Chinese history at the University of Nottingham.

SYED AKBAR HYDER is the director of the Hindi-Urdu Flagship Program and associate professor of Asian studies and Islamic studies at the University of Texas at Austin. He is the author of *Reliving Karbala: Martyrdom in South Asian Memory* (2008) and the coeditor of *Hidden Histories* (2018). His research and teaching focus on literary aesthetics, comparative religion, gender, and sexuality studies across South Asia and the Near East.

RAMINDER KAUR is professor of anthropology and cultural studies based in the School of Global Studies at the University of Sussex. She is the author of *Atomic Mumbai: Living with the Radiance of a Thousand Suns* (2013) and *Performative Politics and the Cultures of Hinduism* (2003, 2005). She is also coauthor of *Diaspora and Hybridity* (with Virinder Kalra and John Hutnyk, 2005) and *Adventure Comics and Youth Cultures in India* (with Saif Eqbal, 2018). She is coeditor of several volumes, a scriptwriter, and artistic director at www.sohayavisions.com.

ROHAN MUKHERJEE is an assistant professor of political science at Yale-NUS College, Singapore. His research has been published in such journals as *Asian Security, India Review, Survival, International Affairs, Global Governance*, and *International Journal*, as well as in edited volumes by Oxford University Press, Stanford University Press, and Brookings Institution Press. He is the coeditor of *Poised for Partnership: Deepening India-Japan Relations in the Asian Century* (2016). His research focuses on rising powers, international security, global governance, and India's foreign and security policies.

SWAPNA KONA NAYUDU is an associate at the Harvard University Asia Center and at the Asia Research Institute, National University of Singapore. Her research interests are in international relations theory, the Cold War in the Third World, peacekeeping, and security studies. She has written about India's international relations in the journals *Cold War History* and *Global Intellectual History* and for the Wilson Center's Cold War International History Project. She is currently revising her doctoral thesis on Indian non-alignment in the Nehru period for publication.

PALLAVI RAGHAVAN is assistant professor of international relations at Ashoka University. Her research interests are in India's early diplomatic history. Her book *A Resolvable Enmity: India's and Pakistan's Early Years* is scheduled for publication in 2019.

SRINATH RAGHAVAN is senior fellow at the Centre for Policy Research and visiting professor at Ashoka University. He is the author of *War and Peace in Modern India* (2010), *1971: A Global History* (2013), and *India's War* (2016). His most recent book is *Fierce Enigmas: A History of the United States in South Asia* (2018).

RAHUL SAGAR is Global Network Associate Professor of Political Science at NYU Abu Dhabi. He is the author of *Secrets and Leaks* (2013) and is currently completing a manuscript on Indian political thought. He has a Ph.D. in government from Harvard University and a B.A. in philosophy, politics, and economics from Balliol College, Oxford University.

WAHEGURU PAL SINGH SIDHU is clinical associate professor at New York University's Center for Global Affairs, where he teaches courses on India, the United Nations, and weapons of mass destruction. He is also a nonresident Senior Fellow at the Brookings Institution and Associate Fellow at the Geneva Centre for Security Policy. His research focuses on India's role in the global order and on addressing nuclear weapon challenges. He is the author of multiple books and articles. His most recent publication is *Shaping the Emerging World: India and the Multilateral Order* (2013). He is also a regular columnist on global strategic issues for *Mint* newspaper.

Index

Acheson, Dean, 23, 27
ahimsa, 234
Ahlberg, Kristin L., 186
Aid India Consortium, 183, 186
Akhtar, Begum, 72
Akhtar, Salim, 69
Aksai Chin, 8, 102, 104–10, 112–14, 117, 119, 121, 167
al-Hallaj, Mansur, 70
Ali, Agha Shahid, 70–71
Aman (film), 12, 199–222
Anandabazaar Patrika, 32
Ardagh alignment of 1897, 102
Ardagh Line, 104
Arms Control Association, 145
Asia and the Cold War, 37, 41, 48
Asian African Conference (April 1955), 41
Atomic Energy Act, 145
Atomic Energy Commission, 145

Baghdad Pact, 29, 32
Bajpai, Girija Shankar, 22–23, 103
Bandung Conference (1955), 7, 32, 41–42
Bass, Gary, 9
Basu, Jyoti, 62
Beattie, Keith, 206
Bergson, Henri, 61
Bhabha, Homi, 8, 43, 128
Bhagavan, Manu, 154, 165
Bharatiya Janata Party (BJP), 229, 243–46; post–Cold War rise, 230–31

Bhargava, G. S., 145
Black, Eugene, 25
Blood, Archer, 9
Boothby, Robert, 3
Bose, Raj Narain, 231–32
Bowles, Chester, 21, 22, 26
Bretton Woods Institutions, 181
Bulganin, Nikolai, 42
Burns, E. L. M., 87
business-state alliance, 191
Byroade, Henry, 21, 29

Carnegie Endowment for International Peace, 145
Caroe, Olaf, 29
Castro, Fidel, 68
Central Treaty Organization (CENTO), 31, 32
Chacko, Priya, 12, 157
Chakravarty, B. N., 143
Chatterjee, Partha, 154, 190
Chatterji, Bankim Chandra, 232, 233, 234
Chatterji, N. C., 238–39
Chaudhuri, Rudra, 154, 165, 229
Chaudhuri, Sachin, 187
Chibber, Vivek, 184
Chinese Communist Party (CCP), 155
Churchill, Winston, 30–31
Cold War, 178–80; economic statecraft, Nehruvian state and, 181–83; Hindu nationalists and, 229–46; India's role

in, 1–2; Nehruvian consensus, 230; new
front in South Asia, 37–38; and religious
nationalists, 12; traditional narratives, 10;
U.N. peace operations during, 81
Communist Party of India, 72, 162
Communist Party of the Soviet Union
(CPSU), 42
CPSU. *See* Communist Party of the Soviet
Union
Cullather, Nick, 183
culture: and diplomacy, 71, 201; post-
documentary, 206

Dalai Lama, 159, 168
Datta, Narendranath. *See* Swami
Vivekananda
Dawn, 31, 32
Dayal, Rajeshwar, 90, 91, 93
decolonization, 29
Desai, Morarji, 114, 115, 164
Deshmukh, C. D., 22, 23
Deshpande, V. G., 240
diplomacy: Bollywood and; culture and,
71, 201; disarmament-related, 141; in the
Third World
diplomatic history of India, 10, 40, 44
Discovery of India, The (Nehru), 209
Drought-Prone Areas Program, 191
Dulles, John Foster, 5
Dutt, Subimal, 38, 45

economic development, and the Cold
War, 153–71; Chinese encounter, 157–61;
Chinese used discussions of, 159; and
international strategy, 166; overview, 153–
57; return of struggle for, 165–69; Soviet
Union and peaceful transition, 161–64;
territorial dispute and, 167
Eighteen-Nation Committee on
Disarmament (ENCD), 127, 138–45;
General Assembly role in, 138–39, 145;
India after 1965 in, 142–45; India before
1965 in, 140–42; multilateral institution,
139
Eisenhower, Dwight, 7, 42, 45
ENCD. *See* Eighteen-Nation Committee
on Disarmament

Engerman, David, 154, 170
Enlai, Zhou, 11, 101, 104–7, 109, 111, 112, 113–
21, 158, 159, 167, 169

Faiz, Faiz Ahmed, 10–11, 57–74; on Africa,
65–66; and Agha Shahid Ali, 70–71;
anti-Zia song, 70; during the Cold
War, 71; as editor, 63; fame, 61–62; first
recited poem, 61; *ghazals* by, 59–60;
joins the Marxists, 71–72; journey to
Cuba, 67–68; left-leaning critics, 72;
poetry assemblies of, 61–62; prison
empowered, 66–67; sent to prison, 63;
shares Ghalib's attitude, 68; source of
emulation, 60; South Asia's diary, 62;
subtitles reference, 72–73; translation
of Hikmet's thoughts, 74; "We Shall
Overcome," 69; won International Lenin
Peace Prize, 71; writing and protest
against Pakistan's chief and the United
States, 64–65
Five Power Resolution, 45
Food for Peace, 186
Ford and Rockefeller Foundations, 183
Foreign Exchange Regulation Act, 189
Frankel, Francine, 154, 161
Freeman, Orville, 186

Gaddis, John Lewis, 19
Gandhi, Indira, 8, 9, 12, 23, 62, 127, 128, 144,
145, 187–93; 1970s as critical juncture,
190–92
Gandhi, Mahatma, 2, 81, 234, 235
Geneva Conference (1954), 37
Ghalib, Mirza, 60
Ghosh, Aurobindo, 233, 234
Glimpses of World History (Nehru), 209
global Cold War, 153
Golwalkar, Madhav Sadashiv, 236
Gopal, Sarvepalli, 112
Grady, Henry F., 21, 28
Great Leap Forward, 164
Green Revolution, 190
Guevara, Che, 68
Guha, Ramachandra, 154
Gujral, I. K., 62

Haksar, P. N., 137, 144
Hammarskjöld, Dag, 81, 82, 88, 90, 91, 93, 94
Haqqani, Hussain, 28
Harder, Anton, 11
Hassan, Mehdi, 72
Hikmet, Nazim, 70, 73, 74
Hindi-Chini Bhai Bhai, 115
Hindu Mahasabha, 229, 237–40; "Hindu Socialism," 240; two-pronged response of, 238
Hindu nationalism, 229, 231, 237, 246
Hindu nationalists, and the Cold War, 229–46; after independence, 235–37; before independence, 231–35; Bharatiya Janata Party, 243–46; Hindu Mahasabha, 237–40; Jan Sangh, 240–43; overview, 229
Hundred Flowers, 162, 165, 170
Hungarian Revolution, 8, 44–45
Hussain, Altaf, 31
Hyder, Syed Akbar, 10

IAEA. See International Atomic Energy Agency
Ikramullah, M., 28
India: and China, 100–121; domestic politics, 108; evolution of boundary policy, 101–6; and internationalism, 2–3, 93, 210; and Japan, 200–216; mediation between superpowers, 38–39; and non-alignment, 7, 20, 32, 38, 40; and nuclear weapons, 126–46; and One World, 83–84, 93, 154, 155, 157, 210; and Pakistan, 5, 8–9, 19–21, 32–33, 57, 61; and peacemaking, 79–92; policy toward Tibet, 102; and the Postwar Global Order, role in Cold War, 1–2, 4, 38; role in Congo, 88–92; and Russia, 38–43; sovereignty, and the Cold War, 3, 8, 114, 238; and the Soviet Union, 36–49; and the United States, 19–33
Indian Communist Party, 168
Indian diplomacy, 3–4, 49
Indian foreign relations, 154
Indian National Congress, 154
Indo-American Technical Agreement, 182
Indo-Pakistani relations, 5, 8–9, 19–21, 32–33, 57, 61
Indo-Soviet relations, 36–49; history of, 36–37; and Nehru, Khrushchev, and the Thaw, 38–47; overview, 36–38; year 1954, 41
Indo-U.S. relations, 19–33
Indus Waters Treaty, 26
International Atomic Energy Agency (IAEA), 137
International Monetary Fund (IMF), 181
Iqbal, Muhammad, 59, 60–61
Ispahani, M. A. H., 27

Jafri, Ali Sardar, 72
Jahan, Noor, 58–58, 61, 72
Jain, A. P., 165
Jan Sangh, 229, 240–43
Jha, C. S., 143–44
Jha, L. K, 144, 187
Jieshi, Jiang, 155, 167
Johnson, Lyndon, 184–85

Kalecki, Michal, 153, 154
Kant, Immanuel, 61
Kaur, Raminder, 12
Khan, Liaquat Ali, 10; appeal for potential in Pakistan's economy, 26; with Dean Acheson, 27; visit to the United States, 19–33
Khan, Rana Liaquat Ali, 27
Khare, N. B., 238
Khilnani, Sunil, 153
Khrushchev, Nikita, 5, 7, 38–47, 108, 156, 161–62, 164, 166, 170
Kissinger, Henry, 9
Komer, Robert, 186
Kongka Pass incident, 110–11
Korean War (1950–1954), 39, 84–86
Koselleck, Reinhart, 100
Kripalani, J. B., 167, 230
Krishnamachari, T. T., 187
Krishnaswamy, Kabilan, 93
Kumar, Mohan, 199
Kumar, Rajendra, 199, 200

Lall, Arthur, 44, 45, 137–38, 142
Land Acquisition Act, 190
Li, Hua-yu
Lie, Trygve, 80

Lilienthal, David, 25
Longju, 107–8, 110, 118
Love in Tokyo (film), 208

MacDonald Line, 104
Mahalanobis, P. C., 185
Malenkov, Georgy, 10, 38, 41
Malihabadi, Josh, 59
Malkani, K. R., 235–36
Manhattan Project, 6
Mankekar, D. R., 23, 100
Marshall Plan, 178
Marx, Karl, 61
Mathai, M. O., 23
Maxwell, Neville, 101
McCain, John, 94
McGhee, George, 31–32
McMahon, Henry, 102
McMahon Line, 102–3, 105–9, 111, 113–16,
    118, 120
McNamara, Robert, 182
Mehta, Asoka, 187
Mehta, G. L., 45
Menon, K. P. S., 38, 39, 40–41, 42, 43, 44,
    47, 49, 84, 103
Menon, V. K. Krishna, 4, 7, 8, 40, 46, 47, 85,
    87, 88, 90–91, 94, 115, 142, 163, 164, 168
Merrill, Dennis, 154
Middle East Command, 30–31
Middle Eastern Defense Organization, 31
Millner, E., 30
Mohiuddin, Makhdum, 73
Montgomery, Bernard L., 29
Mookherjee, Syama Prasad, 235
Morgenthau, Hans, 32
Moscow Economic Conference, 39
Mountbatten, Louis, 29, 113
Muhammad (prophet), 61
Mukherjee, Rohan, 11

Nagy, Imre, 46
Naidu, M. V., 88
Narayan, Jayaprakash, 81, 116
Nasser, Gamal Abdel, 7, 87
NATO. *See* North Atlantic Treaty
    Organization
Nayudu, Swapna Kona, 10, 11, 156, 160

NEFA. *See* North East Frontier Agency
Nehru, Jawaharlal, 2, 82, 85, 100, 128;
    attended Bandung Conference, 41–42;
    and the Cold War, 47; Fabian socialist
    outlook, 2–3; failure for China policy,
    168–69; and Faiz Ahmad Faiz, 10, 62;
    idea of "One World," 83–84, 157; and
    Indo-Soviet relations, 38–47; and
    internationalism, 2–3, 93, 210; meeting
    with Dean Acheson, 23; U.N. General
    Assembly speech, 89–90; visit to the
    United States, 19–33
Nehru, R. K., 104, 115
Nehruvian Consensus, 157, 184–90,
    230; domestic responses, 187–88;
    international pressures, 185–86; political
    and policy flux, 188–89; political and
    policy outcomes, 189–90
Nehruvian Foreign Policy, 38–39, 154
Nehru-Zhou Enlai Summit (1960), 100–121;
    correspondence and clashes, 106–12;
    evolution of India's boundary policy,
    101–6; Nehru agreed to meet Zhou, 112–
    15; opening rounds of, 115–20; overview,
    100–101
Neutral Nations Repatriation Commission
    (NNRC), 85–86
Nietzsche, Friedrich, 61
Nixon, Richard, 9
NNRC. *See* Neutral Nations Repatriation
    Commission
Non-Aligned Movement, 7, 20
Non-alignment and the Cold War, 32
North Atlantic Treaty Organization
    (NATO), 30, 87
North East Frontier Agency (NEFA), 103,
    107, 109, 110, 111, 118, 120
NPT. *See* Nuclear Non-Proliferation
    Treaty
nuclear ambiguity: aspects of India's
    strategy, 137; benefits of, 133; as optimal
    strategy, 130–31; overview, 126–27;
    reactions to Chinese threat and, 131–33
Nuclear Non-Proliferation Treaty (NPT),
    127, 139, 146
nuclear weapons and disarmament,
    126–46; benefits of nuclear ambiguity,

133–35; Eighteen-Nation Committee on Disarmament, 138–45; and international nuclear regime, 137–38; nuclear ambiguity as optimal strategy, 130–31; overview, 126–27; reactions to Chinese threat, 131–33

One World movement, by India, 83–84, 93, 154, 155, 157, 210
ONUC. *See* United Nations Operations in Congo
Oppenheimer, Robert, 6
Organiser, 235

Pact, Baghdad, 29
Pakistan Communist Party, 71
Pakistan Times, 63
Panchsheel (Five Principles) Agreement, 8, 43
Panda, Ankit, 230
Pandit, Vijaya Lakshmi, 3–4, 39, 40, 160
Panikkar, K. M., 102, 104, 157–58, 159
Pant, G. B., 112, 115, 163
Partial Test Ban Treaty (PTBT), 138, 142
Parveen, Abida, 72
PDS. *See* Public Distribution System
peacekeeper, global, 4, 10, 79–95; during the Cold War, 81; during Korean War (1950–1954), 84–86; historical and military drivers, 82–84; normative drivers, 79–82; origins of U.N. peacekeeping, 79–82; United Nations Emergency Force (1956–1967), 86–88; United Nations Operations in Congo (1960–1964), 88–92
"Peace Offensive," 40
Picasso, Pablo, 71
Planning Commission, 187, 188
Prebisch, Raul, 185
Principles for a New Political Party (Malkani), 235
PTBT. *See* Partial Test Ban Treaty
Public Distribution System (PDS), 183
Public Law 480 Act (PL-480), 182

Radhakrishnan, Sarvepalli, 39, 114–15, 116
Raghavan, Pallavi, 10, 11, 155
Raghavan, Srinath, 11, 157, 167, 170

Rahman, M. M., 44
Rajadhyaksha, Ashis, 199
Ram, Malik, 59
Rashtriya Swayamsevak Sangh (RSS), 235
Rau, B. N., 4
Rau, Benegal, 85
Rau, K. Rama, 23
Rawalpindi Conspiracy Case, 63
Rikhye, Indar Jit, 82, 87, 94
ringed system of defense, 30
Rockefeller, Nelson, 182
Roosevelt, Eleanor, 3–4
Rostow, Walt, 185
Russell, Bertrand: in Bollyworld, 199–222; cameo appearance in film *Aman*, 199–222; and Indian affairs, 216–19; and Nehru, 216–20
Russell, Ralph, 72

Sagar, Rahul, 12
Salaria, Gurbachan Singh, 91–92
Sarila, Narendra Singh, 29
Savarkar, Vinayak, 234, 235
Sharma, Balkrishna, 230
Shastri, Lal Bahadur, 126, 128, 184
Shastri, Shiv, 160
Shatra, Lonchen, 102
Shikwah (Iqbal), 60–61
Sidhu, Waheguru Pal Singh, 11
Simla Convention, 102, 115
Singh, Anita Inder, 29
Singh, Kameshwar, 230
Singh, Ram, 239
Singh, Swaran, 115, 118
Sino-Indian relations, 8, 100–121; in 1950s, 153–71
Sino-Indian war (1962), 100–101
Sino-Soviet Treaty of Friendship, 157
60th Parachute Field Ambulance, 85
Small Farmer's Development Agency, 191
Smuts, Jan, 3
Southeast Asia Treaty Organization (SEATO), 32
Stalin, Joseph, 5, 38, 39–40
Stevenson, Adlai, 94
Subramaniam, C., 187
Suez Crisis, 7, 8, 43–44, 86, 87

Superiority of Hinduism to Other Existing Religions, The (Bose), 231
Swami Vivekananda, 232–33, 235, 239

Tata Group, 163
Tata Iron and Steel Corporation, 182
Thakur, Vineet, 4
Thimayya, K. S., 164
Third World, 1
Times of India, 209
Trivedi, Vishnu, 142–43
Truman, Harry, 21, 24; emergency aid to India, 26; policies toward South Asia, 25

UNEF I. *See* United Nations Emergency Force
United Nation (U.N.): General Assembly, 44, 47, 84, 93, 138, 139; Guard, 79; Security Council, 43, 79, 91, 95; Temporary Commission on Korea (1948), 84–85
United Nations Emergency Force (UNEF I), 82, 86–89
United Nations Observer Group, 82

United Nations Operations in Congo (ONUC), 82, 88–92
Universal Declaration of Human Rights (1948), 4
Upadhyaya, Deendayal, 236–37

Vassilyeva, Ludmila, 71
Vyshinsky, Andrey, 38, 40

Warsaw Pact, 44, 46
Wells of Power, The (Caroe), 29
Westad, Odd Arne, 1, 2
Woods, George, 182
World Bank, 163, 181, 183, 184, 185, 186, 192

Xiaoyuan, Liu, 164

Yi, Chen, 116, 118, 169
Yudin, Pavel, 164, 166

Zachariah, Benjamin, 154
Zaheer, Sajjad, 63
Zedong, Mao, 12, 155, 156, 159, 162–64, 167, 168, 169, 170